The
Allyn & Bacon
Guide to Writing
Concise Edition

The Allyn & Bacon Guide to Writing

Concise Edition

FOURTH EDITION

John D. Ramage
Arizona State University

John C. Bean
Seattle University

June Johnson
Seattle University

PEARSON

Longman

New York   San Francisco   Boston
London   Toronto   Sydney   Tokyo   Singapore   Madrid
Mexico City   Munich   Paris   Cape Town   Hong Kong   Montreal

Publisher: Joseph Opiela
Development Editor: Marion B. Castellucci
Marketing Manager: Alexandra Rivas-Smith
Supplements Editors: Teresa Ward/Donna Campion
Media Supplements Editor: Jenna Egan
Production Manager: Donna DeBenedictis
Project Coordination, Text Design, and Electronic Page Makeup:
  Elm Street Publishing Services, Inc.
Cover Design Manager: Wendy Ann Fredericks
Cover Designer: Base Art Co.
Cover Art: Helen Frankenthaler (b. 1928). © *Small's Paradise*, 1964. Acrylic on canvas.
  100 × 93-5/8 in. (254 × 237.7 cm). Smithsonian American Art Museum, Washington, DC/
  Art Resource, NY.
Photo Researcher: Photosearch, Inc.
Senior Manufacturing Buyer: Alfred C. Dorsey
Printer and Binder: RR Donnelley & Sons Company, Crawfordsville
Cover Printer: Phoenix Color Corporation

For permission to use copyrighted material, grateful acknowledgment is made to the copyright holders on pages 377 to 379, which are hereby made part of this copyright page.

Library of Congress Cataloging-in-Publication Data
Ramage, John D.
      The Allyn & Bacon guide to writing / John D. Ramage, John C. Bean, June Johnson.—
Concise ed., 4th ed.
          p.   cm.
      Includes bibliographical references and index.
      ISBN 0-321-29152-2
      1. English language—Rhetoric—Handbooks, manuals, etc. 2. English language—
Grammar—Handbooks, manuals, etc. 3. Report writing—Handbooks, manuals, etc. 4.
College readers. I. Title: Allyn and Bacon guide to writing. II. Bean, John C. III. Johnson,
June. IV. Title.

      PE1408.R18 2006
      808'.042—dc22   2005047617

Please visit us at *http://www.ablongman.com/ramage*

ISBN 0-321-29150-6 (Complete Edition)
ISBN 0-321-29151-4 (Brief Edition)
ISBN 0-321-29152-2 (Concise Edition)

1 2 3 4 5 6 7 8 9 10—DOC—08 07 06 05

Brief Contents

PART ONE
A Rhetoric for College Writers   2

PART TWO
Writing Projects   92

> WRITING TO LEARN

> WRITING TO EXPLORE

> WRITING TO INFORM

> WRITING TO ANALYZE

> WRITING TO PERSUADE

PART THREE

A Guide to Composing and Revising   278

PART FOUR

A Rhetorical Guide to Research   340

Detailed Contents

PART TWO
Writing Projects   92

➤ **WRITING TO LEARN**

➤ WRITING TO INFORM

➤ WRITING TO ANALYZE

PART FOUR

A Rhetorical Guide to Research   340

Writing Projects

Thematic Contents

The Allyn & Bacon Guide to Writing, Fourth Edition, contains 27 essays—14 by professional writers and 13 by students. In addition, the text contains a number of visual texts (advertisements, political photographs, posters, and Web sites) that can lead to productive thematic discussions. These essays and visual texts can be clustered thematically in the following ways:

POPULAR CULTURE, MEDIA, AND ADVERTISING

IDENTITY AND VALUES

PARENTS, CHILDREN, AND FAMILY

NATURE AND ECOLOGY

Preface

We continue to be grateful for the enthusiastic reviews of *The Allyn & Bacon Guide to Writing*. Known for its groundbreaking integration of composition research and rhetorical perspective, *The Allyn & Bacon Guide to Writing* has been hailed as the most successful college rhetoric in more than a decade. The book has been widely admired for its appeal to students, its focus on problem posing, and its distinctive emphasis on writing and reading as rhetorical acts. The book is distinguished by its lively and engaging instruction, practical classroom activities, and effective writing assignments. From all quarters, instructors have praised the book's theoretical coherence and explanatory power, which help students produce interesting, idea-rich essays and help composition teachers create pedagogically effective, challenging, and intellectually stimulating courses. This Concise Edition—based on the fourth edition of *The Allyn & Bacon Guide to Writing*—retains the signature strengths of the text while making substantial improvements based on our continuing research in composition theory and practice, on the needs and interests of our students, and on the pedagogical insights and suggestions of the users of previous editions.

What's New in This Revised Concise Edition

Building on the text's well-established strengths, we have revised the book to increase its flexibility, clarity, usefulness, and student interest. We have particularly responded to reviewers' requests for an expanded treatment of rhetoric in Part One, for more emphasis on rhetorical context in assignments and exercises, for more attention to visuals, and for a greater range of student models. Here is what's new:

- **A revision of Part One, "A Rhetoric for College Writers," aimed at improving students' comprehension of key rhetorical principles.** Rhetorical instruction that in the previous edition was dispersed throughout the writing project chapters has been consolidated into a revised Part One for easier reference and stronger focus. Chapters 1 through 4 now provide students with a more inclusive and powerful overview to rhetoric that will ground their study of college-level writing, reading, and thinking.
- **In Chapter 1, an improved explanation of question asking and problem posing** that leads to more engaged class discussion, higher-quality questions, and improved performance on the chapter's brief writing project. Using short visual and verbal texts on an important new topic—automobiles, fossil fuels, and energy choices—the chapter now provides a cultural context for questioning while connecting with students' personal

experiences. The writing prompt now offers two options, both of which ground the students' questions in a real-world context.

- **In Chapters 2 and 3, a condensing and streamlining of the previous edition's Chapters 2, 3, and 4.** Improved explanations, often updated with newer or better examples, make the rhetorical concepts in these chapters easier to read, understand, and retain. The explanations of freewriting and idea mapping, formerly in Chapter 2, have been moved to Chapter 11 as part of that chapter's explanation of the writing process.

- **A new Chapter 4, "Thinking Rhetorically about How Messages Persuade."** This engaging new chapter gives students the background and explanations needed to think rhetorically about a wide range of verbal and nonverbal texts. A section on rhetorical theory provides a framework for introducing concepts previously delayed until later in the text. Chapter 4 now introduces the classical appeals of *logos, ethos,* and *pathos,* explains angle of vision, introduces strategies for analyzing a text rhetorically, and shows students how they can think rhetorically about nonverbal texts such as images or clothing fashions. These powerful concepts can then be used to enhance rhetorical discussions of readings or assignments throughout Part Two.

- **An expansion of Chapter 8, "Writing an Informative (and Surprising) Essay,"** to include informational reports as well as pieces using a surprising-reversal strategy. Two new student examples have been included to demonstrate the use of field or library research with an informational aim.

- **A new chapter on analysis of visual images and advertisements (Chapter 9, "Analyzing Images").** This chapter introduces students to visual rhetoric, especially as used in advertising—an approach that also opens up many popular culture issues connected to consumerism and to race, gender, and class.

- **Throughout the text, an expanded focus on visual rhetoric.** Striking images appear at the beginning of the major parts of the text with explanatory captions that provoke critical thinking. Examples of visual or visual/verbal texts also appear in numerous For Writing and Class Discussion exercises to provoke interest in how images influence audiences' responses and how they contribute to social conversations and controversies.

- **Eight new student essays and four new professional essays, selected to show a wider range of genres** as well as varying degrees of complexity or challenge. Some of the student essays are from exceptionally strong student writers while others show good work from less skilled writers. Professional essays range from closed-form academic pieces to open-form personal essays. The wide range of genres represented in the Concise Edition can be seen in the list on the inside back cover.

Distinctive Features of the Text

The Concise Edition of *The Allyn & Bacon Guide to Writing, Fourth Edition*, continues to have the following distinctive features:

- **Great flexibility for instructors.** Because the chapters on rhetoric, on writing projects, and on composing strategies have been designed as self-contained modules, users praise the ease with which they can select chapters and order them to fit the goals of their own courses.
- **Classroom-tested writing projects that guide students through all phases of reading and writing processes and make frequent use of collaboration and peer review.** Assignments are designed to promote intellectual growth and to stimulate the kind of critical thinking valued in college courses.
- **Integration of rhetorical theory with composition research.** Writing and reading are treated both as rhetorical acts and as processes of inquiry, problem posing, and critical thinking.
- **Balanced coverage of academic writing and personal and narrative forms,** placing nonfiction writing on a continuum from thesis-driven "closed-form" writing to narrative-based "open-form" writing. The text focuses on closed-form writing for entering most academic, civic, and professional conversations and on open-form writing for artistic or stylistic surprise and for narrating ideas and experiences that resist closed-form structures.
- **Distinctive explanations of closed-form prose based on reader-expectation theory.** These explanations (Chapter 12) are arranged in a sequence of eight minilessons that can be easily integrated into a variety of course structures.
- **Emphasis on teaching students to read rhetorically;** to understand the differences between print and cyberspace sources; to analyze the rhetorical occasion, genre, context, and intended audience of sources; to evaluate sources according to appropriate criteria; and to negotiate the World Wide Web with confidence.
- **Coverage of visual rhetoric and document design** with particular emphasis on Web sites, advertisements, posters, and other texts where words and images work together for rhetorical effect.
- **An attractive four-color design** that enhances the book's visual appeal and presents examples of visual rhetoric and document design in full color.
- **Instructional emphases that meet Writing Program Administrators (WPA) guidelines** for outcome goals in first-year composition courses. (The fourth edition of the *Instructor's Resource Manual* discusses the correlation of the WPA Outcomes Statement and the fourth edition of *The Allyn & Bacon Guide to Writing*.)
- **A friendly, encouraging tone** that respects students and treats them as serious learners.

Structure of *The Allyn & Bacon Guide to Writing,* Concise Edition

Part One, "A Rhetoric for College Writers," provides a conceptual framework for *The Allyn & Bacon Guide to Writing* by showing how inquiring writers pose problems, pursue them through dialectic thinking and research, and try to solve them within a rhetorical context shaped by the writer's purpose, audience, and genre. Chapter 1 explains how writers grapple with both subject matter and rhetorical problems and introduces principles of question asking and the concept of a continuum from closed to open forms of prose. Chapter 2 explains college professors' desire for students to "wallow in complexity" by learning to pose engaging questions, conduct inquiry, and seek surprising thesis statements that must be supported with points and particulars. Chapter 3 shows how a writer's purpose, intended audience, and genre influence decisions about content, structure, style, and document design. Chapter 4 extends the discussion of rhetoric by showing students how messages persuade. After a brief introduction to rhetorical theory, Chapter 4 explains the classical appeals of *logos, ethos,* and *pathos* as well as the concept of angle of vision and various strategies for analyzing texts rhetorically. It concludes by showing students how to think rhetorically about visual images, clothing fashions, and other cultural texts.

Part Two, "Writing Projects," consists of six self-contained assignment chapters focusing on writing to learn, to explore, to inform, to analyze, and to persuade. Each chapter guides students through the processes of generating and exploring ideas, composing and drafting, and revising and editing. Concluding each chapter are "Guidelines for Peer Reviews," which sum up the important features in the assignments and facilitate detailed, helpful peer reviews. The heart of each chapter is a writing project designed to teach students new ways of seeing and thinking. The exploratory exercises in each assignment chapter help students generate ideas for their essays while developing their skills at posing problems, delaying closure, speaking back to texts, valuing alternative points of view, and thinking dialectically.

Part Three, "A Guide to Composing and Revising," comprises two self-contained chapters of nuts-and-bolts strategies for composing and revising thesis-driven, closed-form prose.

Part Four, "A Rhetorical Guide to Research," presents an in-depth discussion of the rhetoric of Web sites and a concise guide to MLA and APA documentation and style, with two student examples of research papers formatted in MLA and APA styles.

Strategies for Using *The Allyn & Bacon Guide to Writing,* Concise Edition

The text's flexible and logical organization makes it easy to design a new syllabus or adapt the text to your current syllabus. Key rhetorical concepts that students should know early in the course are developed in Part One, while explanations of compositional strategies and skills, which students will practice recursively throughout the course, are placed in Part Three.

Although there are many ways to use the Concise Edition of *The Allyn & Bacon Guide to Writing*, the most typical course design calls for students to read material from Part One (Chapters 1–4) during the opening weeks of class. The brief, informal write-to-learn projects in these chapters can be used either for overnight homework assignments or for in-class discussion. For the rest of the course, instructors typically assign writing project chapters from the options available in Part Two (Chapters 5–10). While students are engaged with the writing projects in these chapters, instructors can assign material from the compositional chapters in Part Three to give students greater facility with the writing process. Each of the lessons in Chapter 12 on composing and revising closed-form prose is designed for coverage in a half hour or less of class time. At the same time students are working on a writing project, classroom discussion can alternate between issues related directly to the assignment (invention exercises, group brainstorming, peer review workshops) and those focusing on instructional matter from the rest of the text.

Using the Writing Projects in Part Two

Because each of the six assignment chapters in Part Two is self-contained, instructors can select and organize the writing projects in the way that best fits their course goals and their students' needs. The projects in Chapters 5 and 6 introduce students to the rhetorical ways of observing and reading that underpin mature, academic thinking, showing students how to analyze a text, pose questions about it, and understand and resist the text's rhetorical strategies.

Chapter 7's assignment, an exploratory essay, asks students to narrate their engagement with a problem and their attempts to resolve it. Teachers may want to pair this chapter with the assignment of a researched classical argument (in Chapter 10) and draw on the research skills taught in Chapters 13 and 14. In our own classes, we have found this sequence of assignments successful at equipping students to grapple with the research questions they have posed to produce rich, lively arguments that incorporate their research.

Chapter 8, on informative writing, urges students to reach beyond straightforward reporting by employing a "surprising-reversal" strategy aimed at altering the reader's initial assumptions about a topic. Surprising reversal is a powerful rhetorical move that can be used to enliven almost any kind of informative, analytical, or persuasive prose.

Chapter 9, on analyzing images, introduces students to visual rhetoric and to the analysis of popular culture through advertisements. The chapter teaches students how to analyze photographs and drawings, helping them understand how a given image constructs its subject and persuades viewers. Because advertising opens up discussions of popular culture—including issues of consumerism and of class, race, and gender—this chapter is particularly rich in its potential to interest students.

Chapter 10, on persuasive writing, teaches key concepts of argumentation. Providing a strong introduction to both academic and civic argument, it combines accessible Toulmin and stasis approaches and emphasizes argument as truth seeking and consensus seeking rather than as a win/lose debate.

Supplements for *The Allyn & Bacon Guide to Writing*

The Allyn & Bacon Guide to Writing is supported by a variety of helpful supplements for instructors and students.

For Instructors

- The fourth edition of the *Instructor's Resource Manual* has been revised by Susanmarie Harrington of Indiana University Purdue University Indianapolis. The *Instructor's Resource Manual* integrates emphases for meeting the Writing Program Administrators guidelines for outcome goals in first-year composition courses. It continues to offer detailed teaching suggestions to help both experienced and new instructors; practical teaching strategies for composition instructors in a question-and-answer format; suggested syllabi for courses of various lengths and emphases; chapter-by-chapter teaching suggestions; answers to Handbook exercises; suggestions for using the text with nonnative speakers; suggestions for using the text in an electronic classroom; transparency masters for class use; and annotated bibliographies.
- *The Allyn & Bacon Guide to Writing Companion Website* enables instructors to access online writing exercises, Web links keyed to specific chapters, and teaching tips as well as receive essay assignments directly from students. (http://www.ablongman.com/ramage)
- *The Longman Instructor's Planner* includes weekly and monthly calendars, student attendance and grading rosters, space for contact information, Web references, an almanac, and blank pages for notes.
- *The Allyn & Bacon / Longman Instructor Resource Library*
  - *The Allyn & Bacon Sourcebook for College Writing Teachers,* Second Edition
  - *An Introduction to Teaching Composition in an Electronic Environment*
  - *Comp Tales*
  - *In Our Own Voice: Graduate Students Teach Writing*
  - *The Longman Guide to Community Service: Learning in the English Classroom and Beyond*
  - *Using Portfolios*
  - *Teaching in Progress: Theories, Practices, and Scenarios,* Third Edition
  - *The Longman Guide to Classroom Management*

For Students

- *The Allyn & Bacon Guide to Writing Companion Website* presents chapter summaries, writing exercises, Web links keyed to specific text sections, peer review checklists, student writing samples, and the ability to e-mail exercises to their instructor. (http://www.ablongman.com/ramage)

- NEW! *MyCompLab 2.0 Web Site* (*www.mycomplab.com*) offers all the strengths of 1.0, but adds exciting new features that makes this market-leading site even more useful for composition students and instructors. Access cards to MyCompLab 2.0 can be packaged with *The Allyn & Bacon Guide to Writing* at no additional cost to students. (MyCompLab 2.0 is available in four versions: Web Site, CourseCompass, Blackboard, and WebCT.)

Writing Resources

- *Exchange:* Pearson's online peer and instructor writing review program. Use *Exchange* to comment on student papers at the word, sentence, paragraph, or paper level—or have your students review each other's work.
- NEW! *Process:* Guided assistance through the stages of the writing process, with interactive worksheets and in-depth exercises for each stage.
- NEW! *Activities:* Provides 100 different writing activities in which students respond to videos, images, Web sites, and writing prompts.
- NEW! *Model Documents Gallery:* Over 50 sample papers, reports, and documents from across the curriculum.

Grammar Resources

- NEW! *Diagnostics:* Two new research-based, 50-question diagnostic tests comprehensively assess student skills in basic grammar, sentence grammar, mechanics, punctuation, and style. Results pages provide overall proficiency scores as well as question-by-question feedback.
- *ExerciseZone:* Over 3,600 self-grading practice items cover all major topics of grammar, style, and usage. NEW! Sentence and paragraph editing exercises.
- NEW! *ESL ExerciseZone:* Over 650 self-grading practice exercises for students whose first language is not English.

Research Resources

- *Research Navigator:* Access to credible, reliable sources, including EBSCO's ContentSelect Database and *The New York Times* Search-by-Subject Archive, plus hundreds of pages of material on the research process itself. Includes a new bibliography-maker program.
- *Avoiding Plagiarism:* A self-guided exploration of the issue of plagiarism, these tutorials teach students to recognize plagiarism and avoid its practice in both MLA and APA formats.

Tutor Center

Students using MyCompLab receive complimentary access to Longman's English Tutor Center. Our live, qualified college instructors help students use resources in MyCompLab effectively and will review student papers for organization and consistent grammar errors.

MyDropBox

Instructors who have ordered a MyCompLab Value Pack for their course can receive complimentary access to MyDropBox, a leading online plagiarism detection service.

- *Longman Grammar and Documentation Study Card:* Packed with useful information, this colorful, laminated study card is an 8-page guide to key grammar, punctuation, and documentation skills.
- *The Longman Writer's Portfolio and Student Planner:* This unique portfolio/ planner includes an assessing/organizing area (including a grammar diagnostic test, a spelling quiz, and project planning worksheets), a before and during writing area (including peer review sheets, editing checklists, writing self-evaluations, and a personal editing profile), and an after-writing area (including a progress chart, a final table of contents, and a final assessment).
- *10 Practices of Highly Successful Students:* Murphy's popular supplement helps students learn crucial study skills, offering concise tips for a successful career in college. Topics include time management, test-taking, reading critically, stress, and motivation.
- *The Longman Editing Exercises:* This print supplement allows students to practice correct English in context with dozens of paragraph editing exercises in various topic areas of grammar, style, and punctuation.
- *The Longman Writer's Journal:* Written by Mimi Markus, this journal contains helpful journal writing strategies, sample journal entries by other students, and many writing prompts and topics to get students writing.
- *The Longman Researcher's Journal:* Designed to help students work through the steps involved in writing a research paper, each section contains record-keeping strategies, checklists, graphic organizers, and pages for taking notes from sources.
- *Literacy Library Series:* This series of brief booklets offers informed, detailed guidelines for writing in academic, public, and workplace communities.
- *Analyzing Literature: A Guide for Students:* This supplement provides critical reading strategies, writing advice, and sample student papers to help students interpret and discuss literary works from a variety of genres.
- *Visual Communication,* Second Edition: Susan Hilligoss' popular text introduces document-design principles and features practical discussions of space, type, organization, pattern, graphic elements, and visuals.
- *Discounted Dictionaries and Thesauruses:* The following can be packaged at a discount with *The Allyn & Bacon Guide to Writing:*
  - *The New American Webster Handy College Dictionary,* Third Edition
  - *The Oxford American Desk Dictionary and Thesaurus,* Second Edition
  - *The Oxford Essential Thesaurus*
  - *Merriam-Webster's Collegiate Dictionary,* Tenth Edition

Acknowledgments

We wish to give special thanks to our longtime colleague and friend, Virginia Chappell of Marquette University, who clarified and updated the explanations of MLA and APA formatting and documentation in Chapter 14.

We would like to thank the many scholars and teachers who reviewed *The Allyn & Bacon Guide to Writing* in its various stages. Several scholars gave us chapter-by-chapter advice, and to them we owe our deepest appreciation:

Larry Beason, University of South Alabama
Gregory R. Glau, Arizona State University
Jennifer Liethen Kunka, Francis Marion University
Lisa J. McClure, Southern Illinois University, Carbondale
Wendy Sharer, East Carolina University
Bill Stiffler, Harford Community College
Donna Strickland, University of Missouri—Columbia
Diane S. Thompson, Harrisburg Area Community College
Scott Weeden, Indiana University Purdue University Indianapolis
Debbie J. Williams, Abilene Christian Universit

Many gave us initial advice on how to proceed with the fourth edition:

Hugh Burns, Texas Woman's University
Virginia Chappell, Marquette University
Ron Christiansen, Salt Lake Community College
Gregory R. Glau, Arizona State University
Emily Golson, University of Northern Colorado
Melissa Helquist, Salt Lake Community College
Ruth M. Higgins, Mitchell College
Rosemary B. Johnson, Mitchell College
Michael Kramp, University of Northern Colorado
Bonnie Lenore Kyburz, Utah Valley State College
Lindsay Lewan, Arapahoe Community College
Phillip P. Marzluf, Kansas State University
Sharon James McGee, Southern Illinois University, Edwardsville
Carole Clark Papper, Ball State University
Irving N. Rothman, University of Houston
Wendy Sharer, East Carolina University
Linda Shelton, Utah Valley State College
Suzanne Shumway, North Central Michigan College
Donna Strickland, University of Missouri–Columbia
David Susman, Salt Lake Community College
Scott Weeden, Indiana University Purdue University Indianapolis
Carolyn Young, University of Wyoming

Most of all, we are indebted to our students, who have made the teaching of composition such a joy. We thank them for their insights and for their willingness to engage with problems, discuss ideas, and, as they compose and revise, share with us their frustrations and their triumphs. They have sustained our love of teaching and inspired us to write this book. In particular, we would like to thank a number of students who provided invaluable research assistance for this edition as well as their student perspective on important issues: Jean Bessette and Tiffany Anderson, two of Seattle University's most talented Writing Center consultants.

Finally, John Bean thanks his wife, Kit, also a professional composition teacher, whose dedication to her students as writers and individuals manifests the sustaining values of our unique profession. John also thanks his children, Matthew, Andrew, Stephen, and Sarah, who have grown to adulthood since he began writing textbooks. June Johnson thanks her husband, Kenneth Bube, for his loving support, his interest in teaching, and his expert understanding of the importance of writing in mathematics and the sciences. Finally, she thanks her daughter, Jane Ellen, who has offered encouragement and support in countless ways.

JOHN D. RAMAGE
JOHN C. BEAN
JUNE JOHNSON

The
Allyn & Bacon
Guide to Writing
Concise Edition

A Rhetoric for College Writers

This recent advertisement for the Hummer H2, taken from a surprising bird's-eye-view camera angle, depends on the viewer's memory of what the Hummer looks like from other angles—its power, size, and rugged sleekness. Note the way the bright image of the Hummer dominates the ad and reinforces the confident tone of the slogan: "Like nothing else." Consider the ad-making team's intentions in focusing exclusively on the Hummer itself, in choosing this camera angle, in creating the unusual terrain beneath the vehicle, in placing the tiny words "Lost? Cool" in the top right corner, and in relying on the Hummer's reputation as a versatile, all-terrain vehicle with top-of-the-line quality. Who seems to be the target audience for this ad?

This advertisement is part of the For Writing and Discussion exercise in Chapter 1, on page 11.

LOST? COOL

THE H2. **HUMMER**® LIKE NOTHING ELSE.™   HUMMER.COM

Part 1 A Rhetoric for College Writers

Posing Problems
The Demands of College Writing

It seems to me, then, that the way to help people become better writers is not to tell them that they must first learn the rules of grammar, that they must develop a four-part outline, that they must consult the experts and collect all the useful information. These things may have their place. But none of them is as crucial as having a good, interesting question.

—RODNEY KILCUP, *HISTORIAN*

Our purpose in this introductory chapter is to help you see writers as questioners and problem posers—a view of writing that we believe will lead to your greatest growth as a college-level thinker and writer. In particular, we want you to think of writers as people who pose interesting questions or problems and struggle to work out answers or responses to them. As we show in this chapter, writers pose two sorts of problems: *subject-matter problems* (for example, Should the homeless mentally ill be placed involuntarily in mental hospitals?) and *rhetorical problems* (for example, How much background about the homeless population does my audience need? What is their current attitude about mental institutions? What form and style should I use?).

We don't mean to make this focus on problems sound scary. Indeed, humans pose and solve problems all the time and often take great pleasure in doing so. Psychologists who study critical and creative thinking see problem solving as a productive and positive activity. According to one psychologist, "Critical thinkers are actively engaged with life. [. . .] They appreciate creativity, they are innovators, and they exude a sense that life is full of possibilities."* By focusing first on the kinds of problems that writers pose and struggle with, we hope to increase your own engagement and pleasure in becoming a writer.

In this chapter we introduce you to the following concepts and principles:

- Why a writing course is valuable, with special emphasis on the connection between writing and thinking

---

*Academic writers regularly document their sources. The standard method for documenting sources in student papers and in many professional scholarly articles is the MLA or the APA citation system explained in Chapter 14. In this text we have cited our sources in an "Acknowledgments" section. To find our source for this quotation (or for the quotation from Kilcup above), see the Acknowledgments at the end of the text.

- How writers pose subject-matter problems, in which they wrestle with the complexities of their topics
- How writers pose rhetorical problems, in which they must make decisions about content, organization, and style based on their purpose, audience, and genre
- How the rules of writing vary along a continuum from closed to open prose
- How to ask good subject-matter questions and show how they are problematic and significant

The chapter concludes with a brief writing assignment in which you can try your own hand at proposing a subject-matter question.

Why Take a Writing Course?

Before turning directly to the notion of writers as questioners and problem posers, let's ask why a writing course can be valuable for you.

For some people, being a writer is part of their identity, so much so that when asked, "What do you do?" they are apt to respond, "I'm a writer." Poets, novelists, scriptwriters, journalists, technical writers, grant writers, self-help book authors, and so on see themselves as writers the way other people see themselves as chefs, realtors, bankers, or musicians. But many people who don't think of themselves primarily as writers nevertheless *use* writing—often frequently—throughout their careers. They are engineers writing proposals or project reports; attorneys writing legal briefs; nurses writing patient assessments; business executives writing financial analyses or management reports; concerned citizens writing letters to the editor about public affairs; college professors writing articles for scholarly journals.

In our view, all these kinds of writing are valuable and qualify their authors as writers. If you already identify yourself as a writer, then you won't need much external motivation for improving your writing. But if you have little interest in writing for its own sake and aspire instead to become a nurse, an engineer, a business executive, a social worker, or a marine biologist, then you might question the benefits of taking a writing course.

What are these benefits? First of all, the skills you learn in this course will be directly transferable to your other college courses, where you will have to write papers in a wide variety of styles. Lower-division (general education or core) courses often focus on general academic writing, while upper-division courses in your major introduce you to the specialized writing and thinking of your chosen field. What college professors value are the kinds of questioning, analyzing, and arguing skills that this course will help you develop. You will emerge from this course as a better reader and thinker and a clearer and more persuasive writer, able to meet the demands of different academic writing situations.

Effective writing skills are also essential for most professional careers. To measure the importance of writing to career success, researchers Andrea Lunsford and Lisa Ede surveyed randomly selected members of such professional organizations as the American Consulting Engineers Counsel, the American Institute of Chemists, the American Psychological Association, and the International City

Management Association. They discovered that members of these organizations spend, on average, forty-four percent of their professional time writing, including (most commonly) letters, memos, short reports, instructional materials, and professional articles and essays.

Besides the pragmatic benefits of college and career success, learning to write well can bring you the personal pleasure of a richer mental life. As we show throughout this text, writing is closely allied to thinking and to the innate satisfaction you take in exercising your curiosity, creativity, and problem-solving ability. Writing connects you to others and helps you discover and express ideas that you would otherwise never think or say. Unlike speaking, writing gives you time to think deep and long about an idea. Because you can revise writing, it lets you pursue a problem in stages, with each new draft reflecting a deeper, clearer, or more complex level of thought. In other words, writing isn't just a way to express thought; it is a way to do the thinking itself. The act of writing stimulates, challenges, and stretches your mental powers and, when you do it well, is profoundly satisfying.

Subject-Matter Problems: The Starting Point of Writing

Having made a connection between writing and thinking, we now move to the spirit of inquiry that drives the writing process. From your previous schooling, you are probably familiar with the term *thesis statement*, which is the main point a writer wants to make in an essay. However, you may not have thought much about the question that lies behind the thesis, which is the problem or issue that the writer is wrestling with. An essay's thesis statement is actually the writer's one-sentence summary answer to this question, and it is this question that has motivated the writer's thinking. Experienced writers immerse themselves in subject matter questions in pursuit of answers or solutions. They write to share their proposed solutions with readers who share their interests. As we will show in Chapter 2, introductions to academic essays typically begin with the question or problem that the writer plans to address. In this section we show you more fully the nature of subject matter questions that initiate the writing process.

Shared Problems Unite Writers and Readers

Everywhere we turn, we see writers and readers forming communities based on questions or problems of mutual interest. Perhaps nowhere are such communities more evident than in academe. Many college professors are engaged in research projects stimulated and driven by questions or problems. At a recent workshop for new faculty members, we asked participants to write a brief description of a question or problem that motivated them to write a seminar paper or article. Here are two examples of their responses.

A Biochemistry Professor During periods of starvation, the human body makes physiological adaptations to preserve essential protein mass. Unfortunately, these adaptations don't work well during long-term starvation. After the body depletes its carbohydrate storage, it must shift to depleting protein in order to produce glucose. Eventually, this loss of functional protein leads to metabolic dysfunction and death. Interestingly, several animal species are capable of surviving for extensive periods without food and water while conserving protein and maintaining glucose levels. How do the bodies of these animals accomplish this feat? I wanted to investigate the metabolic functioning of these animals, which might lead to insights into the human situation.

A Journalism Professor Several years ago, I knocked on the wooden front door of the home of an elderly woman in Tucson, Arizona. Tears of grief rolled down her cheeks as she opened the door. The tears turned to anger when I explained that I was a reporter and wished to talk with her about her son's death in jail. Her face hardened. "What right do you have coming here?" I recall her saying. "Why are you bothering me?" Those questions have haunted me throughout my journalism career. Do journalists have the right to intrude on a person's grief? Can they exercise it any time they want? What values do journalists use to decide when to intrude and violate someone's privacy?

Of course these are not new college students speaking about problems they posed; they are college professors recalling problems that fueled a piece of professional writing. We share these problems with you to persuade you that most college professors value question asking and want you to be caught up, as they are, in the spirit of inquiry.

As you progress through your college career, you will find yourself increasingly engaged with questions. All around college campuses you'll find clusters of professors and students asking questions about all manner of curious things—the reproductive cycles of worms and bugs, the surface structure of metals, the social significance of obscure poets, gender roles among the Kalahari Bushmen, the meaning of Balinese cockfighting, the effect of tax structure on economies, the rise of labor unions in agriculture, the role of prostitutes in medieval India, the properties of concrete, and almost anything else a human being might wonder about. A quick review of the magazine rack at any large supermarket reveals that similar communities have formed around everything from hot rods to model railroads, from computers to kayaks to cooking.

At the heart of all these communities of writers and readers is an interest in common questions and the hope for better or different answers. Writers write because they have something new or surprising or challenging to say in response to a question. Readers read because they share the writer's interest in the problem and want to deepen their understanding.

Posing a Problem: A Case Study of a Beginning College Writer

So far we have talked about how professional writers pose problems. In this section we show you how student writer Christopher Leigh posed a problem for an argumentative paper requiring research.

At the start of his process, Christopher was interested in the issue of school violence. Like many of his classmates, Christopher had been disturbed by the massacre at Columbine High School in Littleton, Colorado, in April 1999. When he discussed Columbine with his small group in his first-year composition course, he explained that these killings were especially unsettling for him because Columbine seemed like a safe, middle-class school with no previous record of violence. He wondered what would cause a normal-seeming group of kids to open fire on their classmates.

When he started doing research, he had formulated only a broad question: What can be done to prevent school violence? On his first trip to the library, however, he came across an article on psychological profiling. Here is what he wrote in his journal on that day:

> Today I came across an article in the *New York Times* that disturbed me. It was about psychological profiling, which means that they figure out psychological traits that are apt to indicate a person may become violent. Then they look for kids in the schools that fit those traits. After reading this article, I began to think about whether or not the use of profiles to identify potentially violent students is effective, and if it is somehow a violation of students' rights or privacy. Profiles that use signs such as "antisocial behavior" and "mood swings" may be problematic because almost any student would fit the profiles at some point. Think of all the bad, depressing days that teenagers have. And singling out a student because he or she fits the profile is never going to be able to predict for sure if that student will become violent. I know someone who was suspended for making a joke about a bomb, and even though it was a careless remark, she had no intention of doing harm. So profiling may victimize students who are not violent. Right now my feeling is that profiling in any form is wrong, but I need to learn more about how they are used and if they are effective. Also if they violate students' rights, and how other students feel about them.

> → narrowed quest
> is psychological
> profiling effective
> in inducating
> violence?
> (final Draft pg 363)

After writing this journal entry, Christopher wrote out his new research question as follows: Is psychological profiling an effective way to help reduce school violence? When he discussed this question with his small group, his friends thought it was an interesting question worth researching. The group was divided about profiling. Some thought that schools should do everything they can to identify disturbed classmates and intervene with psychological counseling. Others thought profiling is a total violation of privacy. This division of opinion convinced Christopher that the question was a good one.

We will return to Christopher's story occasionally throughout this text. You can read his final paper in Chapter 14, pages 363–374, where Christopher argues against metal detectors in schools—a moderately changed focus from his initial interest in psychological profiling. You can also read his earlier exploratory paper (Ch. 7, pp. 159–163), which narrates the evolution of his thinking as he researched ways of preventing school violence.

Posing Your Own Subject-Matter Questions

Where do good questions come from and how can you learn to pose them? At the outset, we should say that the kinds of questions we discuss in this chapter may lead you toward new and unfamiliar ways of thinking. Beginning college students typically value questions that have right answers. Students ask their professors questions about a subject because they are puzzled by confusing parts of a text-book, a lecture, or an assigned reading. They hope their professors will explain the confusing material clearly. Their purpose in asking these questions is to eliminate misunderstandings, not to open up controversy and debate. Although basic comprehension questions are important, they are not the kinds of inquiry questions that initiate strong college-level writing and thinking.

The kinds of questions that stimulate the writing most valued in college are open-ended questions that focus on unknowns or invite multiple points of view rather than factual questions that have single right answers. These are what historian Rodney Kilcup refers to when he says that writers should begin with a "good, interesting question" (see the epigraph to this chapter, p. 5). For Kilcup, a good question sets the writer on the path of inquiry, critical thinking, analysis, and argument.

Later in your college career, many of the questions you pursue will come from your chosen major, particularly from controversies, uncertainties, and unknowns within the subject matter of that discipline. Nevertheless, you currently have many other areas of experience or knowledge that can lead to good, interesting questions. Consider, for example, the various communities to which you belong: your dorm or apartment complex; your campus; your city or region of the country; your job or volunteer work; your connection with any religious, sports, or activity group. Consider also your civic role as a citizen of a city, state, nation, and global community. If you read newspapers or magazines, watch television, listen to radio programs, or surf the Internet, you are exposed to problems that merit investigation and critical analysis. Many writers find that questions emerge when they perceive differences between their own views and those of others within a given community or when they discover confusions, gaps, and inconsistencies within information, ideas, or beliefs. Good questions can arise when you do any of the following:

- Discover holes in your knowledge of something
- Note gaps or inconsistencies in the evidence for something, or realize that you and someone else are drawing different conclusions from the same set of facts
- Think about contradictions among different perspectives and different points of view
- Consider why you are dissatisfied with someone else's explanation of a phenomenon, analysis of an event, or solution to a problem
- Feel curious about the cause, consequence, purpose, function, or value of something
- Note discrepancies between the ideal and the real, between what someone values and what he or she does, between the current state of something and your desired state of something

Once you start practicing these ways of thinking, you will see yourself as a more powerful writer able to contribute your own views to a community of readers drawn into conversation by mutual interest in a problem.

Characteristics of Good Subject-Matter Questions

Questions that lead to good college-level writing generally exhibit three main qualities:

- *A good question is problematic.* By problematic, we mean that community members do not currently know the answer or agree on the answer. A question whose answer can be looked up in a reference book or solved by applying a mathematical formula is not problematic.
- *A good question is significant.* In addition, a good question should have something at stake. Writers need to answer their readers' "So what?" question by showing that a problem is worth pursuing. Why does the problem matter? Who are its stakeholders? How will a community gain by considering the writer's answer to the question?
- *A good question is interesting to the writer.* Finally, you as writer need to be genuinely engaged with this question; it has to be a real question for you, a problem in which you feel invested. You can infuse your writing with vitality only when you, the writer, are truly curious about a question or passionately concerned about it.

Our way of thinking about problems has been motivated by the South American educator Paulo Freire, who wanted his students (often poor, illiterate villagers) to become *problematizers* instead of memorizers. Freire opposed what he called "the banking method" of education, in which students deposited knowledge in their memory banks and then made withdrawals during exams. The banking method, Freire believed, left third world villagers passive and helpless to improve their situations in life. He wanted students to ask disturbing questions and then to act on their discoveries. When students are taught to read and write through the banking method, they learn the word *water* by repeating an irrelevant, self-evident sentence such as, "The water is in the well." With Freire's method of teaching literacy, students might learn the word *water* by asking, "Why is the water dirty and who is responsible?" Freire believed that good questions have stakes and that answering the questions can make a difference in the world.

For Writing and Discussion

Your task: Working in small groups or as a whole class, create a list of problematic, significant, and interesting questions about any topic area assigned by your instructor. In the following pages we provide a context for one possible subject: the problem of the world's growing desire for automobiles in the face of a declining supply of fossil fuels. If you choose this topic, derive your questions from your personal experiences with automobiles and your energy knowledge based on reading and observation. For further context, we provide an array of data for you to examine.

(continued)

The seven visual and verbal texts in this data set present a range of perspectives on energy usage and automobiles, yet these texts represent only a small sampling of the views currently being voiced. As you read through the passages and ponder the images and graphics in light of your own personal experiences, look for controversies, inconsistencies, and gaps in knowledge that can prompt you to articulate problems worth exploring.

Some examples of questions: The range of questions you can ask is very wide. You can ask questions based on your own personal experience and observations ("What can we do to make bike riding more popular?" or "How did Hummers or Dodge Ram pickups become prestigious urban vehicles?"), or you can ask questions spinning off the exhibits ("What will happen to our way of life if oil becomes unaffordable?" or "Should the government force people into smaller cars? If so, how?") When your class shares the questions you have produced, you will begin experiencing what it is like to be drawn into inquiry—to feel the pleasure and exhilaration of doing your own critical thinking in response to a problem.

Exhibit 1: The Hummer ad that appears on page 3 as the part opener image for Part One of this text.

Exhibit 2: Excerpt from news story on China

SHIFTING INTO HIGH GEAR

From a nation of bikes and donkey carts, China has shifted to a mobile population in just a generation. Automobile sales on the mainland are doubling almost every year, with all the car makers racing to China to cash in on the world's most revved-up auto market. . . .

China really has been a dream market for the world's auto makers, who have seen profits steadily decline due to gloomy economic conditions around the globe. Except in China.

In 2002, for instance, China sales soared 37 percent, even as overall sales across Europe tumbled seven percent. And, contrary to most of the mainland products, profit margins in China are sky-high, amongst the world's biggest margins.

No wonder all the world's auto makers are established on the mainland. Most arrived less than a decade ago. All are racing to keep apace of demand.

—Source: http://www.gluckman.com/ChinaCars.html

Exhibit 3: Excerpt from the Bush Administration's *National Energy Policy*

Estimates indicate that over the next 20 years, U.S. oil consumption will increase by 33 percent, natural gas consumption by well over 50 percent, and demand for electricity will rise by 45 percent. If America's energy production grows at the same rate as it did in the 1990s we will face an ever-increasing gap.

Increases on this scale will require preparation and action today. Yet America has not been bringing on line the necessary supplies and infrastructure. . . .

A primary goal of the National Energy Policy is to add supply from diverse sources. This means [increasing the domestic production of] oil, gas, and coal. It also means [increasing our use of] hydropower and nuclear power. And it means making greater use of non-hydro renewable sources now available.

Exhibit 4: Excerpt from "Greenpeace Responds to the Bush/Cheney National Energy Policy Task Force"

The Bush/Cheney Task Force's National Energy Policy leads the nation down the wrong road. Though the administration claims to have crafted a long-term solution, the shortsighted policy includes:

- No efforts to cut the nation's global warming pollution
- Massive electric power plant construction—1,300 new polluting fossil fuel and nuclear power plants are proposed
- New oil extraction in ecologically sensitive areas such as the Arctic National Wildlife Refuge and the Rocky Mountains
- More oil refineries, pipelines and electrical transmission lines
- Additional U.S. taxpayer subsidies for the fossil fuel and nuclear industries

And in an effort to hide their true agenda, the Administration proposes:

- Minor efforts toward saving energy through energy efficiency and renewable energy sources

> —Source: http://archive.greenpeace.org/climate/climatecountdown/
> documents/bushrealitycheck.pdf

Exhibit 5: News analysis excerpt

In interviews at the New York International Auto Show this month, top executives of General Motors and the Ford Motor company, both of which make and sell a lot of cars in Europe, reiterated their support for high gasoline taxes—as opposed to stricter fuel economy regulations.

"Anything that can align the individual customer's purchase decisions with society's goals [is] the way to go," Ford's chairman and chief executive, William Clay Ford, Jr., said, adding that his company has previously supported a 50-cent increase in gas taxes. . . .

Mr. Ford said the current regulatory system, which compels automakers to make cars and trucks that meet minimum standards for fuel efficiency, "puts the manufacturer in this tug of war that's unsustainable between what the customer wants and what society says it wants."

In other words, most customers want bigger and faster cars—actually, light-duty trucks like sport utility vehicles—not efficient ones.

—Danny Hakim, "A Fuel-Saving Proposal From Your Automaker: Tax the Gas"
The New York Times (18 April 2004): BU 5

Exhibit 6: From "The Energy Guy Website" (Ray Darby, PE)

Let's look at the case for oil, our most used fuel. Data from the *Energy Information Administration (EIA)* indicates about 981.4 billion barrels of *oil reserves remain* on the planet (it was 1,033 BB when I checked a year earlier?!?). Although this may sound like a lot, the world has consumed about 800 billion barrels of oil thus far. Half of the oil we've used so far has been consumed since 1970—a mere 28 years ago. In addition to the known (verified) oil reserves on the planet, there are an estimated 547 billion more barrels of "technically feasible" oil to recover. That leaves us with a total of 1,528 billion barrels.

(*continued*)

The world consumed about *75 billion barrels* of oil in 1999. In another 38 years from now, at a constant 2% rate of world oil consumption growth we will have used up virtually all of the remaining oil on the planet! . . . Unfortunately, the aforementioned "current rate of world oil consumption growth" is not likely to remain constant at 2%, but increase due to world economic development. For example, the annual *percent change in world oil consumption* (over the preceding year) was 0.8% in 1998, 1.7% in 1999, and 2.4% (estimated) for 2000 . . .

Are we going to run out of oil? No. It will get very expensive long before that! It's just a matter of time and circumstances, supply and demand. As demand continues to grow while reserves continue to decline, it's simply a matter of time before a permanent oil-price spiral begins. The graphic below illustrates how supply problems will begin to limit production. The area under the curve is the total amount of (known) oil remaining on the planet (the dotted line represents production if additional discoveries, which can be reasonably anticipated, are included). Note the peak is estimated to occur around 2010 (only eight short years away)!

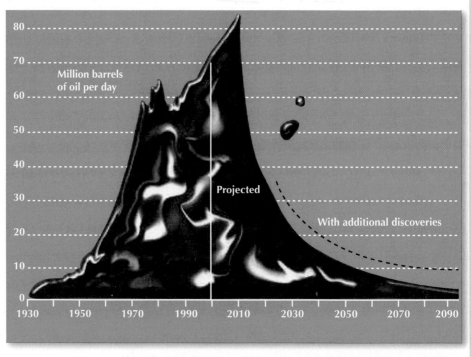

—Source: http://www.theenergyguy.com/IssuesSummary.html

Exhibit 7: Oil consumption table

Map & Graph: Energy: Oil consumption (Top 20 Countries)

View this stat: Per capita   Show map full screen

	Country	Description	Amount
1.	United States	19.7 million barrels per day (2002E)	
2.	Japan	5.4 million barrels per day (2002E)	
3.	China	4.9 million barrels per day (2001E)	
4.	Germany	2.71 million barrels per day (2002E)	
5.	Russia	2.38 million barrels per day; (2001E)	
6.	Brazil	2.2 million barrels per day (2001E)	
7.	India	2.0 million barrels per day (2002E)	
8.	Canada	2.0 million barrels per day (2002E)	
9.	France	1.96 million barrels per day (2002E)	
10.	Mexico	1.93 million barrels per day (2002E)	
11.	Italy	1.87 million barrels per day (2002E)	
12.	United Kingdom	1.7 million barrels per day (2002E)	
13.	Spain	1.5 million barrels per day (2002E)	
14.	Saudi Arabia	1.36 million barrels per day (2002E)	
15.	Indonesia	1,022,000 barrels per day (2001E)	
16.	Taiwan	985,000 barrels per day (2002E)	
17.	Australia	872,000 barrels per day (2001E)	
18.	Singapore	722,000 barrels per day (all imported) (2002E)	
19.	Thailand	715,000 barrels per day (2001E)	
20.	Turkey	635,000 barrels per day (2002E)	
	Total	56.56 million barrels per day	
	Weighted Average	4.26 million barrels per day	

Source: Energy Information Administration, US Department of Energy

Source: http://www.nationmaster.com/red/graph-T/ene_oil_con&int=20

Rhetorical Problems: Reaching Readers Effectively

So far we have been focusing on subject-matter problems. In this section we shift our attention to rhetorical problems.

By rhetorical problems, we refer to a network of questions writers must ask about audience, purpose, and genre (a *genre* is a recurring type of writing with established conventions, such as an academic article, a personal essay, a newspaper feature story, a grant proposal, an article for *Seventeen* or *Rolling Stone*, a

Web page, and so forth). These questions often loom as large for writers as do the subject-matter problems that drive their writing in the first place. Suppose, for example, that you have asked the subject-matter question: To what extent will hydrogen cars be an effective solution to the problem of dwindling fossil fuels? Suppose further that your research casts doubt on hydrogen cars. Consider the number of rhetorical problems you must think about as you sit down to write a draft.

One of our students did a short research project on this question. You can read her paper in Chapter 8, pp. 187–196.

- Who are my readers? How much background do they need on hydrogen cell cars? Do I need to explain how hydrogen cells work?
- Are my readers already interested in the problem of dwindling supply of fossil fuels? Do they believe the world may soon run out of oil, or do they think the supply is endless? Do I need to hook them on this problem?
- Should I take a strong stand against hydrogen cars or just raise some doubts?
- How should I organize my essay to make it most effective?
- Should I write this paper as a formal college research paper or as a more popular magazine-style article?

Subject-matter problems and rhetorical problems are often so closely linked that writers can't address one without addressing the other. You would not even be able to decide on a title, for example, until you decided whether the paper should have an academic or a popular tone.

In Chapters 2 and 3 we discuss in more detail the kinds of rhetorical problems that writers must pose and solve. In this chapter we simply introduce you to one extended example of a rhetorical problem. From a student's point of view, we might call this "the problem of varying rules." From our perspective, we call it a problem of "genre"—or "what kind of prose does my audience expect me to write?"

An Example of a Rhetorical Problem: When to Choose Closed Versus Open Forms

In our experience, beginning college writers are often bothered by the ambiguity and slipperiness of rules governing writing. Many beginning writers wish that good writing followed consistent rules such as "Never use 'I' in a formal paper" or "Start every paragraph with a topic sentence." The problem is that different kinds of writing follow different rules, leaving the writer with rhetorical choices rather than with hard-and-fast formulas for success. To develop this point, we begin by asking you to consider a problem about how writing might be classified.

Read the following short pieces of nonfiction prose. The first is a letter to the editor written by a professional civil engineer in response to a newspaper editorial arguing for the development of wind-generated electricity. The second short piece is entitled "A Festival of Rain." It was written by the American poet and religious writer Thomas Merton, a Trappist monk. After reading the two samples carefully, proceed to the discussion questions that follow.

READINGS

David Rockwood
A Letter to the Editor

1   Your editorial on November 16, "Get Bullish on Wind Power," is based on fantasy rather than fact. There are several basic reasons why wind-generated power can in no way serve as a reasonable major alternative to other electrical energy supply alternatives for the Pacific Northwest power system.

2   First and foremost, wind power is unreliable. Electric power generation is evaluated not only on the amount of energy provided, but also on its ability to meet system peak load requirements on an hourly, daily, and weekly basis. In other words, an effective power system would have to provide enough electricity to meet peak demands in a situation when the wind energy would be unavailable—either in no wind situations or in severe blizzard conditions, which would shut down the wind generators. Because wind power cannot be relied on at times of peak needs, it would have to be backed up by other power generation resources at great expense and duplication of facilities.

3   Secondly, there are major unsolved problems involved in the design of wind generation facilities, particularly for those located in rugged mountain areas. Ice storms, in particular, can cause sudden dynamic problems for the rotating blades and mechanisms which could well result in breakdown or failure of the generators. Furthermore, the design of the facilities to meet the stresses imposed by high winds in these remote mountain regions, in the order of 125 miles per hour, would indeed escalate the costs.

4   Thirdly, the environmental impact of constructing wind generation facilities amounting to 28 percent of the region's electrical supply system (as proposed in your editorial) would be tremendous. The Northwest Electrical Power system presently has a capacity of about 37,000 megawatts of hydro power and 10,300 megawatts of thermal, for a total of about 48,000 megawatts. Meeting 28 percent of this capacity by wind power generators would, most optimistically, require about 13,400 wind towers, each with about 1,000 kilowatt (one megawatt) generating capacity. These towers, some 100 to 200 feet high, would have to be located in the mountains of Oregon and Washington. These would encompass hundreds of square miles of pristine mountain area, which, together with interconnecting transmission facilities, control works, and roads, would indeed have major adverse environmental impacts on the region.

5   There are many other lesser problems of control and maintenance of such a system. Let it be said that, from my experience and knowledge as a professional engineer, the use of wind power as a major resource in the Pacific Northwest power system is strictly a pipe dream.

Thomas Merton
A Festival of Rain

1   Let me say this before rain becomes a utility that they can plan and distribute for money. By "they" I mean the people who cannot understand that rain is a festival, who do not appreciate its gratuity, who think that what has no price has no value, that what cannot be sold is not real, so that the only way to make something *actual* is to place it on the market. The time will come when they will sell you even your rain. At the moment it is still free, and I am in it. I celebrate its gratuity and its meaninglessness.

2   The rain I am in is not like the rain of cities. It fills the woods with an immense and confused sound. It covers the flat roof of the cabin and its porch with insistent and controlled rhythms. And I listen, because it reminds me again and again that the whole world runs by rhythms I have not yet learned to recognize, rhythms that are not those of the engineer.

3   I came up here from the monastery last night, sloshing through the corn fields, said Vespers, and put some oatmeal on the Coleman stove for supper. . . . The night became very dark. The rain surrounded the whole cabin with its enormous virginal myth, a whole world of meaning, of secrecy, of silence, of rumor. Think of it: all that speech pouring down, selling nothing, judging nobody, drenching the thick mulch of dead leaves, soaking the trees, filling the gullies and crannies of the wood with water, washing out the places where men have stripped the hillside! What a thing it is to sit absolutely alone, in a forest, at night, cherished by this wonderful, unintelligible, perfectly innocent speech, the most comforting speech in the world, the talk that rain makes by itself all over the ridges, and the talk of the watercourses everywhere in the hollows!

4   Nobody started it, nobody is going to stop it. It will talk as long as it wants, this rain. As long as it talks I am going to listen.

5   But I am also going to sleep, because here in this wilderness I have learned how to sleep again. Here I am not alien. The trees I know, the night I know, the rain I know. I close my eyes and instantly sink into the whole rainy world of which I am a part, and the world goes on with me in it, for I am not alien to it.

For Writing and Discussion

Working in small groups or as a whole class, try to reach consensus on the following specific tasks:

1. What are the main differences between the two types of writing? If you are working in groups, help your recorder prepare a presentation describing the differences between Rockwood's writing and Merton's writing.
2. Create a metaphor, simile, or analogy that best sums up your feelings about the most important differences between Rockwood's and Merton's writing: "Rockwood's writing is like . . . , but Merton's writing is like. . . . "
3. Explain why your metaphors are apt. How do your metaphors help clarify or illuminate the differences between the two pieces of writing?

Now that you have done some thinking on your own about the differences between these two examples, turn to our brief analysis.

Distinctions between Closed and Open Forms of Writing

David Rockwood's letter and Thomas Merton's mini-essay are both examples of nonfiction prose. But as these examples illustrate, nonfiction prose can vary enormously in form and style. From the perspective of structure, we can place nonfiction prose along a continuum that goes from closed to open forms of writing (see Figure 1.1).

Of our two pieces of prose, Rockwood's letter illustrates tightly closed writing and falls at the far left end of the continuum. The elements that make this writing closed are the presence of an explicit thesis in the introduction (i.e., wind-generated power isn't a reasonable alternative energy source in the Pacific Northwest) and the

FIGURE 1.1 A Continuum of Essay Types: Closed to Open Forms

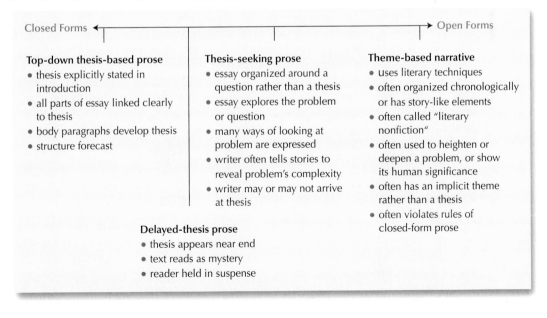

Closed Forms ←   → Open Forms

Top-down thesis-based prose
- thesis explicitly stated in introduction
- all parts of essay linked clearly to thesis
- body paragraphs develop thesis
- structure forecast

Thesis-seeking prose
- essay organized around a question rather than a thesis
- essay explores the problem or question
- many ways of looking at problem are expressed
- writer often tells stories to reveal problem's complexity
- writer may or may not arrive at thesis

Theme-based narrative
- uses literary techniques
- often organized chronologically or has story-like elements
- often called "literary nonfiction"
- often used to heighten or deepen a problem, or show its human significance
- often has an implicit theme rather than a thesis
- often violates rules of closed-form prose

Delayed-thesis prose
- thesis appears near end
- text reads as mystery
- reader held in suspense

writer's consistent development of that thesis throughout the body (i.e., "First and foremost, wind power is unreliable. . . . Secondly, there are major unsolved [design] problems. . . . Thirdly, . . . "). Once the thesis is stated, the reader knows the point of the essay and can predict its structure. The reader also knows that the writer's point won't change as the essay progresses. Because its structure is transparent and predictable, the success of closed-form prose rests entirely on its ideas, which must "surprise" readers by asserting something new, challenging, doubtful, or controversial. It aims to change readers' view of the subject through the power of reason, logic, and evidence. Closed-form prose is what most college professors write when doing their own scholarly research, and it is what they most often expect of their students. It is also the most common kind of writing in professional and business contexts.

Merton's "A Festival of Rain" falls toward the right end of the closed-to-open continuum. It resists reduction to a single, summarizable thesis. Although Merton praises rain, and clearly opposes the consumer culture that will try to "sell" you the rain, it is hard to pin down exactly what he means by "festival" or by rain's "gratuity and its meaninglessness." The main organizing principle of Merton's piece, like that of most open-form prose, is a story or narrative—in this case the story of Merton's leaving the monastery to sleep in the rain-drenched cabin. Rather than announce a thesis and support it with reasons and evidence, Merton lets his point emerge suggestively from his story and his language. Open-form essays still have a focus, but the focus is more like a theme in fiction than like a thesis in argument. Readers may argue over its meaning in the same way that they argue over the meaning of a film or poem or novel.

As you can see from the continuum in Figure 1.1, essays can fall anywhere along the scale. Not all thesis-with-support writing has to be top down, stating its thesis explicitly in the introduction. In some cases writers choose to delay the thesis, creating a more exploratory, open-ended, "let's think through this together" feeling before finally stating the main point late in the essay. In some cases writers explore a problem without *ever* finding a satisfactory thesis, creating an essay that is thesis seeking rather than thesis supporting, an essay aimed at deepening the question, refusing to accept an easy answer. Such essays may replicate their author's process of exploring a problem and include digressions, speculations, conjectures, multiple perspectives, and occasional invitations to the reader to help solve the problem. When writers reach the far right-hand position on the continuum, they no longer state an explicit thesis. Instead, like novelists or short story writers, they embed their points in plot, imagery, dialogue, and so forth, leaving their readers to *infer* a theme from the text.

Where to Place Your Writing along the Continuum

Clearly, essays at opposite ends of this continuum operate in different ways and obey different rules. Because each position on the continuum has its appropriate uses, the writer's challenge is to determine which sort of writing is most appropriate for a given situation.

As you will see in later chapters, the kind of writing you choose depends on your purpose, your intended audience, and your genre (you will recall that a *genre* is a recurring type of writing with established conventions). Thus, if you were writing an analytical paper for an academic audience, you would typically choose a closed-form structure, and your finished product would include elements such as the following:

- An explicit thesis in the introduction
- Forecasting of structure
- Cohesive and unified paragraphs with topic sentences
- Clear transitions between sentences and between parts
- No digressions

But if you were writing an autobiographical narrative about, say, what family means to you, you would probably move toward the open end of the continuum and violate one or more of these conventions (note how extensively Merton violates them). It's not that open-form prose doesn't have rules; it's that the rules are different, just as the rules for jazz are different from the rules for a classical sonata.

For another perspective on how rules vary, consider two frequently encountered high school writing assignments: the five-paragraph theme and the personal-experience narrative (for example, the infamous "What I Did Last Summer" essay). The five-paragraph theme is a by-the-numbers way to teach closed-form, thesis-with-support writing. It emphasizes logical development, unity, and coherence. The five-paragraph structure may emerge naturally if you are writing an argument based on three supporting reasons—an introductory paragraph, three body paragraphs (one for each reason), and a concluding paragraph. Rockwood's letter is a real-world example of a five-paragraph theme even though Rockwood certainly didn't have that format in mind when writing.

In contrast, the "What I Did Last Summer" assignment calls for a different sort of writing, probably an open-form, narrative structure closer to Merton's piece about the night in the rain. Whether the writer chooses a closed-form or an open-form approach depends on the intended audience of the piece and the writer's purpose.

For Writing and Discussion

Do you and your classmates most enjoy writing prose at the closed or more open end of the continuum? Prior to class discussion, work individually by recalling a favorite piece of writing that you have done in the past. Jot down a brief description of the kind of writing this was (a poem, a personal-experience essay, a research paper, a newspaper story, a persuasive argument). Then, working in small groups or as a whole class, report one at a time on your favorite piece of writing and speculate where it falls on the continuum from closed to open forms. Are you at your best in closed-form writing that calls for an explicit thesis statement and logical support? Or are you at your best in more open and personal forms?

Is there a wide range of preferences in your class? If so, how do you account for this variance? If not, how do you account for the narrow range?

Chapter Summary

This chapter introduced you to the notion of writers as questioners and problem posers who wrestle with both subject-matter and rhetorical problems. We have shown how writers start with questions or problems about their subject matter rather than with topic areas, and how they take their time resolving the uncertainties raised by such questions. We saw that writers must ask questions about their rhetorical situation and make decisions about content, form, and style based on their understanding of their purpose, their audience, and their genre. We described how the rules governing writing vary as the writer moves along the continuum from closed to open forms.

The next chapter looks closely at how writers pose problems, pursue them in depth, and then pose answers that bring something new, surprising, or challenging to readers.

BRIEF WRITING PROJECT

We close this chapter with two options for a brief writing project, each aimed at helping you appreciate the value of a "good, interesting question." The first option is the easier of the two and can be done informally. The second option is more formal and yet can be completed in one page.

Option 1: Think of a recent experience in your life that has generated questions for you—for example, reading a book or magazine, watching a film or TV show, participating in a class discussion, or observing an incident in the dorms. Briefly describe the experience and then, based on your ponderings, pose several questions arising from the experience that you think are problematic, significant, and interesting.

Option 2: Write a one-page (double-spaced) essay that poses a question about automobiles and fossil fuels (or some other topic provided by your instructor). Besides explaining your question and providing needed background information, you will need to help readers see (1) why the question is problematic—that is, why it is a genuine problem with no easy right answers—and (2) why the question is significant or worth pursuing—that is, what benefit will come from solving it. Your essay should not answer the question; your purpose is only to ask it.

The goal of these brief writing project options is to give you practice at posing problematic questions. As you will see in Chapter 2, the second option, which focuses on a single question, will give you practice at writing the question-posing part of a typical academic introduction.

Either of these options will anchor your questions in a specific experience, reading, or set of data. The best kinds of questions are neither so broad that they are virtually unanswerable nor so narrow that they have only one right answer. If you can imagine several different ways to answer the questions you ask, you are on the right track. What follows are student examples for each option.

READINGS

Our first reading, by student writer Noel Gaudette, responds to Option 1.

Noel Gaudette
Questions about Genetically Modified Foods

A few weeks ago I was eating breakfast while listening to the news on the radio. One report I heard was about the political and economic tension over shipping genetically modified (GM) food to African nations. One of the concerns of Africans was the long-term safety of GM products. They worried about the food disrupting the natural biological balance we maintain in our bodies from eating traditionally grown foods. While listening to this program, I peered at my food service breakfast of reconstituted eggs, uniform hash browns, perfect-looking sausages, and little cup of bright red ketchup. My orange juice tasted fresh squeezed and my coffee seemed very ordinary. Still, I started to wonder if my breakfast contained genetically modified foods. I began to think of these questions:

1. How do I know if I am eating a GM product? How should consumers be made aware that their food contains GM products? Are these labeled on cans and boxes? If not, should they be?
2. Are the African nations correct in their assumption that GM food is unsafe?
3. What testing has been done on these new GM foods and is it sufficient?
4. To what extent should we promote the development and consumption of GM foods?

Describes the specific experience that generated the questions

Shows how details of the experience caused writer to ponder questions

States specific questions or issues that the writer feels are both problematic and significant

Our second reading, by student writer Brittany Tinker, responds to Option 2.

Brittany Tinker
Can the World Sustain an American Standard of Living?

Yesterday's class discussion about the growing demand for automobiles in China combined with all the problems of smog and air pollution in Beijing raised lots of dilemmas for me. Because the United States and other developed nations are already using up vast quantities of the world's oil, adding oil demands from China and other developing nations will cause the world to deplete its oil even sooner. Moreover, third world development adds even

Hooks reader's interest and provides background

States the question

Begins to show that the question is problematic by presenting one side of her dilemma

Shows the other side of her dilemma

Shows why question is significant

more to the air pollution and global warming caused by consumerism in the United States and other developed countries. So I wonder, what standard of living can the whole world sustain once third world countries expand their own economies?

Part of me hopes that the poor people in second and third world countries can one day enjoy the standard of living that I have had. The disparity between first world and second or third world countries hit me when I visited Nicaragua. Most Nicaraguans live in small, one-room homes made from corrugated tin and cinder blocks. The plumbing is underdeveloped and the electricity is inconstant. Most Nicaraguan families do not have enough food to provide adequate nutrition. But through economic development, I hope that these people can have the comforts that I and many other fortunate Americans have such as hot water, lots of nutritious food, numerous bedrooms, at least one car in the family, paved sidewalks or driveways, and a backyard, swimming pool, or hot tub.

But another part of me sees that my own standard of living may be what's at fault; maybe this model for the good life won't work anymore. If second and third world countries attain the standard of living that I have been lucky enough to have, then air pollution, destruction of forests, global warming, and harm to wildlife, as well as the depletion of oil reserves, will pose even greater risks for the world than they already do. A lot of my classmates seem confident that scientists will discover alternative energy sources and solutions to pollution and global warming so that the whole world can live in comfort. But this pessimistic side of me doesn't share their confidence. Maybe the solution is for Americans to greatly reduce their own consumption and to begin reducing the environmental damage they have already created.

So I am left wondering, Can the world sustain for everybody the standard of living I have enjoyed? This question is significant because there is so much at stake. If our model for the happy life is to have all the American luxuries, then the development of the third world might mean a much speedier destruction of the planet. If we hope to preserve the planet while eliminating the poverty and misery of third world people, then maybe Americans have to develop a new model for happiness. Is it possible for developing countries to find a new path to economic prosperity that shows the developed world a new model of preserving the environment?

Showing Why Your Question Is Problematic and Significant (Option 2)

If you have been assigned the second option for your brief writing project, you will need to show why your question is both problematic and significant. (Doing so helps your readers understand the puzzling nature of your problem and motivates their interest in it.) Some strategies writers can use to show that a question is problematic and significant are given in the following charts.

Strategies for Showing That a Question Is Problematic

POSSIBLE STRATEGY	EXAMPLE
Show how your own (or previous researchers') attempts to solve the problem have failed.	If your problem were "How can our university encourage more students, faculty, and staff to carpool?" you could show how the university's previous attempts to encourage carpooling (reduced-rate parking, privileged parking spots) have failed.
Show different ways that people have attempted to answer the question (different theories or competing explanations) and indicate how no one answer is fully adequate.	If you were puzzled by why Europeans accept much higher fuel prices than Americans do, you could summarize several theories presented by your classmates and show why each one isn't fully convincing.
Show the alternative points of view on an issue.	If your problem were whether to save fossil fuels by building more nuclear power plants, you could summarize the main arguments for and against nuclear power.
Show why an expected or "easy" answer isn't satisfactory.	Suppose you asked, "What is the best alternative to using fossil fuels for generating electricity?" and one of your environmentalist friends says, "All we have to do is put our money into developing wind energy." You could problematize this easy answer by summarizing engineer David Rockwood's objections to the technical feasibility of wind power (see pp. 17–18).
Narrate your own attempts to think through the problem, revealing how none of your possible answers fully satisfied you.	You might use the strategy "Part of me thinks this . . . ; but another part of me thinks this . . . " or "I used to think this, but now I think . . . ." This is the strategy used by Brittany Tinker in the example essay.

Strategies for Showing That a Question Is Significant

POSSIBLE STRATEGY	EXAMPLE
Show how solving the problem will lead to practical, real-world benefits.	If we could figure out how to get people to buy fuel-efficient cars rather than SUVs, we could cut down substantially on fossil fuel use.
Show how solving a small knowledge problem will help us solve a larger, more important knowledge problem.	If we could better understand why Europeans are willing to live with high gasoline prices, we might better understand how cultural values influence consumer behavior.

Planning Your Essay

To help you develop a plan for your Option 2 brief essay, you can make an informal outline or flowchart in which you plan out each of the required parts. Here are some examples of student plans that led to successful question-posing essays on problems other than cars and fossil fuels.

EXAMPLE 1

I would like to question the ethics of interspecies transplants and show why it is not an easy question to answer.

Illustrate question with case of a man who had a transplant of a baboon heart.

View One: Interspecies transplants are unethical. It is unethical to "play God" by taking the organs of one species and placing them into another.

View Two: Interspecies transplants may save lives. Medical research done with the intention of improving human life is ethical.

This is a significant problem because it causes us to question the limits of medical research and to ask what it means to be human.

EXAMPLE 2

I am wondering whether Eminem's music ought to be censored in some way or at least kept out of the hands of children or unknowledgeable listeners.
Show how I am conflicted by all the different points of view:

- I agree that his lyrics are vile, misogynistic, homophobic, and obscene. Children should not be allowed to listen to his music.
- Yet I believe in free speech.
- Also rap is more complex than the general public realizes. Eminem's irony and complexity are often misunderstood. Therefore, serious listeners should have access to his music.
- Additionally, there may be some value just in expressing politically incorrect thoughts, but not if doing so just leads to more hatred.

Explain how I am left with a dilemma about whether or not to censor Eminem and if so, how.
This is an important question because it involves the larger question of individual freedom versus public good.

Exploring Problems, Making Claims

"In management, people don't merely 'write papers,' they solve problems," said [business professor Kimbrough Sherman]. . . . He explained that he wanted to construct situations where students would have to "wallow in complexity" and work their way out, as managers must.

—A. KIMBROUGH SHERMAN, *MANAGEMENT PROFESSOR*

In the previous chapter we introduced you to the role of the writer as a questioner and problem poser. In this chapter, we narrow our focus to thesis-governed writing—the kind of writing most frequently required in college courses and often required in civic and professional life. Thesis-governed writing requires a behind-the-scenes ability to think rigorously about a problem and then to make a claim* that summarizes your "best solution."

In Part Three of this text, "A Guide to Composing and Revising," we give you compositional advice on the actual drafting and revising of a thesis-governed essay. Our goal in this chapter is to stand back from the nuts and bolts of writing to give you some big-picture principles of thesis-governed prose. We believe these principles, which you can transfer across most of your college courses, can significantly improve your writing. Your payoff for reading this chapter will be a marked increase in your ability to write engaging and meaningful prose targeted to the audience of your choice. In particular, you will learn the following:

- How college professors value a kind of thinking that one professor calls "wallow[ing] in complexity"
- How each academic discipline is a field of inquiry and argument, not just a repository of facts and concepts to be learned
- How the thinking process of posing questions and proposing answers is reflected in the introductions of academic articles and how an effective question must engage the interests of your intended audience
- How your thesis statement should contain a surprising element aimed at changing your reader's view of your topic

*In this text we use the words *claim* and *thesis statement* interchangeably. As you move from course to course, instructors typically use one or the other of these terms. Other synonyms for thesis statement include *proposition*, *main point*, or *thesis sentence*.

- How thesis statements are supported by a network of points and particulars
- How you can deepen and complicate your thinking through "the believing and doubting game" (the brief writing project for this chapter)

What Does a Professor Want?

It is important to understand the kind of thinking most college professors want in student writing. Many beginning students imagine that professors want students primarily to comprehend course concepts as taught in textbooks and lectures and to show their understanding on exams. Such comprehension is important, but it is only a starting point. As management professor A. Kimbrough Sherman explains in the epigraph to this chapter, college instructors expect students to wrestle with problems by applying the concepts, data, and thought processes they learn in a course to new situations. As Sherman puts it, students must learn to "wallow in complexity and work their way out."

Learning to Wallow in Complexity

Wallowing in complexity is not what most first-year college students aspire to do. (Certainly that wasn't what we, the authors of this text, had uppermost in our minds when we sailed off to college!) New college students tend to shut down their creative thinking processes too quickly and head straight for closure to a problem. Harvard psychologist William Perry, who has studied the intellectual development of college students, found that few of them become skilled wallowers in complexity until late in their college careers. According to Perry, most students come to college as "dualists," believing that all questions have right or wrong answers, that professors know the right answers, and that the student's job is to learn them. Of course, these beliefs are partially correct. First-year students who hope to become second-year students must indeed understand and memorize mounds of facts, data, definitions, and basic concepts.

But true intellectual growth requires the kind of problematizing we discussed in Chapter 1. It requires students to *do* something with their new knowledge, to apply it to new situations, to conduct the kinds of inquiry, research, analysis, and argument pursued by experts in each discipline. Instead of confronting only questions that have right answers, students need to confront the kinds of open-ended problems we discussed in Chapter 1. Cognitive psychologists call such problems "ill-structured" because they seldom yield a single, correct answer and often require the thinker to operate in the absence of full and complete data.* Your college professors pursue ill-structured problems in their professional writing. The kinds of problems vary from discipline to discipline, but they all require

---

*In contrast, a "well-structured" problem eventually yields a correct answer. Math problems that can be solved by applying the right formulae and processes are well structured. That's why you can have the correct answers in the back of the book.

the writer to use reasons and evidence to support a tentative solution. Because your instructors want you to learn how to do the same kind of thinking, they often phrase essay exam questions or writing assignments as ill-structured problems. They are looking not for one right answer, but for well-supported arguments that acknowledge alternative views. A C paper and an A paper may have the same "answer" (identical thesis statements), but the C writer may have waded only ankle deep into the mud of complexity, whereas the A writer wallowed in it and worked a way out.

What skills are required for successful wallowing? Specialists in critical thinking have identified the following:

1. The ability to pose problematic questions
2. The ability to analyze a problem in all its dimensions—to define its key terms, determine its causes, understand its history, appreciate its human dimension and its connection to one's own personal experience, and appreciate what makes it problematic or complex
3. The ability (and doggedness) to find, gather, and interpret facts, data, and other information relevant to the problem (often involving library, Internet, or field research)
4. The ability to imagine alternative solutions to the problem, to see different ways in which the question might be answered and different perspectives for viewing it
5. The ability to analyze competing approaches and answers, to construct arguments for and against alternatives, and to choose the best solution in light of values, objectives, and other criteria that you determine and articulate
6. The ability to write an effective argument justifying your choice while acknowledging counterarguments

We discuss and develop these skills throughout this text.

In addition to these generic thinking abilities, critical thinking requires what psychologists call "domain-specific" skills. Each academic discipline has its own characteristic ways of approaching knowledge and its own specialized habits of mind. The questions asked by psychologists differ from those asked by historians or anthropologists; the evidence and assumptions used to support arguments in literary analysis differ from those in philosophy or sociology.

What all disciplines value, however, is the ability to manage complexity, and this skill marks the final stage of William Perry's developmental scheme. At an intermediate stage of development, after they have moved beyond dualism, students become what Perry calls "multiplists." At this stage students believe that since the experts disagree on many questions, all answers are equally valid. Professors want students merely to have an opinion and to state it strongly. A multiplist believes that a low grade on an essay indicates no more than that the teacher didn't like his or her opinion. Multiplists are often cynical about professors and grades; to them, college is a game of guessing what the teacher wants to hear. Students emerge into Perry's final stages—what he calls "relativism" and "commitment in relativism"— when they are able to take a position in the face of complexity and to justify that decision through reasons and evidence while weighing and acknowledging contrary reasons and counterevidence. Professor Sherman articulates what is expected at Perry's last stages—wading into the messiness of complexity and working your way back to solid ground.

Seeing Each Academic Discipline as a Field of Inquiry and Argument

When you study a new discipline, you must learn not only the knowledge that scholars in that discipline have acquired over the years, but also the processes they used to discover that knowledge. It is useful to think of each academic discipline as a network of conversations in which participants exchange information, respond to each other's questions, and express agreements and disagreements. The scholarly articles and books that many of your instructors write (or would write if they could find the time) are formal, permanent contributions to an ongoing discussion carried on in print in your college's or university's library. Each book or article represents a contribution to a conversation; each writer agreed with some of his or her predecessors and disagreed with others.

As each discipline evolves and changes, its central questions evolve also, creating a fascinating, dynamic conversation that defines the discipline. At any given moment, scholars are pursuing hundreds of cutting-edge questions in each discipline. Table 2.1 provides examples of questions that scholars have debated over the years as well as questions they are addressing today.

As you study a discipline, you are learning how to enter its network of conversations. To do so, you have to build up a base of knowledge about the discipline, learn its terminology, observe its conversations, read its major works, see how it asks questions, and learn its methods. To help you get a fuller sense of how written "conversation" works within a discipline, the rest of this chapter shows you how a typical academic writer poses a question and then presents and supports his or her proposed answer to the question.

Posing an Engaging Question

In Chapter 1, we said that a thesis statement is the writer's answer to a thesis question. But, as we have suggested, the kinds of questions that engage audiences vary from discipline to discipline or, in popular culture, from magazine to magazine. Let's suppose, for example, that you want to write an essay on rap music. How might your essay differ if you wanted to write it for different courses you might be taking or for different popular media? Here are some examples of rap questions that would interest different audiences:

- *Psychology course:* To what extent does rap music increase misogynistic or homophobic attitudes in listeners?
- *Sociology course:* Based on a random sampling of student interview subjects, how does the level of appreciation for rap music vary by ethnicity, class, age, and gender?

TABLE 2.1 Scholarly Questions in Different Disciplines

Field	Examples of Current Cutting-Edge Questions	Examples of Historical Controversies
Anatomy	What is the effect of a pregnant rat's alcohol ingestion on the development of fetal eye tissue?	In 1628, William Harvey produced a treatise arguing that the heart, through repeated contractions, caused blood to circulate through the body. His views were attacked by followers of the Greek physician Galen.
Literature	To what extent does the structure of a work of literature, for example Conrad's *Heart of Darkness*, reflect the class and gender bias of the author?	In the 1920s, a group of New Critics argued that the interpretation of a work of literature should be based on close examination of the work's imagery and form and that the intentions of the writer and the biases of the reader were not important. These views held sway in U.S. universities until the late 1960s, when they came increasingly under attack by deconstructionists and other postmoderns, who claimed that author intentions and reader's bias were important parts of the work's meaning.
Rhetoric/ Composition	How does hypertext structure and increased attention to visual images in Web-based writing affect the composing processes of writers?	Prior to the 1970s, college writing courses in the United States were typically organized around the rhetorical modes (description, narration, exemplification, comparison and contrast, and so forth). This approach was criticized by the expressivist school associated with the British composition researcher James Britton. Since the 1980s, composition scholars have proposed various alternative strategies for designing and sequencing assignments.
Psychology	What are the underlying causes of gender identification? To what extent are differences between male and female behavior explainable by nature (genetics, body chemistry) versus nurture (social learning)?	In the early 1900s under the influence of Sigmund Freud, psychoanalytic psychologists began explaining human behavior in terms of unconscious drives and mental processes that stemmed from repressed childhood experiences. Later, psychoanalysts were opposed by behaviorists, who rejected the notion of the unconscious and explained behavior as responses to environmental stimuli.

- *Rhetoric/composition course:* What images of rap artists, urban life, and women do the lyrics of rap songs portray?
- *Local newspaper:* Should Bill Cosby be criticized or applauded for attacking "obscene rap music" as an example of bad values that keep poor African-Americans impoverished?
- *Rolling Stone Magazine:* Was the murder of Biggie used to set up a civil war in hip-hop and the Black community?

In each of these cases, the writer understands how readers in a particular community pose questions. The first three examples show differences in the way that psychologists, sociologists, and rhetoric/composition scholars might ask questions about rap music. For newspaper readers, the Bill Cosby question would interest readers who followed the public reaction to Cosby's June 2004 speech to the NAACP in which he criticized young African-Americans for wearing sagging pants, speaking in street slang, and listening to rap. The question about the murder of Biggie actually appeared in the June 7, 2004, issue of *Rolling Stone Magazine*. In all these cases, the writer poses a subject-matter question that connects in some way to the intended readers' values, beliefs, or characteristic ways of thinking.

How a Prototypical Introduction Poses a Question and Proposes an Answer

To show you how academic writers typically begin by asking a question, we will illustrate with a "prototype" introduction from a scholarly journal. A *prototype* is the most typical or generic instance of a class and doesn't constitute a value judgment. For example, a prototype bird might be a robin or blackbird (rather than an ostrich, chicken, hummingbird, or pelican) because these birds seem to exhibit the most typical features of "birdiness." Likewise, a prototype dog would be a medium-sized mutt rather than a Great Dane or toy poodle. The article we have chosen for our illustration comes from a scholarly journal called the *Journal of Popular Culture*. Other articles in this same journal are on topics ranging from *Buffy the Vampire Slayer* to international transformations of Barbie dolls in India or Mexico. In the following introduction, note how the authors first present a question and then move, at the end of the introduction, to their thesis and the overview of their argument. Note also how the question-posing part of the introduction is similar to the question-posing essay one might write for the brief writing project (Option 2) in Chapter 1.

See student writer Brittany Tinker's problem-posing essay on pp. 23–24.

PIT BULL PANIC

Provides background showing dangerous reputation of pit bulls in the media

The news media has long been criticized for being sensationalist as well as biased. One ongoing story that the media has offered their audience is a melodrama regarding the American Pit Bull Terrier (hereafter referred to as "Pit Bull"). The Pit Bull has been portrayed in the past one and a half decades as ". . . the archetype of canine evil, predators of the defenseless. Unpredictable companions that kill and maim without discretion. Walking horror shows bred with an appetite for violence (sic)" (Verzemnieks B6). This news coverage has had profound effects. Pit Bull ownership brings with it consequences not associated with most acquisitions. "These days, buying a Pit Bull means buying into a controversy; Pit Bull owners had better not be afraid of public opinion" (B6). In some places, Pit Bull ownership is not even allowed; in fact, ownership is banned in 75 communities in the United States (Sanchez-Beswick 1). Many insurance companies refuse to insure homeowners with Pit Bulls (V. Richardson 189). A survey done by the American Society for the Prevention of Cruelty to Animals found that 30% of shelters that responded do not adopt out Pit Bulls. Most of these shelters have this policy due to community bans,

Parenthetical citation of sources

but others choose not to (Schultz 36). Obviously these organizations feel that Pit Bulls are dangerous. They are, no doubt, in part influenced by media accounts. The general public also looks to the media for information to warn them of dangers that they need to avoid (De Becker 294–5). The extent to which the public has caught the wave of "Pit Bull panic" is the focus of a study that is presented in this paper.

Presentation of question

Such a panic would be rational if, in fact, Pit Bulls were as dangerous as the media has portrayed. But is the media portrayal of Pit Bulls truly accurate? Advocates feel that Pit Bulls have been unfairly maligned by the media. As Hallum* makes painfully clear, there are always two sides to every story. Additional evidence that Pit Bulls have been unfairly demonized comes from the personal experience of the authors themselves. The authors have worked with dozens of Pit Bulls at a local animal shelter in southern New Jersey. The vast majority of these Pit Bulls have been stray dogs brought in by animal control officers from a neighborhood where residents use Pit Bulls as macho status symbols, over-breed them severely, and are alleged to hold at least occasional informal dog fights. These Pit Bulls do not belong to a special pampered minority who have been given a "genteel" upbringing. Yet, as a breed, they are consistently among the most people-friendly dogs in the shelter.

Provides counterevidence that pit bulls are people friendly (shows why question is problematic)

This paper examines the negative portrayal of the Pit Bull in the media. It offers a theory regarding why such a portrayal has come about. It then discusses the results of a study that examined three major issues regarding Pit Bulls: (1) people's perception of Pit Bulls; (2) attitudes towards legislation designed to place restrictions on Pit Bull ownership; and (3) whether certain variables affect these perceptions and attitudes. This research is important for several reasons. Although our primary purpose is not to prove the ultimate truth about Pit Bulls, we do offer an abundance of evidence to discredit the media's negative portrayals of Pit Bulls. Only by offering counter-evidence can we establish the existence of media bias on this topic. More importantly, we offer an innovative theory of media bias. This theory is not based on the political orientation of journalists. Indeed, many issues covered by the media can be biased for reasons other than political orientation. Furthermore, we examine, for our specific topic, whether the news media actually influences the attitudes of the people it is supposedly informing. Ultimately, media bias should only be worrisome if the public actually believes the misinformation it is exposed to.

Thesis sentences showing purpose of paper and forecasting main parts

Shows why question is significant

—Judy Cohen and John Richardson

This introduction, like most introductions to academic articles, includes the following prototypical features:

- *Focus on a question or problem to be investigated.* In this case the question is stated explicitly: "But is the media portrayal of Pit Bulls truly accurate?" This direct question implies a further question: If the media portrayal of pit bulls is not accurate, then how do we account for the media bias? In many introductions, the question to be investigated is implied rather than stated directly.
- *An explanation of why the question is problematic.* To show that their question is problematic, Cohen and Richardson juxtapose two opposing views: the common media representation of pit bulls as dangerous, countered by their

For a detailed discussion of posing questions in closed-form introductions, see Chapter 12, "Composing and Revising Closed-Form Prose," pp. 318–319.

*Hallum is one of the "advocates" of pit bulls. He is identified in the bibliography at the end of the article as the author of a book entitled *Pit Bull Sting: The Other Side of the Story.*

own personal experience working in animal shelters and by a book by Hallum, a pit bull advocate, showing that pit bulls are "people friendly."

For a detailed discussion of thesis statements, purpose statements, and blueprint statements, see Chapter 12, "Composing and Revising Closed-Form Prose," pp. 319–320.

- *An explanation of why the question is significant.* To show the significance of their question, Cohen and Richardson see two benefits of their research and analysis: First, they hope to rectify public misunderstandings about pit bulls. Second, they hope to offer a new theory about the causes of media bias as a way of helping the public guard itself against misinformation. This explanation addresses the reader's "So what?" question.

- *The writer's tentative "answer" to this question (the essay's "thesis"), which brings something new to the audience.* In closed-form articles the thesis is usually stated explicitly at the end of the introduction. Although Cohen and Richardson do not condense their whole thesis into one sentence, such a thesis is clearly implied: The media have misrepresented pit bulls for reasons that we explain through our innovative theory of media bias.

- *[optional] A mapping statement forecasting the content and shape of the rest of the article ("First X is discussed, then Y, and finally Z").* Cohen and Richardson forecast the shape of their article by identifying its major parts Such forecasting is typical of longer articles, where readers appreciate a roadmap of what is coming. In shorter articles, writers typically omit forecasting or mapping statements.

We have used Cohen and Richardson's article to show how academic writers—in posing a problem and proposing an answer—join an ongoing conversation. The papers you will be asked to write in college will be much stronger if you create the same kind of introduction that poses a problem and then asserts a tentative, risky answer (your thesis), which you will support with reasons and evidence.

Seeking a Surprising Thesis

It is not enough to ask a good question. You also have to have a strong thesis. But what makes a thesis strong?

For one thing, a strong thesis usually contains an element of uncertainty, risk, or challenge. A strong thesis implies a naysayer who could disagree with you. According to composition theorist Peter Elbow, a thesis has "got to stick its neck out, not just hedge or wander. [It is] something that can be quarreled with." Elbow's sticking-its-neck-out metaphor is a good one, but we prefer to say that a strong thesis *surprises* the reader with a new, unexpected, different, or challenging view of the writer's topic. By surprise, we intend to connote, first of all, freshness or newness for the reader. Many kinds of closed-form prose don't have a sharply contestable thesis of the sticking-its-neck-out kind highlighted by Elbow. A geology report, for example, may provide readers with desired information about rock strata in an exposed cliff, or a Web page for diabetics may explain how to coordinate meals and insulin injections during a plane trip across time zones. In these cases, the information is surprising because it brings something new and significant to intended readers.

In other kinds of closed-form prose, especially academic or civic prose addressing a problematic question or a disputed issue, surprise requires an argumentative, risky, or contestable thesis. In these cases also, surprise is not inherent in the material but in the intended readers' reception; it comes from the writer's providing an adequate or appropriate response to the readers' presumed question or problem.

In this section, we present two ways of creating a surprising thesis: (1) trying to change your reader's view of your subject; and (2) giving your thesis tension.

Try to Change Your Reader's View of Your Subject

To change your reader's view of your subject, you must first imagine how the reader would view the subject _before_ reading your essay. Then you can articulate how you aim to change that view. A useful exercise is to write out the "before" and "after" views of your imagined readers:

Before reading my essay, my readers think this way about my topic:

_____

After reading my essay, my readers will think this different way about my

topic: _____

You can change your reader's view of a subject in several ways.* First, you can enlarge it. Writing that enlarges a view is primarily informational; it provides new ideas and data to add to a reader's store of knowledge about the subject. For example, suppose you are interested in the problem of storing nuclear waste (a highly controversial issue in the United States) and decide to investigate how Japan stores radioactive waste from its nuclear power plants. You could report your findings on this problem in an informative research paper. (Before reading my paper, readers would be uncertain how Japan stores nuclear waste. After reading my paper, my readers would understand the Japanese methods, possibly helping us better understand our options in the United States.)

Second, you can clarify your reader's view of something that was previously fuzzy, tentative, or uncertain. Writing of this kind often explains, analyzes, or interprets. This is the kind of writing you do when analyzing a short story, a painting, an historical document, a set of economic data, or other puzzling phenomena or when speculating on the causes, consequences, purpose, or function of something. Suppose, for example, you are analyzing the persuasive strategies used in various perfume ads and are puzzled by an advertisement for Jennifer Lopez's "Still" perfume. Your paper tries to explain how the unusual name "Still" is essential for understanding the verbal and visual aspects of the ad. (Before reading my paper, my readers will be puzzled by what this ad is trying to do. After reading my paper, my readers will see how the words and images of this ad are connected to different meanings of the word "Still.")

*Our discussion of how writing changes a reader's view of the world is indebted to Richard Young, Alton Becker, and Kenneth Pike, _Rhetoric: Discovery and Change_ (New York: Harcourt Brace & Company, 1971).

Another kind of change occurs when an essay actually restructures a reader's whole view of a subject. Such essays persuade readers to change their minds or make decisions. For example, the writers of "Pit Bull Panic," the introduction to which you have just read, want to restructure their readers' thinking about pit bulls. (Before reading our article, readers would think that pit bulls are vicious animals bred to maim and kill. After reading our article, readers will regard pit bulls as people-friendly animals demonized by the media.) Likewise, engineer David Rockwood, in his letter to the editor that we reprinted in Chapter 1 (pp. 17–18), wants to change readers' views about wind power. (Before reading my letter, readers would believe that wind-generated electricity can solve our energy crisis. After reading my letter, they will see that the hope for wind power is a pipe dream.)

Surprise then is the measure of change an essay brings about in a reader. Of course, to bring about such change requires more than just a surprising thesis; the essay itself must persuade the reader that the thesis is sound as well as novel. Later in this chapter, we talk about how writers support a thesis through a network of points and particulars.

Give Your Thesis Tension

Another element of a surprising thesis is tension. By *tension* we mean the reader's sensation of being pulled away from familiar ideas toward new, unfamiliar ones or being pulled in two or more directions by opposing ideas. One of the best ways to create tension in a thesis statement is to begin the statement with an *although* or *whereas* clause: "Whereas most people believe X, this paper asserts Y." The *whereas* or *although* clause summarizes the reader's "before" view of your topic or the counterclaim that your essay opposes; the main clause states the surprising view or position that your essay will support. You may choose to omit the *although* clause from your actual essay, but formulating it first will help you achieve focus and surprise in your thesis. The examples that follow illustrate the kinds of tension we have been discussing and show why tension is a key requirement for a good thesis.

Question	What effect has the cell phone had on our culture?
Thesis without Tension	The invention of the cell phone has brought many advantages to our culture.
Thesis with Tension	Although the cell phone has brought many advantages to our culture, it may also have contributed to an increase in risky behavior among boaters and hikers.
Question	Do reservations serve a useful role in contemporary Native American culture?
Thesis without Tension	Reservations have good points and bad points.
Thesis with Tension	Although my friend Wilson Real Bird believes that reservations are necessary for Native Americans to preserve their heritage, the continuation of reservations actually degrades Native American culture.

In the first example, the thesis without tension (cell phones have brought advantages to our culture) is a truism with which everyone would agree and hence lacks surprise. The thesis with tension places this truism (the reader's "before" view) in an *although* clause and goes on to make a surprising or contestable assertion. The idea that the cell phone contributes to risky behavior among outdoor enthusiasts alters our initial complacent view of the cell phone and gives us new ideas to think about.

In the second example, the thesis without tension may not at first seem tensionless because the writer sets up an opposition between good and bad points. But *almost anything* has good and bad points, so the opposition is not meaningful, and the thesis offers no element of surprise. Substitute virtually any other social institution (marriage, the postal service, the military, prisons), and the statement that it has good and bad points would be equally true. The thesis with tension, in contrast, is risky. It commits the reader to argue that reservations have degraded Native American culture and to oppose the counterthesis that reservations are needed to *preserve* Native American culture. The reader now feels genuine tension between two opposing views.

Tension, then, is a component of surprise. The writer's goal is to surprise the reader in some way, thereby bringing about some kind of change in the reader's view. Here are some specific strategies you can use to surprise a reader:

- Give the reader new information or clarify a confusing concept.
- Make problematic something that seems nonproblematic by showing paradoxes or contradictions within it, by juxtaposing two or more conflicting points of view about it, or by looking at it more deeply or complexly than expected.
- Identify an unexpected effect, implication, or significance of something.
- Show underlying differences between two concepts normally thought to be similar or underlying similarities between two concepts normally thought to be different.
- Show that a commonly accepted answer to a question isn't satisfactory or that a commonly rejected answer may be satisfactory.
- Oppose a commonly accepted viewpoint, support an unpopular viewpoint, or in some other way take an argumentative stance on an issue.
- Propose a new solution to a problem or an unexpected answer to a question.

For Writing and Discussion

It is difficult to create thesis statements on the spot because a writer's thesis grows out of an exploratory struggle with a problem. However, in response to a question one can often propose a possible claim and treat it hypothetically as a tentative thesis statement put on the table for testing. What follows are several problematic questions that we have used as examples in this and the previous chapter, along with some possible audiences that you might consider addressing. Working individually, spend ten minutes considering possible thesis statements

(continued)

that you might pose in response to one or more of these questions. (Remember that these are tentative thesis statements that you might abandon after doing research.) Be ready to explain why your tentative thesis brings something new, enlightening, challenging, or otherwise surprising to the specified readers. Then, working in small groups or as a whole class, share your possible thesis statements. Finally, choose one or two thesis statements that your small group or the whole class thinks are particularly effective and brainstorm the kinds of evidence that would be required to support the thesis.

1. To what extent should the public support genetically modified foods? (possible audiences: readers of health food magazines; general public concerned about food choices; investors in companies that produce genetically modified seeds)
2. Should people be encouraged to drive more fuel-efficient cars? If so, how? (possible audiences: SUV owners; conservative legislators generally in favor of free markets; investors in the automobile industry)
3. What social views—particularly of male success and of women or gays—are promoted by rap music? (possible audiences: consumers of rap music; parents concerned about their children's exposure to rap music; black parents who read about Bill Cosby's speech to the 2004 NAACP convention—see pp. 31–32).
4. Any questions that your class might have developed through discussing Chapter 1.

Here is an example:

Problematic question: What can cities do to prevent traffic congestion?

One possible thesis: Although many people think that building light rail systems won't get people out of their cars, new light rail systems in many cities have attracted new riders and alleviated traffic problems.

Intended audience: Residents of cities concerned about traffic congestion but skeptical about light rail

Kinds of evidence needed to support thesis: Examples of cities with successful light rail systems; evidence that many riders switched from driving cars; evidence that light rail alleviated traffic problems

Supporting Your Thesis with Points and Particulars

Of course, a surprising thesis is only one aspect of an effective essay. An essay must also persuade the reader that the thesis is believable as well as surprising. Although tabloid newspapers have shocking headlines ("Britney Spears Videos Contain FBI Spy Secrets!"), skepticism quickly replaces surprise when you look inside and find the article's claims unsupported. A strong thesis, then, must both surprise the reader and be supported with convincing particulars.

In fact, the particulars are the flesh and muscle of writing and comprise most of the sentences. In closed-form prose, these particulars are connected clearly to points, and the points precede the particulars. In this section, we explain this principle more fully.

How Points Convert Information to Meaning

When particulars are clearly related to a point, the point gives meaning to the particulars, and the particulars give force and validity to the point. Particulars constitute the evidence, data, details, examples, and subarguments that develop a point and make it convincing. By themselves, particulars are simply information—mere data without meaning.

In the following example, you can see for yourself the difference between information and meaning. Here is a list of information:*

- In almost all species on earth, males are more aggressive than females.
- Male chimpanzees win dominance by brawling.
- To terrorize rival troops, they kill females and infants.
- The level of aggression among monkeys can be manipulated by adjusting their testosterone levels.
- Among humans, preliminary research suggests that male fetuses are more active in the uterus than female fetuses.
- Little boys play more aggressively than little girls despite parental efforts to teach gentleness to boys and aggression to girls.

To make meaning out of this list of information, the writer needs to state a point—the idea, generalization, or claim—that this information supports. Once the point is stated, a meaningful unit (point with particulars) springs into being:

> Aggression in human males may be a function of biology rather than culture. In almost all species on earth, males are more aggressive than females. Male chimpanzees win dominance by brawling; to terrorize rival troops, they kill females and infants. Researchers have shown that the level of aggression among monkeys can be manipulated by adjusting their testosterone levels. Among humans, preliminary research suggests that male fetuses are more active in the uterus than female fetuses. Also, little boys play more aggressively than little girls despite parental efforts to teach gentleness to boys and aggression to girls.

Point

Particulars

Once the writer states this point, readers familiar with the biology/culture debate about gender differences immediately feel its surprise and tension. This writer believes that biology determines gender identity more than does culture. The writer now uses the details as evidence to support a point.

To appreciate the reader's need for a logical connection between points and particulars, note how readers would get lost if, in the preceding example, the

*The data in this exercise are adapted from Deborah Blum, "The Gender Blur," *Utne Reader* Sept. 1998: 45–48.

writer included a particular that seemed unrelated to the point ("Males also tend to be taller and heavier than women"—a factual statement, but what does it have to do with aggression?) or if, without explanation, the writer added a particular that seemed to contradict the point ("Fathers play more roughly with baby boys than with baby girls"—another fact, but one that points to culture rather than biology as a determiner of aggression).

Obviously, reasonable people seek some kind of coordination between points and particulars, some sort of weaving back and forth between them. Writing teachers use a number of nearly synonymous terms for expressing this paired relationship: *points/particulars, generalizations/specifics, claims/evidence, ideas/details, interpretations/data, meaning/support.*

How Removing Particulars Creates a Summary

What we have shown, then, is that skilled writers weave back and forth between generalizations and specifics. The generalizations form a network of higher-level and lower-level points that develop the thesis; the particulars (specifics) support each of the points and subpoints in turn. In closed-form prose, the network of points is easily discernible because points are clearly highlighted with transitions, and main points are placed prominently at the heads of paragraphs. (In open-form prose, generalizations are often left unstated, creating gaps where the reader must actively fill in meaning.)

Being able to write summaries and abstracts of articles is an important academic skill. See Chapter 6 on strategies for writing summaries and strong responses.

If you remove most of the particulars from a closed-form essay, leaving only the network of points, you will have written a summary or abstract of the essay. As an example, reread the civil engineer's letter to the editor arguing against the feasibility of wind-generated power (pp. 17–18). The writer's argument can be summarized in a single sentence:

> Wind-generated power is not a reasonable alternative to other forms of power in the Pacific Northwest because wind power is unreliable, because there are major unsolved problems involved in the design of wind-generation facilities, and because the environmental impact of building thousands of wind towers would be enormous.

What we have done in this summary is remove the particulars, leaving only the high-level points that form the skeleton of the argument. The writer's thesis remains surprising and contains tension, but without the particulars the reader has no idea whether to believe the generalizations or not. The presence of the particulars is thus essential to the success of the argument.

For Writing and Discussion

Compare the civil engineer's original letter with the one-sentence summary just given and then note how the engineer uses specific details to support each point. How do these particulars differ from paragraph to paragraph? How are they chosen to support each point?

How to Use Points and Particulars When You Revise

The lesson to learn here is that in closed-form prose, writers regularly place a point sentence in front of detail sentences. When a writer begins with a point, readers interpret the ensuing particulars not as random data but rather as *evidence* in support of that point. The writer depends on the particulars to make the point credible and persuasive.

This insight may help you clarify two of the most common kinds of marginal comments that readers (or teachers) place on writers' early drafts. If your draft has a string of sentences giving data or information unconnected to any stated point, your reader is apt to write in the margin, "What's your point here?" or "Why are you telling me this information?" or "How does this information relate to your thesis?" Conversely, if your draft tries to make a point that isn't developed with particulars, your reader is apt to write marginal comments such as "Evidence?" or "Development?" or "Could you give an example?" or "More details needed."

Don't be put off by these requests; they are a gift. It is common in first drafts for main points to be unstated, buried, or otherwise disconnected from their details and for supporting information to be scattered confusingly throughout the draft or missing entirely. Having to write point sentences obliges you to wrestle with your intended meaning: Just what am I trying to say here? How can I nutshell that in a point? Likewise, having to support your points with particulars causes you to wrestle with the content and shape of your argument: What particulars will make this point convincing? What further research do I need to do to find these particulars? In Part Three of this text, which is devoted to advice about composing and revising, we show how the construction and location of point sentences are essential for reader clarity. Part Three also explains various composing and revising strategies that will help you create effective networks of points and particulars.

For more about the importance of points, see pp. 322–325, which discuss topic sentences in paragraphs.

Chapter Summary

In this chapter we looked at the kind of wallowing in complexity that professors expect from students and saw how academic writing is rooted in subject matter problems. We saw how a prototypical introduction for an academic essay poses a question, explains how the question is problematic and significant, and then states the writer's thesis. We explained how a strong thesis aims to change readers' view of a topic by bringing to the reader something new, surprising, or challenging. Finally we saw how a writer supports a thesis through a network of points and particulars.

BRIEF WRITING PROJECT

Throughout this chapter we have shown the close relationship between a thesis question and a thesis statement. We conclude this chapter with a powerful thinking exercise that will keep you from being satisfied with a thesis statement too

Strategies for doing exploratory writing, composing first drafts, revising, and editing are treated in detail in Part Three of this text, "A Guide to Composing and Revising."

soon. As we have explained, writing is an active process of problem solving involving periods of pondering, researching, note-taking, exploratory writing, talking with others, drafting, and revising. The following exercise, developed by writing theorist Peter Elbow, is called the "believing and doubting game." To play the game, you explore many sides of a problematic question by posing a possible answer and then systemically trying first to believe that answer and then to doubt it. The game, as you will see, stimulates your critical thinking, helping you resist early closure.

Playing the Believing and Doubting Game

Play the believing and doubting game with one of the assertions listed on pages 44–46 (or another assertion provided by your instructor) by freewriting your believing and doubting responses. Spend fifteen minutes believing and then fifteen minutes doubting for a total of thirty minutes.

When you play the believing side of this game, you try to become sympathetic to an idea or point of view. You listen carefully to it, opening yourself to the possibility that it is true. You try to appreciate why the idea has force for so many people; you try to accept it by discovering as many reasons as you can for believing it. It is easy to play the believing game with ideas you already believe in, but the game becomes more difficult, sometimes even frightening and dangerous, when you try believing ideas that seem untrue or disturbing.

The doubting game is the opposite of the believing game. It calls for you to be judgmental and critical, to find fault with an idea rather than to accept it. When you doubt a new idea, you try your best to falsify it, to find counterexamples that disprove it, to find flaws in its logic. Again, it is easy to play the doubting game with ideas you don't like, but it, too, can be threatening when you try to doubt ideas that are dear to your heart or central to your own worldview.

READING

Here is how one student played the believing and doubting game with the following assertion from professional writer Paul Theroux that emphasizing sports is harmful to boys.

Just as high school basketball teaches you how to be a poor loser, the manly attitude towards sports seems to be little more than a recipe for creating bad marriages, social misfits, moral degenerates, sadists, latent rapists and just plain louts. I regard high school sports as a drug far worse than marijuana.

Believing and Doubting Paul Theroux's Negative View of Sports

Believe

1   Although I am a woman I have a hard time believing this because I was a high school basketball player and believe high school sports are *very* important. But here goes. I will try to believe this statement even though I hate it. Let's see. It would seem that I wouldn't have much first-hand experience with how society turns boys into men. I do see though that Theroux is right about some major problems. Through my observations, I've seen many young boys go through humiliating experiences with sports that have left them scarred. For example, a 7-year-old boy, Matt, isn't very athletic and when kids in our neighborhood choose teams, they usually choose girls before they choose Matt. I wonder if he sees himself as a sissy and what this does to him? I have also experienced some first-hand adverse effects of society's methods of turning boys into men. In our family, my dad spent much of his time playing football, basketball, and baseball with my brother. I've loved sports since I was very young so I was eager to play. In order to play with them, I had to play like a boy. Being told you threw or played like a girl was the worst possible insult you could receive. The phrase "be tough" was something I heard repeatedly while I was growing up. Whenever I got hurt, my dad would say, "Be tough." It didn't matter how badly I was hurt, I always heard the same message. Today, I think, I have a very, very difficult time opening up and letting people get to know me, because for so long I was taught to keep everything inside. Maybe sports does have some bad effects.

Doubt

2   I am glad I get to doubt this too because I have been really mad at all the sports bashing that has been going on in class. I think much of what Theroux says is just a crock. I know that the statement "sports builds character" is a cliché, but I really believe it. It seems to me that the people who lash out at sports clichés are those who never experienced these aspects of athletics and therefore don't understand them. No one can tell me that sports didn't contribute to some of my best and most meaningful friendships and growing experiences. I am convinced that I am a better person because through sports I have had to deal with failure, defeat, frustration, sacrificing individual desires for the benefit of the team, and so on. After my last high school basketball game when after many years of mind games, of hating my coach one minute and the next having deep respect for him, of big games lost on my mistakes, of hours spent alone in the gym, of wondering if the end justifies the means, my coach put his arm around me and told me he was proud. Everything, all the pain, frustration, anxiety, fear, and sacrifice of the past years seemed so worthwhile. You might try to tell me that this story

is hackneyed and trite, but I won't listen because it is a part of me, and some thing you will never be able to damage or take away. I think athletes share a special bond. They know what it is like to go through the physical pain of practice time and again. They understand the wide variety of emotions felt (but rarely expressed). They also know what a big role the friendships of teammates and coaches play in an athlete's life.

We admire this writer a great deal—both for the passion with which she defends sports in her doubting section and for the courage of walking in a sports basher's shoes in the believing section. This exercise clearly engaged and stretched her thinking.

We invite you now to stretch your own thinking by playing the believing and doubting game with one of the following assertions. The first set of assertions focuses on the constellation of issues surrounding fossil fuels and energy that we introduced in Chapter 1. The last set gives you other options to explore.

Option 1: Energy Issues

For these energy issues, we have identified the source for each assertion to help you imagine yourself joining a public conversation of ideas already in print.

1. ". . . the car is the greatest modern symbol of American freedom." (John Bragg, "The American Dream: Why Environmentalists Attack the SUV," *Capitalism Magazine Online*)
2. ". . . most customers want bigger and faster cars—actually, light-duty trucks like sport utility vehicles—not efficient ones." ["A Fuel-Saving Proposal from Your Automaker: Tax the Gas," *New York Times* (April 18, 2004): BU 5]
3. "This country must immediately start phasing out its national dependence on fossil fuel [and] support policies to immediately reduce carbon emissions and greenhouse gases . . . ." ("Climate Justice: Indigenous Peoples, Global Warming and Climate Change," Indigenous Environmental Network www.ienearth.org)
4. "The best way to break the back of OPEC [Organization of Petroleum Exporting Countries] is to produce more oil here at home." [Stephen Moore, "Stick a Pump in It," *National Review Online* (May 10, 2004)]
5. "If Congress is serious about ensuring our national security, it should immediately pass legislation to raise fuel economy standards to 40 miles a gallon by 2012 and 55 by 2020." [Robert F. Kennedy, Jr., "Better Gas Mileage, Greater Security," *New York Times* (November 24, 2001)]
6. You can also play the believing and doubting game with advertisements or other visual texts. Consider using the Shell corporate ad (Figure 2.1) or the Adbusters' spoof ad (Figure 2.2) as visual commentary on the oil industry's approach to oil exploration. If you are responding to one of these visual texts, begin by stating the main point of the text in a one-sentence assertion. For example, "The Shell ad says that the oil industry, especially our company, will

FIGURE 2.1 Shell Corporate Ad

WHAT DO WE REALLY NEED IN TODAY'S ENERGY HUNGRY WORLD? MORE GARDENERS.

The Flower Gardens of the Gulf of Mexico. Home to some of the most spectacular banks of coral and sponges to be found in this part of the world.

In fact, this National Marine Sanctuary forms the most northerly reef on the U.S. continental shelf. Which is why, when Shell went looking for oil and natural gas in this region, we looked for help from Jim Ray— a marine biologist and Shell employee.

For some thirty years now, Jim and others just like him have been working to protect this magnificent area and other sensitive marine environments.

They're providing a habitat for all manner of marine life, so everyone from ecologists to school-teachers has the opportunity to study this wonderful world firsthand.

Because at Shell, we focus on energy but that's not our only focus. To find out more, see the Shell Report at www.shell.com.

FIGURE 2.2 Adbusters' Spoof Ad

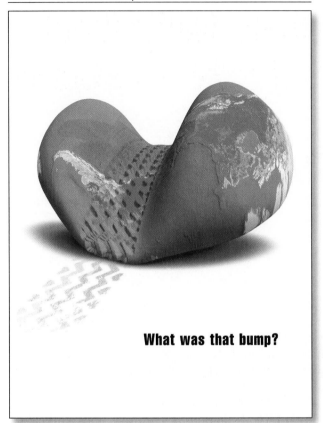

solve the problem of diminishing fossil fuel reserves by using our company's innovative thinking and technological expertise." Then play the believing and doubting game with the assertion.

Option 2: Other Issues

1. Grades are an effective means of motivating students to do their best work.
2. In recent years advertising has made enormous gains in portraying women as strong, independent, and intelligent.
3. To help fight terrorism and promote public safety, individuals should be willing to give up some of their rights.
4. It is often OK to tell a lie.
5. The United States should reinstate the draft.
6. Violent video games are harmful to young people.
7. NASCAR drivers are not real athletes.
8. It is rude to talk on a cell phone in a public place.
9. Hate speech should be forbidden on college campuses.

Thinking Rhetorically about Purpose, Audience, and Genre

It is amazing how much so-called writing problems clear up when the student really cares, when he is realistically put into the drama of somebody with something to say to somebody else.

—JAMES MOFFETT, *WRITING TEACHER AND THEORIST*

In Chapters 1 and 2 we introduced you to rhetorical thinking by showing you how experienced writers think about their audience and purpose as they wrestle with subject-matter questions. They must pose questions that matter to their intended readers and propose claims that bring those readers something new, surprising, or challenging. In all these cases, the writer's subject-matter considerations are influenced by rhetorical context.

In this chapter, we extend the idea of rhetorical thinking by probing three key variables in a writer's rhetorical context: purpose, audience, and genre. While thinking about subject matter, writers also think about rhetorical issues, posing questions about their purpose (What am I trying to accomplish in this paper?), their audience (What are my readers' values and assumptions? What do they already know and believe about my subject?), and genre (What kind of document am I writing? What are its requirements for structure, style, and document design?). We show how your answers to these questions influence many of the decisions you make as a writer. We end by explaining the generic rhetorical context assumed by most teachers for college papers across the disciplines.

In this chapter you will learn the following principles:

- How to think productively about your purpose, audience, and genre
- How to make decisions about structure and style based on your analysis of these elements
- How to adjust your writing on the scale of abstraction to fit your purpose, audience, and genre
- How to recognize and employ document design features appropriate for different genres
- How to understand the generic rhetorical context for most college papers

How Writers Think about Purpose

In this section, we want to help you think more productively about your purpose for writing, which can be examined from several different perspectives: your rhetorical aim, the motivating occasion that gets you going, and your desire to change your reader's view. All three perspectives will help you make your awareness of purpose work for you and increase your savvy as a writer. Let's look at each in turn.

Purpose as Rhetorical Aim

One powerful way to think about purpose is through the general concept of "rhetorical aim." In this text, we identify six different rhetorical aims of writing: to express, to explore, to inform, to analyze and synthesize, to persuade, and to give aesthetic pleasure. Thinking of each piece of writing in terms of one or more of these rhetorical aims can help you understand typical ways that your essay can be structured and developed and can help you clarify your relationship with your audience. The writing projects in Part Two of this text are based on these rhetorical aims.* Table 3.1 gives you an overview of each of the six rhetorical aims and sketches out how the subject matter differs from aim to aim, how the writer's task and relationship to readers differ according to aim, and how a chosen aim affects the writing's genre and its position on the spectrum from open to closed forms.

Purpose as a Response to a Motivating Occasion

Another important way to think about purpose is to think about each piece of writing as a response to a particular motivating occasion. Almost all writing is compelled by some sort of motivating occasion or exigency.† This exigency can be external (someone giving you a task and setting a deadline) or internal (your awareness of a problem stimulating your desire to bring about some change in people's views). Thus, when engineer David Rockwood read a newspaper editorial supporting wind-power projects, his own belief in the impracticality of wind power motivated him to write a letter to the editor in rebuttal (see pp. 17–18). But he also knew that he had to write the letter within one or two days or else it stood no chance of being published. His exigency thus included both internal and external factors.

---

*An additional aim, not quite parallel to these others, is sometimes called "writing-to-learn." When your purpose is writing-to-learn, your writing is aimed at helping you understand an important concept or learn a skill necessary for expert performance in a discipline. Teachers often design writing-to-learn assignments focusing on specific course learning goals. In Part Two of this text, the first two writing projects (for Chapters 5 and 6) are writing-to-learn pieces.
†An *exigency* is an urgent or pressing situation requiring immediate attention. Rhetoricians use the term to describe the event or occasion that causes a writer to begin writing.

TABLE 3.1 Purpose as Rhetorical Aim

Rhetorical Aim	Focus of Writing	What Writers Do	Relationship to Audience	Form and Genres
Express or share	Your own life, personal experiences that you want to make public, reflections	You express your feelings and thoughts (even venting); you write to move others.	You ask readers to see the world your way; you invite them to see connections between your life and theirs; you surprise readers with your experiential insights.	**Form:** Tends to have many open-form features **Sample genres:** Diary or journal; personal essay; literary nonfiction, perhaps using plot, character, image, and symbol
Explore or inquire (Chapter 7)	Subject-matter problems; a significant, problematic question; shows a writer seeking to understand these problems or questions	You ask questions, wade into complexity by posing or deepening a problem, raising new questions, considering alternative views, and showing the limitations of other answers and approaches.	You invite readers on your intellectual journey; you ask readers to think with you, to collaborate in discovering a new understanding of a subject.	**Form:** Follows open form in being narrative based; seeks a thesis rather than supporting one **Sample genres:** Freewriting; idea mapping; journals; notes; formal essays in narrative form dramatizing the writer's thinking about a question
Inform or explain (Chapter 8)	Subject matter on which you present new or needed information based on your own experience or research	You provide information your readers need or want, or you arouse curiosity and then present new, surprising information.	You, as knowledgeable teacher, surprise by enlarging readers' view of a subject; you expect readers to trust your authority and information.	**Form:** Usually has a closed-form structure but could be open form **Sample genres:** Encyclopedia, newspaper, and magazine articles; brochures; instruction booklets; sales reports; technical reports; informative Web sites
Analyze, synthesize, or interpret (Chapter 9)	Subject matter that is problematic and complex and that you can break down into parts and put together in new ways for greater understanding	Using critical thinking and possibly research, you examine parts and their relationships to each other and the whole; you put together ideas from your analyses into a new whole that represents your enlarged, enriched understanding of a subject or issue.	You challenge readers with a new, illuminating way of seeing, thinking about, or understanding your subject; readers may be skeptical, expecting you to support your thesis with good particulars.	**Form:** Typically has a closed-form structure; introduces a question or problem, sketches an answer, and develops this answer with good supporting points and particulars **Sample genres:** Scholarly articles and much other academic writing across the disciplines; critiques; public affairs magazine articles; newspaper feature articles

(continued)

TABLE 3.1 continued

Rhetorical Aim	Focus of Writing	What Writers Do	Relationship to Audience	Form and Genres
Persuade (Chapter 10)	Subject-matter questions that have multiple, controversial answers	You enter a controversy in hopes of persuading readers to accept your own views on a controversial issue; you surprise your readers with reasons and evidence to change their beliefs and actions.	You try to convince your readers, who are like jurors, of the soundness of your position; you must appeal to your readers' values and beliefs and anticipate the objections and alternative views of skeptical readers.	**Form:** Anywhere on the open-to-closed-form spectrum; could be a closed-form argument consisting of logical point-by-point reasons and evidence; could also be an open-form story or collage of emotionally charged scenes **Sample genres:** Letters to the editor; op-ed pieces; policy statements for public affairs magazines and advocacy Web sites; researched academic arguments
Entertain or give aesthetic pleasure	Language itself shaped to convey experience or emotion	You explore the properties of language, using words the way artists use clay and paint; you work with sounds, rhythms, and word images to make readers see and feel.	You seek to entice and move your readers—please, delight, thrill, or disturb them.	**Form:** Open form; literary nonfiction may combine a literary purpose with an expressive or explanatory purpose **Sample genres:** Literary nonfiction; poetry; all genres of fiction

You might think that school is the only place where people are compelled to write. However, some element of external compulsion is present in nearly every writing situation, although this external compulsion is almost never the sole motivation for writing. Consider a middle manager requested by the company vice president to write a report explaining why his division's profits are down. The manager is motivated by several factors: He wants to provide a sound analysis of why profits have declined; he wants to propose possible solutions that will remedy the situation; he wants to avoid looking personally responsible for the dip in profits; he wants to impress the vice president in the hope that she will promote him to upper management; and so on.

College students' motivations for writing can be equally complex: In part, you write to meet a deadline; in part, you write to please the teacher and get a good grade. But ideally you also write because you have become engaged with an intellectual problem and want to say something significant about it. Our point here is that your purposes for writing are always more complex than the simple desire to meet an assignment deadline.

Purpose as a Desire to Change Your Reader's View

Perhaps the most useful way to think about purpose is to focus on the change you want to bring about in your audience's view of the subject. When you are given a college writing assignment, this view of purpose engages you directly with the intellectual problem specified in the assignment. This view of purpose has already been introduced in Chapter 2, where we explained the importance of surprise as a measure of what is new or challenging in your essay. For most essays, you can write a one-sentence, nutshell statement about your purpose.

See Chapter 2, pp. 34–37, for an explanation of surprise in thesis statements.

My purpose is to give my readers a vivid picture of my difficult struggle with Graves' disease.

My purpose is to raise serious doubts about the value of the traditional grading system.

My purpose is to inform my readers about the surprising growth of the marijuana industry in the Midwestern farm states.

My purpose is to explain how Thoreau's view of nature differs in important ways from that of contemporary environmentalists.

My purpose is to persuade the general public that wind-generated electricity is not a practical energy alternative in the Pacific Northwest.

In closed-form academic articles, technical reports, and other business and professional pieces, writers often place explicit purpose statements in their introductions along with the thesis. In most other forms of writing, the writer uses a behind-the-scenes purpose statement to achieve focus and direction but seldom states the purpose explicitly. Writing an explicit purpose statement for a paper is a powerful way to nutshell the kind of change you want to bring about in your reader's view of the subject.

Chapter 12, pp. 319–320, shows you how purpose statements can be included in closed-form introductions.

For Writing and Discussion

This exercise will show you how the concept of "rhetorical aim" can help you generate ideas for an essay. As a class, choose one of the following topic areas or another provided by your instructor. Then imagine six different writing situations in which a hypothetical writer would compose an essay about the selected topic. Let each situation call for a different aim. How might a person write about the selected topic with an expressive aim? An exploratory aim? An informative aim? An analytic aim? A persuasive aim? A literary aim? How would each essay surprise its readers?

automobiles	animals	hospices or nursing homes
homelessness	music	dating or marriage
advertising	energy crisis	sports injuries

(*continued*)

Working on your own or in small groups, create six realistic scenarios, each of which calls for prose in a different category of aim. Then share your results as a whole class. Here are two examples based on the topic "hospices."

Expressive Aim   Working one summer as a volunteer in a hospice for dying cancer patients, you befriend a woman whose attitude toward death changes your life. You write an autobiographical essay about your experiences with this remarkable woman.

Analytic Aim   You are a hospice nurse working in a home care setting. You and your colleagues note that sometimes family members cannot adjust psychologically to the burden of living with a dying person. You decide to investigate this phenomenon. You interview "reluctant" family members in an attempt to understand the causes of their psychological discomfort so that you can provide better counseling services as a possible solution. You write a paper for a professional audience analyzing the results of your interviews.

How Writers Think about Audience

In our discussion of purpose, we already had a lot to say about audience. What you know about your readers—their familiarity with your subject matter, their reasons for reading, their closeness to you, their values and beliefs—affects most of the choices you make as a writer.

The value of moving from old information to new information is explained in Chapter 12, pp. 303–304 and 330–336.

In assessing your audience, you must first consider what, to them, is old information and what is new information. You'll ask questions like these: What in my essay will be familiar and what will be new, challenging, and surprising? How much background will my readers need? What can I assume they know and don't know? What is their current view of my topic that I am trying to change?

As you think about your readers' current views on your topic, you also need to think about their methods and reasons for reading. Imagine that you want to persuade your boss to reconfigure your office's computer network. You've discussed your ideas with her briefly, and she's asked you to write a formal proposal for the next technology meeting. Knowing of her harried environment—people waiting to see her, meetings to attend, e-mails piling up, memos and reports filling her in-box—you use a tightly closed structure for your proposal. Your document must be clear, concise, summarizable, and immediately comprehensible. The same reader in a different mood and setting may turn to a more leisurely kind of prose, say, an article in her favorite magazine or a new book on her favorite subject, where she might enjoy the subtlety and stylistic pleasures of open-form prose.

Now consider how a change in audience can affect the content of a piece. Suppose you want voters in your city to approve a bond issue to build a new baseball stadium. If most members of your audience are baseball fans, you can appeal to their love of the game, the pleasure of a new facility, and so forth. But non-baseball fans won't be moved by these arguments. To reach them, you must tie the new baseball stadium to their values. You can argue that a new stadium will bring new tax revenues to the city, clean up a run-down area, revitalize local businesses, or stimulate the tourist industry. Your purpose remains the same—to persuade taxpayers to fund the stadium—but the content of your argument changes if your audience changes.

In college, you often seem to be writing for an audience of one—your instructor. However, most instructors try to read as a representative of a broader audience. To help college writers imagine these readers, many instructors try to design writing assignments that provide a fuller sense of audience. They may ask you to write for the readers of a particular magazine or journal, or they may create case assignments with built-in audiences (for example, "You are an accountant in the firm of Numbers and Fudge; one day you receive a letter from . . ."). If your instructor does not specify an audience, you can generally assume the audience to be what we like to call "the generic academic audience"—student peers who have approximately the same level of knowledge and expertise in the field as you do, who are engaged by the question you address, and who want to read your writing and be surprised in some way.

Assessing Your Audience

In any writing situation, you can use the following questions to help you make decisions about content, form, and style:

QUESTIONS TO ASK ABOUT AUDIENCE

1. Who is going to read what I write? A specific individual? A specific group with special interests? Or a general readership with wide-ranging interests and backgrounds?
2. What relationship do I have to these readers? Do I and my readers have an informal, friendly relationship or a polite, formal one? Is my readers' expertise in my general subject area greater, less, or equal to mine?
3. How much do my readers already know about the specific problem I address? How much background will I have to provide?
4. How much interest do my readers bring to my topic? Do I need to hook readers with a vivid opening and use special techniques to maintain their interest throughout? Or are they interested enough in the problem I am examining that the subject matter itself will drive their reading? (In persuasive writing, particularly in writing that proposes a solution to a problem, you may need to shock your readers into awareness that the problem exists.)
5. What are my audience's values, beliefs, and assumptions in relation to my topic? If I am writing on a controversial issue, will my readers oppose my position, be neutral to it, or support it? To which of their values, beliefs, or assumptions can I appeal? Will my position unsettle or threaten my audience or stimulate a strong emotional response? (Because a concern for audience is particularly relevant to persuasive writing, we treat these questions in more depth in Chapter 10.)

How to hook your readers' interest through an effective introduction is covered in Chapter 12, pp. 318–319.

Posing these questions will not lead to any formulaic solutions to your writing problems, but it can help you develop strategies that will appeal to your audience and enable you to achieve your purpose.

How Writers Think about Genre

The term *genre* refers to broad categories of writing that follow certain conventions of style, structure, approach to subject matter, and document design. Literary genres include the short story, the novel, the epic poem, the limerick, the sonnet, and so forth. Nonfiction prose has its own genres: the business memo, the technical manual, the scholarly article, the scientific report, the popular magazine article (each magazine, actually, has its own particular conventions), the Web page, the five-paragraph theme (a school genre), the newspaper editorial, the cover letter for a job application, the legal contract, the advertising brochure, and so forth.

The concept of genre creates strong reader expectations and places specific demands on writers. How you write any given letter, report, or article is influenced by the structure and style of hundreds of previous letters, reports, or articles written in the same genre. If you wanted to write for *Reader's Digest*, for example, you would have to use the conventions that appeal to its older, conservative readers: simple language, subjects with strong human interest, heavy reliance on anecdotal evidence in arguments, an upbeat and optimistic perspective, and an approach that reinforces the conservative *ethos* of individualism, self-discipline, and family. If you wanted to write for *Seventeen* or *Rolling Stone*, however, you would need to use quite different conventions.

To illustrate the relationship of a writer to a genre, we sometimes draw an analogy with clothing. Although most people have a variety of different types of clothing in their wardrobes, the genre of activity for which they are dressing (Saturday night movie date, job interview, wedding) severely constrains their choice and expression of individuality. A man dressing for a job interview might express his personality through choice of tie or quality and style of business suit; he probably wouldn't express it by wearing a Hawaiian shirt and sandals. Even when people deviate from a convention, they tend to do so in a conventional way. For example, teenagers who do not want to follow the genre of "teenager admired by adults" form their own genre of purple hair and pierced body parts. The concept of genre raises intriguing and sometimes unsettling questions about the relationship of the unique self to a social convention or tradition.

These same kinds of questions and constraints perplex writers. For example, academic writers usually follow the genre of the closed-form scholarly article. This highly functional form achieves maximum clarity for readers by orienting them quickly to the article's purpose, content, and structure. Readers expect this format, and writers have the greatest chance of being published if they meet these expectations. In some disciplines, however, scholars are beginning to publish more experimental, open-form articles. They may slowly alter the conventions of the scholarly article, just as fashion designers alter styles of dress.

For Writing and Discussion

1. On the previous page we offered you a brief description of the conventions governing *Reader's Digest* articles, which appeal mainly to older, conservative readers. For this exercise, prepare similar descriptions of the conventions that govern articles in several other magazines such as *Rolling Stone, Sports Illustrated, Cosmopolitan, Details, The New Yorker*, or *Psychology Today*. Each person should bring to class a copy of a magazine that he or she enjoys reading. The class should then divide into small groups according to similar interests. Your instructor may supply a few scholarly journals from different disciplines. In preparing a brief profile of your magazine, consider the following:

   - Scan the table of contents. What kinds of subjects or topics does the magazine cover?
   - Look at the average length of articles. How much depth and analysis are provided?
   - Consider the magazine's readership. Does the magazine appeal to particular political or social groups (liberal/conservative, male/female, young/old, white-collar/blue-collar, in-group/general readership)?
   - Look at the advertisements. What kinds of products are most heavily advertised in the magazine? Who is being targeted by these advertisements? What percentage of the magazine consists of advertisements?
   - Read representative pages, including the introductions, of some articles. Would you characterize the prose as difficult or easy? Intellectual or popular? Does the prose use the jargon, slang, or other language particular to a group? Are the paragraphs long or short? How are headings, inserts, visuals, and other page-formatting features used? Is the writing formal or informal?
   - Think about what advice you would give a person who wanted to write a freelance article for this magazine.

2. Imagine that someone interested in hospices (see the example in the For Writing and Discussion exercise on pp. 51–52) wanted to write an article about hospices for your chosen magazine. What approach would the writer have to take to have a hospice-related article published in your magazine? There may be no chance of this happening, but be creative. Here is an example:

   > Ordinarily *Sports Illustrated* would be an unlikely place for an article on hospices. However, *SI* might publish a piece about a dying athlete in a hospice setting. It might also publish a piece about sports memories of dying patients or about watching sports as therapy.

Rhetorical Context and Your Choices about Structure

So far in this chapter, we have examined purpose, audience, and genre as components of a writer's rhetorical context. In this section and the next, our goal is to help you appreciate how these variables influence a writer's choices regarding structure and style. Although there is no formula that allows you to determine an appropriate structure and style based on particular purposes, audiences, and genres, there are some rules of thumb that can help you make decisions. Let's look first at structure.

Because most academic, business, and professional writing uses a closed-form structure, we spend a significant portion of this text advising you how to write such prose. But open-form prose is equally valuable and is often more subtle, complex, and beautiful, so it is good to practice writing at different positions on the continuum. The following advice will help you decide when closed or open forms are more appropriate:

WHEN IS CLOSED-FORM PROSE MOST APPROPRIATE?

- When your focus is on the subject matter itself and your goal is to communicate efficiently to maximize clarity. In these cases, your aim is usually to inform, analyze, or persuade.
- When you imagine your audience as a busy or harried reader who needs to be able to read quickly and process ideas rapidly. Closed-form prose is easy to summarize; moreover, a reader can speed-read closed-form prose by scanning the introduction and then glancing at headings and the openings of paragraphs, where writers place key points.
- When the conventional genre for your context is closed-form writing and you choose to meet, rather than break, readers' expectations.
- When you encounter any rhetorical situation that asks you to assert and support a thesis in response to a problem or question.

WHEN IS A MORE OPEN FORM DESIRABLE?

- When you want to delay your thesis rather than announce it in the introduction (for example, to create suspense). A delayed-thesis structure is less combative and more friendly; it conveys an unfolding "let's think through this together" feeling.
- When your aim is expressive, exploratory, or literary. These aims tend to be served better through narrative rather than through thesis-with-support writing.
- When you imagine your audience reading primarily for enjoyment and pleasure. In this context you can often wed a literary purpose to another purpose.
- When the conventional genre calls for open-form writing—for example, autobiographical narratives, character sketches, or personal reflective pieces. Popular magazine articles often have a looser, more open structure than do scholarly articles or business reports.

- When you are writing about something that is too complex or messy to be captured in a fixed thesis statement, or when you feel constrained by the genre of thesis with support.

Rhetorical Context and Your Choices about Style

Writers need to make choices not only about structure but also about style. By *style*, we mean the choices you make about how to say something. Writers can say essentially the same thing in a multitude of ways, each placing the material in a slightly different light, subtly altering meaning, and slightly changing the effect on readers. In this section we illustrate more concretely the many stylistic options open to you and explain how you might go about making stylistic choices.

Factors That Affect Style

As we shall see, style is a complex composite of many factors. We can classify the hundreds of variables that affect style into four broad categories:

1. *Ways of shaping sentences:* long/short, simple/complex, many modifiers/few modifiers, normal word order/frequent inversions or interruptions, mostly main clauses/many embedded phrases and subordinate clauses
2. *Types of words:* abstract/concrete, formal/colloquial, unusual/ordinary, specialized/general, metaphoric/literal, scientific/literary
3. *The implied personality projected by the writer (often called* voice *or* persona): expert/layperson, scholar/student, outsider/insider, political liberal/conservative, neutral observer/active participant
4. *The writer's implied relationship to the reader and the subject matter (often called* tone): intimate/distant, personal/impersonal, angry/calm, browbeating/sharing, informative/entertaining, humorous/serious, ironic/literal, passionately involved/aloof

Recognizing Different Styles and Voices

When discussing style, rhetoricians often use related terms such as *voice* and *persona*. We can distinguish these terms by thinking of style as analyzable textual features on a page (length and complexity of sentences, level of abstraction, and so forth) and of voice or persona as the reader's impression of the writer projected from the page. Through your stylistic choices, you create an image of yourself in your readers' minds. This image can be cold or warm, insider or outsider, humorous or serious, detached or passionate, scholarly or hip, antagonistic or friendly, and so forth.

What style you adopt depends on your purpose, audience, and genre. Consider, for example, the following thought exercise: Suppose you are interested in the subject of flirting. (Perhaps you have asked a research question such as the following: How has concern about sexual harassment affected views on flirting in the workplace? Or, When is flirting psychologically and emotionally healthy?) You decide to do library research on flirting and are surprised by the different styles and genres you encounter. Here are the opening paragraphs of three different articles that discuss flirting—from a scholarly journal, from a fairly intellectual special interest magazine, and from a popular magazine devoted to women's dating and fashion. At the moment, we are considering only differences in the verbal styles of these articles. Later in this chapter, we reproduce the actual opening pages of two of these articles as they originally appeared in order to discuss document design.

SCHOLARLY JOURNAL

[*From* The Journal of Sex Research]

Sexual Messages: Comparing Findings from Three Studies

Sexual socialization is influenced by a wide range of sources, including parents, peers, and the mass media (Hyde & DeLameter, 1997). In trying to understand the process by which young people acquire their sexual beliefs, attitudes, and behaviors, the study of media provides information about potential socializing messages that are an important part of everyday life for children and adolescents (Greenberg, Brown, & Buerkel-Rothfuss, 1993). The significance of media content in this realm stems from a number of unique aspects surrounding its role in the lives of youth, including its early accessibility and its almost universal reach across the population.

Electronic media, and television in particular, provide a window to many parts of the world, such as sexually related behavior, that would otherwise be shielded from young audiences. Long before many parents begin to discuss sex with their children, answers to such questions as "When is it OK to have sex?" and "With whom does one have sexual relations?" are provided by messages delivered on television. These messages are hardly didactic, most often coming in the form of scripts and plots in fictional entertainment programs. Yet the fact that such programs do not intend to teach sexual socialization lessons hardly mitigates the potential influence of their portrayals.

—Dale Kunkel, Kirstie M. Cope, and Erica Biely

SPECIAL INTEREST MAGAZINE

[*From* Psychology Today]

The New Flirting Game

"It may be an ages-old, biologically-driven activity, but today it's also played with artful self-awareness and even conscious calculation" [opening lead in large, all-caps text].

To hear the evolutionary determinists tell it, we human beings flirt to propagate our genes and to display our genetic worth. Men are constitutionally predisposed to flirt with the healthiest, most fertile women, recognizable by their biologically correct waist-hip ratios. Women favor the guys with dominant demeanors, throbbing muscles and the most resources to invest in them and in their offspring.

Looked at up close, human psychology is more diverse and perverse than the evolutionary determinists would have it. We flirt as thinking individuals in a particular culture at a particular time. Yes, we may express a repertoire of hardwired nonverbal expressions and behaviors—staring eyes, flashing brows, opened palms—that resemble those of other animals, but unlike other animals, we also flirt with conscious calculation. We have been known to practice our techniques in front of the mirror. In other words, flirting among human beings is culturally modulated as well as biologically driven, as much art as instinct.

—Deborah A. Lott

WOMEN'S DATING AND FASHION MAGAZINE

[*From* Cosmopolitan]

Flirting with Disaster

"I'd never be unfaithful, but . . ." [opening lead in very large type].

"You're in love and totally committed—or are you? You dirty danced with a cute guy at the office party, and make an effort to look sexy for the man in the coffee shop. Are you cheating without knowing it?" [second lead in large type]

I think I've been cheating on my partner. Let me explain. I went out clubbing recently with a really good friend, a guy I've known for years. We both love to dance. [. . .] [W]henever we get together, there comes a moment, late in the evening, when I look at him and feel myself beginning to melt. [. . .] This is not the way people who are "just friends" touch each other.

[. . .] So I suppose the question is, at what point does flirting stop being harmless fun and become an actual betrayal of your relationship?

—Lisa Sussman and Tracey Cox

For Writing and Discussion

Working in small groups or as a whole class, analyze the differences in the styles of these three samples.

1. How would you describe differences in the length and complexity of sentences, in the level of vocabulary, and in the degree of formality?
2. How do the differences in styles create different voices, personas, and tones?
3. Based on clues from style and genre, who is the intended audience of each piece? What is the writer's purpose? How does each writer hope to surprise the intended audience with something new, challenging, or valuable?
4. How are the differences in content and style influenced by differences in purpose, audience, and genre?

Rhetorical Context and Your Choices along the Scale of Abstraction

In Chapter 2, we explained how writers use particulars—examples, details, numerical data, and other kinds of evidence—to support their points. We said that strong writing weaves back and forth between points and particulars; points give meaning to particulars and particulars flesh out and develop points, making them credible and convincing. However, the distinction between points and particulars is a matter of context. The same sentence might serve as a point in one context and as a particular in another. What matters is the relative position of words and sentences along a scale of abstraction. As an illustration of such a scale, consider the following list of words descending from the abstract to the specific:

Clothing→footwear→shoes→sandals→Birkenstocks→my old hippie Birkenstocks with salt stains

Where you pitch a piece of writing on this scale of abstraction helps determine its style, with high-on-the-scale writing creating an abstract or theoretical effect and low-on-the-scale writing creating a more vivid and concrete effect. In descriptive and narrative prose, writers often use sensory details that are very low on the scale of abstraction. Note how shifting down the scale improves the vividness of the following passage:

Mid-scale The awkward, badly dressed professor stood at the front of the room.
Low on the scale At the front of the room stood the professor, a tall, gawky man with inch-thick glasses, an enormous Adam's apple, an old brown-striped jacket, burgundy and gray plaid pants, a silky vest with what appeared to be "scenes from an aquarium" printed on it, and a tie with blue koalas.

The details in the more specific passage help you experience the writer's world. They don't just tell you that the professor was dressed weirdly; they *show* you.

In closed-form prose such specific sensory language is less common, so writers need to make choices about the level of specificity that will be most effective based on their purpose, audience, and genre. Note the differences along the level of abstraction in the following passages:

PASSAGE 1: FAIRLY HIGH ON SCALE OF ABSTRACTION

Point sentence

Particulars high on scale of abstraction

Although lightning produces the most deaths and injuries of all weather-related accidents, the rate of danger varies considerably from state to state. Florida has twice as many deaths and injuries from lightning strikes as any other state. Hawaii and Alaska have the fewest.

—Passage from a general interest informative article on weather-related accidents

PASSAGE 2: LOWER ON SCALE OF ABSTRACTION

Point sentence

Florida has twice as many deaths and injuries from lightning strikes as any other state, with many of these casualties occurring on the open spaces of golf courses.

Florida golfers should carefully note the signals of dangerous weather conditions such as darkening skies, a sudden drop in temperature, an increase in wind, flashes of light and claps of thunder, and the sensation of an electric charge on one's hair or body. In the event of an electric storm, golfers should run into a forest, get under a shelter, get into a car, or assume the safest body position. To avoid being the tallest object in an area, if caught in open areas, golfers should find a low spot, spread out, and crouch into a curled position with feet together to create minimal body contact with the ground.

Particulars at midlevel on scale

Particulars at lower level on scale

—Passage from a safety article aimed at Florida golfers

Both of these passages are effective for their audience and purpose. Besides sensory details, writers can use other kinds of particulars that are low on the scale of abstraction such as quotations or statistics. Civil engineer David Rockwood uses low-on-the-scale numerical data about the size and number of wind towers to convince readers that wind generation of electricity entails environmental damage.

See Rockwood's letter to the editor, pp. 17–18.

Other kinds of closed-form writing, however, often remain high on the scale. Yet even the most theoretical kind of prose will move back and forth between several layers on the scale. Your rhetorical decisions about level of abstraction are important because too much high-on-the-scale writing can become dull for readers, while too much low-on-the-scale writing can seem overwhelming or pointless. Each of the assignment chapters in Part Two of this text gives advice on finding the right kinds and levels of particulars to support each essay.

For Writing and Discussion

The following exercise will help you appreciate how details can be chosen at different levels of abstraction to serve different purposes and audiences. Working in small groups or as a whole class, invent details at appropriate positions on the scale of abstraction for each of the following point sentences.

1. The big game was a major disappointment. You are writing an e-mail message to a friend who is a fan (of baseball, football, basketball, another sport) and missed the game; use midlevel details to explain what was disappointing.
2. Although the game stunk, there were some great moments. Switch to low-on-the-scale details to describe one of these "great moments."
3. Advertising in women's fashion magazines creates a distorted and unhealthy view of beauty. You are writing an analysis for a college course on popular culture; use high-to-midlevel details to give a one-paragraph overview of several ways these ads create an unhealthy view of beauty.
4. One recent ad, in particular, conveys an especially destructive message about beauty. Choose a particular ad and describe it with low-on-the-scale details.
5. In United States politics, there are several key differences between Republicans and Democrats. As part of a service learning project, you are creating a page on "American Politics" for a Web site aimed at helping

(continued)

international students understand American culture. Imagine a two-columned bulleted list contrasting Republicans and Democrats and construct two or three of these bullets. Choose details at an appropriate level on the scale of abstraction.

6. One look at Pete's pickup, and you knew immediately he was an in-your-face Republican (Democrat). You are writing a feature story for your college newspaper about Pete, a person who has plastered his pickup with political signs, bumper stickers, and symbols. Choose details at an appropriate level on the scale of abstraction.

Rhetorical Context and Your Choices about Document Design

When thinking about structure, style, and genre, writers also need to consider document design. Document design refers to the visual features of a text. The "look" of a document is closely bound to the rhetorical context, to the way writers seek to communicate with particular audiences for particular purposes, and to the audience's expectations for that genre of writing. In this section, we explain the main components of document design that you will encounter as a reader.

Historically, the use of images to convey information is more important than we may realize. Alphabets, for example, derived from picture drawings, and in earlier centuries, when only a small portion of the population could read, images—such as on signs—were an important means of communication. Now in the twenty-first century, some cultural critics theorize that we are moving from a text-based culture to an image-based culture. These critics speculate that visual communication has become more important, partly because of the increased pace of life, the huge volume of information that bombards us daily, and the constantly improving technology for creating better and more varied electronic images. We rely more heavily on information transmitted visually, and we depend on receiving that information more quickly. Visual details become a shorthand code for conveying this information concisely, quickly, and vividly. The visual details of document design are part of a code for recognizing genres and part of audience expectations that writers must meet.

As a writer, you are often expected to produce manuscript (typed pages of text) rather than a publication-ready document. When your task is to produce manuscript, your concerns for document design usually focus on margins, font style and size, location of page numbers, and line spacing. As an academic writer, you generally produce manuscripts following the style guidelines of the Modern Language Association (MLA), the American Psychological Association (APA), or some other scholarly organization. In business and professional settings, you employ different kinds of manuscript conventions for writing letters, memoranda, or reports.

Chapter 14 explains MLA and APA conventions.

Instead of producing manuscript, today's writers are sometimes asked to use desktop publishing software to produce camera-ready or Web-ready documents that have a professional visual appeal (such as a pamphlet or brochure, a Web page, a poster, a marketing proposal that incorporates visuals and graphics, or some other piece with a "professionally published" look). Occasionally in your manuscript documents, you may want to display ideas or information visually— for example, with graphs, tables, or images.

Key Components of Document Design

The main components of document design are use of type, use of space and layout, use of color, and use of graphics or images.

Use of Type

Type comes in different typeface styles, or fonts, that are commonly grouped in three font families: serif fonts that have tiny extensions on the letters, which make them easier to read for long documents; sans serif fonts that lack these extensions on the letters and are good for labels, headings, and Web documents; and specialty fonts, often used for decorative effect, that include script fonts and special symbols. Common word processing programs usually give you a huge array of fonts. Some examples of different fonts are shown in the box on page 64.

Fonts also come in different sizes, measured in points (one point = 1/72 of an inch). Much type in printed texts is set in ten or twelve points. In addition, fonts can be formatted in different ways: boldface, italics, underlining, or shading.

Font style and size contribute to the readability and overall impression of a text. Scholarly publications use few, plain, and regular font styles that don't draw attention to the type. Their use of fonts seeks to keep the readers' focus on the content of the document, to convey a serious tone, and to maximize the readers' convenience in grappling with the ideas of the text. (Teachers regularly expect a conservative font such as CG Times, Times New Roman, or Courier New for academic papers. Were you to submit an academic paper in a specialty or scripted font, you'd make a "notice me" statement, analogous to wearing a lime green jumpsuit to a college reception.) In academic papers, boldface can be used for headings and italics for occasional emphasis, but otherwise design flourishes are seldom used.

Popular magazines, on the other hand, tend to use fonts playfully and artistically, using a variety of fonts and sizes to attract readers' attention initially and to make a document look pleasingly decorative on the page. Although the body text of articles is usually the same font throughout, the opening page often uses a variety of fonts and sizes, and font variations may occur throughout the text to highlight key ideas for readers who are reading casually or rapidly.

Examples of Font Styles

Font Style	Font Name	Example
Serif fonts	Times New Roman	Have a good day!
	Courier New	Have a good day!
Sans serif fonts	Arial	Have a good day!
	Century Gothic	Have a good day!
Specialty fonts	Monotype Corsiva	*Have a good day!*
	Symbol	Ηαϖε α γοοδ δαψ!

Use of Space and Layout of Documents

Layout refers to how the text is formatted on the page. Layout includes the following elements:

- The size of the page itself
- The proportion of text to white space
- The arrangement of text on the page (single or multiple columns, long or short paragraphs, spaces between paragraphs)
- The size of the margins
- The use of justification (alignment of text with the left margin or both margins)
- The placement of titles
- The use of headings and subheadings to signal main and subordinate ideas and main parts of the document
- The spacing before and after headings
- The use of numbered or bulleted lists
- The use of boxes to highlight ideas or break text into visual units

Academic and scholarly writing calls for simple, highly functional document layouts. Most scholarly journals use single or double columns of text that are justified at both margins to create a regular, even look. (In preparing an academic manuscript, however, justify only the left-hand margin, leaving the right margin ragged.) Layout—particularly the presentation of titles and headings and the formatting of notes and bibliographic data—is determined by the style of the individual journal, which treats all articles identically. The layout of scholarly documents strikes a balance between maximizing the amount of text that fits on a page and ensuring readability by using headings and providing adequate white space in the margins.

In contrast, popular magazines place text in multiple columns that are often varied and broken up by text in boxes or by text wrapped around photos or drawings. Readability is important, but so is visual appeal and entertainment: Readers must enjoy looking at the pages. Many popular magazines try to blur the distinction between content and advertising so that ads become part of the visual appeal. This is why, in fashion magazines, the table of contents is often buried a dozen or more pages into the magazine. The publisher wants to coax readers to look at the ads as they look for the contents. (In contrast, the table of contents for most academic journals is on the cover.)

Use of Color

Colors convey powerful messages and appeals, even affecting moods. While manuscripts are printed entirely in black, published documents often use color to identify and set off main ideas or important information. Color-tinted boxes can indicate special features or allow magazines to print different but related articles on the same page.

Academic and scholarly articles and books use color minimally, if at all, relying instead on different font styles and sizes to make distinctions in content. Popular magazines, on the other hand, use colors playfully, artistically, decoratively, and strategically to enhance their appeal and, thus, their sales. Different colors of type may be used for different articles within one magazine or within articles themselves. Some articles may be printed on colored paper to give variety to the whole magazine.

The rhetorical use of visuals is introduced in Chapter 4, pp. 85–87. More detailed discussion of drawings and photographs appears in Chapter 9.

Use of Graphics or Images

Graphics include visual displays of information such as tables, line graphs, bar graphs, pie charts, maps, cartoons, illustrations, and photos.

As with the use of type, space, and color, the use of graphics indicates the focus, seriousness, function, and complexity of the writing. In scientific articles and books, many of the important findings of the articles may be displayed in complex, technical graphs and tables. Sources of information for these graphics are usually prominently stated, with key variables clearly labeled. In the humanities and social sciences, content-rich photos and drawings also tend to be vital parts of an article, even the subject of the analysis.

Popular magazines typically use simple numeric visuals (for example, a colorful pie chart or a dramatic graph) combined with decorative use of images, especially photos. If photos appear, it is worthwhile to consider how they are used. For example, do photos aim to look realistic and spontaneous like documentary photos of disaster scenes, sports moments, or people at work, or are they highly constructed, aesthetic photos? (Note that many political photos are meant to look spontaneous but are actually highly scripted—for example, a photograph of the president mending a fence with a horse nearby.) Are they concept (thematic) photos meant to illustrate an idea in an article (for example, a picture of a woman surrounded by images of pills, doctors, expensive medical equipment, and wrangling employers and insurance agents, to illustrate an article on health care costs)? The use of photos and illustrations can provide important clues about a publication's angle of vision, philosophy, or political leaning. For example, the *Utne Reader* tends to use many colored drawings rather than photos to illustrate its articles. These funky drawings with muted colors suit the magazine's liberal, socially progressive, and activist angle of vision.

Examples of Different Document Designs

In our earlier discussion of style, we reprinted the opening paragraphs of three articles on flirting. Figures 3.1 and 3.2 show the opening pages of two of these articles as they appeared in *The Journal of Sex Research* and *Psychology Today* (*Cosmopolitan*

FIGURE 3.1 Opening Page from Article in *The Journal of Sex Research*

Sexual Messages on Television: Comparing Findings From Three Studies

Dale Kunkel, Kirstie M. Cope, and Erica Biely

University of California Santa Barbara

Television portrayals may contribute to the sexual socialization of children and adolescents, and therefore it is important to examine the patterns of sexual content presented on television. This report presents a summary view across three related studies of sexual messages on television. The content examined ranges from programs most popular with adolescents to a comprehensive, composite week sample of shows aired across the full range of broadcast and cable channels. The results across the three studies identify a number of consistent patterns in television's treatment of sexual content. Talk about sex and sexual behaviors are both found frequently across the television landscape, although talk about sex is more common. Most sexual behaviors tend to be precursory in nature (such as physical flirting and kissing), although intercourse is depicted or strongly implied in roughly one of every eight shows on television. Perhaps most importantly, the studies find that TV rarely presents messages about the risks or responsibilities associated with sexual behavior.

Sexual socialization is influenced by a wide range of sources, including parents, peers, and the mass media (Hyde & DeLameter, 1997). In trying to understand the process by which young people acquire their sexual beliefs, attitudes, and behaviors, the study of media provides information about potential socializing messages that are an important part of everyday life for children and adolescents (Greenberg, Brown, & Buerkel-Rothfuss, 1993). The significance of media content in this realm stems from a number of unique aspects surrounding its role in the lives of youth, including its early accessibility and its almost universal reach across the population.

Electronic media, and television in particular, provide a window to many parts of the world, such as sexually-related behavior, that would otherwise be shielded from young audiences. Long before many parents begin to discuss sex with their children, answers to such questions as "When is it OK to have sex?" and "With whom does one have sexual relations?" are provided by messages delivered on television. These messages are hardly didactic, most often coming in the form of scripts and plots in fictional entertainment programs. Yet the fact that such programs do not intend to teach sexual socialization lessons hardly mitigates the potential influence of their portrayals.

While television is certainly not the only influence on sexual socialization, adolescents often report that they use portrayals in the media to learn sexual and romantic scripts and norms for sexual behavior (Brown, Childers, & Waszak, 1990). Indeed, four out of ten (40%) teens say they have gained ideas for how to talk to their boyfriend or girlfriend about sexual issues directly from media portrayals (Kaiser Family Foundation, 1998).

Just as it is well established that media exposure influences social behaviors such as aggression and social stereotyping, there is a growing body of evidence documenting the possible effects of sexual content on television (Huston, Wartella, & Donnerstein, 1998). For example, two studies have reported correlations between watching television programs high in sexual content and the early initiation of sexual intercourse by adolescents (Brown & Newcomer, 1991; Peterson, Moore, & Furstenberg, 1991), while another found heavy television viewing to be predictive of negative attitudes toward remaining a virgin (Courtright & Baran, 1980). An experiment by Bryant and Rockwell (1994) showed that teens who had just viewed television dramas laden with sexual content rated descriptions of casual sexual encounters less negatively than teens who had not viewed any sexual material.

Another important aspect of sexual socialization involves the development of knowledge about appropriate preventative behaviors to reduce the risk of infection from AIDS or other sexually-transmitted diseases. When teenagers begin to engage in sexual activity, they assume the risk of disease as well as the risk of unwanted pregnancy, and it appears that many lack adequate preparation to avoid such negative consequences.

Two Americans under the age of 20 become infected with HIV every hour (Office of National AIDS Policy, 1996). Almost one million teenagers become pregnant every year in the United States (Kirby, 1997). In the face of these sobering statistics, it is important to consider the extent to which media portrayals engage in or overlook concerns such as these, which are very serious issues in the lives of young people today.

In summary, media effects research clearly suggests that television portrayals contribute to sexual socialization.

The Family Hour Study was supported by the Henry J. Kaiser Family Foundation (Menlo Park, CA) and Children Now (Oakland, CA). The Teen Study was the Master's Thesis for Kirstie M. Cope. The V-Chip Study was supported by the Henry J. Kaiser Family Foundation. The authors wish to thank Carolyn Colvin, Ed Donnerstein, Wendy Jo Farinola, Ulla Foehr, Jim Potter, Vicky Rideout, and Emma Rollin, each of whom made significant contributions to one or more of the studies summarized here.

Address correspondence to Dr. Dale Kunkel, Department of Communication, University of California Santa Barbara, Santa Barbara, CA 93106; e-mail: kunkel@ahshaw.ucsb.edu.

FIGURE 3.2 Opening Page from Article in *Psychology Today*

THE NEW

Flirting Game

IT MAY BE AN AGES-OLD, BIOLOGICALLY-DRIVEN ACTIVITY, BUT TODAY IT'S ALSO PLAYED WITH ARTFUL SELF-AWARENESS AND EVEN CONSCIOUS CALCULATION.

By Deborah A. Lott

To hear the evolutionary determinists tell it, we human beings flirt to propagate our genes and to display our genetic worth. Men are constitutionally predisposed to flirt with the healthiest, most fertile women, recognizable by their biologically correct waist-hip ratios. Women favor the guys with dominant demeanors, throbbing muscles and the most resources to invest in them and their offspring.

Looked at up close, human psychology is more diverse and perverse than the evolutionary determinists would have it. We flirt as thinking individuals in a particular culture at a particular time. Yes, we may express a repertoire of hardwired non-verbal expressions and behaviors—staring eyes, flashing brows, opened palms—that resemble those of other animals, but unlike other animals, we also flirt with conscious calculation. We have been known to practice our techniques in front of the mirror. In other words, flirting among human beings is culturally modulated as well as biologically driven, as much art as instinct.

In our culture today, it's clear that we do not always choose as the object of our desire those people the evolutionists might deem the most biologically desirable. After all, many young women today find the pale, androgynous, scarcely muscled yet emotionally expressive Leonardo DiCaprio more appealing than the burly Tarzans (Arnold Schwartzenegger, Bruce Willis, etc.) of action movies. Woody Allen may look nerdy but he's had no trouble winning women—and that's not just because he has material resources, but because humor is also a precious cultural commodity. Though she has no breasts or hips to speak of, Ally McBeal still attracts because there's ample evidence of a quick and quirky mind.

In short, we flirt with the intent of assessing potential lifetime partners, we flirt to have easy, no-strings-attached sex, and we flirt when we are not looking for either. We flirt because, most simply, flirtation can be a liberating form of play, a game with suspense and ambiguities that brings joys of its own. As Philadelphia-based social psychologist Tim Perper says, "Some flirters appear to want to prolong the interaction because it's pleasurable and erotic in its own right, regardless of where it might lead."

Here are some of the ways the game is currently being played.

TAKING The Lead

When it comes to flirting today, women aren't waiting around for men to make the advances. They're taking the lead. Psychologist Monica Moore, Ph.D. of Webster University in St. Louis, Missouri, has spent more than 2000 hours observing women's flirting maneuvers in restaurants, singles bars and at parties. According to her findings, women give non-verbal cues that get a flirtation rolling fully two-thirds of the time. A man may think he's making the first move because he is the one to literally move from wherever he is to the woman's side, but usually he has been summoned.

By the standards set out by evolutionary psychologists, the women who attract the most

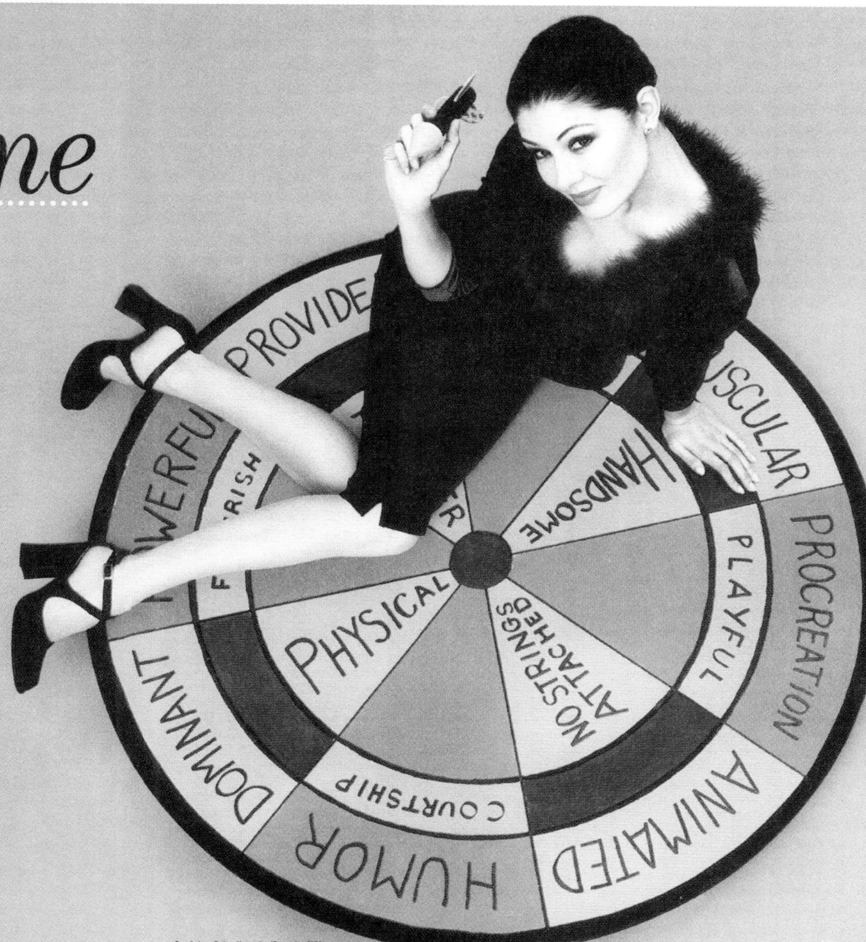

42 PHOTOGRAPHY BY FRANK VERONSKY

Psychology Today November/December 1998

would not permit these images in its opening two-page spread to be reproduced for this textbook. However, we describe the opening pages in some detail in the For Writing and Discussion exercise below, discussion question 4).

For Writing and Discussion

Working individually or in small groups, analyze how content, style, genre, and document design are interrelated in these articles.

1. How does the document design of each article—its use of fonts, layout, color, and graphics—identify each piece as a scholarly article or an article in a popular magazine? From your own observation, what are typical differences in the document design features of an academic article and a popular magazine article? For example, how are fonts and color typically used in articles in women's and men's fashion magazines?

2. What makes the style and document design of each article appropriate for its intended audience and purpose?

3. What is the function of the abstract (article summary) at the beginning of the academic journal article? What is the function of the large-font "leads" at the beginning of popular articles?

4. Consider the photographs that accompany popular magazine articles. To illustrate the concept of flirting as potential cheating, the opening page (not shown) of the *Cosmopolitan* article, quoted on page 59, features a two-page spread showing a beautiful, young, mysterious woman in a low-cut dress that shows her glistening tan skin. She is looking seriously but coyly at the reader, and behind her are shadowy images of handsome men in loosely buttoned white shirts and sports coats. Think about the photograph in the *Psychology Today* article shown in Figure 3.2. Is it a realistic, candid "documentary" photo? Is it a scripted photo? Is it a concept photo aimed at illustrating the article's thesis or question? What aspects of the *Psychology Today* photo appeal to psychological themes and interests and make it appropriate for the content, audience, and genre of the article? How do you think photos accompanying *Cosmopolitan* articles differ from photos accompanying articles in *Psychology Today?*

5. When you download an article from an electronic database (unless it is in pdf format), you often lose visual cues about the article's genre such as document design, visuals, and so forth. Even when an article is in pdf format, you lose cues about its original print context—the kind of magazine or journal the article appeared in, the magazine's layout and advertisements, and its targeted audience. How do these visual cues in the original print version of an article provide important contextual information for reading the article and using it in your own research? Why do experienced researchers prefer the original print version of articles rather than downloaded articles whenever possible?

A Generic Rhetorical Context for College Writing

How can you transfer this chapter's discussion of rhetorical context, style, and document design to the writing assignments you typically receive in college? Our general advice is to pay attention to cues about purpose, audience, and genre in your instructors' assignments and, when in doubt, to ask your instructors questions about their expectations. Our specific advice is that you should assume a "default" or "generic" rhetorical context unless the assignment suggests something different.

What Do We Mean by a "Default" or "Generic" Rhetorical Context?

We have spent years studying the assignments of professors across the curriculum and have found that, unless they specify otherwise, instructors generally assume the following context:

- *Purpose.* Generally, instructors want you to write a closed-form, thesis-governed essay in response to a problem the instructor provides or to a problem that you must pose yourself. The most common rhetorical aims are informative, analysis/synthesis, or persuasion.
- *Audience.* Generally, instructors ask you to write to fellow classmates who share approximately the same level of expertise in a discipline as you do. Your goal is to say something new and challenging to this audience (but not necessarily to the instructor, who has a much higher level of expertise).
- *Genre.* Generally, instructors expect you to follow the manuscript requirements of the discipline, often MLA or APA style. Instructors vary considerably, however, in how much they care about exact formats.

Given this generic context, what is an appropriate writer's voice for college papers? For most college assignments, we recommend that students approximate their natural speaking voices to give their writing a conversational academic style. By "natural," we mean a voice that strives to be plain and clear while retaining the engaging quality of a person who is enthusiastic about the subject.

Of course, as you become an expert in a discipline, you often need to move toward a more scholarly voice. For example, the prose in an academic journal article can be extremely dense in its use of technical terms and complex sentence structure, but expert readers in that field understand and expect this voice. Students sometimes try to imitate a dense academic style before they have achieved the disciplinary expertise to make the style sound natural. The result can seem pretentiously stilted and phony. Writing with clarity and directness within your natural range will usually create a more effective and powerful voice.

Besides striving for a natural voice, you need to be aware of subtle features of your prose that project your image to readers. For example, in an academic article, the overt function of documentation and a bibliography is to enable other scholars to track down your cited sources. But a covert function is to create an air

See Chapter 14 on citing and documenting sources professionally.

of authority for you, the writer, to assure readers that you have done your professional work and are fully knowledgeable and informed. Judicious use of the discipline's specialized language and formatting can have a similar effect. Your image is also reflected in your manuscript's form, appearance, and editorial correctness. Sloppy or inappropriately formatted manuscripts, grammatical errors, misspelled words, and other problems send a signal to the reader that you are unprofessional.

Assignments That Specify Different Rhetorical Contexts

Although the majority of college writing assignments assume the generic rhetorical context we have just described, many ask students to write in different genres and styles. At our own universities, for example, some professors ask students to link their writing to service-learning projects by creating Web sites, pamphlets, brochures, proposals, or news stories related to the organizations they are serving. Others ask students to role-play characters in a case study—writing as a marketing manager to a corporate policy board or as a lobbyist to a legislator. Still others ask students to write short stories using course ideas and themes or to create imaginary dialogues between characters with different points of view on a course issue. When you get such assignments, enter into their spirit. You'll usually be rewarded for your creative ability to imagine different voices, genres, and styles.

Chapter Summary

In this chapter we have looked at how experienced writers think rhetorically about purpose, audience, and genre. We began by examining how writers think productively about each of these elements in their rhetorical context, and then we considered how variations in purpose, audience, and genre influence a writer's choices about structure, style, and document design. We concluded with a brief discussion of the generic rhetorical context assumed in most college writing assignments.

BRIEF WRITING PROJECT

This assignment asks you to try your hand at translating a piece of writing from one rhetorical context to another. As background, you need to know that each month's *Reader's Digest* includes a section called "News from the World of Medicine," which contains one or more mini-articles reporting on recent medical research. The writers of these pieces scan articles in medical journals, select items of potential interest to the general public, and translate them from a formal, scientific style into a popular style. Here is a typical example of a *Reader's Digest* mini-article:

COMPLETE ARTICLE FROM *READERS DIGEST*

"For Teeth, Say Cheese," Penny Parker

Cheese could be one secret of a healthy, cavity-free smile, according to a recent study by a professor of dentistry at the University of Alberta in Edmonton, Canada.

In the study, John Hargreaves found that eating a piece of hard cheese the size of a sugar cube at the end of a meal can retard tooth decay. The calcium and phosphate present in the cheese mix with saliva and linger on the surface of the teeth for up to two hours, providing protection against acid attacks from sweet food or drink.

Now compare this style with the formal scientific style in the following excerpts, the introduction and conclusion of an article published in the *New England Journal of Medicine*.

EXCERPTS FROM SCIENTIFIC ARTICLE IN A MEDICAL JOURNAL

From "Aspirin as an Antiplatelet Drug," Carlo Patrono

Introduction: The past 10 years have witnessed major changes in our understanding of the pathophysiologic mechanisms underlying vascular occlusion and considerable progress in the clinical assessment of aspirin and other antiplatelet agents. The purpose of this review is to describe a rational basis for antithrombotic prophylaxis and treatment with aspirin. Basic information on the molecular mechanism of action of aspirin in inhibiting platelet function will be integrated with the appropriate clinical pharmacologic data and the results of randomized clinical trials. . . .

Conclusions: Aspirin reduces the incidence of occlusive cardiovascular events in patients at variable risk for these events. Progress in our understanding of the molecular mechanism of the action of aspirin, clarification of the clinical pharmacology of its effects on platelets, and clinical testing of its efficacy at low doses have contributed to a downward trend in its recommended daily dose. The present recommendation of a single loading dose of 200–300 mg followed by a daily dose of 75–100 mg is based on findings that this dose is as clinically efficacious as higher doses and is safer than higher doses. The satisfactory safety profile of low-dose aspirin has led to ongoing trials of the efficacy of a combination of aspirin and low-intensity oral anti-coagulants in high-risk patients. Finally, the efficacy of a cheap drug such as aspirin in preventing one fifth to one third of all important cardiovascular events should not discourage the pharmaceutical industry from attempting to develop more effective antithrombotic drugs, since a sizeable proportion of these events continue to occur despite currently available therapy.

Assume that you are a writer of mini-articles for the medical news section of *Reader's Digest*. Translate the findings reported in the article on aspirin into a *Reader's Digest* mini-article.

Although the style of the medical article may seem daunting at first, a little work with a good dictionary will help you decipher the whole passage. We've reproduced excerpts from the article's introduction and all of the final section labeled "Conclusions." These two sections provide all the information you need for your mini-article.

Thinking Rhetorically about How Messages Persuade

A way of seeing is also a way of not seeing.

—KENNETH BURKE, *RHETORICIAN*

Every time an Indian villager watches the community TV and sees an ad for soap or shampoo, what they notice are not the soap and shampoo but the lifestyle of the people using them, the kind of motorbikes they ride, their dress and their homes.

—NAYAN CHANDA, *INDIAN-BORN EDITOR OF YALEGLOBAL ONLINE MAGAZINE*

Throughout Part One, we have focused on writing as a rhetorical act. When writers think rhetorically, they are aware of writing to an audience for a purpose within a genre. We have explained how writers pose both subject-matter questions and rhetorical questions, which are closely inter-linked: Subject-matter questions must engage their audience's interests, and proposed solutions to these questions must bring something new, surprising, or challenging to that audience.

In this final chapter of Part One, we hope to expand your understanding of a writer's choices by focusing on the particular ways that messages persuade. We will use the words *message* and *persuade* in the broadest sense to refer to the success or failure of any communication act, including nonverbal acts, such as one's choices about clothing or music. Throughout this chapter we will ask: What makes a given message successful or unsuccessful in achieving its intended effect? What choices can a person make to increase the effectiveness of a message? The payoffs for doing this kind of rhetorical thinking are wide-ranging. Not only will such thinking make you a more powerful communicator, but it will also help you be a better reader, observer, and listener. When you understand how messages achieve their effects, you will be better prepared to analyze and evaluate those messages and to make your own choices about whether to resist them or accede to them.

A classic illustration of rhetorical thinking is this little thought exercise:

THOUGHT EXERCISE ON RHETORICAL THINKING

Suppose you attended a fun party on Friday night. (You get to choose what constitutes "fun" for you.) Now imagine two people asking you what you did on Friday night. Person A is your best friend, who missed the party. Person B is your grandmother. How would your descriptions of Friday night differ?

Clearly there isn't just one way to describe this party. Your description will be shaped by your purpose and by the values and concerns of your intended audience. Along the way, you will have to make rhetorical decisions such as the following:

- What kind of image of myself should I project? (For your friend you might construct yourself as a party animal; for Grandma you might construct yourself as a demure, soda-sipping observer of the party action.)
- What details should I include or leave out? (Does Grandma really need to know that the neighbors called the police?)
- How much emphasis do I give the party? (Your friend might want a complete description of every detail. Grandma might only want assurance that you are having some fun at college.)
- What words should I choose? (The colorful slang you use with your friend might not be appropriate for Grandma.)

You'll note that our comments about your rhetorical choices are shaped by common assumptions about friends and grandmothers. You might actually have a party-loving grandma and a geeky best friend, in which case Grandma might want the party details while your friend prefers talking about gigabytes or modern poetry. No matter the case, your rhetorical decisions are shaped by your particular knowledge of your audience and context.

What we hope to do in this chapter is extend your basic awareness of rhetorical thinking so that you can apply it to any communication act—from reading primary sources in a history class to analyzing the use of visual images in a Web site. Here is what you will learn in this chapter:

- How an introductory knowledge of rhetorical theory can extend your ability to think rhetorically
- How writers use appeals to *logos, ethos,* and *pathos* to increase the effectiveness of their texts
- How writers construct an "angle of vision" in a text, which you as a reader can learn to identify and analyze
- How you can apply the skills of rhetorical analysis to any cultural "text" such as photographs, clothing, tattoos, or other communicative acts
- How the ability to think rhetorically can deepen your skills as a reader and writer

A Brief Introduction to Rhetorical Theory

Rhetoric is the study of how human beings use language and other symbols to influence the attitudes, beliefs, and actions of others. The study of rhetoric can help people write, speak, read, and listen more effectively. At its deepest level, rhetoric aims to improve human communities by enabling people, through better cooperative dialogue, to find the best solutions to complex problems.

Rhetoric and Symbolic Action

One prominent twentieth-century rhetorician, Kenneth Burke, calls rhetoric "a symbolic means of inducing cooperation in beings that by nature respond to symbols." To understand what Burke means by responding to symbols, consider the difference in flirting behavior between peacocks and humans. When peacocks flirt, they spread their beautiful tails, do mating dances, and screech weirdly to attract females, but the whole process is governed by instinct. Peacocks don't have to choose among different symbolic actions such as buying an Armani tail versus buying a Wal-Mart tail or driving to the mating grounds in the right car. Unlike a peacock, a flirting human must make symbolic choices, all of which involve consequences. Consider how what you wear might contribute to the effectiveness of your flirting behavior (For males: Feedlot cap? Do-rag? Preppy sweater? Baggy, low-riding pants? For females: Skirt and stockings? Low-cut jeans, halter top, and belly ring? Gothic makeup, black dress, and open-fingered black gloves?). Each of these choices sends signals about the groups you identify with. Your choice of language (for example, big words versus street slang) or conversation topics (football versus art films) gives further hints of your identity and values. All these choices carry symbolic significance about the identity you wish to project to the world. Rhetoricians study, among other things, how these symbols are constructed within a given culture and how they operate to persuade audiences toward certain beliefs or actions.

For Writing and Discussion

Working in small groups or as a whole class, construct a flirting scenario for two or more of the following situations. For each case, indicate how you think the participants would be dressed. How would they talk? What accessories or other items (watches, jewelry, backpacks/briefcases, bicycles/skateboards/cars, and so forth) might be included in the scene? What might be a typical flirting "move"? You might want to write up your scenario as a short dramatic scene, indicating how the characters look and what the characters say and do.

- High school students in the parking lot after a football game
- Couple standing in line for tickets at a foreign art film festival
- New college students in a dorm cafeteria
- Upscale urban singles bar
- Typical gathering place at your college or university
- Other situation of your choice

Inducing Cooperation: Rhetoric as Inquiry and Persuasion

Another important part of Burke's definition of *rhetoric* is his emphasis on cooperation. The art of rhetoric—to the extent that it results in more productive human conversation—is a foundation of democracy, for it enables humans to settle their differences through dialogue rather than war. When the art of rhetoric works well, it induces cooperation among persons with divergent views, who, in conversation, move back and forth between the modes of inquiry and persuasion. Let us show you in more detail what we mean.

One of our two modes is *inquiry,* which we might define as the pursuit of the best solutions to complex problems. Imagine a conversation of several speakers, each with differing points of view on an important question. Here is how Kenneth Burke describes such a conversation when its participants are persons of good will guided by the skills of rhetoric:

> A rhetorician, I take it, is like one voice in a dialogue. Put several such voices
> together, with each voicing its own special assertion, let them act upon one another
> in cooperative competition, and you get a dialectic that, properly developed, can
> lead to the views transcending the limitations of each.

Burke's point here is that dialectic conversation can lead to the discovery of new and better ideas. Human beings engaged in exchange of reasoned arguments can discover better ways of seeing and hence better solutions to shared problems.

For the conversation to work, however, each participant must be willing to voice his or her own views. This requirement leads to the other mode in our schema: the mode of *persuasion*. Perhaps the most famous definition of rhetoric comes from the Greek philosopher Aristotle, who defined it as "the ability to see, in any particular case, all the available means of persuasion." An effective speaker's task, within Aristotle's view, is to try to persuade listeners to accept the speaker's views on a question of action or belief. If we imagine the interaction of several speakers, each proposing different answers to the question, and if we imagine all the speakers listening to each other respectfully and open-mindedly,* we can see how productive human conversation could emerge.

The conversation works to develop new and better answers because, as rhetoricians understand, *no one person's point of view can be the whole truth.* This is the fundamental insight of rhetoric—that there is always more than one way to tell the same story. (Recall our opening thought exercise in which you were asked to describe the same party to two different audiences.) Each participant's persuasive argument always, by necessity, reflects an emphasis on some facts and values and a corresponding de-emphasis on other facts and values. Each argument—including our own—has characteristic insights and blind spots. Thinking rhetorically thus encourages us to value a diversity of views—to be willing to assert and justi-

---

*For now we are imagining an ideal situation where responsible arguers listen respectfully to each other and are willing to revise their original views. Shortly we will discuss more typical real-world situations where vested interests and the drive for power create nonideal contexts.

fy our own views but also to listen critically and to shift our own point of view in light of other ways of seeing the world.

To see how inquiry and persuasion work together, consider what happens in an ideal class discussion. Suppose an instructor gives students an open-ended discussion question such as, "Why doesn't Hamlet rush to his revenge?" or "To what extent was Louis XIV a good king?" If no one proposes an answer, no conversation takes place: Students simply wait in embarrassed silence for the instructor to tell them what to think. If everyone simply asserts his or her own initial opinion, the conversation stops after each student speaks. Productive discussion occurs only if students are willing to support their views with reasonable arguments and only if these arguments differ in fundamental ways so that students begin seeing "all the available means of persuasion." Soon students begin shifting their initial views, influenced by others' arguments, and find new and better positions to which they can commit themselves. As can be seen in the following list, the rhetorician's view of a productive conversation matches the criteria for effective class discussions established by researchers who study critical thinking:

CRITERIA FOR AN EFFECTIVE CLASS DISCUSSION

Students challenge one another for reasons and examples.

Students offer counterexamples, counterinstances, and counterarguments.

Students piggyback on one another's comments.

Students identify the function of their comments (e.g., "I would like to comment on A, add to B, or disagree with C").

Students view themselves as scholars discussing worthwhile materials.

Students search for and present relationships between the subject under discussion and other relevant school subjects and outside experiences.

Students relate the specific subject under discussion to more general principles.

Students ask relevant and sequential questions.

Students don't take things for granted, but ask for justification.

Students ask for clarification (e.g., "What do you mean?").

—Source: Matthew Lipman, Paper Presented at Connecticut
Critical Thinking Conference, 1985.

For Writing and Discussion

Working in groups, construct your own view of what constitutes a good class discussion. To what extent does your vision of a good class discussion match the criteria listed by Matthew Lipman? What advice would you give teachers and fellow students for improving the effectiveness of class discussions?

Persuasion and Power

So far we have been discussing an ideal rhetorical situation where open-minded participants are committed to inquiry. This view is often too rosy. In many public and personal controversies, vested interests fuel the argument. Participants aren't interested in inquiry but in victory for their own claims. They look for evidence only to support their own views, they don't listen to alternative arguments, and they close themselves off from new ideas. In such an environment, a skeptic might regard rhetoric simply as the art of bombast and propaganda—the ability to create reasonable-sounding arguments that actually serve the private interests of the arguer.

The defense against abuses of rhetoric is faith in your own power to analyze and weigh persuasive messages. Rhetorical thinking helps you become aware of vested interests, private agendas, suppressed evidence, and various kinds of bias in texts and take these into account as you weigh alternative points of view. That a clinical trial showing the value of a new medication was funded by a drug company or that arguments in favor of nuclear power plants often come from the nuclear industry doesn't mean that you should dismiss these views. Rather, your obligation is to seek out alternative voices and bring these voices into the dialogue. Our hope is that this brief introduction to rhetorical theory will help you become a more responsible inquirer who *does* listen to contrary views and who therefore resists early closure (which means not making up your mind based on the first forceful argument you read). Such a thinker understands the responsibilities and pleasures of productive conversation.

The Appeals to *Logos*, *Ethos*, and *Pathos*

We have seen how rhetoric involves both inquiry and persuasion. We next consider how participants in a written or oral conversation can make their contributions as persuasive as possible in order to win people's consideration of their ideas. In this section we explain Aristotle's three "appeals" that writers and speakers can use to increase the effectiveness of their messages: the appeals to *logos*, *ethos*, and *pathos*. These appeals are particularly important in argument when one takes a directly persuasive aim. But all kinds of messages, including writing with an expressive, informative or analytic aim, can be strengthened by a conscious and competent use of these appeals.

A fuller discussion of these classical appeals appears in Chapter 10, "Writing a Classical Argument," pp. 254–256.

Developing the habit of examining how these appeals are functioning in texts and being able to employ these appeals in your own writing will substantially enhance your ability to read and write rhetorically. Let's look briefly at each of these strategies:

- *Logos* is the appeal to reason. It refers to the quality of the message itself—to its internal consistency, to its clarity in asserting a thesis or point, and to the quality of reasons and evidence used to support the point.

- *Ethos* is the appeal to the character of the speaker/writer. It refers to the speaker/writer's trustworthiness and credibility. One can often increase the *ethos* of a message by being knowledgeable about the issue, by appearing thoughtful and fair, by listening well, and by being respectful of alternative points of view. A writer's accuracy and thoroughness in crediting sources and professionalism in caring about the format, grammar, and neat appearance of a document are part of the appeal to *ethos.*
- *Pathos* is the appeal to the sympathies, values, beliefs, and emotions of the audience. Appeals to *pathos* can be made in many ways. *Pathos* can often be enhanced through evocative visual images, frequently used in Web sites, posters, and magazine or newspaper articles. In written texts, the same effects can be created through vivid examples and details, through connotative language, and through empathy with the audience's beliefs and values.

To see how these three appeals are interrelated, you can visualize a triangle with points labeled *Message, Audience,* and *Writer or Speaker.* Rhetoricians study how effective communicators consider all three points of this *rhetorical triangle.* (See Figure 4.1.)

We encourage you to ask questions about the appeals to *logos, ethos,* and *pathos* every time you examine a text. For example, is the appeal to *logos* weakened by the writer's use of scanty and questionable evidence? Has the writer made a powerful appeal to *ethos* by documenting her sources and showing that she is an authority on the issue? Has the writer relied too heavily on appeals to *pathos* by

FIGURE 4.1 Rhetorical Triangle

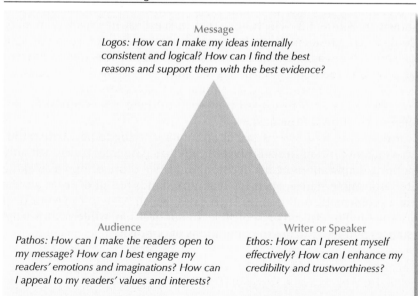

Message
Logos: How can I make my ideas internally consistent and logical? How can I find the best reasons and support them with the best evidence?

Audience
Pathos: How can I make the readers open to my message? How can I best engage my readers' emotions and imaginations? How can I appeal to my readers' values and interests?

Writer or Speaker
Ethos: How can I present myself effectively? How can I enhance my credibility and trustworthiness?

using numerous heart-wringing examples? Later chapters in this textbook will help you use these appeals well in your own writing as well as analyze these appeals in others' messages.

Angle of Vision

Another key insight of rhetoric, one that we mentioned at the beginning of this chapter, is the awareness that there is always more than one way to tell the same story and that no single way of telling it constitutes the whole truth. A writer's thesis necessarily commits a writer to a particular view of a subject that emphasizes some facts and values and de-emphasizes others. This particular point of view we call "angle of vision."

Recognizing the Angle of Vision in a Text

By saying that the writer writes from an "angle of vision," we mean that the writer cannot take a godlike stance that allows a universal, all-seeing, completely true, and whole way of knowing. Rather, the writer looks at the subject from a certain location, or, to use another metaphor, the writer wears a lens that colors or filters the topic in a certain way. The angle of vision, lens, or filter determines what part of a topic gets "seen" and what remains "unseen," what gets included or excluded from the writer's essay, what gets emphasized or de-emphasized, and so forth. It even determines what words get chosen out of an array of options— for example, whether you say "affirmative action" or "reverse discrimination," "terrorist" or "freedom fighter," "public servant" or "politician."

A good illustration of angle of vision is the political cartoon on stem cell research shown in Figure 4.2, which appeared in national newspapers in early summer 2001 when President Bush was contemplating his stance on federal funding for stem cell research. As the cartoon shows, nobody sees stem cells from a universal position. Each stakeholder has an angle of vision that emphasizes some aspects of stem cell research and de-emphasizes or censors other aspects. In the chart on page 82, we try to suggest how each of these angles of vision produces a different "picture" of the field.

In this cartoon, President Bush is cast as an inquirer trying to negotiate multiple perspectives. The cartoon treats Bush satirically—as if he were concerned only with the political implications of his decision. But if we think of him as seeking an ethically responsible stance, then his dilemma stands for all of us as writers confronting a problematic question. In such cases, we all have to forge our own individual stance and be ethically responsible for our decision, while acknowledging other stances and recognizing the limitations of our own.

FIGURE 4.2 Political Cartoon Illustrating Angle of Vision

Where do our stances come from? The stance we take on questions is partly influenced by our life experiences and knowledge, by our class and gender, by our ethnicity and sexual orientation, by our personal beliefs and values, and by our ongoing intentions and desires. But our stance can also be influenced by our rational and empathic capacity to escape from our own limitations and see the world from different perspectives, to imagine the world more fully. We have the power to take stances that are broader and more imaginative than our original limited vision, but we also never escape our own roots and situations in life.

The brief writing project at the end of this chapter will help you understand the concept of "angle of vision" more fully. Your instructor might also assign Chapter 5, which explores angle of vision in more depth.

The exercise on page 82 will help you understand the concept of "angle of vision" more fully.

Angle of Vision on Stem Cell Research

Angle of Vision	Words or Phrases Used to Refer to Stem Cells	Particulars that get "Seen" or Emphasized
Disease sufferer	Cluster of tiny cells that may help repair damaged tissues or grow new ones	The diseases that may be cured by stem cell research; the suffering of those afflicted; scientists as heroes; shelves of frozen stem cells; cells as objects that would just be thrown out if not used for research; emphasis on cures
Priest	Embryo as potential human life formed by union of sperm and egg	Moral consequences of treating human life as means rather than ends; scientists as Dr. Frankensteins; single embryo as potential baby
Scientist	Blastocysts, which are better suited for research than adult stem cells	Scientific questions that research would help solve; opportunities for grants and scholarly publication; emphasis on gradual progress rather than cures
Businessperson	New area for profitable investments	Potential wealth for company that develops new treatments for diseases or injuries
President Bush (at time of cartoon, Bush was uncertain of his stance)	Afraid to say "cluster of cells," "embryo," or "blastocyst" because each term has political consequences	Political consequences of each possible way to resolve the stem cell controversy; need to appease supporters from the Right without appearing callous to sufferers of diseases; need to woo Catholic vote

For Writing and Discussion

Background: Suppose that you are a management professor who is regularly asked to write letters of recommendation for former students. One day you receive a letter from a local bank requesting a confidential evaluation of a former student, one Uriah Rudy Riddle (U. R. Riddle), who has applied for a job as a management trainee. The bank wants your assessment of Riddle's intelligence, aptitude, dependability, and ability to work with people. You haven't seen U. R. for several years, but you remember him well. Here are the facts and impressions you recall about Riddle:

- Very temperamental student, seemed moody, something of a loner
- Long hair and very sloppy dress—seemed like a misplaced street person; often twitchy and hyperactive
- Absolutely brilliant mind; took lots of liberal arts courses and applied them to business
- Wrote a term paper relating different management styles to modern theories of psychology—the best undergraduate paper you ever received. You gave it an A+ and remember learning a lot from it yourself.
- Had a strong command of language—the paper was very well written
- Good at mathematics; could easily handle all the statistical aspects of the course
- Frequently missed class and once told you that your class was boring
- Didn't show up for the midterm. When he returned to class later, he said only that he had been out of town. You let him make up the midterm, and he got an A.
- Didn't participate in a group project required for your course. He said the other students in his group were idiots.
- You thought at the time that Riddle didn't have a chance of making it in the business world because he had no talent for getting along with people.
- Other professors held similar views of Riddle—brilliant, but rather strange and hard to like; an odd duck.

You are in a dilemma because you want to give Riddle a chance (he's still young and may have had a personality transformation of some sort), but you also don't want to damage your own professional reputation by falsifying your true impressions.

Individual task: Working individually for ten minutes or so, compose a brief letter of recommendation assessing Riddle; use details from the list to support your assessment. Role-play that you have decided to take a gamble with Riddle and give him a chance at this career. Write as strong a recommendation as possible while remaining honest. (To make this exercise more complex, your instructor might ask half the class to role-play a negative angle of vision in which you want to warn the bank against hiring Riddle without hiding his strengths or good points.)

Task for group or whole-class discussion: Working in small groups or as a whole class, share your letters. Pick out representative examples ranging from the most positive to the least positive and discuss how the letters achieve their different rhetorical effects. If your intent is to support Riddle, to what extent does honesty compel you to mention some or all of your negative memories? Is it possible to mention negative items without emphasizing them? How?

Analyzing Angle of Vision

Chapter 5, "Seeing Rhetorically," develops this connection between seeing and interpretation in more detail.

Just as there is more than one way to describe the party you went to on Friday night, there is more than one way to write a letter of recommendation for U. R. Riddle. The writer's angle of vision determines what is "seen" or "not seen" in a given piece of writing—what gets slanted in a positive or negative direction, what gets highlighted, what gets thrown into the shadows. As rhetorician Kenneth Burke claims, "A way of seeing is also a way of not seeing." Note how the writer controls what the reader "sees." As Riddle's professor, you might in your mind's eye see Riddle as long-haired and sloppy, but if you don't mention these details in your letter, they remain unseen to the reader. Note too that your own terms "long-haired and sloppy" interpret Riddle's appearance through the lens of your own characteristic way of seeing—a way that perhaps values business attire and clean-cut tidiness. Another observer might describe Riddle's appearance quite differently, thus seeing what you don't see.

In an effective piece of writing, the author's angle of vision often works so subtly that unsuspecting readers—unless they learn to think rhetorically—will be drawn into the writer's spell and believe that the writer's prose conveys the "whole picture" of its subject rather than a limited picture filtered through the screen of the writer's perspective. To understand more clearly how an angle of vision is constructed, you can analyze the language strategies at work. Some of these strategies—which writers employ consciously or unconsciously to achieve their intended effects—are as follows:

WAYS THAT WRITERS CONSTRUCT AN ANGLE OF VISION

- *Writers can state their meaning or intentions directly.* For example, your letter for U. R. Riddle might say, "Riddle would make an excellent bank manager" or "Riddle doesn't have the personality to be a bank manager."
- *Writers can select details that support their intended effect and omit those that don't.* If your intention is to support Riddle, you can include all the positive data about Riddle and omit the negative data (or vice versa if your letter opposes his candidacy). Instead of outright omission of data, you can de-emphasize some details while highlighting others.
- *Writers can choose words that frame the subject in a desired way or that have desired connotations.* For example, if you call Riddle "an independent thinker who doesn't follow the crowd," you frame him positively within a value system that favors individualism. If you call him "a loner who thinks egocentrically," you frame him negatively within a value system that favors consensus and social skills. Also, words can have connotations that serve to channel the reader's response in an intended direction. You thus could call Riddle either "forthright" or "rude" depending on your angle of vision.
- *Writers can use metaphors, similes, or analogies to create an intended effect.* For example, to suggest that Riddle has perhaps outgrown his earlier alienation from classmates, you might call him a "late-bloomer socially." But if you

see him out of place in a bank, you might say that Riddle's independent spirit would feel "caged in" by the routine of a banker's life.

- *Writers can vary sentence structure to emphasize or de-emphasize ideas and details.* Details can get emphasized or de-emphasized depending on where they appear in a sentence or paragraph. For example, material gets emphasized if it appears at the end of a long sentence, in a short sentence surrounded by long sentences, or in a main clause rather than a subordinate clause. Consider the difference between saying, "Although Riddle had problems relating to other students in my class, he is a brilliant thinker" versus "Although Riddle is a brilliant thinker, he had problems relating to other students in my class." The first sentence emphasizes his brilliance, the second his poor people skills.

The brief writing assignment at the end of this chapter will give you further practice in analyzing angle of vision.

Thinking Rhetorically about Any Cultural "Text"

To us, one of the most pleasurable aspects of rhetorical thinking is analyzing the rhetorical power of visual images or identifying rhetorical factors in people's choices about clothing, watches, cars, tattoos, and other consumer items.

Visual Rhetoric

Just as you can think rhetorically about texts, you can think rhetorically about photographs, drawings, paintings, statues, buildings, and other visual images. In Chapter 9, we deal extensively with visual rhetoric, explaining how color, perspective, cropping, camera angle, foreground/background, and other visual elements work together to create a persuasive effect. In this chapter, we intend only to introduce you to the concept of visual rhetoric and to suggest its importance. Consider, for example, the persuasive power of famous photographs from the war in Iraq. Early in the war, several widely publicized images, particularly the film footage of the toppling of the statue of Saddam Hussein and the "Mission Accomplished" photograph of President Bush wearing a pilot's flight suit on the deck of the aircraft carrier *Abraham Lincoln,* served to consolidate public support of the war. Later, certain images began eating away at public support. For example, an unauthorized picture of flag-draped coffins filling the freight deck of a military transport plane focused attention on those killed in the war. Particularly devastating for supporters of the war were the images of American prison guards sexually humiliating Iraqi prisoners in the Abu Ghraib prison. Images like these stick in viewers' memories long after specific texts are forgotten.

An illuminating example of the rhetorical power of paintings and photographs is evident in our cultural discussions of health care. In the early and middle decades of

FIGURE 4.3 A Norman Rockwell Painting of a Family Doctor

FIGURE 4.4 A Modern High-Tech Image of a Doctor

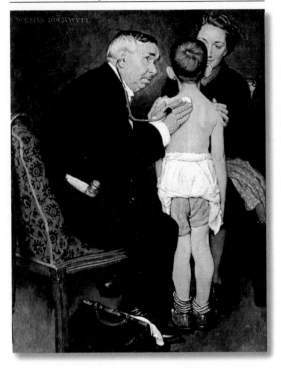

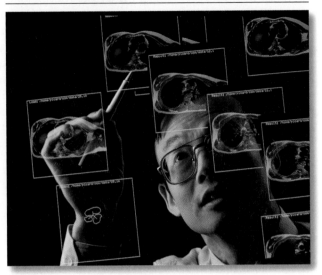

"Doc Melhorn and the Pearly Gates" by Norman Rockwell, inside illustration from The Saturday Evening Post, December 24, 1938. Printed by permission of the Norman Rockwell Family Agency. Copyright © 1938 the Norman Rockwell Family Entities.

the twentieth century, a powerful concept of the "family doctor" emerged. This "family doctor" was envisioned as a personal, caring individual—usually a fatherly or grandfatherly male—with a stethoscope around his neck and a little black bag for making house calls. This image was deeply embedded in the American psyche through a series of paintings by Norman Rockwell, several of which were reproduced on the cover of the influential *Saturday Evening Post* (see Figure 4.3).

These paintings are now part of our cultural nostalgia for a simpler era and help explain some of the cultural resistance in the United States to impersonal HMOs, where medical decisions seem made by insurance bureaucrats. Yet, we also want our doctors to be high-tech. In the last few decades, the image of doctors in the popular imagination, especially furthered by advertising, has shifted away from idealized Norman Rockwell scenes to images of highly specialized experts using the latest technological equipment. Figure 4.4 suggests the kinds of high-tech imagery that now characterizes popular media portrayal of doctors. However, in many current articles about health care in the United States, the

Norman Rockwell paintings of the family doctor are still invoked to represent an older ideal about what people are looking for in their doctors.

The point we want to make in this brief introduction to visual rhetoric is that images make arguments. The Norman Rockwell painting and the high-tech photograph work rhetorically to influence an audience's view of what a doctor should be. The competing images of doctors serve the interests of different groups with different views about the role of medicine in our culture.

For Writing and Discussion

Working in small groups or as a whole class, explore your answers to the following questions:

1. How do the Norman Rockwell painting and the contemporary photograph work to create different images of doctors? What are the values conveyed by the Rockwell painting? What are the values conveyed by the photograph?
2. Why is it in the interest of HMOs and insurance companies to portray high-tech images of doctors? How might the influence of the Norman Rockwell view of doctors serve the interests of alternative health care providers such as naturopathic physicians?

The Rhetoric of Clothing and Other Consumer Items

Not only do visual images have rhetorical power, but so also do many of our consumer choices. We choose our clothes, for example, not only to keep ourselves covered and warm but also to project our identification with certain social groups. For example, if you want to be identified as a skate-boarder, a preppy socialite, a gang member, a pickup-driving NASCAR fan, or a junior partner in a corporate law firm, you know how to select clothes and accessories that convey that identification. The way you dress communicates where you fit (or how you want to be perceived as fitting) within a class and social structure. For the most part, clothing codes are arbitrary, based on a system of differences. For example, there is no universal "truth" saying that long baggy basketball shorts are more attractive than short basketball shorts or that cargo pants are more beautiful than stirrup pants, even though one style may feel current and one out-of-date.

How do these symbolic codes get established? They can be set by fashion designers, by advertisers, or by trendy groups or individuals. The key to any new clothing code is to make it look different in some distinctive way from an earlier code or from a code of another group. Sometimes clothing codes develop to show rebellion against the values of parents or authority figures. At other times they develop to show new kinds of group identities.

Clothing codes are played on in conscious ways in fashion advertisements so that consumers become very aware of what identifications are signaled by different styles and brands. This aspect of consumer society is so ubiquitous that one of the marks of growing affluence in third-world countries is people's attention to the rhetoric of consumer goods. Consider the second epigraph to this chapter, which indicates that villagers in India watching TV ads notice not only the soap or shampoo but also the brands of motorbikes and the lifestyles of the people in the ads. Buying a certain kind of consumer good projects a certain kind of status or group or class identity. Our point, from a rhetorical perspective, is that in making a consumer choice, many people are concerned not only with the quality of the item itself but also with the symbolic messages that the item sends to different audiences. Note that the same item can send quite different messages to different groups: A Rolex watch might enhance one's credibility at a corporate board meeting while undercutting it at a barbecue for union workers. Or consider the clothing choices of preteen girls who want to dress like female pop rock stars. They often do so to fit in with their friends, perhaps unaware of the whole array of cultural messages that these clothes convey to other social groups.

For Writing and Discussion

Working in small groups or as a whole class, do a rhetorical analysis of the consumer items shown in Figures 4.5, 4.6, 4.7, and 4.8.

1. In each case, see if you can reach consensus on why persons might have chosen a particular way of dressing. How does the clothing style project a desire to identify with certain groups or to shock or reject certain groups? How do the clothing choices help establish and enhance the wearer's sense of identity?
2. When you and your friends make consumer purchases, to what extent are you swayed by the internal quality of the item (its materials and workmanship) versus the rhetorical messages it sends to an audience (its signals about social identity and standing)? (Note: Advertisers have long known that consumers, when queried, say: "I buy to please myself." However, advertisers' extensive psychological research suggests that consumers are intensely aware of audience: "I buy to maintain and project a certain way of being perceived by others.")
3. How does the rhetoric of clothing extend to other consumer items such as cars, vacations, recreational activities, home furnishings, music, and so forth?

Chapter Summary

In this chapter we explained Kenneth Burke's definition of *rhetoric* as the use of language and other symbols to produce cooperation among humans. We saw how rhetoric operates under the modes of inquiry and persuasion and how,

FIGURE 4.5

FIGURE 4.6

FIGURE 4.7

FIGURE 4.8

under ideal conditions, an exchange of different perspectives can lead reasonable people toward better solutions to problems. We also introduced the classical appeals of *logos, ethos,* and *pathos* as strategies for increasing the effectiveness of messages. Next we explained the concept of angle of vision. Any text necessarily looks at its subject from a perspective that emphasizes some details while minimizing others. We also showed you how to analyze angle of vision by considering the writer's word choices and the selection and arrangement of evidence. Finally, we explained how you can apply rhetorical thinking to visual images and to various kinds of consumer choices.

BRIEF WRITING PROJECT

Background and Readings

This brief writing project will give you practice at analyzing the angle of vision in different texts. This assignment focuses on two passages about nuclear power plants. Read the two passages; then we will describe your writing task.

The first passage is from the Bush administration's *National Energy Policy: Reliable, Affordable, and Environmentally Sound Energy for America's Future.* The document was written by an energy task force chaired by Vice President Dick Cheney. This passage is an overview paragraph on nuclear power from the opening chapter of the document; the last sentence of the passage is from a later section on recommendations for increasing energy supplies:

PASSAGE 1

Nuclear power plants serve millions of American homes and businesses, have a dependable record for safety and efficiency, and discharge no greenhouse gases into the atmosphere. As noted earlier, these facilities currently generate 20 percent of all electricity in America, and more than 40 percent of electricity generated in 10 states in the Northeast, South, and Midwest. Other nations, such as Japan and France, generate a much higher percentage of their electricity from nuclear power. Yet the number of nuclear plants in America is actually projected to decline in coming years, as old plants close and none are built to replace them. . . . [Later the Cheney document makes the following recommendation:] Provide for the safe expansion of nuclear energy by establishing a national repository for nuclear waste, and by streamlining licensing of nuclear power plants.

The second passage is from an op-ed piece by columnist Marianne Means, published on April 12, 2001, by Hearst Newspapers. It was entitled "Bush, Cheney Will Face Wall of Opposition If They Try to Resurrect Nuclear Power."

PASSAGE 2

Washington—Vice President Dick Cheney, head of the presidential task force studying our energy needs, favors building new nuclear power plants—and he's oddly casual about it.

The industry has been moribund in this country since the partial meltdown at Three Mile Island more than two decades ago set off fierce emotional resistance to an unreliable technology capable of accidentally spreading deadly radiation. No new plants have been ordered since then. Only 20 percent of our electricity is generated by nuclear power.

But President Bush has instructed Cheney to look into the prospect of resurrecting and developing nuclear power as a major part of a broad new energy policy. Cheney argues that modern, improved reactors operate safely, economically and efficiently. "It's one of the safest industries around," he says unequivocally.

There remains, however, a little problem of how to dispose of the plants' radioactive waste. Cheney concedes that issue is still unsolved. "If we're going to go forward with nuclear power, we need to find a way to resolve it," he said Sunday in an NBC "Meet the Press" interview.

No state wants to be the repository of the more than 40,000 tons of high-level nuclear waste currently accumulating at 103 commercial reactor sites around the country. This spent fuel is so deadly it can remain a potential threat to public health and safety for thousands of years. A leak could silently contaminate many miles of groundwater that millions of people depend on.

Your task: Contrast the differences in angle of vision in these two passages by analyzing how they create their different rhetorical effects. Consider factors such as overt statements of meaning, selection/omission of details, connotations of words and figures of speech, and sentence emphasis. To help guide your analysis, reread the section "Analyzing Angle of Vision" on pages 84–85. Your goal here is to explain to your readers how these two passages create different impressions of nuclear power.

PART

2

Writing Projects

This ad for the United States Army highlights qualities traditionally associated with patriotic military service to the country: respect,
honor, and courage. Note that this poster does not depict soldiers in
uniform on a battlefield or in the midst of a drill. Consider the way
the images of the father and daughter and the words in this ad connect character-building, family relationships, the Army, and success.
Think about how gender functions in this ad by focusing on the
young woman's long hair, tasteful makeup, and earnest manner.
This advertisement is part of an exercise in Chapter 9.

YOU TAUGHT HER ABOUT RESPECT, HONOR AND COURAGE. IS IT ANY SURPRISE THAT NOW SHE WANTS TO USE THEM?

She'll experience the most challenging training, use the latest technology and get the strongest support. Every drill and every mission will reinforce in her that character always leads to success. Encourage her to consider becoming a Soldier — AN ARMY OF ONE®.

GOARMY.COM U.S.ARMY

AN ARMY OF ONE

Part 2 Writing Projects

Seeing Rhetorically
The Writer as Observer

About Seeing Rhetorically

Earlier in your school career, you may have been asked in an English class to write a description of a scene as if you were painting a picture of it in words. As you observed your scene carefully, trying to use sensory details to appeal to sight, sound, touch, smell, and even taste, you might have imagined that you were creating a true and objective description of your scene. But consider what happens to a description assignment if we give it a rhetorical twist. Suppose we asked you to write *two* descriptions of the same scene from two different perspectives or angles of vision (caused, say, by different moods or intentions) and then to analyze how the two descriptions differed. We could then ask you to reflect on the extent to which any description of a scene is objective as opposed to being shaped by the observer's intentions, experiences, beliefs, or moods.

Our goal in this chapter is to help you understand more fully the rhetorical concept of "angle of vision," which we introduced in Chapter 4. Learning to ask *why* a text includes certain details and not others and to ponder *how* a text creates its dominant impression will help you analyze any text more critically and understand the complex factors that shape what a writer sees.

> Angle of vision is explained on pp. 80–85.

Your writing assignment for this chapter belongs to a category that we call "writing-to-learn." Many instructors from across the disciplines use writing-to-learn assignments intended to help students understand important disciplinary concepts. The assignment in this chapter, while teaching you about angle of vision, also shows you some of the subtle ways that language and perception are interconnected.

Exploring Rhetorical Observation

One of the intense national debates of the last few years has been whether the federal government should permit oil exploration in the Coastal Plain of the Arctic National Wildlife Refuge (ANWR). Arguments for and against drilling in the ANWR have regularly appeared in newspapers and magazines, and numerous advocacy groups have created Web sites to argue their cases. Nearly every argument contains descriptions of the ANWR that operate rhetorically to advance the writer's position. In the following exercise, we ask you to analyze the angle of vision of these verbal and visual depictions of the ANWR—that is, to analyze how these photographs and descriptions "see" the ANWR. We ask you to consider how different descriptions of the ANWR can be used to support different views of oil exploration. After examining the following data set of five verbal or visual texts, proceed to the questions under "Analyzing the Exhibits" (p. 99).

Exhibit 1: Web Page of the Arctic Power Advocacy Group
This text, with photograph labeled "Wildlife grow accustomed to oil operations at Prudhoe Bay" (Figure 5.1), is part of a pamphlet produced by Arctic Power, an advocacy group in favor of drilling for oil. We accessed this pamphlet through the organization's Web site.

FIGURE 5.1 Bears on Pipeline

Wildlife grow accustomed to oil operations at Prudhoe Bay.

ANWR has the nation's best potential for major additions to U.S. oil supplies

Most geologists think the Coastal Plain of the Arctic National Wildlife Refuge has the best prospects for major additions to U.S. domestic oil supply. This is the part of ANWR set aside by Congress in 1980 for further study of its petroleum potential. There is a good chance that very large oil and gas fields, equal to the amount found at Prudhoe Bay further west, could be discovered in ANWR's Coastal Plain.

The Coastal Plain has very attractive geology and lies between areas of the Alaska North Slope and the Canadian Beaufort Sea where there have been major oil and gas discoveries. Oil and gas deposits have been discovered near ANWR's western border, and a recent oil discovery may result in the first pipeline built to the western boundary of the Coastal Plain.

Although the Coastal Plain was reserved for study of its oil potential, Congress must act to open it for oil and gas exploration. Alaskans and residents of the North Slope, including the Inupiat community of Kaktovik, within ANWR, widely support exploring the Coastal Plain.

Exhibit 2: Photograph from a Pro-Environment Newspaper Op Ed Piece
The photograph of the polar bears in Figure 5.2 accompanied a newspaper op-ed column entitled "Arctic Wildlife Refuge: Protect This Sacred Place."

FIGURE 5.2 Polar Bear with Cubs

Exhibit 3: Photograph Juxtaposing Alaskan Wildlife and Industry
This photograph, showing caribou crossing a road in front of a semi, typifies the Alaskan conflict over preserving nature versus the increasing presence of people and economic development (Figure 5.3).

FIGURE 5.3 Caribou and Truck

Exhibit 4: Photograph and Description on the Arctic Power Web Site
This photograph (Figure 5.4) and passage appeared on the Web site for Arctic Power, a pro-exploration advocacy group.

FIGURE 5.4 ANWR Coastal Plain

[The facts about ANWR] are not as pretty or as emotionally appealing [as the descriptions of ANWR by anti-exploration writers]. But they are important for anyone involved in the ANWR debate. On the coastal plain, the Arctic winter lasts for 9 months. It is dark continuously for 56 days in midwinter. Temperatures with the wind chill can reach –110 degrees F. It's not pristine. There are villages, roads, houses, schools, and military installations. It's not a unique Arctic ecosystem. The coastal plain is only a small fraction of the 88,000 square miles that make up the North Slope. The same tundra environment and wildlife can be found throughout the circumpolar Arctic regions. The 1002 Area [the legal term for the plot of coastal plain being contested] is flat. That's why they call it a plain. [. . .]

Some groups want to make the 1002 Area a wilderness. But a vote for wilderness is a vote against American jobs.

Exhibit 5: Excerpt from a Newspaper Feature Article
The following passage is the opening of a newspaper feature article in which freelance writer Randall Rubini describes his bicycle tour through the Prudhoe Bay Area of Alaska.

The temperature is 39 degrees. The going is slow but finally I am in motion. The bike churns through big rocks and thick gravel that occasionally suck the wheels to a dead halt.

Sixty miles to the east lies the Arctic National Wildlife Refuge, a place ARCO [a major oil-refining company] describes as "a bleak and forbidding land where temperatures plunge to more than 40 degrees below zero and the sun is not seen for nearly two months each year." To me the refuge is 19.5 million acres of unspoiled wilderness believed to contain crude oil and natural gas fields.

Prudhoe Bay production is on the decline, and oil corporations are salivating over the prospect of drilling on the 125-mile-long stretch of coastal plain within the refuge.

The area is a principal calving ground for the 180,000-member porcupine caribou herd that annually migrates to the windswept plain, seeking relief from insects.

The refuge also provides habitat for grizzlies, wolves, musk oxen, wolverines, and arctic foxes. Polar bears hunt over the ice and come ashore. Millions of waterfowl, seabirds, and shorebirds nest here.

Analyzing the Exhibits

Working in small groups or as a whole class, try to reach consensus answers to the following questions:

1. Which photographs do you think create visual claims opposing oil exploration in the ANWR? Which create visual claims supporting oil exploration? What is the verbal argument underlying each of these photos?
2. As we explained in Chapter 4, angle of vision focuses readers' attention on some details of a scene rather than on others; it accounts for what is "seen" and "not seen" by a given writer. What do the opponents of oil exploration tend to "see" and "not see" when they describe the ANWR? What do the proponents of oil exploration tend to "see" and "not see"?
3. When opponents of oil exploration mention oil companies or oil wells, they often try to plant a quick negative picture in the reader's mind. What rhetorical strategies, such as making direct statements and using highly connotative words, do the anti-exploration writers use to give a negative impression of oil companies?
4. In contrast, how do supporters of oil exploration try to create positive feelings about drilling in the ANWR?

WRITING PROJECT

Your writing project for this chapter is to write two descriptions and a self-reflection. The assignment has two parts.*

---

*For this assignment, we are indebted to two sources: (1) Richard Braddock, *A Little Casebook in the Rhetoric of Writing* (Englewood Cliffs, NJ: Prentice-Hall, 1971); and (2) Kenneth Dowst, "Kenneth Dowst's Assignment," *What Makes Writing Good?* eds. William E. Coles, Jr., and James Vopat (Lexington, MA: D.C. Heath, 1985), pp. 52–57.

Part A: Find an indoor or outdoor place where you can sit and observe for fifteen or twenty minutes in preparation for writing a focused description of the scene that will enable your readers to see what you see. Here is the catch: You are to write *two* descriptions of the scene. Your first description must convey a favorable impression of the scene, making it appear pleasing or attractive. The second description must convey a negative, or unfavorable, impression, making the scene appear unpleasant or unattractive. Both descriptions must contain only factual details and must describe exactly the same scene from the same location at the same time. It's not fair, in other words, to describe the scene in sunny weather and then in the rain or otherwise to alter factual details. Each description should be one paragraph long (approximately 125–175 words).

Part B: Self-reflection on What You Learned (300–400 words): Attach to your two descriptions a self-reflection about what you have learned from doing this assignment. This self-reflection should include your own rhetorical analysis of your two descriptions and explain some of the insights you have gained into the concepts of "angle of vision" and "seeing rhetorically."

Strategies for doing a rhetorical analysis were introduced in Chapter 4, pp. 84–85, and are explained further on pp. 103–106.

Part A of the assignment asks you to describe the same scene in two different ways, giving your first description a positive tone and the second description a negative one. You can choose from any number of scenes: the lobby of a dormitory or apartment building, a view from a park bench or a window, a favorite (or disliked) room, a scene at your workplace, a busy street, a local eating or drinking spot, whatever. A student example of two contrasting scenes written for this assignment is found on pages 105–106. Part B of the assignment asks you to write a self-reflection in which you do a rhetorical analysis of your two descriptions and explore what you have learned from this exercise about seeing rhetorically. An excerpt from a student self-reflection, written for this assignment, is found on page 112. Because this assignment results in a thought exercise rather than in a self-contained essay requiring an introduction, transitions between parts, and so forth, you can label your sections simply "Descriptions" and "Self-Reflection."

Understanding Observational Writing

In this section, we elaborate on the concept of angle of vision. We explore what factors influence angle of vision and show how a writer's angle of vision shapes the language he or she chooses, or, to put it inversely, how the chosen language both conveys and creates the angle of vision. We also examine the complex relationship between perception and belief by explaining how previous knowledge, cultural background, interests, and values influence perceptions.

Considering the Factors That Shape Perception

On the face of it, terms such as *observation, perception,* and *seeing* seem nonproblematic. Objects are objects, and the process of perceiving an object is immediate and automatic. However, perception is never a simple matter. Consider what we call "the expert-novice phenomenon": Experts on any given subject notice details about that subject that the novice overlooks. An experienced bird-watcher can distinguish dozens of kinds of swallows by subtle differences in size, markings, and behaviors, whereas a non-bird-watcher sees only a group of birds of similar size and shape. Similarly, people observing an unfamiliar game (for example, an American watching cricket or a Nigerian watching baseball) don't know what actions or events have meaning and, hence, don't know what to look for.

In addition to prior knowledge, cultural differences affect perception. An American watching two Japanese business executives greet each other might not know that they are participating in an elaborate cultural code of bowing, eye contact, speech patterns, and timing of movements that convey meanings about social status. An Ethiopian newly arrived in the United States and an American sitting in a doctor's office will see different things when the nurse points to one of them to come into the examination room: The American notices nothing remarkable about the scene; he or she may remember what the nurse was wearing or something about the wallpaper. The Ethiopian, on the other hand, is likely to remember the nurse's act of pointing, a gesture of rudeness used in Ethiopia only to beckon children or discipline dogs. Again, observers of the same scene see different things.

Your beliefs and values can also shape your perceptions, often creating blind spots. You might not notice data that conflict with your beliefs and values. Or you might perceive contradictory data at some level, but if they don't register in your mind as significant, you disregard them. Consider, for example, how advocates of gun control focus on a child's being accidentally killed because the child found a loaded firearm in Dad's sock drawer, while opponents of gun control focus on burglaries or rapes being averted because the home owner had a pistol by the bedside. The lesson here is that people note and remember whatever is consistent with their worldview much more readily than they note and remember inconsistencies. What you believe is what you see.

Another factor determining what you see is mood. We know that when people are upbeat they tend to see things through "rose-colored glasses"—a cliché with a built-in reference to angle of vision. When you are in a good mood, you see the flowers in a meadow. When you are depressed, you see the discarded wrappers from someone's pack of gum.

More direct and overt is the influence of rhetorical purpose. Consider again the case of the Arctic National Wildlife Refuge mentioned earlier in this chapter. In the passage by Randall Rubini (p. 98), the author juxtaposes his own view of the ANWR as an "unspoiled wilderness" against ARCO's view of the ANWR as a "'bleak and forbidding land.'" Note how each way of seeing the ANWR serves the political purposes of the author. Opponents of oil exploration focus on the unspoiled beauty of the land, listing fondly the names of different kinds of animals that live there. What remains "unseen" in their descriptions are the native villages and military installations on the Coastal Plain and any references to economic issues, the U.S. need for domestic oil, or jobs. In contrast, supporters of oil exploration shift the focus from the caribou herds (their descriptions don't "see" the animals), to the bleak and frigid landscape and the native communities that would benefit from jobs.

This example suggests the ethical dimension of description. Rhetorical purpose entails responsibility. All observers must accept responsibility for what they see and for what they make others see because their descriptions can have real-world consequences—for example, no jobs for a group of people or potential harm to an animal species and an ecosystem. We should reiterate, however, that neither perspective on the ANWR is necessarily dishonest; each is true in a limited way. In any description, writers necessarily—whether consciously or unconsciously—include some details and exclude others. But the writer's intent is nevertheless to influence the reader's way of thinking about the described phenomenon, and ethical readers must be aware of what is happening. By noting what is *not there,* readers can identify a piece's angle of vision and analyze it. The reader can see the piece of writing not as the whole truth but as one person's perspective that can seem like the whole truth if one simply succumbs to the text's rhetorical power.

Finally, let's look at one more important factor that determines angle of vision—what we might call a writer's "guiding ideology" or "belief system." We touched on this point earlier when we showed how one's belief system can create blind spots. Let's examine this phenomenon in more depth by seeing how different beliefs about the role of women in primitive societies cause two anthropologists to describe a scene in different ways. What follows are excerpts from the works of two female anthropologists studying the role of women in the !Kung tribe* of the African Kalahari Desert (sometimes called the "Bushmen"). Anthropologists have long been interested in the !Kung because they still hunt and forage for food in the manner of their prehistoric ancestors.

Here is how anthropologist Lorna Marshal describes !Kung women's work:

MARSHAL'S DESCRIPTION

Women bring most of the daily food that sustains the life of the people, but the roots and berries that are the principal plant foods of the Nyae Nyae !Kung are apt to be tasteless, harsh and not very satisfying. People crave meat. Furthermore, there is only drudgery in digging roots, picking berries, and trudging back to the encampment with heavy loads and babies sagging in the pouches of the karosses: there is no splendid excitement and triumph in returning with vegetables.

—Lorna Marshal, *The !Kung of Nyae Nyae*

---

*The word *!Kung* is preceded by an exclamation point in scholarly work to indicate the unique clicking sound of the language.

And here is how a second anthropologist describes women's work:

DRAPER'S DESCRIPTION

A common sight in the late afternoon is clusters of children standing on the edge of camp, scanning the bush with shaded eyes to see if the returning women are visible. When the slow-moving file of women is finally discerned in the distance, the children leap and exclaim. As the women draw closer, the children speculate as to which figure is whose mother and what the women are carrying in the karosses. [. . .]

!Kung women impress one as a self-contained people with a high sense of self-esteem. There are exceptions—women who seem forlorn and weary—but for the most part, !Kung women are vivacious and self-confident. Small groups of women forage in the Kalahari at distances of eight to ten miles from home with no thought that they need the protection of the men or of the men's weapons should they encounter any of the several large predators that also inhabit the Kalahari.

—P. Draper, "!Kung Women: Contrasts in Sexual Egalitarianism in Foraging and Sedentary Contexts"

As you can see, these two anthropologists "read" the !Kung society in remarkably different ways. Marshal's thesis is that !Kung women are a subservient class relegated to the heavy, dull, and largely thankless task of gathering vegetables. In contrast, Draper believes that women's work is more interesting and requires more skill than other anthropologists have realized. Her thesis is that there is an egalitarian relationship between men and women in the !Kung society.

The source of data for both anthropologists is careful observation of !Kung women's daily lives. But the anthropologists are clearly not seeing the same thing. When the !Kung women return from the bush at the end of the day, Marshal sees their heavy loads and babies sagging in their pouches, whereas Draper sees the excited children awaiting the women's return.

So which view is correct? That's a little like asking whether the ANWR is an "unspoiled wilderness" or a " 'bleak and forbidding land.' " If you believe that women play an important role in !Kung society, you "see" the children eagerly awaiting the women's return at the end of the day, and you note the women's courage in foraging for vegetables "eight to ten miles from home." If you believe that women are basically drudges in this culture, then you "see" the heavy loads and babies sagging in the pouches of the karosses. The details of the scene, in other words, are filtered through the observer's interpretive screen.

Conducting a Simple Rhetorical Analysis

Our discussion of two different views of the ANWR and two different views of the role of women in !Kung society shows how a seemingly objective description of a scene reflects a specific angle of vision that can be revealed through analysis. Rhetorically, a description subtly persuades the reader toward the author's angle of vision. This angle of vision isn't necessarily the author's "true self" speaking, for authors *create* an angle of vision through rhetorical choices they make while composing. We hope you will discover this insight for yourself while doing the assignment for this chapter.

In this section we describe five textual strategies writers often use (consciously or unconsciously) to create the persuasive effect of their texts. Each strategy creates textual differences that you can discuss in your rhetorical analysis.

For a more complete explanation of these five strategies, see Chapter 4's discussion of how an angle of vision is constructed on pp. 80–82.

Strategies for Creating a Persuasive Effect

Strategy 1: State your meaning or intended effect directly.

Example: The first anthropologist says that "there is only drudgery in digging roots" while the second anthropologist says, "!Kung women impress one as a self-contained people with a high sense of self-esteem." The first writer casts her view in negative terms while the second announces a more positive perspective.

Strategy 2: Select details that convey your intended effect and omit those that don't.

Example: The first anthropologist, Marshal, selects details about the tastelessness of the vegetables and the heaviness of the women's loads, creating an overall impression of women's work as thankless and exhausting. Draper, the second anthropologist, selects details about excitement of the children awaiting their mothers' return and the fearlessness of the mothers as they forage "eight to ten miles from home," creating an impression of self-reliant women performing an essential task.

Strategy 3: Choose words with connotations that convey your intended effect.

Example: Marshal chooses words connoting listlessness and fatigue such as *drudgery, trudging, heavy,* and *sagging.* Draper chooses words connoting energy: The children *scan* the bush, *leap and exclaim,* and *speculate,* while the women *forage.*

Strategy 4: Use figurative language (metaphors, similes, and analogies) that conveys your intended effect.

Example: Rubini writes that oil companies are "salivating" for new oil-drilling opportunities (p. 99). He equates oil companies with drooling dogs, giving readers an unpleasant vision of the oil companies' eagerness to get at the ANWR's oil reserves.

Strategy 5: Use sentence structure to emphasize and de-emphasize your ideas.

Example: Marshal uses sentence structure to create a negative impression of the !Kung women's plant-gathering role:

> Women bring most of the daily food that sustains the life of the people, but the roots and berries that are the principal plant foods of the Nyae Nyae !Kung are apt to be tasteless, harsh and not very satisfying. People crave meat.

The short sentence following the long sentence receives the most emphasis, giving readers the impression that meat is more important than the women's vegetables.

For Writing and Discussion

What follows is a student example of two contrasting descriptions written for the assignment in this chapter. Read the descriptions carefully. Working individually, analyze the descriptions rhetorically to explain how the writer has created contrasting impressions through overt statements of meaning, selection and omission of details, word choice, figurative language, and sentence structure. (You will do the same thing for your own two descriptions in Part B of the assignment.) Spend approximately ten minutes doing your own analysis of this example and taking notes. Then, working in small groups or as a whole class, share your analyses, trying to reach agreement on examples of how the writer has created different rhetorical effects by using the five strategies just explained.

Description 1: Positive Effect The high ceiling and plainness of this classroom on the second floor of the Administration Building make it airy, spacious, and functional. This classroom, which is neither dusty and old nor sterile and modern, has a well-used, comfortable feel like the jeans and favorite sweater you put on to go out for pizza with friends. Students around me, who are focused on the assignment, read the instructor's notes on the chalkboard, thumb through their texts, and jot down ideas in their notebooks spread out on the spacious two-person tables. In the back of the room, five students cluster around a table and talk softly and intently about the presentation they are getting ready to make to the class. Splashes of spring sunshine filtering through the blinds on the tall windows brighten the room with natural light, and a breeze pungent with the scent of newly mown grass wafts through the open ones, sweeps over the students writing at their desks, and passes out through the door to the hall. As I glance out the window, I see a view that contributes to the quiet harmony of the environment: bright pink and red rhododendron bushes and manicured beds of spring flowers ring the huge lawn where a few students are studying under the white-blossomed cherry trees.

Description 2: Negative Effect The high ceiling of this classroom on the second floor of the Administration Building cannot relieve the cramped, uncomfortable feeling of this space, which is filled with too many two-person tables, some of them crammed together at awkward angles. A third of the chalkboard is blocked from my view by the bulky television, VCR, and overhead projector that are stacked on cumbersome carts and wreathed in electrical cords. Students around me, working on the assignment, scrape their chairs on the bare linoleum floor as they try to see the chalkboard where some of the instructor's notes are blotted out by the shafts of sunlight piercing through a few bent slats in the blinds. In the back of the room, five students cluster around a table, trying to talk softly about their presentation, but their voices

(continued)

bounce off the bare floors. Baked by the sun, the classroom is so warm that the instructor has allowed us to open the windows, but the wailing sirens of ambulances racing to the various hospitals surrounding the campus distract us. The breeze, full of the smell of mown lawn, brings warm air from outside into this stuffy room. Several students besides me gaze longingly out the window at the bright pink and red rhododendrons in the garden and at the students reading comfortably in the shade under the white-blossomed cherry trees.

READINGS

The reading for this chapter consists of two eyewitness accounts of an event that occurred on the Congo River in Africa in 1877.* The first account is by the famous British explorer Henry Morton Stanley, who led an exploration party of Europeans into the African interior. The second account is by the African tribal chief Mojimba, as told orally to a Belgian missionary, Fr. Frassle, who recorded the story. The conflicting accounts suggest the complexity of what happens when different cultures meet for the first time.

Clash on the Congo: Two Eyewitness Accounts

Henry Morton Stanley's Account

1   We see a sight that sends the blood tingling through every nerve and fibre of the body . . . a flotilla of gigantic canoes bearing down upon us. A monster canoe leads the way . . . forty men on a side, their bodies bending and swaying in unison as with a swelling barbarous chorus they drive her down towards us . . . the warriors above the manned prow let fly their spears. . . . But every sound is soon lost in the ripping crackling musketry. . . . Our blood is up now. It is a murderous world, and we feel for the first time that we hate the filthy vulturous ghouls who inhabit it. . . . We pursue them . . . and continue the fight in the village streets with those who have landed, hunt them out into the woods, and there only sound the retreat, having returned the daring cannibals the compliment of a visit.

Mojimba's Account

2   When we heard that the man with the white flesh was journeying down the [Congo] we were open-mouthed with astonishment. . . . He will be one of our brothers who were drowned in the river. . . . We will prepare a feast, I

---

*These readings are taken from Donald C. Holsinger, "A Classroom Laboratory for Writing History," *Social Studies Review* 31.1 (1991): 59–64. The role-playing exercise following the readings is also adapted from this article.

ordered, we will go to meet our brother and escort him into the village with rejoicing! We donned our ceremonial garb. We assembled the great canoes. . . . We swept forward, my canoe leading, the others following, with songs of joy and with dancing, to meet the first white man our eyes had beheld, and to do him honor. But as we drew near his canoes there were loud reports, bang! bang! And fire-staves spat bits of iron at us. We were paralyzed with fright . . . they were the work of evil spirits! "War! That is war!" I yelled. . . . We fled into our village—they came after us. We fled into the forest and flung ourselves on the ground. When we returned that evening our eyes beheld fearful things: our brothers, dead, dying, bleeding, our village plundered and burned, and the water full of dead bodies. The robbers and murderers had disappeared.

Thinking Critically about the *Two Accounts*

Our purpose in presenting these two accounts is to raise the central problem examined in this chapter: the rhetorical nature of observation—that is, how observation is shaped by values, beliefs, knowledge, and purpose and therefore represents an angle of vision or one perspective.

1. How do the two accounts differ?

2. What is common to both accounts? Focusing on common elements, try to establish as many facts as you can about the encounter.

3. How does each observer create a persuasive effect by using one or more of the five strategies described on page 104 (overt statement of meaning, selection/omission of details, connotations of words, figurative language, ordering and shaping of sentences)?

4. What differences in assumptions, values, and knowledge shape these two interpretations of events?

5. As a class, try the following role-playing exercise:
   Background: You are a newspaper reporter who has a global reputation for objectivity, accuracy, and lack of bias. You write for a newspaper that has gained a similar reputation and prides itself on printing only the truth. Your editor has just handed you two eyewitness accounts of an incident that has recently occurred in central Africa. You are to transform the two accounts into a brief front-page article (between sixty and ninety words) informing your readers what happened. You face an immediate deadline and have no time to seek additional information.
   Task: Each class member should write a sixty- to ninety-word newspaper account of the event, striving for objectivity and lack of bias. Then share your accounts.

6. As a class, play the believing and doubting game with this assertion: "It is possible to create an objective and unbiased account of the Congo phenomenon."

Composing Your Essay

Since the assignment for this chapter has two parts—Part A, calling for two contrasting descriptions, and Part B, calling for a self-reflection—we address each part separately.

Exploring Rationales and Details for Your Two Descriptions

To get into the spirit of this unusual assignment, you need to create a personal rationale for why you are writing two opposing descriptions. Our students have been successful imagining any one of the following three rationales:

Rationales for Writing Opposing Descriptions

Different moods: One approach is to imagine observing your scene in different moods. How could I reflect a "happy" view of this scene? How could I reflect a "sad" view of this scene? Be sure, however, to focus entirely on a description of the scene, not on your mood itself. Let the mood determine your decisions about details and wording, but don't put yourself into the scene. The reader should infer the mood from the description.

Verbal game: Here you see yourself as a word wizard trying consciously to create two different rhetorical effects for readers. In this scenario, you don't worry how you feel about the scene but how you want your reader to feel. Your focus is on crafting the language to influence your audience in different ways.

Different rhetorical purposes: In this scenario, you imagine your description in service of some desired action. You might want authorities to improve an ugly, poorly designed space (for example, a poorly designed library reading room). Or you might want to commend someone for a particularly functional space (for example, a well-designed computer lab). In this scenario, you begin with a strongly held personal view of your chosen scene—something you want to commend or condemn. One of your descriptions, therefore, represents *the way you really feel*. Your next task is to see this same scene from an opposing perspective. To get beyond your current assessment of the scene—to recognize aspects of it that are inconsistent with your beliefs—you need to "defamiliarize" it, to make it strange. Artists sometimes try to disrupt their ordinary ways of seeing by drawing something upside down or by imagining the scene from the perspective of a loathsome character—whatever it takes to wipe away "the film of habit" from the object.

The student who wrote the example on pages 105–106 worked from this last rationale. She disliked one of her classrooms, which she found unpleasant and detrimental to learning. In choosing this place, she discovered that she valued college classrooms that were well equipped, comfortable, quiet, modernized, reasonably roomy, and unaffected by outside weather conditions. It was easy for her to write the negative description of this room, which used descriptive details showing how the scene violated all her criteria. However, she had trouble writing the positive description until she imagined being inside the head of someone totally different from herself.

Generating Details

Once you have chosen your scene, you need to compose descriptions that are rich in sensory detail. You might imagine yourself in descriptive partnership with a recently blinded friend in which you become your friend's eyes, while your friend—having newly heightened senses of hearing, touch, and smell—can notice nonsight details that you might otherwise miss. In your writing, good description should be packed with sensory detail—sights, sounds, smells, textures, even on occasion tastes—all contributing to a dominant impression that gives the description focus.

After you have chosen a subject for your two descriptions, observe it intensely for fifteen or twenty minutes. One way to train yourself to notice sensory details is to create a two-column sensory chart. As you observe your scene, note details that appeal to each of the senses and then try describing them, first positively (left column) and then negatively (right column). One student, observing a scene in a local tavern, made these notes in her sensory chart:

Positive Description	Negative Description
Taste	**Taste**
salted and buttered popcorn	salty, greasy popcorn
frosty pitchers of beer	half-drunk pitchers of stale, warm beer
big bowls of salted-in-the-shell peanuts on the tables	mess of peanut shells and discarded pretzel wrappers on tables and floor
Sound	**Sound**
hum of students laughing and chatting	din of high-pitched giggles and various obnoxious frat guys shouting at each other
the jukebox playing oldies but goodies from the early Beatles	jukebox blaring out-of-date music

[She continued with the other senses of odor, touch, and sight]

Shaping and Drafting Your Two Descriptions

Once you have decided on your rationale for the two descriptions, observed your scene, and made your sensory chart, compose your two descriptions. You will need to decide on an ordering principle for your descriptions. It generally makes sense to begin with an overview of the scene to orient your reader.

From the park bench near 23rd and Maple, one can watch the people strolling by the duck pond.

By eight o'clock on any Friday night, Pagliacci's Pizzeria on Broadway becomes one of the city's most unusual gathering places.

Then you need a plan for arranging details. There are no hard-and-fast rules here, but there are some typical practices. You can arrange details in the following ways:

- By spatially scanning from left to right or from far to near
- By using the written equivalent of a movie zoom shot: begin with a broad overview of the scene, then move to close-up descriptions of specific details

Compose your pleasant description, selecting and focusing on details that convey a positive impression. Then compose your unpleasant description. Each description should comprise one fully developed paragraph (125–175 words).

Using *Show* Words Rather than *Tell* Words

In describing your scenes, use *show* words rather than *tell* words. *Tell* words interpret a scene without describing it. They name an interior, mental state, thus telling the reader what emotional reaction to draw from the scene.

TELL WORDS

There was a *pleasant* tree in the backyard.
There was an *unpleasant* tree in the backyard.

In contrast, *show* words describe a scene through sensory details appealing to sight, sound, smell, touch, and even taste. The description itself evokes the desired effect without requiring the writer to state it overtly.

SHOW WORDS

A *spreading elm* tree *bathed* the backyard with *shade.* [evokes positive feelings]
An *out-of-place elm, planted too close to the house, blocked our view* of the *mountains.* [evokes negative feelings]

The "scale of abstraction" is explained in Chapter 3, pp. 60–61.

Whereas *show* words are particulars that evoke the writer's meaning through sensory detail, *tell* words are abstractions that announce the writer's intention directly (strategy 1 on p. 104). An occasional *tell* word can be useful, but *show* words operating at the bottom of the "scale of abstraction" are the flesh and muscle of descriptive prose.

Inexperienced writers often try to create contrasting impressions of a scene simply by switching *tell* words.

WEAK: OVERUSE OF *TELL* WORDS

The smiling merchants happily talked with customers trying to get them to buy their products. [positive purpose]
The annoying merchants kept hassling customers trying to convince them to buy their products. [negative purpose]

In this example, the negative words *annoying* and *hassling* and the positive words *smiling* and *happily* are *tell* words; they state the writer's contrasting intentions, but they don't describe the scene. Here is how the student writer revised these passages using *show* words.

STRONG: CONVERSION TO *SHOW* WORDS

One of the merchants, selling thick-wooled Peruvian sweaters, nodded approvingly as a woman tried on a richly textured blue cardigan in front of the mirror. [positive purpose]

One of the merchants, hawking those Peruvian sweaters that you find in every open-air market, tried to convince a middle-aged woman that the lumpy, oversized cardigan she was trying on looked stylish. [negative purpose]

Here are some more examples taken from students' drafts before and after revision:

Draft with *Tell* Words	Revision with *Show* Words
Children laugh and point animatedly at all the surroundings.	Across the way, a small boy taps his friend's shoulder and points at a circus clown.
The wonderful smell of food cooking on the barbecue fills my nose.	The tantalizing smell of grilled hamburgers and buttered corn on the cob wafts from the barbecue area of the park, where men in their cookout aprons wield forks and spatulas and drink Budweisers.
The paintings on the wall are confusing, dark, abstract, demented, and convey feelings of unhappiness and suffering.	The paintings on the wall, viewed through the smoke-filled room, seem confusing and abstract—the work of a demented artist on a bad trip. Splotches of black paint are splattered over a greenish-yellow background like bugs on vomit.

Revising Your Two Descriptions

The following checklist of revision questions will help you improve your first draft:

1. *How can I make my two descriptions more parallel—that is, more clearly about the same place at the same time?* The rules for the assignment ask you to use only factual details observable in the same scene at the same time. It violates the spirit of the assignment to have one scene at a winning basketball game and the other at a losing game. Your readers' sense of pleasure in comparing your two descriptions will be enhanced if many of the same details appear in both descriptions.

2. *Where can I replace* tell *words with* show *words?* Inexperienced writers tend to rely on *tell* words rather than give the reader sensory details and visual impressions. Find words that deliver prepackaged ideas to the reader (*pleasant, happy, depressing, annoying, pretty,* and so forth) and rewrite those sentences by actually describing what you see, hear, smell, touch, and taste. Pay particular attention to this advice if you are choosing "different moods" as your rationale for two descriptions.

3. *How can I make the angle of vision in each description clearer? How can I clarify my focus on a dominant impression?* Where could you use words with vividly appropriate connotations? Where could you substitute specific words for general ones? For example, consider synonyms for the generic word *shoe.* Most people wear shoes, but only certain people wear spiked heels or riding boots. Among words for kinds of sandals, *Birkenstocks* carries a different connotation from *Tevas* or *strappy espadrilles with faux-metallic finish.* Search your draft for places where you could substitute more colorful or precise words for generic words to convey your dominant impression more effectively.

Generating and Exploring Ideas for Your Self-Reflection

Part B of this Writing Project asks you to write a self-reflection about what you have learned. Your reflection should begin with a rhetorical analysis of your two descriptions in which you explain how you created your positive versus negative effects. Focus on how you used the strategies introduced in Chapter 4 (pages 84–85) and summarized in the chart "Strategies for Creating a Persuasive Effect" on page 104. In the rest of your self-reflection, explore what you have learned from reading this chapter and doing this exercise. You are invited to consider questions like these:

- What rationale or scenario did you use for explaining to yourself why one might write opposing descriptions (different moods? verbal game? different rhetorical purposes? something else?) Which description was easier for you to write and why?
- What new insights did you come away with? Specifically, what have you learned about the concept "angle of vision" and about ways writers can influence readers? What, if anything, was disturbing or challenging about the concepts developed in this chapter?
- Throughout this text we urge you to read rhetorically, that is, to be aware of how a text is constructed to influence readers. How has this chapter advanced your ability to read rhetorically?

To illustrate self-reflection, we reproduce here a portion of the self-reflection written by the student who wrote the two descriptions on pages 105–106.

SELECTIONS FROM A STUDENT'S SELF-REFLECTION

In writing the two descriptions, I used most of the strategies for creating rhetorical effects discussed in the text. In deliberately changing my angle of vision from positive to negative, I realized how much the connotation of individual words can convey particular ideas to readers. For example, in the positive description to get across the idea of a comfortably studious environment, I used words such as "airy," "spacious," "focused," and "quiet harmony." But in my negative description, I wanted readers to feel the unpleasantness of this room so I used words like "cramped," "crammed," "blocked," and "bulky." I also created different effects by including or excluding certain details. For example, in the positive description, I mentioned the "splashes of sunshine" coming through the window, but in the negative description

I mentioned the wailing sirens of ambulances. [She continues with this rhetorical analysis, explaining and illustrating the other strategies she used.]

I learned a lot from doing this assignment. In writing my two descriptions, I found it helpful both to imagine different moods and different rhetorical purposes. It was easy for me to write the negative view of my classroom because I often get irritated with the problems in this room—the discomfort, inconvenience, and noise. It was much harder to write the positive view. In fact, I couldn't do so until I imagined looking at the room from someone else's perspective. To do so, I imagined that a fellow student was interviewing me on the question, How could the classroom facilities on our campus be improved? I role-played telling this person what I really like in a classroom and then tried to give these features to the room.

What amazed me is that both of my descriptions are factually true but create totally different effects that depend on the observer's perspective. Writing my two descriptions made me think about how much power writers have to influence readers' thinking. . . .

[In the rest of her self-reflection, she explains further what she learned from this assignment and also notes how she has begun to notice similar rhetorical strategies being used in some of her recent reading.]

GUIDELINES FOR PEER REVIEWS

Instructions for peer reviews are provided in Chapter 11 (pp. 293–294).

For the Writer

Prepare two or three questions you would like your peer reviewer to address while responding to your draft. The questions can focus on some aspect of your draft that you are uncertain about, on one or more sections where you particularly seek help or advice, on some feature that you particularly like about your draft, or on some part you especially wrestled with. Write out your questions and give them to your peer reviewer along with your draft.

For the Reviewer

To write a peer review for a classmate, use your own paper, numbering your responses to correspond to the question numbers. At the head of your paper, place the author's name and your own name, as shown.

Author's Name: _____

Peer Reviewer's Name: _____

I. Read the draft at a normal reading speed from beginning to end. As you read, do the following:
   A. Place a wavy line in the margin next to any passages that you find confusing, that contain something that doesn't seem to fit, or that otherwise slow down your reading.
   B. Place a "Good!" in the margin next to any passages where you think the writing is particularly strong or interesting.

II. Read the draft again slowly and answer the following questions by writing brief explanations of your answers:

A. The two descriptions

1. How could the two descriptions be made more parallel or more detailed and vivid? How might the writer sharpen or clarify the angle of vision in each description?

2. Where could the writer replace *tell* words with *show* words? How could the writer use *show* words more effectively? How could the writer include more sensory details appealing to more of the senses?

3. If the writer has used only one or two of the strategies for creating contrast (direct statement of meaning, selection of details, word choice, figurative language, sentence structure), how might he or she use other strategies?

B. Self-reflection

1. How might the writer improve the effectiveness of the rhetorical analysis? How many strategies does the writer include? Where might the writer use more or better examples to illustrate the chosen strategies? What might the writer add or clarify?

2. What does the writer say he or she has learned from doing this assignment? How could the writer's insights be expanded, explained more clearly, or developed more thoroughly?

III. Rhetorical considerations

A. *Purpose, audience,* and *genre:* How do differences in organization and style in Parts A and B reveal the writer's awareness of differences in purpose, audience, and genre?

B. *Logos, ethos,* and *pathos:* How might the writer improve the ideas in this draft, particularly in Part B? What image of the writer emerges in Parts A and B? How might the writer improve this image? How effectively does the writer appeal to the readers' feelings, emotions, and desires?

IV. If the writer has prepared questions for you, respond to his or her inquiries.

V. Sum up what you see as the chief strengths and problem areas of this draft.

A. Strengths

B. Problem areas

VI. Read the draft one more time. Place a check mark in the margin wherever you notice problems in grammar, spelling, or mechanics (one check mark per problem).

Reading Rhetorically
The Writer as Strong Reader

About Reading Rhetorically

Many new college students are surprised by the amount, range, and difficulty of reading they have to do in college. Every day they are challenged by reading assignments ranging from scholarly articles and textbooks on complex subject matter to primary sources such as Plato's dialogues or Darwin's *Voyage of the Beagle*.

The goal of this chapter is to help you become a more powerful reader of academic texts, prepared to take part in the conversations of the disciplines you study. To this end, we explain two kinds of thinking and writing essential to your college reading:

- Your ability to listen carefully to a text, to recognize its parts and their functions, and to summarize its ideas
- Your ability to formulate strong responses to texts by interacting with them, either by agreeing with, interrogating, or actively opposing them

To interact strongly with texts, you must learn how to read them both with and against the grain. When you read *with the grain* of a text, you see the world through its author's perspective, open yourself to the author's argument, apply the text's insights to new contexts, and connect its ideas to your own experiences and personal knowledge. When you read *against the grain* of a text, you resist it by questioning its points, raising doubts, analyzing the limits of its perspective, or even refuting its argument. We say that readers who respond strongly to texts in this manner read *rhetorically*; that is, they are aware of the effect a text is intended to have on them, and they critically consider that effect, entering into or challenging the text's intentions.

Exploring Rhetorical Reading

As an introduction to rhetorical reading, we would like you to read Dr. Andrés Martin's "On Teenagers and Tattoos," which appeared in the *Journal of the American Academy of Child and Adolescent Psychiatry*, a scholarly publication. Before reading the article, complete the following opinion survey. Answer each question using a 1–5 scale, with 1 meaning "strongly agree" and 5 meaning "strongly disagree."

1. For teenagers, getting a tattoo is like following any other fad such as wearing the currently popular kind of shoe or hairstyle.
2. Teenagers get tattoos primarily as a form of asserting independence from parents and other adults.
3. Teenagers get tattoos on the spur of the moment and usually don't consider the irreversibility of marking their skin.
4. Teenagers who get tattoos are expressing deep psychological needs.
5. A psychiatry journal can provide useful insights into teen choices to tattoo their bodies.

When you have finished rating your degree of agreement with these statements, read Martin's article, using whatever note-taking, underlining, or highlighting strategies you normally use when reading for a class. When you have finished reading, complete the exercises that follow.

READING

Andrés Martin, M.D.
On Teenagers and Tattoos

The skeleton dimensions I shall now proceed to set down are copied verbatim from my right arm, where I had them tattooed: as in my wild wanderings at that period, there was no other secure way of preserving such valuable statistics.

—Melville/*Moby Dick CII*

1   Tattoos and piercings have become a part of our everyday landscape. They are ubiquitous, having entered the circles of glamour and the mainstream of fashion, and they have even become an increasingly common feature of our urban youth. Legislation in most states restricts professional tattooing to adults older than 18 years of age, so "high end" tattooing is rare in children and adolescents, but such tattoos are occasionally seen in older teenagers. Piercings, by comparison, as well as self-made or "jailhouse" type tattoos, are not at all rare among adolescents or even among schoolage children. Like hairdo, makeup, or baggy jeans, tattoos and piercings can be subject to fad influence or peer pressure in an effort toward group affiliation. As with any other fashion statement, they can be construed as bodily aids in the inner struggle toward identity consolidation, serving as adjuncts to the defining and sculpting of the self by means of external manipulations. But unlike most other body decorations, tattoos and piercings are set apart by their irreversible and permanent nature, a quality at the core of their magnetic appeal to adolescents.

2   Adolescents and their parents are often at odds over the acquisition of bodily decorations. For the adolescent, piercings or tattoos may be seen as personal and beautifying statements, while parents may construe them as oppositional and enraging affronts to their authority. Distinguishing bodily adornment from self-mutilation may indeed prove challenging, particularly when a family is in disagreement over a teenager's motivations and a clinician is summoned as the final arbiter. At such times it may be most important to realize jointly that the skin can all too readily become but another battleground for the tensions of the age, arguments having less to do with tattoos and piercings than with core issues such as separation from the family matrix. Exploring the motivations and significance underlying tattoos (Grumet, 1983) and piercings can go a long way toward resolving such differences and can become a novel and additional way of getting to know teenagers. An interested and nonjudgmental appreciation of teenagers' surface presentations may become a way of making contact not only in their terms but on their turfs: quite literally on the territory of their skins.

3   The following three sections exemplify some of the complex psychological underpinnings of youth tattooing.

Identity and the Adolescent's Body

4   Tattoos and piercing can offer a concrete and readily available solution for many of the identity crises and conflicts normative to adolescent development. In using such decorations, and by marking out their bodily territories, adolescents can support their efforts at autonomy, privacy, and insulation. Seeking individuation, tattooed adolescents can become unambiguously demarcated from others and singled out as unique. The intense and often disturbing reactions that are mobilized in viewers can help to effectively keep them at bay, becoming tantamount to the proverbial "Keep Out" sign hanging from a teenager's door.

5   Alternatively, [when teenagers feel] prey to a rapidly evolving body over which they have no say, self-made and openly visible decorations may restore adolescents' sense of normalcy and control, a way of turning a passive experience into an active identity. By indelibly marking their bodies, adolescents can strive to reclaim their bearings within an environment experienced as alien, estranged, or suffocating or to lay claim over their evolving and increasingly unrecognizable bodies. In either case, the net outcome can be a resolution to unwelcome impositions: external, familial, or societal in one case; internal and hormonal in the other. In the words of a 16-year-old girl with several facial piercings, and who could have been referring to her body just as well as to the position within her family, "If I don't fit in, it is because *I* say so."

Incorporation and Ownership

6   Imagery of a religious, deathly, or skeletal nature, the likenesses of fierce animals or imagined creatures, and the simple inscription of names are some of the time-tested favorite contents for tattoos. In all instances, marks

become not only memorials or recipients for clearly held persons or concepts; they strive for incorporation, with images and abstract symbols gaining substance on becoming a permanent part of the individual's skin. Thickly embedded in personally meaningful representations and object relations, tattoos can become not only the ongoing memento of a relationship, but at times even the only evidence that there ever was such a bond. They can quite literally become the relationship itself. The turbulence and impulsivity of early attachments and infatuations may become grounded, effectively bridging oblivion through the visible reality of tattoos.

7   *Case Vignette.* A, a 13-year-old boy, proudly showed me his tattooed deltoid. The coarsely depicted roll of the dice marked the day and month of his birth. Rather disappointed, he then uncovered an immaculate back, going on to draw for me the great "piece" he envisioned for it. A menacing figure held a hand of cards: two aces, two eights, and a card with two sets of dates. A's father had belonged to "Dead Man's Hand," a motorcycle gang named after the set of cards (aces and eights) that the legendary Wild Bill Hickock had held in the 1890s when shot dead over a poker table in Deadwood, South Dakota. A had only the vaguest memory of and sketchiest information about his father, but he knew he had died in a motorcycle accident: the fifth card marked the dates of his birth and death.

8   The case vignette also serves to illustrate how tattoos are often the culmination of a long process of imagination, fantasy, and planning that can start at an early age. Limited markings, or relatively reversible ones such as piercings, can at a later time scaffold toward the more radical commitment of a permanent tattoo.

The Quest for Permanence

9   The popularity of the anchor as a tattoo motif may historically have had to do less with guild identification among sailors than with an intense longing for rootedness and stability. In a similar vein, the recent increase in the popularity and acceptance of tattoos may be understood as an antidote or counterpoint to our urban and nomadic lifestyles. Within an increasingly mobile society, in which relationships are so often transient—as attested by the frequencies of divorce, abandonment, foster placement, and repeated moves, for example—tattoos can be a readily available source of grounding. Tattoos, unlike many relationships, can promise permanence and stability. A sense of constancy can be derived from unchanging marks that can be carried along no matter what the physical, temporal, or geographical vicissitudes at hand. Tattoos stay, while all else may change.

10   *Case Vignette.* A proud father at 17, B had had the smiling face of his 3-month-old baby girl tattooed on his chest. As we talked at a tattoo convention, he proudly introduced her to me, explaining how he would "always know how beautiful she is today" when years from then he saw her semblance etched on himself.

11   The quest for permanence may at other times prove misleading and offer premature closure to unresolved conflicts. At a time of normative uncertain-

ties, adolescents may maladaptively and all too readily commit to a tattoo and its indefinite presence. A wish to hold on to a current certainty may lead the adolescent to lay down in ink what is valued and cherished one day but may not necessarily be in the future. The frequency of self-made tattoos among hospitalized, incarcerated, or gang-affiliated youths suggests such motivations: a sense of stability may be a particularly dire need under temporary, turbulent, or volatile conditions. In addition, through their designs teenagers may assert a sense of bonding and allegiance to a group larger than themselves. Tattoos may attest to powerful experiences, such as adolescence itself, lived and even survived together. As with *Moby Dick's* protagonist Ishmael, they may bear witness to the "valuable statistics" of one's "wild wandering(s)": those of adolescent exhilaration and excitement on the one hand; of growing pains, shared misfortune, or even incarceration on the other.

12   Adolescents' bodily decorations, at times radical and dramatic in their presentation, can be seen in terms of figuration rather than disfigurement, of the natural body being through them transformed into a personalized body (Brain, 1979). They can often be understood as self-constructive and adorning efforts, rather than prematurely subsumed as mutilatory and destructive acts. If we bear all of this in mind, we may not only arrive at a position to pass more reasoned clinical judgment, but become sensitized through our patients' skins to another level of their internal reality.

References

Brain, R. (1979). *The Decorated Body*. New York: Harper & Row.
Grumet, G. W. (1983). Psychodynamic implications of tattoos. *Am J Orthopsychiatry*, 53:482–492.

Thinking Critically about "On Teenagers and Tattoos"

1. Summarize in one or two sentences Martin's main points.

2. Freewrite a response to this question: In what way has Martin's article caused me to reconsider my answers to the opinion survey?

3. Working in small groups or as a whole class, compare the note-taking strategies you used while reading this piece. (a) How many people wrote marginal notes? How many underlined or highlighted? (b) Compare the contents of these notes. Did people highlight the same passage or different passages? (c) Individually, look at your annotations and highlights and try to decide why you wrote or marked what you did. Share your reasons for making these annotations. The goal of this exercise is to make you more aware of your thinking processes as you read.

4. Working as a whole class or in small groups, share your responses to the questionnaire and to the postreading questions. To what extent did this article

change people's thinking about the reasons teenagers choose to tattoo their bodies? What were the most insightful points in this article?

5. Assume that you are looking for substantial, detailed information about teenagers and tattooing. What parts of this article leave you with unanswered questions? Where is more explanation needed?

WRITING PROJECT

Write a "summary/strong response" essay that includes: (a) a summary (approximately 150–250 words) of a reading specified by your instructor and (b) a strong response to that reading in which you speak back to that reading from your own critical thinking, personal experience, and values. As you formulate your own response, consider both the author's rhetorical strategies and the author's ideas. Think of your response as your analysis of how the text tries to influence its readers rhetorically and how your wrestling with the text has expanded and deepened your thinking about its ideas.

The skills this assignment develops are crucial for academic writers. You will learn how to summarize an article (or book), including how to quote brief passages, how to use attributive tags to cue your reader that you are reporting someone else's ideas rather than your own, and how to cite the article using (in this case) the Modern Language Association (MLA) documentation system. Because writing summaries and producing strong responses are important writing-to-learn skills, you will draw on them any time you are asked to speak back to or critique a text. These skills are also needed for writing exploratory essays, analysis and synthesis essays, researched arguments, and any other scholarly work that uses sources. In learning how to summarize a text and interact with it in writing, you are learning how to contribute your own ideas to a conversation. Weak readers passively report what other people have said. Strong readers see themselves as contributors to the conversation, capable of analyzing and evaluating texts, speaking back to other authors, and thinking actively for themselves.

Understanding Rhetorical Reading

In this section we explain why college-level reading is often difficult for new students and offer suggestions for improving your reading process based on the reading strategies of experts. We then show you the importance of reading a text both with the grain and against the grain—skills you need to summarize a text and respond to it strongly.

What Makes College-Level Reading Difficult?

The difficulty of college-level reading stems in part from the complexity of the subject matter. Whatever the subject—from international monetary policies to the intricacies of photosynthesis—you have to wrestle with new and complex materials that might perplex anyone. But in addition to the daunting subject matter, several other factors contribute to the difficulty of college-level reading:

- *Vocabulary.* Many college-level readings—especially primary sources—contain unfamiliar technical language that may be specific to an academic discipline: for example, the terms *identity consolidation, normative, individuation,* and *object relations* in the Martin text or words like *existentialism* and *Neoplatonic* in a philosophy textbook. In academia, words often carry specialized meanings that evoke a whole history of conversation and debate that may be inaccessible, even through a specialized dictionary. You will not fully understand them until you are initiated into the disciplinary conversations that gave rise to them.
- *Unfamiliar rhetorical context.* As we explained in Part One, writers write to an audience for a purpose arising from some motivating occasion. Knowing an author's purpose, occasion, and audience will often clarify confusing parts of a text. For example, you can understand the Martin article more easily if you know that its author, writing in a scientific journal, is offering advice to psychiatrists about how to counsel tattooed teens and their families. A text's internal clues can sometimes help you fill in the rhetorical context, but often you may need to do outside research.
- *Unfamiliar genre.* In your college reading, you will encounter a range of genres such as textbooks, trade books, scholarly articles, scientific reports, historical documents, newspaper articles, op-ed pieces, and so forth. Each of these makes different demands on readers and requires a different reading strategy.
- *Lack of background knowledge.* Writers necessarily make assumptions about what their readers already know. Your understanding of Martin, for example, would be more complete if you had a background in adolescent psychology and psychiatric therapy.

For Writing and Discussion

The importance of background knowledge can be easily demonstrated any time you dip into past issues of a newsmagazine or try to read articles about an unfamiliar culture. Consider the following passage from a 1986 *Newsweek* article. How much background knowledge do you need before you can fully comprehend this passage? What cultural knowledge about the United States would a student from Ethiopia or Indonesia need?

(continued)

Throughout the NATO countries last week, there were second thoughts about the prospect of a nuclear-free world. For 40 years nuclear weapons have been the backbone of the West's defense. For almost as long American presidents have ritually affirmed their desire to see the world rid of them. Then, suddenly, Ronald Reagan and Mikhail Gorbachev came close to actually doing it. Let's abolish all nuclear ballistic missiles in the next 10 years, Reagan said. Why not all nuclear weapons, countered Gorbachev. OK, the president responded, like a man agreeing to throw in the washer-dryer along with the house.

What if the deal had gone through? On the one hand, Gorbachev would have returned to Moscow a hero. There is a belief in the United States that the Soviets need nuclear arms because nuclear weapons are what make them a superpower. But according to Marxist-Leninist doctrine, capitalism's nuclear capability (unforeseen by Marx and Lenin) is the only thing that can prevent the inevitable triumph of communism. Therefore, an end to nuclear arms would put the engine of history back on its track.

On the other hand, Europeans fear, a nonnuclear United States would be tempted to retreat into neo-isolationism.

—*Robert B. Cullen, "Dangers of Disarming,"* Newsweek

Working in small groups or as a class, identify words and passages in this text that depend on background information or knowledge of culture for complete comprehension.

Using the Reading Strategies of Experts

In Chapter 11, we describe the differences between the writing processes of experts and those of beginning college writers. There are parallel differences between the reading processes of experienced and inexperienced readers, especially when they encounter complex materials. In this section we describe some expert reading strategies that you can begin applying to your reading of any kind of college-level material.

Reconstruct the Text's Rhetorical Context

Before and as you read a text, ask questions about the author's audience, purpose, genre, and motivating occasion. Any piece of writing makes more sense if you think of its author as a real person writing for some real purpose in a real historical context.

If you read an article that has been anthologized (as in the readings in this textbook), note any information you are given about the author, publication data, and genre. Try to reconstruct the author's original motivation for writing. How have audience, purpose, and genre shaped this text?

Make Marginal Notes as You Read

Expert readers seldom use highlighters, which encourage passive, inefficient reading; instead, they make extensive marginal notes as they read. Advice on writing marginal notes is given throughout this chapter.

Get in the Dictionary Habit

When you can't tell a word's meaning from context, get in the habit of looking it up. One strategy is to make small check marks next to words you're unsure of; then look them up after you're done so as not to break your concentration.

Vary Your Reading Speed to Match Your Reading Goals

Unlike novices, experienced readers vary their reading speeds and strategies according to their goals. In other words, experienced readers know when to slow down or speed up. Robert Sternberg, a cognitive psychologist, discovered that novice readers tend to read everything at about the same pace, no matter what their purpose. In contrast, experienced readers vary their reading speed significantly depending on whether they are scanning for a piece of information, skimming for main ideas, reading deliberately for complete comprehension, or reading slowly for detailed analysis. Knowing when to speed up or slow down—especially if you are doing a research project and trying to cover lots of ground—can make your reading more efficient.

If a Text Is Complex, Read in a "Multidraft" Way

It may be comforting for you to know that expert readers struggle with difficult texts the same way you do. Often, experienced readers reread a text two or three times, treating their first readings like first drafts. They hold confusing passages in mental suspension, hoping that later parts of the essay will clarify earlier parts. The ironic point here is that sometimes you have to speed up to slow down. If you are lost in a passage, try skimming ahead rapidly, looking at the opening sentences of paragraphs and at any passages that sum up the writer's argument or that help clarify the argument's structure. Pay particular attention to the conclusion, which often ties the whole argument together. This rapid "first-draft reading" helps you see the text's main points and overall structure, thus providing a background for a second reading. The passage that puzzled you the first time might now be clearer.

Reading With the Grain and Against the Grain

The reading and thinking strategies that we have just described enable skilled readers to interact strongly with texts. Your purpose in using these strategies is to read texts both with the grain and against the grain, a way of reading that is analogous to the believing and doubting game we introduced in Chapter 2. This concept is so important that we have chosen to highlight it separately here.

For an explanation of the believing and doubting game, see pp. 42–46.

When you read with the grain of a text, you practice what psychologist Carl Rogers calls "empathic listening," in which you try to see the world through the author's eyes, role-playing as much as possible the author's intended readers by adopting their beliefs and values and acquiring their background knowledge. Reading with the grain is the main strategy you use when you summarize a text, but it comes into play also when you develop a strong response. When making with-the-grain points, you support the author's thesis with your own arguments and examples, or apply or extend the author's argument in new ways.

When you read against the grain of a text, you challenge, question, resist, and perhaps even rebut the author's ideas. You are a resistant reader who asks unanticipated questions, pushes back, and reads the text in ways unforeseen by the author. Reading against the grain is a key part of creating a strong response. When you make against-the-grain points, you challenge the author's reasoning, sources, examples, or choice of language. You generate counterexamples, present alternative lines of reasoning, deny the writer's values, or raise points that the writer has overlooked or specific data that the writer has omitted.

Strong readers develop their ability to read in both ways—with the grain and against the grain. Throughout the rest of this chapter, we show you different ways to practice and apply these strategies.

Understanding Summary Writing

In this section we explain techniques for writing an effective summary of a text. Summary writing fosters a close encounter between you and the text and demonstrates your understanding of it. When you write a summary, you practice reading with the grain of a text. You "listen" actively to the text's author, showing that you understand the author's point of view by restating his or her argument as completely and fairly as possible. Summary writing is an essential academic skill, regularly used in research writing of any kind, where you often present condensed views of other writers' arguments, either as support for your own view or as alternative views that you must analyze or respond to.

Reading for Structure and Content

In writing a summary, you must focus on both its structure and its content. In the following steps, we recommend a process that will help you condense a text's ideas into an accurate summary. As you become a more experienced reader and writer, you'll follow these steps without thinking about them.

Step 1:   The first time through, read the text fairly quickly for general meaning. If you get confused, keep going; later parts of the text might clarify earlier parts.

Step 2:   Reread the text carefully. As you read, write gist statements in the margins for each paragraph. A *gist statement* is a brief indication of the paragraph's function or purpose in the text or a brief summary of the paragraph's content. Sometimes it is helpful to think of these two kinds of gist statements as "what it does" statements and "what it says" statements.* A "what it does" statement specifies the paragraph's function—for example, "summarizes an opposing view," "introduces

---

*For our treatment of "what it does" and "what it says" statements, we are indebted to Kenneth A. Bruffee, *A Short Course in Writing*, 2nd ed. (Cambridge, MA: Winthrop, 1980).

another reason," "presents a supporting example," "provides statistical data in support of a point," and so on. A "what it says" statement captures the main idea of a paragraph by summarizing the paragraph's content. The "what it says" statement is the paragraph's main point, in contrast to its supporting ideas and examples. Sometimes an explicit topic sentence makes the main point easy to find, but often you have to extract the main point by shrinking an argument down to its essence. In some cases, you may be uncertain about the main point. If so, select the point that you think a majority of readers would agree is the main one.

When you first practice detailed readings of a text, you might find it helpful to write complete *does* and *says* statements on a separate sheet of paper rather than in the margins until you develop the internal habit of appreciating both the function and content of parts of an essay. Here are *does* and *says* statements for selected paragraphs of Andrés Martin's essay on teenage tattooing:

Paragraph 1: *Does:* Introduces the subject and sets up the argument. *Says:* The current popularity of tattoos and piercings is partly explained as an aid toward finding an identity, but the core of their appeal is their irreversible permanence.

Paragraph 2: *Does:* Narrows the focus and presents the thesis. *Says:* To counsel families in disagreement over tattoos, psychiatrists should exhibit a nonjudgmental appreciation of teen tattoos and use them to understand teenagers better.

Paragraph 4: *Does:* Discusses the first complex motivation behind youth tattooing. *Says:* Teens use tattoos to handle identity crises and to establish their uniqueness from others.

Paragraph 5: *Does:* Elaborates on the first motivation, the identity issue. *Says:* Tattoos provide teens with a sense of control over their changing bodies and over an environment perceived as adverse and domineering.

Paragraph 11: *Does:* Complicates the view of teens' use of tattoos to find permanence and belonging. *Says:* Although tattoos may unrealistically promise the resolution to larger conflicts, they may at least record the triumphs and miseries of adolescent turbulence, including gang and prison experience.

Paragraph 12: *Does:* Sums up the perspective and advice of the article. *Says:* Psychiatrists should regard adolescent tattoos positively as adornment and self-expression and employ tattoos to help understand teens' identities and sense of reality.

You may occasionally have difficulty writing a *says* statement for a paragraph because you may have trouble deciding what the main idea is, especially if the paragraph doesn't begin with a closed-form topic sentence. One way to respond to this problem is to formulate the question that you think the paragraph answers. If you think of chunks of the text as answers to a logical progression of questions, you can often follow the main ideas more easily. Rather than writing *says* statements in the margins, therefore, some readers prefer writing *says* questions. *Says* questions for the Martin text may include the following: What is the most constructive approach clinicians can take to teen tattooing when these tattoos have become the focus of family conflict? What psychological needs and problems are teenagers acting out through their tattoos? Why does the permanence of tattoos appeal to young people?

No matter which method you use—*says* statements or *says* questions—writing gist statements in the margins is far more effective than underlining or highlighting in helping you recall the text's structure and argument.

Step 3:   After you have analyzed the article paragraph by paragraph, try locating the article's main divisions or parts. In longer closed-form articles, writers often forecast the shape of their essays in their introductions or use their conclusions to sum up main points. Although Martin's article is short, it uses both a forecasting statement and subheads to direct readers through its main points. The article is divided into several main chunks as follows:

- Introductory paragraphs, which establish the problem to be addressed and narrow the focus to a clinical perspective (paragraphs 1–2)
- A one-sentence organizing and predicting statement (paragraph 3)
- A section explaining how tattoos may help adolescents establish a unique identity (paragraphs 4–5)
- A section explaining how tattoos help teens incorporate onto their bodies a symbolic ownership of something important to them (paragraphs 6–8)
- A section explaining how tattoos represent and satisfy teens' search for permanence (paragraphs 9–11)
- A conclusion that states the thesis explicitly and sums up Martin's advice to fellow psychiatrists (paragraph 12)

Outlines and tree diagrams are discussed in Chapter 12, pp. 309–314.

Instead of listing the sections, you might prefer to make an outline or tree diagram of the article showing its main parts.

The same basic procedures can work for summarizing a book, but you will need to modify them to fit a much longer text. For instance, you might write "what it does" and "what it says" statements for chapters or parts of a book. In summarizing a book, you might pay special attention to the introduction and conclusion of the book. In the introduction, usually authors state their motivation for writing the book and often put forth their thesis and the subtheses that the subsequent chapters of the book develop and explain. Chapter titles and chapter introductions often restate the author's subtheses and can help you identify main ideas to include in a book summary.

Producing the Summary

Once you have written gist statements or questions in the margins and clarified the text's structure by creating an outline or diagram, you are ready to write a summary. Typically, summaries range from 100 to 250 words, but sometimes writers compose summaries as short as one sentence. The order and proportions of your summary can usually follow the order and proportions of the text. However, if the original article has a delayed thesis or other characteristics of open-form writing, you can rearrange the order and begin with the thesis. With prose that has many open-form features, you may also have to infer points that are more implied than expressed.

A summary of another author's writing—when it is incorporated into your own essay—makes particular demands on you, the writer. Most of all, writing a summary challenges you to convey the main ideas of a text—ideas that are often complex—in as few and as clear words as you can. We tell our students that writing a summary is like having a word budget: you have only so many words (say, a 250- or 100-word limit), and you have to spend them wisely. In addition, a successful summary should do all of the following:

CRITERIA FOR AN EFFECTIVE SUMMARY

- Represent the original article accurately and fairly.
- Be direct and concise, using words economically.
- Remain objective and neutral, not revealing your own ideas on the subject but, rather, only the original author's points.
- Give the original article balanced and proportional coverage.
- Use your own words to express the original author's ideas.
- Keep your reader informed through attributive tags (such as *according to Martin* or *Martin argues that*) that you are expressing someone else's ideas, not your own.
- Possibly include quotations for a few key terms or ideas from the original, but quote sparingly.
- Be a unified, coherent piece of writing in its own right.
- Be properly cited and documented so that the reader can find the original text.

Some of these criteria for a successful summary are challenging to meet. For instance, to avoid interjecting your own opinions, note whether the verbs in your attributive tags reflect a bias. Consider the difference between *Smith argues* and *Smith rants* or between *Brown asserts* and *Brown leaps to the conclusion*. In each pair, the second verb, by moving beyond neutrality, reveals your own judgment of the author's ideas.

When you incorporate a summary into your own writing, it is particularly important to distinguish between the author's ideas and your own—hence the importance of frequent attributive tags, which tell the reader that these ideas belong to Smith or Jones or Brown rather than to you. If you choose to copy any of the author's words directly from the text, you need to use quotation marks and cite the quotation using an appropriate documentation system.

Chapter 14 explains how to work sources smoothly into your own writing and avoid plagiarism.

The following example, which summarizes Martin's article on teenagers and tattoos, uses the MLA documentation system.

Summary of Martin Article

In "On Teenagers and Tattoos," published in the <u>Journal of the American Academy of Child and Adolescent Psychiatry</u>, Dr. Andrés Martin advises fellow psychiatrists to think of teenage tattooing not as a fad or as a form of self-mutilation but as an opportunity for clinicians to understand teenagers better. <u>Martin examines three different reasons</u> that teenagers get tattoos. <u>First, he argues</u> that tattoos help teenagers establish unique identities

Identification of the article, journal, and author

Thesis of article

Attributive tag

Transition

Attributive tag

Transition and attributive tag ——— by giving them a sense of control over their evolving bodies and over an environment perceived as adverse and domineering. <u>Second, he believes</u> that a tattooed image often symbolizes the teen's

Transition and attributive tag ——— relationship to a significant concept or person, making the relationship more visible and real. <u>Finally, says Martin</u>, because

Inclusion of short quotation from article. MLA documentation style; number in parentheses indicates page number of original article where quotation is found ——— teens are disturbed by modern society's mobility and fragmentation and because they have an "intense longing for rootedness and stability" (118), the irreversible nature of tattoos may give them a sense of permanence. <u>Martin concludes</u> that tattoos can be a

Attributive tag ——— meaningful record of survived teen experiences. <u>He encourages</u>

Attributive tag ———

Another short quotation therapists to regard teen tattoos as "self-constructive and adorning efforts," rather than as "mutilatory and destructive

Brackets indicate that the writer changed the material inside the brackets to fit the grammar and context of the writer's own sentence ——— acts" (119) and suggests that tattoos can help therapists understand "another level of [<u>teenagers'</u>] internal reality" (119). [195 words]

Works Cited

Martin article cited completely using MLA documentation form; in a formal paper, the "works cited" list begins on a new page ——— Martin, Andrés. "On Teenagers and Tattoos." <u>Journal of the American Academy of Child and Adolescent Psychiatry</u> 36 (1997): 860–61. Rpt. in <u>The Allyn & Bacon Guide to Writing</u>. John D. Ramage, John C. Bean, and June Johnson. 4th ed. New York: Longman, 2006. 116–119.

For Writing and Discussion

Imagine that the context of a research paper you are writing calls for a shorter summary of the Martin article than the one presented here (which is approximately 195 words, including attributive tags). To practice distilling the main ideas of an article to produce summaries of different lengths, first write a 100-word summary of "On Teenagers and Tattoos." Then reduce your summary further to 50 words. Discuss the principles you followed in deciding what to eliminate or how to restructure sentences to convey the most information in the fewest number of words.

Understanding Strong Response Writing

We have said that summary writing is an essential academic skill. Equally important is strong response writing in which you join the text's conversation and speak back to it. If a strong reading means to engage a text actively, both assenting to an author's ideas and questioning them, what exactly do you write about when you compose a strong response? To appreciate our answer to this question, you need to know the various ways that strong responses are assigned across the curriculum.

Kinds of Strong Responses

A strong response is one of the most common writing assignments you will encounter in college courses. However, teachers vary in what they mean by a "strong response," and they often use different terms for the same basic kind of assignment. Our conversations with instructors from across the disciplines suggest that there are three common kinds of strong response assignments:

- *Analysis or critique assignment.* Here your job is to analyze and critique the assigned reading. You discuss how a text is constructed, what rhetorical strategies it employs, and how effectively its argument is supported. Suppose, for example, that you are asked to critique an article, appearing in a conservative business journal, that advocates oil exploration in the Arctic National Wildlife Refuge (ANWR). For this kind of strong response, you'd be expected to analyze the article's rhetorical strategies (for example, How is it shaped to appeal to a conservative, business-oriented audience? How has the writer's angle of vision filtered the evidence for its arguments?) and evaluate its argument (for example, What are the underlying assumptions and beliefs on which the argument is based? Is the logic sound? Is the evidence accurate and up-to-date?). When you analyze and critique a reading, you focus on the text itself, giving it the same close attention that an art critic gives a painting, a football coach gives a game film, or a biologist gives a cell formation. This close attention can be with the grain, noting the effectiveness of the text's rhetorical strategies, or against the grain, discussing what is ineffective or problematic about these strategies. Or an analysis might point out both the strengths of and the problems with a text's rhetorical strategies.
- *"Your own views" assignment.* Here the instructor expects you to present your own views on the reading's topic or issue—for example, to give your own views on oil exploration in the ANWR, to support or challenge the writer's views, to raise new questions, and otherwise to add your voice to the ANWR conversation. This kind of strong response invites you to read both with and against the grain. A with-the-grain reading supports all or some of the article's arguments but supplies additional reasons or new evidence,

directs the argument to a different audience, extends the argument to a different context, or otherwise adds your own support to the writer's views. An against-the-grain reading attempts to challenge all or part of the writer's argument, to raise doubts in the audience, to show flaws in the writer's reasoning, and to support your own views as they arise from your personal experience, observation, other reading, and wrestling with the author's ideas.

- *A blended assignment that mixes both kinds of responses.* Here the instructor expects you to respond in both ways—to analyze and critique the article but also to engage the writer's ideas by developing your own views on the topic. As a writer, you can emphasize what is most important to you, but the paper should contain elements of analysis and critique as well as your own views on the issue. The assignment for this chapter calls for this kind of blended strong response, but your instructor can specify what kind of emphasis he or she desires.

Instructors also vary in their preferences for the tone and structure of strong response essays. Some instructors prefer the term *reflection paper* rather than *strong response*—a term that invites you to write a personal response with an open-form structure and an expressive or exploratory purpose. In a reflection paper, the instructor is particularly interested in how the reading has affected you personally—what memories it has triggered, what personal experiences it relates to, what values and beliefs it has challenged, and so forth. Other instructors prefer closed-form strong responses with an explicit thesis statement, an analytical or persuasive purpose, and a more academic tone.

The assignment in this chapter calls for a closed-form strong response with a clear thesis statement. Your instructor, however, may modify the assignment to fit the goals of his or her course or the curriculum at your university.

Student Example of a Summary/Strong Response Essay

Before giving you some tips on how to discover ideas for your strong response, we show you an example of a student essay for this chapter: a summary/strong response essay. Note that the essay begins by identifying the question under discussion: Why do teenagers get tattoos? It then summarizes the article by Andrés Martin.* Immediately following the summary, the student writer states his thesis, followed by the strong response, which contains both rhetorical points and points about the causes of teenage tattooing.

WHY DO TEENAGERS GET TATTOOS? A RESPONSE TO ANDRÉS MARTIN

Sean Barry (student)

Introduces topic and sets context

My sister has one. My brother has one. I have one. Just take a stroll downtown and you will see how commonplace it is for someone to be decorated with tattoos and hung with piercings. In fact, hundreds of teenagers, every day, allow themselves

---

*In this essay the student writer uses a shortened version of his 195-word summary that was used as an illustration on pages 127–128.

to be etched upon or poked into. What's the cause of this phenomenon? Why do so many teenagers get tattoos?

Dr. Andrés Martin has answered this question from a psychiatrist's perspective in his article "On Teenagers and Tattoos," published in the Journal of the American Academy of Child and Adolescent Psychiatry. Martin advises fellow psychiatrists to think of teenage tattooing as a constructive opportunity for clinicians to understand teenagers better. Martin examines three different reasons that teenagers get tattoos. First, he argues that tattoos help teenagers establish unique identities by giving them a sense of control over their evolving bodies and over an environment perceived as adverse and domineering. Second, he believes that a tattooed image often symbolizes the teen's relationship to a significant concept or person, making the relationship more visible and real. Finally, says Martin, because teens are disturbed by modern society's mobility and fragmentation and because they have an "intense longing for rootedness and stability" (118), the irreversible nature of tattoos may give them a sense of permanence. Martin concludes that tattoos can be a meaningful record of survived teen experiences. Although Martin's analysis has relevance and some strengths, I think he overgeneralizes and over-romanticizes teenage tattooing, leading him to overlook other causes of teenage tattooing such as commercialization and teenagers' desire to identify with a peer group as well as achieve an individual identity.

Summary of Martin's article

Thesis statement

Some of Martin's points seem relevant and realistic and match my own experiences. I agree that teenagers sometimes use tattoos to establish their own identities. When my brother, sister, and I all got our tattoos, we were partly asserting our own independence from our parents. Martin's point about the symbolic significance of a tattoo image also connects with my experiences. A Hawaiian guy in my dorm has a fish tattooed on his back, which he says represents his love of the ocean and the spiritual experience he has when he scuba dives.

With-the-grain point in support of Martin's ideas

Martin, speaking as a psychiatrist to other psychiatrists, also provides psychological insights into the topic of teen tattooing even though this psychological perspective brings some limitations, too. In this scholarly article, Martin's purpose is to persuade fellow psychiatrists to think of adolescent tattooing in positive rather than judgmental terms. Rather than condemn teens for getting tattoos, he argues that discussion of the tattoos can provide useful insights into the needs and behavior of troubled teens (especially males). But this perspective is also a limitation because the teenagers he sees are mostly youths in psychiatric counseling, particularly teens struggling with the absence of or violent loss of a parent and those who have experience with gangs and prison terms. This perspective leads him to overgeneralize. As a psychological study of a specific group of troubled teens, the article is informative. However, it does not apply as well to most teenagers who are getting tattoos today.

Rhetorical point about Martin's audience, purpose, and genre that has both with-the-grain and against-the-grain elements

Besides overgeneralizing, Martin also seems to romanticize teenage tattooing. Why else would a supposedly scientific article begin and end with quotations from Moby Dick? Martin seems to imply a similarity between today's teenagers and the sailor hero Ishmael who wandered the seas looking for personal identity. In quoting Moby Dick, Martin seems to value tattooing as a suitable way for teenagers to record their experiences. Every tattoo, for Martin, has deep significance. Thus, Martin casts tattooed teens as romantic outcasts, loners, and adventurers like Ishmael.

Against-the-grain rhetorical point: Barry analyzes use of quotations from Moby Dick

In contrast to Martin, I believe that teens are influenced by the commercial nature of tattooing, which has become big business aimed at their age group. Every movie or television star or beauty queen who sports a tattoo sends the commercial message that tattoos are cool: "A tattoo will help you be successful, sexy, handsome, or attractive like us." Tattoo parlors are no longer dark dives in seedy, dangerous parts of cities, but

Transition to writer's own analysis

Against-the-grain point: writer's alternative theory

appear in lively commercial districts; in fact, there are several down the street from the university. Teenagers now buy tattoos the way they buy other consumer items.

Against-the-grain point: writer's second theory

Furthermore, Martin doesn't explore teenagers' desire not only for individuality but also for peer group acceptance. Tattooing is the "in" thing to do. Tattooing used to be defiant and daring, but now it is popular and more acceptable among teens. I even know a group of sorority women who went together to get tattoos on their ankles. As tattooing has become more mainstreamed, rebels/trendsetters have turned to newer and more outrageous practices, such as branding and extreme piercings. Meanwhile, tattoos bring middle-of-the-road teens the best of both worlds: a way to show their individuality and simultaneously to be accepted by peers.

Conclusion and summary

In sum, Martin's research is important because it examines psychological responses to teen's inner conflicts. It offers partial explanations for teens' attraction to tattoos and promotes a positive, noncritical attitude toward tattooing. But I think the article is limited by its overgeneralizations based on the psychiatric focus, by its tendency to romanticize tattooing, by its lack of recognition of the commercialization of tattooing, and by its underemphasis on group belonging and peer pressure. Teen tattooing is more complex than even Martin makes it.

Works Cited

Complete citation of article in MLA format

Martin, Andrés. "On Teenagers and Tattoos." Journal of the American Academy of Child and Adolescent Psychiatry 36 (1997): 860–61. Rpt. in The Allyn & Bacon Guide to Writing. John D. Ramage, John C. Bean, and June Johnson. 4th ed. New York: Longman, 2006. 116–119.

In the student example just shown, Sean Barry illustrates a blended strong response that intermixes rhetorical analysis of the article with his own views on tattooing. He analyzes Martin's article rhetorically by pointing out some of the limitations of a psychiatric angle of vision and by showing the values implications of Martin's references to *Moby Dick*. He adds his own ideas to the conversation by supporting two of Martin's points using his own personal examples. But he also reads Martin against the grain by arguing that Martin, perhaps influenced by his romantic view of tattoos, fails to appreciate the impact on teenagers of the commercialization of tattooing and the importance of peer group acceptance. Clearly, Sean Barry illustrates what we mean by a strong reader. In the next section on question-asking strategies, we help you begin developing the same skills.

Questions for Analyzing and Critiquing a Text

Now that you have read a sample student essay, let's consider questions you can ask to generate ideas for your own strong response. This section focuses on analyzing and critiquing a text and also offers ideas that can help you analyze texts that are partly or largely visual texts. The next section focuses on exploring your own views of the text's subject matter.

The concept of "angle of vision" is explained in Chapter 4, pp. 80–85. See also Chapter 5 where the concept is developed in more detail.

You may find that analyzing and critiquing a text represents a new kind of critical thinking challenge. At this stage in your academic career, we aren't expecting you to be an expert at this kind of thinking. Rather, the strong response assignment will help you begin learning this skill—to see how texts work, how they are written from an angle of vision, how they may reinforce or clash with your own views, and so forth.

A strong response focused on the rhetorical features of a text looks at how the text is constructed to achieve its writer's purpose. Here are sample questions you can ask to help you analyze and critique a text. (We have illustrated them with examples from a variety of texts read by our own students in recent years.) Of course, you don't have to address all these questions in your strong response. Your goal is to find a few of these questions that particularly illuminate the text you are critiquing.

Sample Questions for Analyzing and Critiquing

Questions about purpose and audience.   What is the author's purpose and audience in this text? How clearly does this text convey its purpose and reach its audience?

WHAT TO WRITE ABOUT
Explain your author's purpose and intended audience and show how the author appeals to that audience. Explain how choice of language and use of examples appeal to the values and beliefs of the intended audience. In critiquing the text, you might show how the article is effective for the intended audience but has gaping holes for those who don't share these values and beliefs.

HYPOTHETICAL EXAMPLE
In "Why Johnny Can't Read, but Yoshio Can," Richard Lynn, writing for the conservative magazine the *National Review*, tries to persuade readers that the United States should adopt Japanese methods of education. He appeals to a conservative audience by using evidence and examples that support conservative beliefs favoring competition, discipline, and high academic achievement.

Questions about the text's genre.   How has the genre of the text influenced the author's style, structure, and use of evidence? How might this genre be effective for certain audiences but not for others?

WHAT TO WRITE ABOUT
Show how certain features of the text can be explained by the genre of the work. Show how this genre contributes to the effectiveness of the piece for certain audiences but also has limitations.

HYPOTHETICAL EXAMPLE
Naomi Wolf's essay "The Beauty Myth" is actually the introduction to her book *The Beauty Myth*. Therefore, it presents her major thesis and subtheses for the whole book and only begins to provide supporting evidence for these points. This lack of development might make some readers question or reject her argument.

Questions about the author's style.   How do the author's language choices contribute to the overall impact of the text?

WHAT TO WRITE ABOUT
Discuss examples of images, figures of speech, and connotations of words that draw the reader into the writer's perspective and support the writer's points. In your critique, show how language choices can be effective for some audiences but not for others.

HYPOTHETICAL EXAMPLE
In his chapter "Where I Lived, and What I Lived For" from his book *Walden*, Henry David Thoreau describes his closeness to nature in vivid poetic language. His celebration of the beauty and wonder of nature makes readers reevaluate their indifference or utilitarian attitudes toward nature. Scientific readers might be put off, however, by his romanticism.

(continued)

Questions about the appeal to *logos*, the logic of the argument.   Does the argument seem reasonable? Do the points all relate to the thesis? Are the points well supported? Are there any obvious flaws or fallacies in the argument?

WHAT TO WRITE ABOUT
Describe the argument's logical structure and analyze whether it is reasonable and well supported. Also point out places where the argument is weak or fallacious.

HYPOTHETICAL EXAMPLE
Lynn attributes the success of Japanese students to three main causes: (1) High competition, (2) a national curriculum, and (3) strong cultural incentives to excel in school. These points are well supported with evidence. But his argument that this system should be adopted in the United States is flawed because he doesn't see the dangers in the Japanese system or appreciate the cultural differences between the two countries.

Questions about the author's use of evidence.   Does the evidence come from reputable sources? Is it relevant to the points it supports? Is it appropriately up-to-date? Is it sufficiently broad and representative?

WHAT TO WRITE ABOUT
Describe the sources of evidence in an argument and determine their reliability. Pay particular attention to limitations or narrowness in these data. Point out whether the information is up-to-date, relevant, and compelling. Point out whether the author actually provides data for the argument.

HYPOTHETICAL EXAMPLE
In his book *The McDonaldization of Society*, sociologist George Ritzer elaborates on his thesis that the fast-food industry has come to dominate all of American society. Some readers might say that Ritzer pushes his provocative thesis too far. His discussion of health care, education, and reproductive technology is brief, general, and not developed with specific data.

Questions about the appeal to *ethos* and the credibility of the author.   How does the author try to persuade readers that he or she is knowledgeable and reliable? Is the author successful in appearing credible and trustworthy?

WHAT TO WRITE ABOUT
Discuss features of the text that increase the reader's confidence in the author's knowledge and trustworthiness or that help the intended audience "identify" with the writer. Point out problems with the author's reliability, responsible use of sources, and fair treatment of alternative views.

HYPOTHETICAL EXAMPLE
In her article "The Gender Blur" in the liberal magazine *Utne Reader*, Deborah Blum establishes credibility by citing numerous scientific studies showing that she has researched the issue carefully. She also tells personal anecdotes about her liberal views, establishing credibility with liberal audiences.

Sample Questions for Analyzing and Critiquing *continued*

Questions about the appeal to *pathos*.   How does the author appeal to the readers' emotions, sympathies, and values? Do these appeals to *pathos* enhance the rhetorical power of the text?

WHAT TO WRITE ABOUT
Explain how the author uses description, vivid examples, short narratives or scenarios, figurative language, or moving quotations to tap the emotions and sympathies of the audience and appeal to readers' values and beliefs. Explain whether these appeals to *pathos* are controlled and fitting or excessive and heavy-handed.

HYPOTHETICAL EXAMPLE
Compassionate Living, a brochure by the advocacy organization People for the Ethical Treatment of Animals (PETA), disturbs readers with vivid descriptions of animal suffering; however, these descriptions are so extreme in their appeals to *pathos* that they may offend readers who love animals and therefore lose their support.

Questions about the author's angle of vision.   What does the text reveal about the author's values and beliefs? What is excluded from the author's text? What other perspectives could a writer take on this topic?

WHAT TO WRITE ABOUT
Analyze the author's angle of vision or interpretive filter. Show what the text emphasizes and what it leaves out. Show how this angle of vision is related to certain key values or beliefs.

HYPOTHETICAL EXAMPLE
Dr. Andrés Martin, a psychiatrist, takes a clinical perspective on tattooed adolescents. He writes for fellow psychiatrists, and he uses his teen patients as the subject of his analysis. He does not consider more typical tattooed teenagers who do not need psychiatric therapy. If he had interviewed a wider range of teenagers, he might have reached different conclusions.

Questions for Analyzing and Critiquing a Visual-Verbal Text

In our increasingly visual world, many genres of texts—advocacy sites on the Web, public affairs advocacy ads, advertisements, posters for political and environmental campaigns, brochures, and leaflets—combine verbal and visual elements. As we discuss in Chapter 4, visual images such as photographs, drawings, and paintings can also be read rhetorically, and indeed may do much of the rhetorical work of a visual-verbal text.

Visual-verbal texts are often rhetorically complex and very interesting to examine and critique. A strong response to a visual-verbal text might examine how well the text connects with the intended audience, carries out its purposes, and fulfills readers' expectations for its genre. In critiquing a visual-verbal text, you

In Chapter 9, we explain visual rhetoric in more detail, especially such features as the composition of images, camera angle, and use of color.

might consider how well the words and images collaborate to strengthen the appeal to *logos*. For example, does this combination convey the main point clearly? The features of document design—use of type, layout, color, and images or graphics discussed in Chapter 3—are also extremely important in visual-verbal texts. Images can make powerful appeals to *pathos*, persuading through their appeal to readers' emotions, values, and beliefs. Many visual-verbal texts can also be discussed in terms of their appeal to *ethos* by focusing on how reliable and credible the creator of the text appears to be. Furthermore, these texts often reveal their angle of vision in interesting ways through the dominant impressions they convey and the ideas they ignore or exclude.

In a summary/strong response essay on a visual-verbal text, the summary would capture for readers the main points of the piece and would briefly describe the text's visual features. For a strong response, most of the questions that you would ask of a verbal text could apply to a visual-verbal text; however, here are some questions that might be particularly relevant to a text with visual elements.

Sample Questions for Analyzing and Critiquing Visual-Verbal Texts

Questions about use of type, layout, color, and image.   Which of these design features is important in this text? How are these features used? How are they effective?

WHAT TO WRITE ABOUT	HYPOTHETICAL EXAMPLE
Explain what is distinctive about any or several of these visual features. Explain how these features work for the intended audience and contribute to the author's purpose. In critiquing the text, you might discuss how the visual features work to change the audience's views. You might comment on the problems or strengths of these features.	A poster on nicotine addiction by Project ALERT, a drug prevention program for middle schools, uses colors to make the poster stick in viewers' minds and create an alarmist tone. The use of unpleasant greens, oranges, and golds with the word "ADDICTING" in white overprinting gives a strong, memorable impression of illness and danger.

Questions about the relationship between image and verbal text and the appeals to *logos* and *pathos*.   How much rhetorical work do the visual images perform in this text? How do the images and words work together in this text? Are words more important than images?

WHAT TO WRITE ABOUT	HYPOTHETICAL EXAMPLE
Explain whether words comment on the images or images illustrate the words. Discuss whether the words are labels and slogans connected to the images or presentations of the author's main points. Explain how the image or images in this piece convey the main point and affect the emotions and sympathies of the audience. Discuss whether the use of image is appropriate and effective or unnecessary, unfitting, or overdone.	In the Project ALERT poster on nicotine addiction, the cartoon imaginatively illustrates the concept of addiction and does all the persuasive work of the poster. All the features of this image—the cartoon figure, the burning ramp the figure is running on, and the unreachable package of cigarettes dangling from a stick—convey the poster's idea of addiction as frustration, desperation, and insatiability. The image works equally on the viewers' emotions, evoking a sense of danger.

Questions about the author's angle of vision and contribution to the social conversation.   How is an angle of vision constructed in this text? Does the text make a useful contribution to a discussion of this issue?

WHAT TO WRITE ABOUT	HYPOTHETICAL EXAMPLE
Explain how the author's angle of vision shapes and filters the message of the text. Discuss what is included in and excluded from the text. Discuss whether the angle of vision limits the appeal of the text.	The brochure *Compassionate Living*, by People for the Ethical Treatment of Animals (PETA), poses and responds to eighteen questions about humans' treatment of animals. While the brochure provides clear, vivid answers to the questions and the photos illustrate these points, readers sense that the brochure emphasizes and amasses incidents of cruelty and excludes all other perspectives.

Questions for Developing Your Own Views about the Text's Subject Matter

As you are analyzing and critiquing a text, you also want to imagine how you might speak back to the text's ideas. Look for ways to join the text's conversation using your own critical thinking, personal experience, observations, reading, and knowledge.

In responding to a text's ideas, you will most likely include both with- and against-the-grain points. Strong readers know how to build on a text's ideas and extend them to other contexts. They are also open to challenging or disturbing ideas and try to use them constructively rather than simply dismiss them. Strong readers, in other words, try to believe new ideas as well as doubt them. In speaking back to a text's ideas in your strong response, you will have to decide how affirming of or resistant to those ideas you want to be.

Here are questions you can use to help you generate ideas:

Question: Which of the author's points do you agree with?

WHAT TO WRITE ABOUT	HYPOTHETICAL EXAMPLE
Build on or extend the author's points with supporting evidence from personal experience or knowledge (with the grain).	Build on Dr. Andrés Martin's ideas by discussing examples of acquaintances who have marked significant moments in their lives (graduation, career changes, divorces) by getting tattoos.

(*continued*)

Sample Questions for Generating Your Own Views on the Topic *continued*

Question: What new insights has the text given you?

WHAT TO WRITE ABOUT
Illustrate your insights with examples
(with the grain).

HYPOTHETICAL EXAMPLE
Explore Martin's idea that some teens use
tattoos as a form of bonding by
discussing the phenomenon of women in
college sororities getting tattoos together.

Question: Which of the author's points do you disagree with?

WHAT TO WRITE ABOUT
Provide your own counterpoints and
counterexamples (against the grain).

HYPOTHETICAL EXAMPLE
Challenge Martin's views by showing
that tattooing has become a
commonplace mainstream, middle-class
phenomenon among teens.

Question: What gaps or omissions do you see in the text? What has the author over-looked?

WHAT TO WRITE ABOUT
Point out gaps. Supply your own theory
for why these gaps exist. Explain the
value of your own perspective, which
includes what the author has excluded or
overlooked (against the grain).

HYPOTHETICAL EXAMPLE
Point out that Martin's views leave out
the role that parents play in teens'
decisions to get tattoos. Explain how
rebellion has influenced some of your
friends.

Question: What questions or problems does the text raise for you? How has it trou-bled you or expanded your views?

WHAT TO WRITE ABOUT
Show how the text causes you to
question your own values, assumptions,
and beliefs; show also how you question
the author's beliefs and values (with the
grain and against the grain).

HYPOTHETICAL EXAMPLE
Martin's highly sympathetic attitude
toward tattoos portrays body modification
as positive, creative, and psychologically
constructive, yet he glosses over health
risks and long-term costs.

Question: In what contexts can you see the usefulness of the text? What applications can you envision for it?

WHAT TO WRITE ABOUT
Explore the applicability and
consequences of the text or explore its
limitations (with the grain or against the
grain).

HYPOTHETICAL EXAMPLE
Martin's theory that troubled teens are
seeking control over their bodies and
their identities through getting tattoos is
one important voice in the social
conversation about tattoos. However, he
doesn't explore why tattooing and
piercing have become so popular in the
last ten years. The relationship between
fads and fashions and deeper
psychological factors could lead to
further research.

Rereading Strategies to Stimulate Thinking for a Strong Response

Earlier in the chapter, we presented general strategies to help you become an experienced reader. Now we turn to specific rereading strategies that will stimulate ideas for your strong response. Reread your assigned text, and as you do so, try the following strategies.

Step Up Your Marginal Note Taking, Making With-the-Grain and Against-the-Grain Comments

Writing a strong response requires a deep engagement with texts, calling on all your ability to read with the grain and against the grain. As you reread your text, make copious marginal notes looking for both with-the-grain and against-the-grain responses. Figure 6.1 shows Sean Barry's marginal comments on the opening page of Martin's article. Observe how the notes incorporate with-the-grain and against-the-grain responses and show the reader truly talking back to and interacting with the text.

Identify Hot Spots in the Text

Most texts will create "hot spots" for you (each reader's hot spots are apt to be different). By "hot spot" we mean a quotation or passage that you especially notice because you agree or disagree with it or because it triggers memories or other associations. Perhaps the hot spot strikes you as particularly thought provoking. Perhaps it raises a problem or is confusing yet suggestive. Mark all hot spots with marginal notes. After you've finished reading, find these hot spots and freewrite your responses to them in a reading journal.

Write Questions Triggered by the Text

Almost any text triggers questions as you read. A good way to begin formulating a strong response is simply to write out several questions that the text caused you to think about. Then explore your responses to those questions through freewriting. Sometimes the freewrite will trigger more questions.

Articulate Your Difference from the Intended Audience

In some cases you can read strongly by articulating how you differ from the text's intended audience. As we showed in Chapter 3, experienced writers try to imagine their audience. They ask: What are my audience's values? How interested in and knowledgeable about my topic is my audience? Eventually, the author makes decisions about audience—in effect "creates" the audience—so that the text reveals both an image of the author and of its intended reader.

Your own experiences, arising from your gender, class, ethnicity, sexual orientation, political and religious beliefs, interests, values, and so forth, may cause

See pp. 52–54 for a discussion of audience analysis.

FIGURE 6.1 Student Marginal Notes on Martin's Text

Andrés Martin, M.D.
on Teenagers and Tattoos

The skeleton dimensions I shall now proceed to set down are copied verbatim from my right arm, where I had them tattooed: as in my wild wanderings at that period, there was no other secure way of preserving such valuable statistics.

—Melville/ *Moby-Dick CII*

Tattoos and piercings have become a part of our everyday landscape. They are ubiquitous, having entered the circles of glamour and the mainstream of fashion, and they have even become an increasingly common feature of our urban youth. Legislation in most states restricts professional tattooing to adults older than 18 years of age, so "high end" tattooing is rare in children and adolescents, but such tattoos are occasionally seen in older teenagers. Piercings, by comparison, as well as self-made or "jailhouse" type tattoos, are not at all rare among adolescents or even among schoolage children. Like hairdo, makeup, or baggy jeans, tattoos and piercings can be subject to fad influence or peer pressure in an effort toward group affiliation. As with any other fashion statement, they can be construed as bodily aids in the inner struggle toward identity consolidation, serving as adjuncts to the defining and sculpting of the self by means of external manipulations. But unlike most other body decorations, tattoos and piercings are set apart by their irreversible and permanent nature, a quality at the core of their magnetic appeal to adolescents.

Adolescents and their parents are often at odds over the acquisition of bodily decorations. For the adolescent, piercings or tattoos may be seen as personal and beautifying statements, while parents may construe them as oppositional and enraging affronts to their authority. Distinguishing bodily adornment from self-mutilation may indeed prove challenging, particularly when a family is in disagreement over a teenager's motivations and a clinician is summoned as the final arbiter. At such times it may be most important to realize jointly that the skin can all too readily become but another battleground for the tensions of the age, arguments having less to do with tattoos and piercings than with core issues such as separation from the family matrix. Exploring the motivations and significance underlying tattoos (Grumet, 1983) and piercings can go a long way toward resolving such differences and can become a novel and additional way of getting to know teenagers. An interested and nonjudgmental appreciation of teenagers' surface presentations may become a way of making contact not only in their terms but on their turfs: quite literally on the territory of their skins.

The following three sections exemplify some of the complex psychological underpinnings of youth tattooing.

Marginal notes (left):
- Quotation from a novel?
- Larger tattooing scene?
- I like the phrase "the defining and sculpting of the self"—sounds creative, like art
- Which teenagers? All teenagers?
- Good open-minded, practical approach to teen tattoos

Marginal notes (right):
- A strange beginning for a scientific article
- What do 19th-century sailors have to do with 21st-century teens?
- 1
- Idea here: the body as a concrete record of experience?
- This idea is surprising and interesting. It merits lots of discussion.
- 2
- These terms show the main opposing views on tattoos.
- Is he speaking only to psychiatrists? Does this clinical perspective have other applications?
- 3 I like Martin's focus on complexity

you to feel estranged from the author's imagined audience. If the text seems written for straight people and you are gay, or for Christians and you are a Muslim or an atheist, or for environmentalists and you grew up in a small logging community, you may well resist the text. Sometimes your sense of exclusion from the intended audience makes it difficult to read a text at all. For example, a female student of our acquaintance once brought a class to a standstill by slamming the course anthology on her desk and exclaiming, "How can you people stand reading this patriarchal garbage!" She had become so irritated by the authors' assumption that all readers shared their male-oriented values that she could no longer bear to read the selections.

When you differ significantly from the text's assumed audience, you can often use this difference to question the author's underlying assumptions, values, and beliefs.

For Writing and Discussion

What follows is a short passage by writer Annie Dillard in response to a question about how she chooses to spend her time. This passage often evokes heated responses from our students.

> I don't do housework. Life is too short. . . . I let almost all my indoor plants die from neglect while I was writing the book. There are all kinds of ways to live. You can take your choice. You can keep a tidy house, and when St. Peter asks you what you did with your life, you can say, "I kept a tidy house, I made my own cheese balls."

Individual task: Read the passage and then briefly freewrite your reaction to it.

Group task: Working in groups or as a whole class, develop answers to the following questions:

1. What values does Dillard assume her audience holds?
2. What kinds of readers are apt to feel excluded from that audience?
3. If you are not part of the intended audience for this passage, what in the text evokes resistance?

Articulate Your Own Purpose for Reading
You may sometimes read a text against the grain if your purposes for reading differ from what the author imagined. Normally you read a text because you share the author's interest in a question and want to know the author's answer. In other words, you usually read to join the author's conversation. But suppose that you

wish to review the writings of nineteenth-century scientists to figure out what they assumed about nature (or women, or God, or race, or capitalism). Or suppose that you examine a politician's metaphors to see what they reveal about his or her values, or analyze *National Geographic* for evidence of political bias. In these cases, you will be reading against the grain of the text. In a sense, you would be blindsiding the authors—while they are talking about topic X, you are observing them for topic Y. This method of resistant reading is very common in academia.

READINGS

For this chapter, we offer a provocative essay arguing for an individual's right to smoke balanced by a spoof advertisement opposing smoking. Together the verbal essay and the visual argument introduce you to the public controversy over smoking and individual rights. The smoking essay, by writer and journalist Florence King, first appeared in 1990 in *National Review,* a news commentary magazine with a conservative readership. Although it has many closed-form features, its open-form style and powerful narrative voice invite strong responses from a wide spectrum of viewpoints. Because your task is to summarize your assigned piece and respond strongly to it, we omit the questions for analysis that typically accompany readings elsewhere in this text.

Florence King
I'd Rather Smoke than Kiss

1   I am a woman of 54 who started smoking at the late age of 26. I had no reason to start earlier; smoking as a gesture of teenage rebellion would have been pointless in my family. My mother started at 12. At first her preferred brands were the Fatimas and Sweet Caporals that were all the rage during World War I. Later she switched to Lucky Strike Greens and smoked four packs a day.

2   She made no effort to cut down while she was pregnant with me, but I was not a low-birth-weight baby. The Angel of Death saw the nicotine stains on our door and passed over. I weighed nine pounds. My smoke-filled childhood was remarkably healthy and safe except for the time Mama set fire to my Easter basket. That was all right, however, because I was not the Easter-basket type.

3   I probably wouldn't have started smoking if I had not been a writer. One day in the drugstore I happened to see a display of Du Maurier English cigarettes in pretty red boxes with a tray that slid out like a little drawer. I thought the boxes would be ideal for keeping my paperclips in, so I bought two.

4   When I got home, I emptied out the cigarettes and replaced them with paperclips, putting the loose cigarettes in the desk drawer where the loose paperclips had been scattered. Now the cigarettes were scattered. One day, spurred by two of my best traits, neatness and thrift, I decided that the cigarettes were messing up the desk and going to waste, so I tried one.

5   It never would have happened if I had been able to offer the Du Mauriers to a lover who smoked, but I didn't get an addicted one until after I had become addicted myself. When he entered my life it was the beginning of a uniquely pleasurable footnote to sex, the post-coital cigarette.

6   Today when I see the truculent, joyless faces of anti-tobacco Puritans, I remember those easy-going smoking sessions with that man: the click of the lighter, the brief orange glow in the darkness, the ashtray between us— spilling sometimes because we laughed so much together that the bed shook.

7   A cigarette ad I remember from my childhood said: "One of life's great pleasures is smoking. Camels give you all of the excitement of choice tobaccos. Is enjoyment good for you? You just bet it is." My sentiments exactly. I believe life should be savored rather than lengthened, and I am ready to fight the misanthropes among us who are trying to make me switch.

8   A *misanthrope* is someone who hates people. Hatred of smokers is the most popular form of closet misanthropy in America today. Smokists don't hate the sin, they hate the sinner, and they don't care who knows it.

9   Their campaign never would have succeeded so well if the alleged dangers of smoking had remained a problem for smokers alone. We simply would have been allowed to invoke the Right to Die, always a favorite with democratic lovers of mankind, and that would have been that. To put a real damper on smoking and make it stick, the right of others not to die had to be invoked somehow so "passive smoking" was invented.

10 The name was a stroke of genius. Just about everybody in America is passive. Passive Americans have been taking it on the chin for years, but the concept of passive smoking offered them a chance to hate in the land of compulsory love, a chance to dish it out for a change with no fear of being called a bigot. The right of self-defense, long since gone up in smoke, was back.

Smokers on the Run

11 The big, brave Passive Americans responded with a vengeance. They began shouting at smokers in restaurants. They shuddered and grimaced and said "Ugh!" as they waved away the impure air. They put up little signs in their cars and homes: at first they said, "Thank You for Not Smoking," but now they feature a cigarette in a circle slashed with a red diagonal. Smokists even issue conditional invitations. I know—I got one. The woman said, "I'd love to have you to dinner, but I don't allow smoking in my home. Do you think you could refrain for a couple of hours?" I said, "Go—yourself," and she told everybody I was the rudest person she had ever met.

12 Smokists practice a sadistic brutality that would have done Vlad the Impaler proud. *Washington Times* columnist and smoker Jeremiah O'Leary was the target of two incredibly baleful letters to the editor after he defended the habit. The first letter said, "Smoke yourself to death, but please don't smoke me to death," but it was only a foretaste of the letter that followed:

Jeremiah O'Leary's March 1 column, "Perilous persuaders . . . tenacious zealots," is a typical statement of a drug addict trying to defend his vice.

To a cigarette smoker, all the world is an ashtray. A person who would never throw a candy wrapper or soda can will drop a lit cigarette without a thought.

Mr. O'Leary is mistaken that nonsmokers are concerned about the damage smokers are inflicting on themselves. What arrogance! We care about living in a pleasant environment without the stench of tobacco smoke or the litter of smokers' trash.

If Mr. O'Leary wants to kill himself, that is his choice. I ask only that he do so without imposing his drug or discarded filth on me. *It would be nice if he would die in such a way that would not increase my health-insurance rates* [my italics].

13   The expendability of smokers has also aroused the tender concern of the Federal Government. I was taking my first drag of the morning when I opened the *Washington Post* and found myself starting at this headline: NOT SMOKING COULD BE HAZARDOUS TO PENSION SYSTEM. MEDICARE, SOCIAL SECURITY MAY BE PINCHED IF ANTI-TOBACCO CAMPAIGN SUCCEEDS, REPORT SAYS.

14   The article explained that since smokers die younger than non-smokers, the Social Security we don't live to collect is put to good use, because we subsidize the pensions of our fellow citizens like a good American should. However, this convenient arrangement could end, for if too many smokers heed the Surgeon General's warnings and stop smoking, they will live too long and break the budget.

15   That, of course, is not how the government economists phrased it. They said:

The implications of our results are that smokers "save" the Social Security system hundreds of billions of dollars. Certainly this does not mean that decreased smoking would not be socially beneficial. In fact, it is probably one of the most cost-effective ways of increasing average longevity. It does indicate, however, that if people alter their behavior in a manner which extends life expectancy, then this must be recognized by our national retirement program.

16   At this point the reporter steps in with the soothing reminder that "the war on tobacco is more appropriately cast as a public-health crusade than as an attempt to save money." But then we hear from Health Policy Center economist Gio Gori, who says: "Prevention of disease is obviously something we should strive for. But it's not going to be cheap. We will have to pay for those who survive."

17   Something darkling crawls out of that last sentence. The whole article has a die-damn-you undertow that would make an honest misanthrope wonder if perhaps a cure for cancer was discovered years ago, but due to cost-effectiveness considerations . . .

18   But honest misanthropes are at a premium that no amount of Raleigh coupons can buy. Instead we have tinpot Torquemadas like Ahron

Leichtman, president of Citizens against Tobacco Smoke, who announced after the airline smoking bans: "CATS will next launch its smoke-free airports project, which is the second phase of our smoke-free skies campaign." Representative Richard J. Durbin (D., Ill.) promised the next target will be "other forms of public transportation such as Amtrak, the inter-city bus system, and commuter lines that receive federal funding." His colleague, Senator Frank Lautenberg (D., N.J.), confessed, "We *are* gloating a little bit," and Fran Du Melle of the Coalition on Smoking OR Health, gave an ominous hint of things to come when she heralded the airline ban as "only one encouraging step on the road to a smoke-free society."

Health Nazis

19   These remarks manifest a sly, cowardly form of misanthropy that the Germans call *Schadenfreude*: pleasure in the unhappiness of others. It has always been the chief subconscious motivation of Puritans, but the smokists harbor several other subconscious motivations that are too egregious to bear close examination—which is precisely what I will now conduct.

20   Study their agitprop and you will find the same theme of pitiless revulsion running through nearly all of their so-called public-service ads. One of the earliest showed Brooke Shields toweling her wet hair and saying disgustedly, "I hate it when somebody smokes after I've just washed my hair. Yuk!" Another proclaimed, "Kissing a smoker is like licking an ashtray." The latest, a California radio spot, asks: "Why sell cigarettes? Why not just sell phlegm and cut out the middle man?"

21   Fear of being physically disgusting and smelling bad is the American's worst nightmare, which is why bathsoap commercials never include the controlled-force shower nozzles recommended by environmentalists in *their* public-service ads. The showering American uses oceans of hot water to get "ZESTfully clean" in a sudsy deluge that is often followed by a deodorant commercial.

22   "Raise your hand, raise your hand, raise your hand if you're SURE!" During this jingle we see an ecstatically happy assortment of people from all walks of life and representing every conceivable national origin, all obediently raising their hands, until the ad climaxes with a shot of the Statue of Liberty raising hers.

The New Greenhorns

23   The Statue of Liberty has become a symbol of immigration, the first aspect of American life the huddled masses experienced. The second was being called a "dirty little" something-or-other as soon as they got off the boat. Deodorant companies see the wisdom in reminding their descendants of the dirty-little period. You can sell a lot of deodorant that way. Ethnics get the point directly; WASPs get it by default in the subliminal reminder that, historically speaking, there is no such thing as a dirty little WASP.

24   Smokers have become the new greenhorns in the land of sweetness and health, scapegoats for a quintessentially American need, rooted in our

fabled Great Diversity, to identify and punish the undesirables among us. Ethnic tobacco haters can get even for past slurs on their fastidiousness by refusing to inhale around dirty little smokers; WASP tobacco haters can once again savor the joys of being the "real Americans" by hurling with impunity the same dirty little insults their ancestors hurled with impunity.

25   The tobacco pogrom serves additionally as the basis for a class war in a nation afraid to mention the word "class" aloud. Hating smokers is an excellent way to hate the white working class without going on record as hating the white working class.

26   The anti-smoking campaign has enjoyed thumping success among the "data-receptive," a lovely euphemism describing the privilege of spending four years sitting in a classroom. The ubiquitous statistic that college graduates are two-and-a-half times as likely to be non-smokers as those who never went beyond high school is balm to the data-receptive, many of whom are only a generation or two removed from the lunch-bucket that smokers represent. Haunted by a fear of falling back down the ladder, and half-believing that they deserve to, they soothe their anxiety by kicking a smoker as the proverbial hen-pecked husband soothed his by kicking the dog.

27   The earnest shock that greeted the RJR Reynolds Uptown marketing scheme aimed at blacks cramped the vituperative style of the data-receptive. Looking down on blacks as smokers might be interpreted as looking down on blacks as blacks, so they settled for aping the compassionate concern they picked up from the media.

28   They got their sadism-receptive bona fides back when the same company announced plans to target Dakota cigarettes at a fearsome group called "virile females."

29   When I first saw the headline I thought surely they meant me: what other woman writer is sent off to a book-and-author luncheon with the warning, "Watch your language and don't wear your Baltimore Orioles warm-up jacket." But they didn't. Virile females are "Caucasian females, 18 to 24, with no education beyond high school and entry-level service or factory jobs."

30   Commentators could barely hide their smirks as they listed the tractor pulls, motorcycle races, and macho-man contests that comprise the leisure activities of the target group. Crocodile tears flowed copiously. "It's blue-collar people without enough education to understand what is happening

to them," mourned Virginia Ernster of the University of California School of Medicine. "It's pathetic that these companies would work so hard to get these women who may not feel much control over their lives." George Will, winner of the metaphor-man contest, wrote: "They use sophisticated marketing like a sniper's rifle, drawing beads on the most vulnerable, manipulable Americans." (I would walk a mile to see Virginia Ernster riding on the back of George Will's motorcycle.)

31   Hating smokers is also a guiltless way for a youth-worshipping country to hate old people, as well as those who are merely over the hill—especially middle-aged women. Smokers predominate in both groups because we saw Bette Davis's movies the same year they were released. Now we catch *Dark Victory* whenever it comes on television just for the pleasure of watching the scene in the staff lounge at the hospital when Dr. George Brent and all the other doctors light up.

32   Smoking is the only thing that the politically correct can't blame on white males. Red men started it, but the cowardly cossacks of the anti-tobacco crusade don't dare say so because it would be too close for comfort. They see no difference between tobacco and hard drugs like cocaine and crack because they don't wish to see any. Never mind that you will never be mugged by someone needing a cigarette; hatred of smokers is the conformist's substitute for the hatred that dare not speak its name. Condemning "substance abuse" out of hand, without picking and choosing or practicing discrimination, produces lofty sensations of democratic purity in those who keep moving farther and farther out in the suburbs to get away from . . . smokers.

Our second text is a spoof advertisement, "Welcome to Malboro Country," that appears on the Web site for Adbusters.org. Adbusters is a media foundation with a global network that sponsors a Web site and a magazine dedicated to this purpose: "We want folks to get mad about corporate disinformation, injustices in the global economy, and any industry that pollutes our physical and mental commons" (http://adbusters.org/information/guidelines/). As you think about this ad, you might recall the hallmark features of Marlboro ads. What images have made those ads famous?

Adbusters.org
"Welcome to Malboro Country"

Composing Your Summary/Strong Response Essay

Generating and Exploring Ideas for Your Summary

After you have selected the piece you will use for this assignment, your first task is to read it carefully to get as accurate an understanding of the article as you can. Remember that summarizing is the most basic and preliminary form of reading with the grain of a text.

1. The first time through, read the piece for general meaning. Follow the argument's flow without judgment or criticism, trying to see the world as the author sees it.

2. Reread the piece slowly, paragraph by paragraph, writing "what it does" or "what it says" gist statements in the margins for each paragraph or writing out the question that you think each paragraph answers. We recommend that you supplement these marginal notations by writing out a complete paragraph-by-paragraph *does/says* analysis modeled after our example on page 125.

3. After you've analyzed the piece paragraph by paragraph, locate the argument's main divisions or parts and create an outline or tree diagram of the main points.

If you need to summarize a visual-verbal text such as a poster, advertisement, public affairs advocacy ad, Web page, or brochure, you can adapt the same processes you use for a verbal text piece to this kind of text. Of course, your summary will be longer for more complex texts such as Web pages and brochures than for posters. Examine the parts and record what each part contributes to the whole piece (similar to "what it does" statements). Basically, you are describing each part of the text. Imagine that you are describing the visual elements for someone who hasn't seen the document. For example, here is a brief summary of a brochure from People for the Ethical Treatment of Animals (PETA):

> The PETA brochure, *Compassionate Living*, consists of five pages. The front of the brochure states the title and shows inviting pictures of animals. The next ten panels of the brochure present questions the organization thinks its audience might ask such as, "What's wrong with animal experimentation?" and provides answers and photos of animal cruelty illustrating the answers. The final panel of the brochure describes PETA and has a membership and donation form. Its main argument is that . . . [here you would summarize the main ideas from the panels]

Shaping, Drafting, and Revising Your Summary

Once you have analyzed the article carefully paragraph by paragraph and understand its structure, you are ready to write a draft. If the piece you are summarizing is closed form, you can generally follow the order of the original article, keeping the proportions of the summary roughly equivalent to the proportions of the article. Begin the essay by identifying the question or problem that the reading addresses. Then state the article's purpose or thesis and summarize its argument point by point. If the article has a delayed thesis or some features of open-form prose, then you may have to rearrange the original order to create a clear structure for readers. For a summary of a visual-verbal text, blend your comments about the visual and verbal elements into a paragraph that enables readers to visualize the images, comprehend its parts, and understand the main points of its message.

Count the number of words in your first draft to see whether you are in the 150–250 word range specified by the assignment. When you revise your summary, follow the criteria presented on page 127. Also use the Guidelines for Peer Reviews (pp. 151–152) as a checklist for revision.

Generating and Exploring Ideas for Your Strong Response

After you have written your summary, which demonstrates your full understanding of the text, you are ready to write your strong response. Use the questions and specific reading strategies discussed on pages 132–138 to help you generate ideas. The following questions put this advice into a quick checklist. Look for the questions that most stimulate your thinking and try freewriting your responses.

- Who is the text's intended audience? How is the author trying to change that audience's view of his or her topic? What rhetorical strategies intended to influence the audience most stand out?
- How do I differ from the intended audience? How are my purposes for reading different from what the author imagined?
- How have the author's rhetorical strategies affected me?
- How have the author's ideas affected me? How have they extended or complicated my own thinking? What do I agree with? What can I support?
- How can I question the author's data, evidence, and supporting arguments? If I am not persuaded by the author's ideas and evidence, why not? What is missing? What can be called into question?
- What is excluded from the author's text? What do these exclusions tell me about the author's value system or angle of vision?
- How can I question the author's values, beliefs, and assumptions? Conversely, how does the text cause me to question my own values, beliefs, and assumptions?
- How has the author changed my view of the topic? What do I have to give up or lose in order to change my view? What do I gain?
- How can I use the author's ideas for my own purposes? What new insights have I gained? What new ways of thinking can I apply to another context?

Writing a Thesis for a Strong Response Essay

See Chapter 2, pp.
34–38, for a
discussion of
surprising thesis
statements.

A thesis for a strong response essay should map out for readers the points that you want to develop and discuss. These points should be risky and contestable; your thesis should surprise your readers with something new or challenging. Your thesis might focus entirely on with-the-grain points or entirely on against-the-grain points, but most likely it will include some of both. Avoid tensionless thesis statements such as "This article has both good and bad points."

Here are some thesis statements that students have written for strong responses in our classes. Note that each thesis includes at least one point about the rhetorical strategies of the text.

EXAMPLES OF SUMMARY/STRONG RESPONSE THESIS STATEMENTS

- In "The Beauty Myth," Naomi Wolf makes a very good case for her idea that the beauty myth prevents women from ever feeling that they are good enough; however, Wolf's argument is geared too much toward feminists to be persuasive for a general audience, and she neglects to acknowledge the strong social pressures that I and other men feel to live up to male standards of physical perfection.

- Although Naomi Wolf in "The Beauty Myth" uses rhetorical strategies persuasively to argue that the beauty industry oppresses women, I think that she overlooks women's individual resistance and responsibility.

- Although the images and figures of speech that Thoreau uses in his chapter "Where I Lived, and What I Lived For" from *Walden* wonderfully support his argument that nature has valuable spiritually renewing powers, I disagree with his antitechnology stance and with his extreme emphasis on isolation as a means to self-discovery.

- In "Where I Lived, and What I Lived For" from *Walden*, Thoreau's argument that society is missing spiritual reality through its preoccupation with details and its frantic pace is convincing, especially to twenty-first century audiences; however, Thoreau weakens his message by criticizing his readers and by completely dismissing technological advances.

- Although the brochure *Compassionate Living* by People for the Ethical Treatment of Animals (PETA) uses the design features of layout, color, and image powerfully, its extreme examples, its quick dismissal of alternative views, and its failure to document the sources of its information weaken its appeal to *ethos* and its overall persuasiveness.

Revising Your Strong Response

In revising your strong response, you will find that peer reviews are especially helpful, both in generating ideas and in locating places that need expansion and development. As you revise, think about how well you have incorporated ideas from your initial explorations and how you can make your essay clearer and more meaningful to readers.

GUIDELINES FOR PEER REVIEWS

Instructions for peer reviews are provided in Chapter 11 (pp. 293–294).

For the Writer
Prepare two or three questions you would like your peer reviewer to address while responding to your draft. The questions can focus on some aspect of your draft that you are uncertain about, on one or more sections where you particularly seek help or advice, on some feature that you particularly like about your draft, or on some part you especially wrestled with. Write out your questions and give them to your peer reviewer along with your draft.

For the Reviewer

I. Read the draft at normal reading speed from beginning to end. As you read, do the following:

   A. Place a wavy line in the margin next to any passages where you get confused or find something that doesn't seem to fit or otherwise slowed down your reading.

   B. Place a "Good!" in the margin next to any passages where you think the writing is particularly strong or interesting.

II. Read the draft again slowly and answer the following questions by writing brief explanations of your answers.

   A. The summary

      1. How could the summary be more comprehensive, balanced, and accurate?

      2. Where could it be more fair and neutral?

      3. How could it use attributive tags more effectively?

      4. How could it include and cite quotations more effectively?

      5. What would make the summary read more smoothly?

   B. The strong response

      1. How could the writer's thesis statement be clearer in setting up several focused points about the text's rhetorical strategies and ideas?

      2. How could the body of the strong response follow the thesis more closely?

      3. How could the rhetorical points and "your own views" points engage more specifically and deeply with the text?

      4. Where do you as a reader need more clarification or support for the writer's rhetorical points and subject-matter points?

      5. How could the strong response be improved by adding points, developing points, or making points in a different way?

III. Rhetorical considerations

   A. *Purpose, audience,* and *genre*: This draft should fit the genre of academic writing. Its purpose is to summarize and critique a reading for an audience interested in the reading's subject matter. How well does the draft fit the genre of academic writing? How effectively does it meet its purpose for its intended audience? How could the writer be more effective in communicating his or her critique and response to the intended readers?

   B. *Logos, ethos,* and *pathos*: How convincing or effective is the logical or conceptual aspect of this draft? How has the writer shown his or her knowledgeable and responsible treatment of the reading? How has the writer connected with the values and sympathies of the intended readers? How could the writer improve these dimensions of the draft?

IV. If the writer has prepared questions for you, respond to his or her inquiries.

V. Sum up what you see as the chief strengths and problem areas of this draft.

   A. Strengths

   B. Problem areas

VI. Finally, read the draft one more time. This time place a check mark in the margin next to any places where you noticed problems in grammar, spelling, or mechanics. (One check mark per problem.)

Writing an Exploratory Essay

About Exploratory Writing

In Chapter 1, we said that to grow as a writer you need to love problems—to pose them and to live with them. Most academic writers testify that writing projects begin when they become engaged with a question or problem and commit themselves to an extensive period of exploration. During exploration, writers may radically redefine the problem and then later alter or even reverse their initial thesis.

As we noted in Chapter 2, however, inexperienced writers tend to truncate this exploratory process, committing themselves hastily to a thesis to avoid complexity. College professors say that this tendency hinders their students' intellectual growth. Asserting a thesis commits you to a position. Asking a question, on the other hand, invites you to contemplate multiple perspectives, entertain new ideas, and let your thinking evolve. As management professor A. Kimbrough Sherman puts it, to grow as thinkers, students need "to 'wallow in complexity' and work their way out" (p. 27).

To illustrate his point, Sherman cites his experience in a management class where students were asked to write proposals for locating a new sports complex in a major U.S. city. To Sherman's disappointment, many students argued for a location without first considering all the variables—impact on neighborhoods, building costs and zoning, availability of parking, ease of access, attractiveness to tourists, aesthetics, and so forth—and without analyzing how various proposed locations stacked up against the criteria they were supposed to establish. The students reached closure without wallowing in complexity.

The assignment in this chapter asks you to dwell with a problem, even if you can't solve it. You will write an essay with an exploratory purpose; its focus will be a question rather than a thesis. The body of your paper will be a narrative account of your thinking about the problem—your attempt to examine its complexity, to explore alternative solutions, and to arrive at a solution or answer. Your exploration will generally require outside research, so many instructors will assign Part Four, "A Rhetorical Guide to Research," along with this chapter. The paper will be relatively easy to organize because it follows a chronological structure, but you will have nothing to say—no process to report—unless you discover and examine your problem's complexity.

Exploratory essays can be composed in two ways—what we might call the "in-process" strategy and the "retrospective" strategy. When following the first strategy, writers compose the body of their essays during the actual process of thinking and researching. When writing page 4, for example, they don't know what they will be thinking by page 9. In contrast, when composing retrospectively, writers look back over their process from the vantage point of a completed journey. Their goal, when writing with an exploratory aim, is to reproduce their process, taking the readers, as it were, on the same intellectual and emotional journey they have just traveled. The first strategy yields genuine immediacy—like a sequence of journal entries written in the midst of the action. The second strategy, which allows for more selection and shaping of details, yields a more artistically designed essay.

Exploratory essays occur only occasionally in academic journals and almost never in business or professional life, where readers need thesis-driven arguments and reports. However, exploratory essays exist in embryo in the research journals or lab notebooks of scholars. Scholars sometimes revise their journals into stand-alone exploratory essays that take readers into the kitchen of academic discovery. The exploratory form underlies Plato's dialogues as well as the musings of the Renaissance French writer Michel de Montaigne, whose term *essai* (meaning a "try" or "attempt") leads to the English word *essay*. The power of exploratory writing as a stand-alone genre can be seen in such books as Jon Krakauer's *Into the Wild*, which recounts the author's attempt to fathom the mystery of Chris McCandless, a bright young graduate from Emory University who abandoned conventional life and "disappeared" into the Alaska wilderness, where he was eventually found dead in an abandoned school bus. Who was Chris McCandless?, Krakauer asks. What motivated him? The book records Krakauer's exploration—a collage of personal narrative intermixed with interviews, musings on his reading, and frequent theorizing. This chapter introduces you to thinking processes behind this powerful form.

Exploring Exploratory Writing

Through our work in writing centers, we often encounter students disappointed with their grades on essay exams or papers. "I worked hard on this paper," they tell us, "but I still got a lousy grade. What am I doing wrong? What do college professors want?"

To help you answer this question, consider the following two essays written for a freshman placement examination in composition at the University of Pittsburgh, in response to the following assignment:

> Describe a time when you did something you felt to be creative. Then, on the basis of the incident you have described, go on to draw some general conclusions about "creativity."

How would you describe the differences in thinking exhibited by the two writers? Which essay do you think professors rated higher?

ESSAY A

I am very interested in music, and I try to be creative in my interpretation of music. While in high school, I was a member of a jazz ensemble. The members of the ensemble were given chances to improvise and be creative in various songs. I feel that this was a great experience for me, as well as the other members. I was proud to know that I could use my imagination and feelings to create music other than what was written.

Creativity to me means being free to express yourself in a way that is unique to you, not having to conform to certain rules and guidelines. Music is only one of the many areas in which people are given opportunities to show their creativity. Sculpting, carving, building, art, and acting are just a few more areas where people can show their creativity.

Through my music I conveyed feelings and thoughts which were important to me. Music was my means of showing creativity. In whatever form creativity takes, whether it be music, art, or science, it is an important aspect of our lives because it enables us to be individuals.

ESSAY B

Throughout my life, I have been interested and intrigued by music. My mother has often told me of the times, before I went to school, when I would "conduct" the orchestra on her records. I continued to listen to music and eventually started to play the guitar and the clarinet. Finally, at about the age of twelve, I started to sit down and to try to write songs. Even though my instrumental skills were far from my own high standards, I would spend much of my spare time during the day with a guitar around my neck, trying to produce a piece of music.

Each of these sessions, as I remember them, had a rather set format. I would sit in my bedroom, strumming different combinations of the five or six chords I could play, until I heard a series which sounded particularly good to me. After this, I set the music to a suitable rhythm (usually dependent on my mood at the time), and ran through the tune until I could play it fairly easily. Only after this section was complete did I go on to writing lyrics, which generally followed along the lines of the current popular songs on the radio.

At the time of the writing, I felt that my songs were, in themselves, an original creation of my own; that is, I, alone, made them. However, I now see that, in this sense of the word, I was not creative. The songs themselves seem to be an oversimplified form of the music I listened to at the time.

In a more fitting sense, however, I *was* being creative. Since I did not purposely copy my favorite songs, I was, effectively, originating my songs from my own "process of creativity." To achieve my goal, I needed what a composer would call "inspiration" for my piece. In this case the inspiration was the current hit on the radio. Perhaps, with my present point of view, I feel that I used too much "inspiration" in my songs, but, at the time, I did not.

Creativity, therefore, is a process which, in my case, involved a certain series of "small creations" if you like. As well, it is something the appreciation of which varies with one's point of view, that point of view being set by the person's experience, tastes, and his own personal view of creativity. The less experienced tend to allow for less originality, while the more experienced demand real originality to classify something a "creation." Either way, a term as abstract as this is perfectly correct, and open to interpretation.

Working as a whole class or in small groups, analyze the differences between Essay A and Essay B. What might cause college professors to rate one essay higher than the other? What would the writer of the weaker essay have to do to produce an essay more like the stronger?

WRITING PROJECT

Choose a question, problem, or issue that genuinely perplexes you. At the beginning of your exploratory essay, explain why you are interested in this chosen problem and why you have been unable to reach a satisfactory answer. Then write a first-person, chronologically organized, narrative account of your thinking process as you investigate your question through research, talking with others, and doing your own reflective thinking. Your research might involve reading articles or other sources assigned by your instructor, doing your own library or Internet research, or doing field research through interviews and observations. As you reflect on your research, you can also draw on your own memories and experiences. Your goal is to examine your question, problem, or issue from a variety of perspectives, assessing the strengths and weaknesses of different positions and points of view. By the end of your essay, you may or may not have reached a satisfactory solution to your problem. You will be rewarded for the quality of your exploration and thinking processes. In other words, your goal is not to answer your question but to report on the process of wrestling with it.

This assignment asks you to dwell on a problem—and not necessarily to solve that problem. Your problem may shift and evolve as your thinking progresses. What matters is that you are actively engaged with your problem and demonstrate why it is problematic.

Your instructor may choose to combine this writing project with a subsequent one (for example, a research paper based on one of the assignments in the remaining chapters in Part Two) to create a sustained project in which you write two pieces on the same topic. If so, then the essay for this chapter will prepare you to write a later analytical or persuasive piece. Check with your instructor to make sure that your chosen question for this project will work for the later assignment.

Understanding Exploratory Writing

See the discussion of aims in Table 3.1, pp. 49–50.

As we have explained, this assignment calls for an essay with an *exploratory aim*. Exploratory writing generally has an open-form structure. The writer does not assert a thesis and forecast a structure in the introduction (typical features of closed-form prose) because the writer's purpose is to present the process of exploration itself—to write *thesis-seeking* rather than *thesis-supporting* prose. Instead of following a closed-form, points-first structure, the essay narrates chronologically the process of the author's thinking about the problem.

The Essence of Exploratory Prose: Considering Multiple Solutions

The essential move of an exploratory essay is to consider multiple solutions to a problem or multiple points of view on an issue. The writer defines a problem, poses a possible solution, explores its strengths and weaknesses, and then *moves* on to consider another possible solution.

To show a mind at work examining multiple solutions, let's return to the two student essays you examined in the previous exploratory activity (p. 154). The fundamental difference between Essay A and Essay B is that the writer of Essay B treats the concept of "creativity" as a true problem. Note that the writer of Essay A is satisfied with his or her initial definition:

> Creativity to me means being free to express yourself in a way that is unique to you, not having to conform to certain rules and guidelines.

The writer of Essay B, however, is *not* satisfied with his or her first answer and uses the essay to think through the problem. This writer remembers an early creative experience—composing songs as a twelve-year-old:

> At the time of the writing, I felt that my songs were, in themselves, an original creation of my own; that is, I, alone, made them. However, I now see that, in this sense of the word, I was not creative. The songs themselves seem to be an oversimplified form of the music I listened to at the time.

This writer distinguishes between two points of view: "On the one hand, I used to think *x*, but now, in retrospect, I think *y*." This move forces the writer to go beyond the initial answer to think of alternatives.

The key to effective exploratory writing is to create a tension between alternative views. When you start out, you might not know where your thinking process will end up; at the outset you might not have formulated an opposing, countering, or alternative view. Using a statement such as "I used to think . . . , but now I think" or "Part of me thinks this . . . , but another part thinks that . . . " forces you to find something additional to say; writing then becomes a process of inquiry and discovery.

The second writer's dissatisfaction with the initial answer initiates a dialectic process that plays one idea against another, creating a generative tension. In contrast, the writer of Essay A offers no alternative to his or her definition of creativity. This writer presents no specific illustrations of creative activity (such as the specific details in Essay B about strumming the guitar) but presents merely space-filling abstractions ("Sculpting, carving, building, art, and acting are just a few more areas where people can show their creativity"). The writer of Essay B scores a higher grade, not because the essay creates a brilliant (or even particularly clear) explanation of creativity; rather, the writer is rewarded for thinking about the problem dialectically.

We use the term *dialectic* to mean a thinking process often associated with the German philosopher Hegel, who said that each thesis ("My act was creative") gives rise to an antithesis ("My act was not creative") and that the clash of these opposing perspectives leads thinkers to develop a synthesis that incorporates some features of both theses ("My act was a series of 'small creations' "). You initiate dialectic thinking any time you play Elbow's believing and doubting game or use other strategies to place alternative possibilities side by side.

See Chapter 2, pp. 42–46, for an explanation of the believing and doubting game.

Essay B's writer uses a dialectic thinking strategy that we might characterize as follows:

1. Regards the assignment as a genuine problem worth puzzling over.
2. Considers alternative views and plays them off against each other.
3. Looks at specifics.
4. Continues the thinking process in search of some sort of resolution or synthesis of the alternative views.
5. Incorporates the stages of this dialectic process into the essay.

For Writing and Discussion

1. According to writing theorist David Bartholomae, who analyzed several hundred student essays in response to the placement examination question on page 154, almost all the highest scoring essays exhibited a similar kind of dialectic thinking. How might the writer of the first essay expand the essay by using the dialectic thinking processes just described?
2. Working individually, read each of the following questions and write out your initial opinion or one or two answers that come immediately to mind.

   - Given the easy availability of birth control information and the ready availability of condoms, why do you think there are so many teenage pregnancies?
   - Why do U.S. students, on average, lag so far behind their European and Asian counterparts in scholastic achievement?
   - Should women be assigned to combat roles in the military?
   - The most popular magazines sold on college campuses around the country are women's fashion and lifestyle magazines such as *Glamour*, *Seventeen*, and *Cosmopolitan*. Why are these magazines so popular? Is there a problem with these magazines being so popular? (Two separate questions, both of which are worth exploring dialectically.)

3. Choose one of the preceding questions or one assigned by your instructor and freewrite for five or ten minutes using one or more of the following to stimulate dialectic thinking:
   I used to think _____, but now I think _____.
   Part of me thinks _____, but another part of me thinks _____.
   On some days I think _____, but on other days I think _____.

The first answers that come to mind are _____, but as I think further I see _____.

My classmate thinks _____, but I think _____.

Your goal here is to explore potential weaknesses or inadequacies in your first answers, and then to push beyond them to think of new or different answers. Feel free to be wild and risky in posing possible alternative solutions.

4. As a whole class, take a poll to find out what the most common first-response answers are for each of the questions. Then share alternative solutions generated by class members during the freewriting. The goal is to pose and explore answers that go beyond or against the grain of the common answers. Remember, there is little point in arguing for an answer that everyone else already accepts.

READINGS

In this section we include a student essay that illustrates writing with an exploratory purpose. Student writer Christopher Leigh explores the problem of preventing school violence. You read about Christopher's early exploration of this problem in Chapter 1. By the end of his first-year writing course, he had developed his ideas into a researched argument opposing metal detectors in the schools. Christopher's argument against metal detectors is our sample student research paper in Chapter 14.

Christopher's early journal entry is shown on p. 9. His researched argument is on pp. 363–374.

Christopher Leigh (student)
An Exploration of How to Prevent Violence in Schools

1   The April 20, 1999, shootings at Columbine High School in Littleton, Colorado, left me, as well as people across America, in a state of shock and disbelief. The terrifying incidents made my friends and me wonder what had driven the two high school students to commit such a horrible crime. Most of all, we wanted to know what was being done to prevent incidents like this from happening again.

2   For the exploratory paper I knew I wanted to write on some aspect of school violence, such as what causes it or what can be done to prevent it, and I decided to focus on the ways that schools are working to prevent violence.

3   While I was searching through newspaper articles on Lexis-Nexis Academic Universe, I discovered a New York Times article by Timothy Egan that captured my interest. The article deals with the practice of profiling in high schools to identify potentially violent students. The profiles contain a list of behaviors and warning signs that may indicate that a student is

troubled and prone to violence. Egan quotes former President Clinton, who said, "We must all do more to recognize and look for the early warning signals that deeply troubled young people send often before they explode into violence" (1). Within days, Egan writes, national organizations had distributed lists of characteristics, which included signs such as mood swings, drug/alcohol use, and fondness for violent television. I noted in my journal that the problem with these checklists is that they describe almost every person at some point in adolescence. However, I could also see why kids who fit the profiles for many of the traits should be closely watched; any adolescent who is often depressed and uses drugs or alcohol is likely to be troubled. But a kid could be depressed, troubled, and abusive of drugs or alcohol and yet pose no threat. Would being labeled as "potentially violent" only further alienate or anger the student?

4   The article really made me question how I felt about profiling. On the one hand, I believe that profiling in any form is wrong and defies the very principles upon which our country is built. Just as racial profiling singles out innocent people based on the color of their skin, profiling in schools targets those who do not fit social norms of acceptable behavior. On the other hand, I agree that violence in schools is a problem that needs to be addressed, and preventive measures that may help should be thoroughly considered.

5   After reading this article, I began to think about various issues surrounding profiling, such as whether profiling is effective and whether it violates students' rights. I decided to search for articles that specifically addressed these issues.

6   Unfortunately, after much searching I couldn't find any articles addressing whether or not profiling is effective, nor could I find any discussion of whether it violates civil rights. However, using Ebscohost I found an article in US News and World Report that raises another important issue related to profiling. Its author, Mary Lord, shows that many schools use profiling to identify kids who need counseling, but that fewer than ten percent of schools have mental health professionals available to deal with the kids once they have been identified (57). Lord also describes a student who was arrested for writing an essay about blowing up the school but then rebuilding it to make it state of the art (55). At this point I began to see more clearly why the issue of profiling is problematic. The student described in Lord's article had no intention of causing any harm, but his careless use of words in his essay resulted in an arrest and suspension, which was later rescinded when the school acknowledged its wrongdoing. The student then noted that he avoids writing essays and speaks less often in class as a result of the incident (Lord 55). I can understand that schools have good intentions—to prevent violence by providing troubled kids with counseling—but in this case, the school did not provide counseling and instead suspended him. Furthermore, if most schools do not have the resources to provide counseling, it seems pointless to try to identify potentially violent students.

7   Lord's article referred to an FBI report dealing with prevention of school violence, so I wanted to find out more about it. I found a newspaper article by David Vise and Kenneth Cooper, who write that the FBI report advises schools not to use profiling to identify potentially violent students because actual incidents of school violence are so rare. Instead, they write, the report calls for the use of profiling only when some threat of violence has already occurred (Vise and Cooper A3). I was relieved to learn that the FBI is opposed to the general use of profiling. The article by Mary Lord that I had read earlier had given me the false impression that the FBI report supported profiling, but now I see that the FBI supports profiling only in the case of an actual threat. Nevertheless, many schools still misuse the profiles.

8   I decided that I shouldn't use any more magazines or newspapers due to their potential bias and omission of important information. I next went to find the full FBI report on school violence. The report, published by the FBI Academy's National Center for the Analysis of Violent Crime, can be found on the agency's Web site and can be read in its original format using Acrobat Reader. The report is written by Mary O'Toole, PhD, who headed the investigation. She proposes that schools set up a system of professionals who can be called in to assess threats and determine their severity and risk (United States 5). I found the report impressively comprehensive, even though it does not explain how schools should go about setting up a threat-assessment program. Although the report repeatedly warns schools not to use profiles alone, it still lists pages of characteristics of potentially violent kids, which seemed to me to be an invitation to misuse the report. The way I see it, school administrators will read the report, recognize the complexity of the proposal, and simply take the easiest course of action, which is to remove the profiles from context and use them on their own.

9   One aspect of O'Toole's report really struck me. She shows how the media misrepresent school violence by treating it as a widespread, frequent phenomenon and by portraying school shooters in a stereotypical way (United States 4). I have always felt strongly about the negative power of mass media, so I decided to investigate this lead. I found a brief article in Professional School Counseling entitled "Unsafe Schools: Perception or Reality?" The article's author, Tony Del Prete, writes that people tend to "overanalyze and sensationalize [incidents] to the point of hysteria" (375). He observes that the media inaccurately portray violence as a plague in American society, when in actuality school violence has steadily declined since 1993. After reading this article, I concluded that the media devote so much coverage to incidents such as the one at Columbine High that the public adopts an it-could-happen-to-anyone view of school violence. This attitude creates a panicked need to find a simplistic and crude solution, such as profiling or installing metal detectors in schools where there are no previous incidents of violence.

10   Despite my discovery that the frequency of school violence has been exaggerated, I believe that violence is a real problem, and methods of prevention

should be implemented to maintain safe schools. Del Prete concludes his article by suggesting that the best approach is to create a more friendly community atmosphere in schools by eliminating harassment and reducing competition. Even though it too seems like a simplistic solution, I feel that making schools friendlier and educating teens about the harmful effects of a hostile environment are keys to improving the state of our schools.

11   I then began to think about how other forms of preventing school violence, such as metal detectors, might have a negative impact on the school environment. Metal detectors are a popular form of violence prevention, yet their increasing presence in schools is troubling. I began searching the Web to find out more about metal detectors. One article, entitled "Districts Should Proceed Cautiously on Metal Detectors," from the New York State School Board's Web site, points out that most schools equipped with the devices cannot check every student due to the large numbers of people arriving at once, so it is practically impossible to ensure that weapons do not enter school buildings. The article also notes that metal detectors do not address the nature of the problem of violence, and that schools should be more concerned with "creating a climate that teaches peaceful resolution" ("Districts"). However, a poll conducted by Charlotte.com, a North Carolina newspaper-affiliated Web site, showed that eighty-one percent of local residents approved of metal detectors in schools (Ly and Toosi). Despite the public demand for metal detectors in schools, I feel that they might actually have a negative effect in reducing school violence because they make schools seem like prisons and damage the feeling of community. At this point I was becoming more and more convinced that the best way to reduce violence is to make schools more friendly and less hostile.

12   I decided to try to find one more article about ways to make schools less hostile environments. I went back to the educational journals and found an article by Scott Poland, whose name appeared in many of the other sources I found. The author, who is the president of the National Association of School Psychologists, also calls for an effort to personalize our schools and hire more professionals to help counsel kids who may be troubled (45). He writes that most counselors are already overworked and are required to do things such as scheduling that take away from their attention to the students. Poland also emphasizes that it is important for teachers to form strong relationships with their students. He suggests that teachers set aside a small amount of time each day to interact with students, and he discourages schools from cutting extracurricular programs that may help students feel connected to the school (46). From my point of view, Poland's article offers the most encouraging and perhaps the most promising solution to prevent school violence. Yet Poland's solution can't be done cheaply. I remembered an article that I had scanned briefly earlier in my research process, and I decided to return to it for a closer look. This

article, "America Skips School," explains that until Americans recognize the importance of education by paying teachers higher salaries, public schools will continue to become less and less effective (Barber 45). My research on preventing violence in schools has shown me that now we have another big reason to invest more in public education. If teachers can and should play a significant role in creating a positive school community, then they should be compensated for this additional responsibility. After all, if teachers don't know the first thing about their students, there is no way they are going to be able to know who is in need of help and who is not. By developing relationships with students on a personal level, teachers will be able to sense when a student is in trouble and can take steps to reach out to that student. The need for more counselors is also crucial to provide students with help if a teacher thinks it is necessary.

13   I believe that this exploratory paper has helped me clarify my own thinking about school violence. I am now convinced that the media have instigated a panic about school violence, leading in many cases to counterproductive approaches like psychological profiling and metal detectors. When it comes time to write my major argument paper, I plan to show that these approaches only increase students' sense of alienation and hostility. The most important approach is to make schools more friendly, communal, and personal. We must ensure that troubled students are provided with the help they need, rather than treating them like criminals.

Works Cited

Barber, Benjamin. "America Skips School." <u>Harper's</u> Nov. 1993: 39–46.

Del Prete, Tony. "Unsafe Schools: Perception or Reality?" <u>Professional School Counseling</u> 3 (2000): 375–76.

"Districts Should Proceed Cautiously on Metal Detectors." <u>New York State School Boards Association</u>. 22 May 2000. 16 Aug. 2001 <http://www.nyssba.org/adnews/employee/employee052200.3.html>.

Egan, Timothy. "The Trouble with Looking for Signs of Trouble." <u>New York Times</u> 25 Apr. 1999, sec. 4: 1.

Lord, Mary. "The Violent Kid Profile: A Controversial New Technique for Beating Violence in Schools." <u>US News & World Report</u> 11 Oct. 1999: 56–57.

Ly, Phuong, and Nahal Toosi. "Many Favor Metal Detectors." <u>Charlotte Observer</u>. 19 Nov. 2000. 16 Aug. 2001 <http://www.charlotte.com/observer/special/poll98/0804metal.htm>.

Poland, Scott. "The Fourth R—Relationships." <u>American School Board Journal</u> 187.3 (2000): 45–46.

United States. Dept. of Justice. Fed. Bureau of Investigation. <u>The School Shooter: A Threat Assessment Perspective</u>. By Mary O'Toole. 2000. 16 Aug. 2001 <http://www.fbi.gov/publications/school/school2.pdf>.

Vise, David, and Kenneth Cooper. "FBI Opposes the Use of Profiling of Students." <u>Washington Post</u> 7 Sept. 2000: A3.

Thinking Critically about "An Exploration of How to Prevent Violence in Schools"

1. Exploratory papers usually narrate both the evolution of the writer's thinking and the physical actions the writer takes to do the actual research. In Christopher's case, approximately what percentage of the total paper focuses on Christopher's research processes and what percentage on ideas? When he switches from a summary of a research source to his own thinking or from his own thinking to a description of his next action, how does he write transitions that keep the reader from getting lost?
2. Trace the evolution of Christopher's ideas in this paper. Does his thinking evolve in an ordered and understandable way, or does it seem random and directionless? Explain your reasoning.
3. Read Christopher's argument against metal detectors in the schools on pages 363–374. What connections do you see between his final argument and his earlier exploratory paper? What new research did he do for his final argument? What material from his exploratory paper is omitted from the final argument? In your own words, how does the difference in purpose (exploration versus persuasion) lead to different structures for the two papers?
4. What do you see as the chief strengths and weaknesses of Christopher's exploration of how to prevent school violence?

Composing Your Exploratory Essay

Generating and Exploring Ideas

Your process of generating and exploring ideas is, in essence, the *subject matter* of your exploratory paper. This section helps you get started and keep going.

Keeping a Research Log

Since this assignment asks you to create a chronologically organized account of your thinking process, you need to keep a careful, detailed record of your investigation. The best tool for doing so is a research log or journal in which you take notes on your sources and record your thinking throughout the process.

As you investigate your issue, keep a chronologically organized account that includes notes on your readings, interviews, and significant conversations, as well as explorations of how each of these sources, new perspectives, or data influence your current thinking. Many writers keep a double-entry notebook that has a "notes" section in which to summarize key points, record data, copy potentially usable quotations verbatim, and so forth and a "reflections" section in which to write a strong response to each reading, exploring how it advanced your think-ing, raised questions, or pulled you in one direction or another.

As you write your exploratory essay, your research log will be your main source for details—evidence of what you were thinking at regular intervals throughout the process.*

For an example of double-entry notes, see "Sam's Research Log Entry on *Newsweek* Article" on pp. 167–168.

Exploring Possible Problems for Your Essay

Your instructor may assign a specific problem to explore. If not, then your first step is to choose a question, problem, or issue that currently perplexes you. Perhaps a question is problematic to you because you haven't studied it (How serious is the problem of global warming? How can we keep pornography on the Internet away from children?) or because the available factual data seem conflict-ing and inconclusive (Should postmenopausal women take supplemental estro-gen?) or because the problem or issue draws you into an uncomfortable conflict of values (Should we legalize drugs? Should the homeless mentally ill be placed involuntarily in state mental hospitals?).

The key to this assignment is to choose a question, problem, or issue *that truly perplexes you*. The more clearly readers sense your personal engagement with the problem, the more likely they are to be engaged by your writing. Note: If your instructor pairs this assignment with a later one, be sure that your question is appropriate for the later assignment. Check with your instructor.

Here are several exercises to help you think of ideas for this essay:

Exploration Exercise 1.   In your research log, make a list of issues or problems that both interest and perplex you. Then choose two or three of your issues and freewrite about them for five minutes or so, exploring questions such as these: Why am I interested in this problem? What makes the problem problematic? What makes this problem significant? Share your list of questions and your freewrites with friends and classmates. Discussing questions with friends often stimulates you to think of more questions yourself or to sharpen the focus of questions you have already asked.

To show how a question is problematic and significant, see Chapter 1, pp. 24–25.

Exploration Exercise 2.   If your exploratory essay is paired with a subsequent assignment, look at the invention exercises for that assignment to help you ask a question that fits the context of the final paper you will write.

Exploration Exercise 3.   A particularly valuable kind of problem to explore for this assignment is a public controversy. Often such issues involve complex dis-agreements about facts and values that merit careful, open-ended exploration.

---

*For those of you majoring in science or engineering, this research log is similar to the laboratory notebooks that are required parts of any original research in science or industry. Besides recording in detail the progress of your research, these notebooks often serve as crucial data in patent applications or liability lawsuits. Doctors and nurses keep similar logs in their medical records file for each patient. This is a time-honored practice. In Mary Shelley's early-nineteenth-century novel *Frankenstein*, the monster learns about the process of his creation by reading Dr. Frankenstein's laboratory journal.

This assignment invites you to explore and clarify where you stand on such complex public issues as gay marriages, overcrowded prisons, the USA Patriot Act, racial profiling, the electoral college, Internet censorship and privacy issues, and so forth. These issues make particularly good topics for persuasive papers or formal research papers, if either is required in your course. For this exercise, look through a current newspaper or weekly newsmagazine, and in your research log make a list of public issues that you would like to know more about. Use the following trigger question:

I don't know where I stand on the issue of _____ .

Share your list with classmates and friends.

Formulating a Starting Point

After you've chosen a problem or issue, write a research log entry identifying the problem or issue you have chosen and explaining why you are perplexed by and interested in it. You might start out with a sharp, clearly focused question (for example, "Should the United States legalize the medical use of marijuana?"). Often, however, formulating the question turns out to be part of the *process* of writing the exploratory paper. Many writers don't start with a single, focused question but rather with a whole cluster of related questions swimming in their heads. This practice is all right—in fact, it is healthy—as long as you have a direction in which to move after the initial starting point. Even if you do start with a focused question, it is apt to evolve as your thinking progresses.

For this exercise, choose the question, problem, or issue you plan to investigate and write a research log entry explaining how you got interested in that question and why you find it both problematic and significant. This will be the *starting point* for your essay; it might even serve as the rough draft for your introduction. Many instructors will collect this exploration as a quick check on whether you have formulated a good question that promises fruitful results.

Here is how one student, Sam, wrote the starting point entry for his research log:

SAM'S STARTING POINT RESEARCH LOG ENTRY

I want to focus on the question of whether women should be allowed to serve in combat units in the military. I became interested in the issue of women in combat through my interest in gays in the military. While I saw that gays in the military was an important political issue for gay rights, I, like many gays, had no real desire to be in such a macho organization. But perhaps that was just the point—we had the opportunity to break stereotypes and attack areas most hostile to us.

Similarly, I wonder whether feminists see women in combat as a crucial symbolic issue for women's rights. (I wonder too whether it is a *good* symbol, since many women value a less masculine approach to the world.) I think my instinct right now is that women should be allowed to serve in combat units. I think it is wrong to discriminate against women. Yet I also think America needs to have a strong military. Therefore, I am in a quandary. If putting women in combat wouldn't harm our military power, then I am fully in favor of women in combat. But if it would hurt our military power, then I have to make a value judgment. So I guess I have a lot to think about as I research this issue. I decided to focus on the women issue rather than the gay issue because it poses more of a dilemma for me. I am absolutely in favor of gays in the military, so I am not very open-minded about *exploring* that issue. But the women's issue is more of a problem for me.

Continuing with Research and Dialectic Thinking

After you have formulated your starting point, you need to proceed with research, keeping a research log that records both your reading notes and your strong response reflections to each reading.

After Sam wrote his starting point entry, he created an initial bibliography by searching one of his college library's licensed databases. He decided to try keeping his research log in a double-entry, notes/reflections format. What follows is his research log entry for the first article he read, a piece from *Newsweek*.*

SAM'S RESEARCH LOG ENTRY ON *NEWSWEEK* ARTICLE

Notes

Hackworth, David H. "War and the Second Sex." *Newsweek* 5 Aug. 1991: 24–28.

- Ideals in conflict are equality and combat readiness.
- Acknowledges women's bravery, competence, and education (uses the Gulf War as an example). Admits that there are some women as strong and fit as the strongest men (gives some examples), but then argues that allowing even these women in combat is the type of experimentation that the army doesn't need right now. (He says women already have plenty of jobs open to them in noncombat units.)
- Biggest problem is "gender norming"—having different physical standards for men and women. A 22-year-old female is allowed three more minutes than a 22-year-old male to run two miles; men have to climb a 20-foot rope in 30 seconds; women can take 50 seconds.
- One of Hackworth's big values is male bonding. He points to "male bonding" as a key to unit cohesion. Men have been socialized to think that women must be protected. He uses Israel as an example:

  > "The Israeli Army put women on the front lines in 1948. The experiment ended disastrously after only three weeks. It wasn't that the women couldn't fight. It was that they got blown apart. Female casualties demoralized the men and gutted unit cohesion." (pp. 26–27)

- Another major problem is pregnancy causing women to leave a unit. He says that 10 to 15 percent of servicewomen wear maternity uniforms in a given year. During the Gulf War, pregnancy rates soared. 1200 pregnant women

*Note on dates: The next four pages follow Sam's research process conducted in 1996 during former President Clinton's first term of office when the issues of gays in the military and women in combat were being highly debated. Some of Sam's research data refer to combat evidence gathered during the first Gulf War (Operation Desert Storm, 1991) when U.S. and coalition forces liberated Kuwait from Iraq's occupation under Saddam Hussein.

were evacuated from the gulf (p. 28) during the war. On one destroyer tender, 36 female crew members got pregnant (p. 28). These pregnancies leave vacancies in a unit that can destroy its effectiveness.

- He claims that women soldiers themselves had so many complaints about their experiences in the Gulf War (fraternization, sexual harassment, lack of privacy, primitive living conditions) that they said "don't rush to judgment on women in combat" (p. 28).

Reflections

Some challenging points, but not completely convincing. His biggest reason for opposing women in combat is harm to unit morale, but this isn't convincing to me. The Israeli example seems like unconvincing evidence seeing how those soldiers' attitudes in 1948 reflected a much different society.

Issue of pregnancy is more convincing. A pregnant woman, unlike a father-to-be, cannot continue to fill her role as a combat soldier. I was shocked by the number of pregnancies during the Gulf War and by the extent (although Hackworth doesn't give statistics) of the fraternization (he says the army passed out over a million condoms—p. 28).

I am also bothered by the gender-norming issue. It seems to me that there ought to be some absolute standards of strength and endurance needed for combat duty and the military ought to exclude both men and women who don't meet them. This would mean that a lower percentage of women than men would be eligible, but is that discrimination?

Where do I now stand? Well, I am still leaning toward believing that women should be allowed to serve in combat, but I see that there are a number of subquestions involved. Should physical standards for combat positions be the same for men and women? Will the presence of women really hurt morale in a mostly male unit? Should women be given special consideration for their roles as mothers? How serious a problem is pregnancy? I also see another problem: Should physically eligible women be *required* (e.g., drafted) to serve in combat the same way men are drafted into combat positions? And I still want to know whether this is a crucial issue for the women's rights movement.

In the next section we see how Sam converts material from his research log into a draft of his exploratory essay.

Shaping and Drafting

Your exploratory essay should offer accounts of your search procedures (useful conversations with friends, strategies for tracking down sources, use of indexes or computer searches, strokes of good fortune at stumbling on good leads, and so forth) and your thought processes (what you were discovering, how your ideas were evolving). Drawing on your research log, you can share your frustration when a promising source turned out to be off the mark or your perplexity when a conversation with a friend over late-night espresso forced you to rethink your views. Hook your readers by making your exploratory essay read like a detective story. Consider giving your account immediacy by quoting your thoughts at the very moment you wrote a log entry. The general shape of an exploratory essay can take the following pattern:

1. Starting point: You describe your initial problem, why you are interested in it, why it is problematic, why it is worth pursuing.
2. New input: You read an article, interview someone, pose an alternative solution.
   a. Summarize, describe, or explain the new input.
   b. Discuss the input, analyzing or evaluating it, playing the believing and doubting game with it, exploring how this input affects your thinking.
   c. Decide where to go next—find an alternative view, pursue a subquestion, seek more data, and so forth.
3. More new input: You repeat step 2 for your next piece of research.
4. Still more new input.
5. Ending point: You sum up where you stand at the point when the paper is due, how much your thinking about the issue has changed, whether or not you've reached a satisfactory solution.

Here is how Sam converted his starting point entry (pp. 166–167) and his first research entry (pp. 167–168) into the opening pages of his exploratory essay:

SHOULD WOMEN BE ALLOWED TO SERVE IN COMBAT UNITS?

Sam Scofield

At first, I wanted to explore the issue of gays in the military. But since I am a gay man I already knew where I stood on that issue and didn't find it truly problematic *for myself*. So I decided to shift my question to whether women should be allowed to serve in combat units. I wasn't sure whether feminists see the issue of women in combat the same way that gays see the military issue. Is it important to the feminist cause for women to be in combat? Or should feminists seek a kind of political order that avoids combat and doesn't settle issues through macho male behavior? In my initial thinking, I was also concerned about maintaining our country's military strength. In my "starting point" entry of my research log, I recorded the following thoughts:

> If putting women in combat wouldn't harm our military power, then I am fully in favor of women in combat. But if it would hurt our military power, then I have to make a value judgment.

So I decided that what I should do first is find some general background reading on the women in combat question. I went to the library, plugged the key words "woman and combat" into our online Infotrac database, and found more than a dozen entries. I went to the stacks and found the most familiar magazine in my initial list: *Newsweek*.

I began with an article by a retired Air Force colonel, David H. Hackworth. Hackworth was opposed to women in combat and focused mainly on the standard argument I was expecting—namely that women in combat would destroy male bonding. He didn't provide any evidence, however, other than citing the case of Israel in 1948:

> The Israeli Army put women on the front lines in 1948. The experiment ended disastrously after only three weeks. It wasn't that the women couldn't fight. It was that they got blown apart. Female casualties demoralized the men and gutted unit cohesion. (26–27)

However, this argument wasn't very persuasive to me. I thought that men's attitudes had changed a lot since 1948 and that cultural changes would allow us to get used to seeing both men and women as *people* so that it would be equally bad—or equally bearable—to see either men or women wounded and killed in combat.

But Hackworth did raise three points that I hadn't anticipated, and that really set me thinking. First he said that the military had different physical fitness requirements for men and women (for example, women had three minutes longer to run two miles than did men [25]). As I said in my research log, "It seems to me that there ought to be some absolute standards of strength and endurance needed for combat duty and the military ought to exclude both men and women who don't meet them." A second point was that an alarming number of female soldiers got pregnant in the Gulf War (1200 pregnant soldiers had to be evacuated [28]) and that prior to the war about ten to fifteen percent of female soldiers were pregnant at any given time (28). His point was that a pregnant woman, unlike a father-to-be, cannot continue to fill her role as a combat soldier. When she leaves her unit, she creates a dangerous gap that makes it hard for the unit to accomplish its mission. Finally, Hackworth cited lots of actual women soldiers in the Gulf War who were opposed to women in combat. They raised issues such as fraternization, sexual harassment, lack of privacy, and primitive living conditions.

Although Hackworth didn't turn me against wanting women to be able to serve in combat, he made the issue much more problematic for me. I now realized that this issue contained a lot of subissues, so I decided to focus first on the two major ones for me: (1) How important is this issue to feminists? This concern is crucial for me because I want to support equal rights for women just as I want to do so for gays or ethnic minorities. And (2) How serious are the pregnancy and strength-test issues in terms of maintaining military strength?

As I read the rest of the articles on my list, I began paying particular attention to these issues. The next article that advanced my thinking was. . . .

Revising

Because an exploratory essay describes the writer's research and thinking in chronological order, most writers have little trouble with organization. When they revise, their major concern is often to improve their essay's interest level by keeping it focused and lively. Exploratory essays grow tedious if the pace crawls too slowly or if extraneous details appear. They also tend to become too long, so that condensing and pruning become key revision tasks. The draft here is actually Sam's second draft; the first draft was a page longer and incorporated many more details and quotations from the Hackworth article. Sam eliminated these because he realized that his purpose was not to report on Hackworth but to describe the evolution of his own thinking. By condensing the Hackworth material, Sam saved room for the ideas he discovered later.

Peer reviewers can give you valuable feedback about the pace and interest level of an exploratory piece. They can also help you achieve the right balance between external details (how you did the research, to whom you talked, where you were) and mental details (what you were thinking about). As you revise, make sure you follow proper stylistic conventions for quotations and citations.

Conventions for quotations and citations are explained in Chapter 14.

GUIDELINES FOR PEER REVIEWS

Instructions for peer reviews are provided in Chapter 11 (pp. 293–294).

For the Writer

Prepare two or three questions you would like your peer reviewer to address while responding to your draft. The questions can focus on some aspect of your draft that you are uncertain about, on one or more sections where you particularly seek help or advice, on some feature that you particularly like about your draft, or on some part you especially wrestled with. Write out your questions and give them to your peer reviewer along with your draft.

For the Reviewer

I. Read the draft at a normal reading speed from beginning to end. As you read, do the following:
   A. Place a wavy line in the margin next to any passages that you find confusing, that contain something that doesn't seem to fit, or that otherwise slow down your reading.
   B. Place a "Good!" in the margin next to any passages where you think the writing is particularly strong or interesting.
II. Read the draft again slowly and answer the following questions by writing brief explanations of your answers.
   A. Posing the problem:
      1. How might the title be improved to identify the problem more accurately or to better engage your interest?
      2. How has the writer tried to show that the problem is interesting, problematic, and significant? How could the writer engage you more fully with the initial problem?
      3. How does the writer provide cues that the writer's purpose is to explore a question rather than argue a thesis? How might the opening section of the paper be improved?
   B. Narrating the exploration:
      1. Is the body of the paper organized chronologically so that you see the gradual development of the writer's thinking? Where does the writer provide chronological transitions? Are there confusing shifts from past

tense to present tense? If so, how might the chronological structure of the paper be made clearer?

2. How has the writer revealed the stages or changes in his or her thinking about the problem?

3. Part of an exploratory paper involves summarizing the argument of each new research source. Where in this draft is a summary of a source particularly clear and well developed? Where are summary passages that seem undeveloped or unclear? How could these passages be improved?

4. Another part of an exploratory paper involves the writer's strong response to each source—evidence of the writer's own critical thinking and questioning. Where are the writer's own ideas particularly strong and effective? Where are the writer's own ideas undeveloped or weak? What additional ideas or perspectives do you think the writer should consider?

5. Has the writer done enough research to explore the problem? Can you make suggestions for further research?

6. How might the ending of the paper better sum up the evolution of the writer's thinking or better clarify why the writer has or has not resolved the problem?

III. Rhetorical considerations

A. *Purpose, audience,* and *genre:* Where in this draft has the writer made a special effort to follow an exploratory purpose and to construct an essay that engages reflectively with sources? What has the writer done to interest readers in his or her dialectic exploration of this problem?

B. *Logos, ethos,* and *pathos:* How has the writer treated and structured the discussion of ideas in this essay? To what extent has the writer effectively conveyed his or her reliability, knowledge, and fairness in identifying, citing, and discussing sources throughout this draft? How does the writer connect this exploration to the interests and values of his audience? Where would you recommend improvements in appeals to *logos, ethos,* and *pathos?*

IV. If the writer has prepared questions for you, respond to his or her inquiries.

V. Sum up what you see as the chief strengths and problem areas of this draft:

A. Strengths

B. Problem areas

VI. Read the draft one more time. Place a check mark in the margin wherever you notice problems in grammar, spelling, or mechanics (one check mark per problem).

Writing an Informative (and Surprising) Essay

About Informative (and Surprising) Writing

As a reader, you regularly encounter writing with an informative aim, ranging from the instruction booklet for an MP3 player to a newspaper feature story on the African AIDS crisis. Informative documents include encyclopedias, cookbooks, news articles, instruction booklets, voters' pamphlets, and various kinds of reports, as well as informative Web sites and magazine articles. In some informative prose, visual representations of information such as diagrams, photographs, maps, tables, and graphs can be as important as the prose itself.

Informative Writing and the Audience's Reasons for Reading

A useful way to begin thinking about informative writing is to classify it according to the reader's motivation for reading. From this perspective, we can place informative prose in three categories.

In the first category, readers are motivated by an immediate need for information such as the need to program a VCR, study for a driver's test, or, in a more complex instance, make a major repair on an aircraft engine using the technical documentation supplied by the manufacturer. In these need-to-know instances, what readers want from informative prose is precision, accuracy, and clarity.

In the second category, readers are motivated by their own curiosity about a subject. For example, readers might turn to encyclopedias for information on the rings of Saturn or to newspapers or Internet news services for the latest information on the war against terror. In the academic world, scholars value annotated bibliographies and literature reviews, which provide important information that summarizes recent scholarship on a disciplinary problem.

Informative writing in these two categories does not necessarily contain a contestable thesis. Documents are organized effectively, of course, but they often follow a chronological step-by-step organization (as in a recipe) or an "all-about" topic-by-topic organization (as in an encyclopedia article on, say, Pakistan divided into "Geography," "Climate," "Population," "History," and so forth). The writer provides factual information about a subject without necessarily shaping the information specifically to support a thesis.

In contrast, the third category of informative writing *is* thesis-based and is therefore aligned with other kinds of thesis-based prose. The thesis brings new or surprising information to readers who aren't initially motivated by a need-to-know occasion or by their own curiosity. In fact, readers might not be initially interested in the writer's topic at all, so the writer's first task is to hook readers' interest—often by having an effective opening that arouses curiosity, hints that readers' current knowledge about a topic might have holes or gaps, and motivates their desire to learn something new, surprising, or different. Such pieces are commonly encountered in newspaper feature stories or in magazine articles where the reader is enticed by an intriguing title and interest-grabbing opening paragraphs. An excellent strategy for creating this motivation to read is the technique of "surprising reversal," which we explain in the next section.

The Rhetorical Power of "Surprising Reversal"

This third category of informative writing provides an excellent place to introduce a powerful rhetorical strategy that we call *surprising reversal.* Throughout this text, we have encouraged the habit of considering alternative answers to a question. The surprising-reversal strategy is directly linked to this way of thinking. Using this strategy, you contrast your new, surprising answer to a question with the targeted audience's common answer, creating tension between your own thesis and one or more alternative views. Its basic template is as follows: "Many people believe X (common view), but I am going to show Y (new, surprising view)." The concept of surprising reversal spurs the writer to go beyond the commonplace to change the reader's view of a topic.

The broad aims of writing, including the aims of informing, analyzing, and persuading, are discussed in Table 3.1, pp. 49–50.

This surprising-reversal strategy works as well for the aims of analysis and persuasion as it does for the informative aim. As we discussed in Chapter 2, writers of thesis-based prose usually try to change a reader's view in one of three ways, corresponding to three of the broadly defined aims of writing:

1. *Informative aim: enlarging* readers' views of a topic by providing new information or otherwise teaching them something about the topic they didn't know ("Many people think that security for supply lines in Iraq is provided by U.S. soldiers, but my research reveals that security is often provided by privately hired mercenaries.")

2. *Analytical or interpretive aim: clarifying* readers' views of a topic by bringing critical thinking to bear on problematic data or on a problematic text ("The students in my dorm think that this jeans ad reveals a liberated woman, but my own analysis of this ad shows that the woman fulfills traditional gender stereotypes.")

3. *Persuasive aim: restructuring* readers' views on a topic by urging them to choose the writer's position rather than a competing position on a controversial issue ("Many people believe the United States should continue to depend on an all-volunteer army, but I argue that the U.S. should reinstitute the draft.")

The concept of tension in a thesis statement is discussed in Chapter 2, pp. 36–38.

The surprising-reversal pattern occurs whenever you contrast your reader's original view of a topic with your own new or surprising view. Its power is that it automatically gives your thesis tension. It pushes your view up against the commonplace or expected views that are likely to be shared by your audience. In this chapter, the Option B writing project (p. 178) invites you to use the surprising-reversal strategy for an informative aim. But this strategy also works for the aims of analysis or persuasion. You may find yourself using variations of this strategy for many of the other essays you write for this course and throughout your college career.

Exploring Informative (and Surprising) Writing

Let's say that you have just watched an old James Bond movie featuring a tarantula in Bond's bathroom. Curious about tarantulas, you do a quick Web search and retrieve the following short informative pieces. Read each one, and then proceed to the questions that follow.

READINGS

Our first mini-article comes from the Web site EnchantedLearning.com, a commercial site aimed at providing interesting, fact-filled learning lessons for children.

EnchantedLearning.com
Tarantulas

Jaws that move up and down (unlike most tarantulas)
Mexican Red-Kneed **Tarantula**
Tarsus
Metatarsus
Pedipalps (palps) feelers
Tibia
Femur
White bands
White bands
8 tiny eyes that can only detect light vs. dark
Orange-red "knees"
Black, hairy Cephalothorax (Prosoma) -Contains brain, jaws, eyes, stomach, and leg attachments
White bands
Pedicel (waist)
8 hairy black legs tipped with tiny claws -Each leg has 7 segments
Spinnerets (silk glands)
Black, hairy abdomen (Opisthosoma) -Contains guts, heart, reproductive organs, silk glands
©EnchantedLearning.com   5 to 5.5 inch (13-14 cm) leg span

1   Tarantulas are large hairy spiders that live in warm areas around the world, including South America, southern North America, southern Europe, Africa, southern Asia, and Australia. The greatest concentration of tarantulas is in South America. There are about 300 species of tarantulas. The biggest

tarantula is *Pseudotherathosa apophysis,* which has a leg span of about 13 inches (33 cm). These arachnids have a very long life span; some species can live over 30 years.

2 **Habitat:** Some tarantulas live in underground burrows; some live on the ground, and others live in trees. They live in rain forests, deserts, and other habitats.

3 **Diet:** Tarantulas are carnivores (meat-eaters). They eat insects (like grasshoppers and beetles), other arachnids, small reptiles (like lizards and snakes), amphibians (like frogs), and some even eat small birds. Tarantulas kill their prey using venomous fangs; they also inject a chemical into the prey that dissolves the flesh. Tarantulas can crush their prey using powerful mouthparts. No person has ever died of a tarantula bite.

4 **Anatomy:** Tarantulas have a hairy two-part body and very strong jaws (with venomous fangs). They have eight hairy legs; each leg has 2 tiny claws at the end and a cushioning pad behind the claws. The hairs on the body and legs are sensitive to touch, temperature, and smell. Tarantulas have a hard exoskeleton and not an internal skeleton.

The second mini-article comes from the Web site of the University of Washington's Burke Museum. The author of this piece is the curator of arachnids at the Burke Museum.

Rod Crawford
Myths about "Dangerous" Spiders

1 **Myth: Tarantulas are dangerous or deadly to humans.**

2 **Fact:** Outside of southern Europe (where the name is used for a wolf spider, famous in medieval superstition as the alleged cause of "tarantella" dancing), the word tarantula is most often used for the very large, furry spiders of the family Theraphosidae.

3 Hollywood is squarely to blame for these spiders' toxic-to-humans reputation. Tarantulas are large, photogenic and easily handled, and therefore have been very widely used in horror and action-adventure movies. When some "venomous" creature is needed to menace James Bond or Indiana Jones, to invade a small town in enormous numbers, or to grow to gigantic size and prowl the Arizona desert for human prey, the special-effects team calls out the tarantulas!

4 In reality, the venom of these largest-of-all-spiders generally has **very low toxicity to humans.** I myself was once bitten by a Texan species and hardly even felt it. None of the North American species or those commonly kept as pets are considered to pose even a mild bite hazard. There are some reports that a few tropical species may have venom more toxic to vertebrates, but human bite cases haven't been reported, so we can't know for sure.

European tarantula

Lycosa tarentula
Southern Europe; body length 2–3 cm
(photo: Manuel J. Cabrero)
Click image to enlarge

Pink toe tarantula

Avicularia avicularia
Brazil to Trinidad; body length 6–7 cm
(photo by Ron Taylor)
Click image to enlarge

Both the European wolf spiders (**left**), originally called tarantulas, and the theraphosid spiders (**right**), often kept as pets and called tarantulas now, have been reputed dangerous to humans. They aren't.

5   The only health hazard posed by keeping pet tarantulas comes from the irritating chemicals on the hairs of the abdomen, which can cause skin rashes or inflammation of eyes and nasal passages. To prevent such problems, simply keep tarantulas away from your face and wash your hands after handling one.

6   Compared to common pets such as dogs, tarantulas are not dangerous at all. (For more information see the American Tarantula Society.)

Thinking Critically about "Tarantulas" and "Myths about 'Dangerous' Spiders"

1. Why do you think the reading from EnchantedLearning.com uses a diagram of a tarantula while the Burke Museum Web site uses photographs? How is each choice connected to the piece's targeted audience and purpose?
2. How would you describe the difference in organizational strategies for each of the readings? To us, one of these has an "all-about" topic-by-topic structure while the other has a thesis-based structure. Which is which? How is this difference connected to the targeted audience and purpose? How does the difference affect the way details are selected and arranged?

3. One might suppose that informational writing would be unaffected by the writer's angle of vision—that facts would simply be facts and that informational pieces on the same topic would contain the same basic information. Yet these two short pieces give somewhat different impressions of the tarantula. For example, how do these readings differ in the way they portray the bite of the tarantula? How else do they differ in overall effect?

WRITING PROJECT

To suggest some of the range of informative prose, we offer two writing-project options. The first of these asks you to report the results of your own data-gathering research project.

Option A: Short Informative Report. Write a short informative report based on data you have gathered from observations, interviews, or your own questionnaire. Aim your paper at readers of a popular magazine or newspaper. The introduction of your paper should engage your readers' interest in your question. The body of your paper should present your results, which in many cases can also be displayed visually in a table or graph as well as in prose.

This assignment asks you to report the results of your own research data gathered through observation, interviews, or questionnaires. Write your paper in a popular magazine style for a popular audience. For an example of a student paper written for Option A, see Kerri Ann Matsumoto's "How Much Does It Cost to Go Organic?", which Kerri Ann formatted to have the appearance of a magazine article (p. 183). Typical research questions for this assignment might be "How do college students spend their time during a typical week?" (questionnaire or interview study) or "What microorganisms are present in water samples from three area ponds?" (observation study in conjunction with an ecology class).

Option B: Informative Paper Using Surprising Reversal. Using your personal experience or library/Internet research as a source of information, write a short informative essay using the surprising-reversal pattern. Imagine an audience of readers who hold a mistaken or overly narrow view of your topic. Your purpose is to give them a new, surprising view.

Depending on the wishes of your instructor, this assignment can draw primarily on personal experience (for an example, see Cheryl Carp's essay, "Behind Stone Walls," pp. 184–185) or on library or Internet research (for an example, see Shannon King's "How Clean and Green Are Hydrogen Fuel-Cell Cars?" pp. 187–196). In either case, the assignment asks you to enlarge your reader's view of a subject in a surprising way. The introduction of your essay should engage your reader's interest in a question and provide needed context and background. Next, explain the common or popular answer to your question. Then give your own surprising answer that you develop with information derived from your personal experience or from library/Internet research. To create the "surprising-reversal" feel, consider delaying your thesis until after you have given your audience's common, expected answer to your opening question. This delay in presenting the thesis creates a more open-form feel that readers often find engaging.

For this assignment, avoid controversial issues requiring persuasive rather than informative writing. When writing persuasive prose, you imagine a resistant reader who may argue back. With informative prose, you imagine a more trusting reader, willing to learn from your experience or research. Although you hope to enlarge your reader's view of a topic, you aren't necessarily saying that your audience's original view is wrong, nor are you initiating a debate. For example, suppose a writer wanted to develop the following claim: "Many of my friends think that having an alcoholic mother would be the worst thing that could happen to you, but I will show that my mother's disease forced our family closer together." In this case the writer isn't arguing that alcoholic mothers are good or that everyone should have an alcoholic mother. Rather, the writer is simply offering readers a new, unexpected, and expanded view of what it might be like to have an alcoholic mother.

Finally, note that you do not need to be an expert on your topic, only to be more informed than your target audience. Your surprising information doesn't have to be surprising to everyone. For example, the claim that tarantula bites are harmless may be surprising to naïve viewers of a James Bond film but not to experts on spiders.

Understanding Informative (and Surprising) Writing

Informative Reports

The term *report* has numerous meanings. Students often come to college with inadequate models of what constitutes a strong academic report. For example, the "book reports" often assigned in high school aren't really "reports" in an academic sense and are quite different from professional book reviews written by scholars and critics. Likewise a "report" on Ethiopia done for a high school civics class

For further explanation of the difference between "all-about" structures and thesis-based structures, see Chapter 12, pp. 305–308.

may have been largely paraphrased from an encyclopedia, Web site, or other secondary source. In each of these cases, the report typically had an "all-about" structure rather than a problem-thesis structure—that is, the reports were organized by a sequence of topics rather than by points in support of a thesis.

Sometimes college instructors do give assignments asking primarily for repackaged all-about information. For example, a math instructor might ask you to report on a famous mathematician, or an art instructor might assign a report on cubism or impressionism—assignments that can lead primarily to paraphrasing of secondary sources. Such assignments can expand students' knowledge of a subject area, but they teach very little about the actual inquiry strategies of scholars in a discipline. As a general rule, college professors value informative reports based on the writer's own original research—reading primary documents or doing field or laboratory research—rather than on paraphrasing reference sources. The Option A assignment for this chapter, which asks you to produce new information based on your own field research, is thus a higher-level assignment than an all-about paper gleaned from secondary references.

For our purposes, we will define "report" as any document that presents the results of a fact-finding or data-gathering investigation. Some reports limit themselves to presenting newly discovered information, while others push further by analyzing or interpreting the information in an effort to understand causes, consequences, functions, or purposes. Such informative reports, which often have a thesis-driven rather than an all-about structure, can be of intense interest to researchers or decision makers. Scholars, for example, eagerly await the results of government reports on census or economic data, just as business leaders make crucial decisions based on sales or operations reports. In many disciplinary fields, scholarly writing includes informational reports as well as analyses and arguments. For example, a biologist might catalog the beetles found in a certain forest environment or an anthropologist might describe a fertility ritual in a tribal society. No report, of course, will be just pure information. The data will always be screened through the writer's angle of vision. But in informational reports, the writer's primary focus is on clear presentation of research findings.

Informative Writing Using Surprising Reversal

Because writing that uses the surprising-reversal strategy has a thesis, it is useful to understand more clearly the difference between "all-about" informative writing and "thesis-based" informative writing. Consider, for example, the difference between the EnchantedLearning.com Web site on tarantulas (pp. 175–176) and the Burke Museum piece on "Myths about 'Dangerous' Spiders" (pp. 176–177). The EnchantedLearning.com piece is a short "all-about" report organized under the topic headings "Habitat," "Diet," and "Anatomy." The creator of the Web site may simply have adapted an encyclopedia article on tarantulas into a format for children. In contrast, the Burke Museum piece by Rod Crawford is thesis based. Crawford wishes to refute the myth that "[t]arantulas are dangerous or deadly to humans." He does so by providing information on the low toxicity of tarantula venom to humans and the relative painlessness of bites. All of Crawford's data focus on the potential danger of tarantulas. There are no data about habitat, diet, or other aspects of tarantula life—material that would be included if this were an all-about report. Because the piece also includes data about misconceptions of tarantulas, it follows the basic pattern of surprising reversal: "Many people believe (because of Hollywood movies) that tarantulas are toxic to humans, but I will show that tarantulas are not dangerous at all."

Because of its power to hook and sustain readers, examples of surprising-reversal essays can be found in almost any publication—from scholarly journals to easy-reading magazines. Here, for example, are abstracts of several articles from the table of contents of the *Atlantic Monthly*.

"REEFER MADNESS" BY ERIC SCHLOSSER

Marijuana has been pushed so far out of the public imagination by other drugs, and its use is so casually taken for granted in some quarters of society, that one might assume it had been effectively decriminalized. In truth, the government has never been tougher on marijuana offenders than it is today. In an era when violent criminals frequently walk free or receive modest jail terms, tens of thousands of people are serving long sentences for breaking marijuana laws.

"THE SEX-BIAS MYTH IN MEDICINE" BY ANDREW G. KADAR

A view has gained wide currency that men's health complaints are taken more seriously than those of women, and that medical research has benefited men more than it has women. "In fact," the author writes, "one sex does appear to be favored in the amount of attention devoted to its medical needs. . . . That sex is not men, however."

"MIDLIFE MYTHS" BY WINIFRED GALLAGHER

The idea that middle age is a dismal stage of life—scarred by traumas of personal crisis and physical change—is both firmly entrenched and almost completely untrue. The image in many Americans' minds, the author writes, is derived "not from the ordinary experiences of most people but from the unusual experiences of a few."

Each of these articles asserts a surprising, new position that counters a commonly held view.

Commonly Held, Narrow, or Inaccurate View	Surprising View
Because marijuana laws are no longer enforced, marijuana use has effectively become decriminalized.	The government has never been tougher on marijuana offenders than it is today.
More research dollars are spent on men's diseases than on women's diseases.	The reverse is true: more money is spent on women's diseases.
Middle age is a dismal stage of life.	The widespread notion of midlife crises is a myth based on the unusual experiences of the few.

A similar pattern is often found in scholarly academic writing, which typically has the following underlying shape:

> Whereas other scholars say X, Y, or Z, my research reveals Q.

Because the purpose of academic research is to advance knowledge, an academic article almost always shows the writer's new view against a background of prevailing views (what other scholars have said). This kind of tension is what often makes thesis-based writing memorable and provocative.

READINGS

The readings for this chapter include both a short informational report and surprising-reversal informative essays. Our first reading, by student writer Kerri Ann Matsumoto, responds to the Option A writing project for this chapter. We reproduce it on page 183 to show how Kerri Ann formatted the paper to look like a popular magazine article.

Thinking Critically about "How Much Does It Cost to Go Organic?"

1. In our teaching, we have discovered that students appreciate the concept of genre more fully if they occasionally "desktop publish" a manuscript to look like a magazine article, poster, or brochure rather than a standard double-spaced academic paper. If Kerri Ann had been an actual freelance writer, she would have submitted this article double-spaced with attached figures, and the magazine publisher would have done the formatting. Compare Kerri Ann's document design for "How Much Does It Cost to Go Organic?" with the document design of Shannon King's informative report on hydrogen fuel-cell cars, pages 187–196, which follows the format required by the American Psychological Association for scholarly papers. How does document design itself signal differences in genre? To what extent has Kerri Ann made this article *sound* like a popular magazine article as well as look like one?
2. Do you think Kerri Ann used visual graphics effectively in her essay? How might she have revised the graphics or the wording to make the paper more effective?
3. Do you think it is worth the extra money to go organic? How would you make your case in an argument paper with a persuasive aim?

HOW MUCH DOES IT COST TO GO ORGANIC?

Kerri Ann Matsumoto

Organic foods, grown without pesticides, weed killers, or hormone additives, are gaining popularity from small privately owned organic food stores to large corporate markets. With the cost of living rising, how much can a family of four afford to pay for organically grown food before it becomes too expensive?

To find out more information about the cost of organic foods, I went to the Rainbow Market, which is a privately owned organic food store, and to a nearby Safeway. I decided to see what it would cost to create a stir-fry for a family of four. I estimated that the cost of organic vegetables for the stir-fry would cost $3.97. Non-organic vegetables for the same stir-fry, purchased at Safeway, would cost $2.37. If we imagined our family eating the same stir fry every night for a year, it would cost $1,499 for organic and $865 for non-organic for a difference of $584.

After pricing vegetables, I wanted to find out how much it would cost to add to the stir-fry free-range chicken fed only organic feeds, as opposed to non-organic factory farmed chicken. For good quality chicken breasts, the organic chicken was $6.99 per pound and the non-organic was $3.58 per pound. Projected out over a year, the organic chicken would cost $5,103 compared to $2,613 for non-organic chicken.

My research shows that over the course of one year it will cost $6,552 per year to feed our family organic stir-fry and $3,478 for non-organic for a difference of $3,074. If a family chose to eat not only organic dinner, but also all organic meals, the cost of food would sharply increase.

Before going to the Rainbow Market I knew that the price of organic foods was slightly higher than non-organic. However, I did not expect the difference to be so great. Of course, if you did comparison shopping at other stores, you might be able to find cheaper organic chicken and vegetables. But my introductory research suggests that going organic isn't cheap.

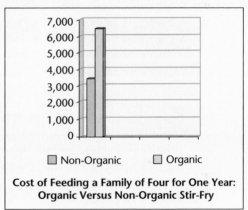

Cost of Feeding a Family of Four for One Year: Organic Versus Non-Organic Stir-Fry

Comparative Cost of Ingredients in an Organic Versus Non-Organic Stir-Fry				
	Vegetables per day	Chicken per day	Total per day	Total per year
Organic	$3.97	$13.98	17.95	$6552
Non-Organic	$2.37	$ 7.16	9 .53	$3478

If we add the cost of chicken and vegetables together (see the table and the graph), we can compute how much more it would cost to feed our family of four organic versus non-organic chicken stir-fry for a year.

Is it worth it? Many people today have strong concerns for the safety of the foods that they feed to their family. If you consider that organic vegetables have no pesticides and that the organic chicken has no growth hormone additives, the extra cost may be worth it. Also if you are concerned about cruelty to animals, free-range chickens have a better life than caged chickens. But many families might want to spend the $3,074 difference in other ways. If you put that money toward a college fund, within ten years you could save over $30,000. So how much are you willing to pay for organic foods?

Our second reading is by student writer Cheryl Carp, whose experience with volunteer outreach in a maximum-security prison enabled her to enlarge her readers' views of prisoners with life sentences. This paper, which uses the surprising-reversal strategy, illustrates how personal experiences can be used for an informative aim.

Cheryl Carp (student)
Behind Stone Walls

1   For about eight hours out of every month I am behind the stone walls of the Monroe State Penitentiary. No, that's not the sentencing procedure of some lenient judge; I am part of a group of inmates and outsiders who identify themselves as Concerned Lifers. Concerned Lifers is an organization operating both inside and outside of prison walls. Inside Monroe there are close to thirty men who take part in the organization and its activities, all of whom have been given life sentences. Concerned Lifers outside the prison visit the prisoners, take part in the organization's meetings, and then split into various small groups for personal conversation. I became involved in this exciting group as a personal sponsor (able to visit the prison alone for special activities) after attending my first meeting inside Monroe State Penitentiary. That first drive to Monroe seemed to take forever. Looking out the window of that twelve-seater van filled with apprehensive first-time volunteers, I kept my eyes on the evening sky and tried to imagine what it would be like to be shut up in prison for life, never to see this beautiful scenery again. I was not scared, but I was nervous and could feel my pulse rate steadily rise as I began to see the green and white road signs to the prison. As the van slowly climbed the hill to the guard tower at the top, I wondered what it would be like to visit this maximum security prison.

2   Many people believe that visiting a prison would be frightening. Most people typically picture dangerous men lurking in every corner. The guards are yelling and the men are fighting; the men are covered with tattoos, probably carrying concealed razor blades and scowling menacingly. People think that prisons are a haven for rampant homosexuality and illegal drugs. Common belief is that the inmates are like locked animals, reaching out between the iron bars of their cages. These men are seen as sex-starved, eagerly waiting for a female body to enter their domain. The atmosphere is one of suspense, with sub-human men ready at any moment to break free and run. People I've spoken to express a fear of danger to themselves and almost a threat to their lives. They wonder how I have the nerve to do it.

3   But visiting a prison to me is an uplifting experience, far from frightening. Since that initial visit, I have returned many times to organize and participate in a clown group. The clown group is made up of about twenty of the inmates in the Concerned Lifers group and myself. The prisoners meet and rehearse once a week, and I join them every other week to critique their progress, give them pointers, and do various exercises to improve their ability.

4   The only frightening part of a visit is getting through all the guards and their red tape. Last week I drove up the hill to the guard tower, identified myself and my affiliation, and was told to "park to the left" by a disembodied voice coming from a loudspeaker. After going through many metal security doors, being checked by a metal detector that even picks up the nails in your shoes, and being escorted by numerous guards, I finally got to be with the people I had come to see.

5   The most enjoyable, exciting, and friendly time I spend at the prison is the time I spend with the boys. These people are no longer "the prisoners" or "the inmates," but are now individuals. Visiting the prison is not a frightening experience because the men inside become people, people full of emotions, creativity, and kindness. These qualities are evident in the activities and projects these men become involved in or initiate themselves. For example, one young lifer named Ken became interested in Japanese paper folding—origami. In order to pursue his interest in origami, he requested a book on the subject from the prison librarian and proceeded to teach himself. A few weeks later, I saw origami creations everywhere—flowers, dragons, and birds—all made by the guys and all done carefully and beautifully. Ken had taught his fellow inmates. Another great thing that this group has undertaken is the sponsorship of four children through an orphan relief program. The men make almost nothing at their various jobs within the prison, but what they do make they are more than willing to share, something many of us never seem to "get around to."

6   It is true that the men value the presence of a female, but not for sexual reasons. The men inside Monroe are hungry for outside companionship and understanding. They're hungry for a woman's viewpoint and conversation. They have treated me as a friend, valued my conversation, and never made sexual advances. The men behind the walls are reaching through their bars not menacingly, but pleadingly—begging the outside world to take a good look at them. The men need to be looked at as people and as fellow humans in this world. Most of them are aching for a second chance at life and relationships. This is not a place for outsiders to fear, but a place to which outsiders can bring light, hope, and understanding.

7   My point is not to condone the crimes that these men may have committed in the past, but to look to the present and the future by seeing these men not as "inmates," but as individual people trying to succeed in the kind of life they now have to live.

Thinking Critically about "Behind Stone Walls"

1. What is the audience that Cheryl Carp imagines?
2. For this audience, what is the common view of prisoners that Cheryl Carp attempts to reverse?
3. What is her own surprising view?
4. What are the strengths and weaknesses of Cheryl's essay?

The next reading, by student writer Shannon King, is a short research paper using the surprising-reversal strategy. Shannon's paper uses research data to enlarge her readers' understanding of hydrogen fuel cell vehicles by showing that hydrogen fuel is not as pollution-free as the general public believes. We reproduce the paper to illustrate the manuscript form required by the American Psychological Association (APA) for scholarly papers. A brief explanation of APA documentation format and style is found on pages 375–376.

Hydrogen Fuel-Cell Cars   1

How Clean and Green Are Hydrogen Fuel-Cell Cars?

Shannon King

June 15, 2004

Hydrogen Fuel-Cell Cars   2

How Clean and Green Are Hydrogen Fuel-Cell Cars?

The United States is embroiled in a controversy over energy and pollution. We are rapidly using up the earth's total supply of fossil fuels, and many experts think that children being born today will experience the end of affordable oil. One energy expert (Roberts, 2004) believes that serious oil shortages will start occurring by 2015 when the world's demand for oil will outstrip the world's capacity for further oil production. An equally serious problem is that the burning of fossil fuels spews carbon dioxide into the atmosphere, which increases the rate of global warming.

One hopeful way of addressing these problems is to develop hydrogen fuel cell cars. According to the author of the fuel cell pages on the How Stuff Works Web site (Nice, n.d.), a fuel cell is "an electrochemical energy conversion device that converts hydrogen and oxygen into water, producing electricity and heat in the process." A hydrogen-fueled car is therefore an electric car, powered by an electric motor. The car's electricity is

Hydrogen Fuel-Cell Cars   3

generated by a stack of fuel cells that act like
a battery. In the hydrogen fuel cell, the
chemicals that produce the electricity are
hydrogen from the car's pressurized fuel tank,
oxygen from the air, and special catalysts
inside the fuel cell. The fuel cell releases no
pollutants or greenhouse gases. The only waste
product is pure water.

To what extent will these pollution-free
fuel cells be our energy salvation? Are they
really clean and green?

Many people think so. The development of
hydrogen fuel cells has caused much excitement. I
know people who say we don't need to worry about
running out of oil because cars of the future
will run on water. One recent *New York Times*
advertisement produced by General Motors (2004)
has as its headline, "Who's driving the hydrogen
economy?" The text of the ad begins by saying
"The hydrogen economy isn't a pipe dream. . . .
The hydrogen economy is the endgame of a multi-
faceted strategy General Motors set in motion
years ago, with steps that are real, progressive,
and well-underway." The Web site for the Hydrogen
Fuel Cell Institute includes a picture of a

crystal clear blue sky landscape with a large
letter headline proclaiming "At long last, a
technology too long overlooked promises to
transform society." At the bottom of the picture
are the words, "Offering clean & abundant power,
hydrogen-based fuel cells could soon end our
reliance on oil and minimize emissions of
pollution and global-warming gases." According to
CNN News (2004), the Bush administration has
proposed devoting 1.7 billion dollars of federal
funds to developing hydrogen fuel cells. The
biggest nationally known proponent of hydrogen
fuel cells is California Governor Arnold
Schwarzenegger, who signed an Executive Order
that California's "21 interstate freeways shall
be designated as the 'California Hydrogen Highway
Network.'" (California, 2004, p. 2). In this
executive order, Schwarzenegger envisions

> a network of hydrogen fueling stations along
> these roadways and in the urban centers that
> they connect, so that by 2010, every
> Californian will have access to hydrogen
> fuel, with a significant and increasing
> percentage produced from clean, renewable
> sources. (p. 2)

Hydrogen Fuel-Cell Cars   5

Schwarzenegger's optimism about the hydrogen highway sums up the common view that hydrogen is a clean alternative energy source that is abundant throughout nature. All we have to do is bottle it up, compress it, and transport it to a network of new "gas stations" where the gas being pumped is hydrogen.

But what I discovered in my research is that hydrogen is not as green as most people think. Although hydrogen fuel cells appear to be an environmentally friendly alternative to fossil fuels, the processes for producing hydrogen actually require the use of fossil fuels. The problem is that pure hydrogen doesn't occur naturally on earth. It has to be separated out from chemical compounds containing hydrogen, and that process requires other forms of energy. What I discovered is that there are only two major ways to produce hydrogen. The first is to produce it from fossil fuels by unlocking the hydrogen that is bonded to the carbon in coal, oil, or natural gas. The second is to produce it from water through electrolysis, but the power required for electrolysis would also come mainly from burning fossil fuels. These problems make hydrogen fuel cell cars look less clean and green than they first appear.

One approach to creating hydrogen from fossil fuels is to use natural gas. According to Wald (2003), natural gas is converted to hydrogen in a process called "steam reforming." Natural gas (made of hydrogen and carbon atoms) is mixed with steam (which contains hydrogen and oxygen atoms) to cause a chemical reaction that produces pure hydrogen. But it also produces carbon dioxide, which contributes to global warming. According to Wald, if fuel cell cars used hydrogen from steam reforming, they would emit 145 grams of global warming gases per mile compared to 374 grams an ordinary gas-powered car would emit. The good news is that using hydrogen power would cut carbon emissions by more than half. The bad news is that these cars would still contribute to global warming and consume natural gas. Moreover, Wald suggests that the natural gas supply is limited and that natural gas has many better, more efficient uses than converting it to hydrogen.

Another method for producing hydrogen would come from coal, which is the cheapest and most

Hydrogen Fuel-Cell Cars   7

abundant source of energy. However, the current
method of generating electricity by burning coal is
the leading source of carbon dioxide emission. At
Ohio University, engineers state we still have
enough coal to last us 250 years and that we should
find some better uses for coal. The engineers have
received a 4 million dollar federal grant to
investigate the production of hydrogen from coal.
They plan on mixing coal with steam, air, and oxygen
under high temperatures and pressure to produce
hydrogen and carbon monoxide ("Ohio University
aims," 2003). But this too would generate greenhouse
gases and is a long way off from producing results.

The next likely source of hydrogen is to
produce it directly from water using a device
called an electrolyzer. Wald explains that the
electrolyzer sends an electrical current through
water to break down the water molecule into
hydrogen and oxygen atoms. Creating hydrogen
through electrolysis sounds like a good idea
because the only waste product emitted into the
atmosphere is oxygen, and there is nothing harmful
about oxygen. But the hazardous environmental
impact is not in the electrolysis reaction, but in
the need to generate electricity to run the

electrolyzer. If the electricity to run the electrolyzer came from the current electrical grid, which gets half its energy from burning coal, the carbon dioxide emissions for a fuel cell car would be 436 grams per mile—17% worse than the current emissions for gasoline powered cars (Wald). One way to avoid these emissions would be to run the electrolyzer with wind-generated or nuclear-powered electricity. But wind power would be able to produce only a small fraction of what would be needed for large-scale use of hydrogen as fuel, and nuclear power brings with it a whole new set of problems including disposal of nuclear waste.

Although there seem to be various methods of producing hydrogen, the current sources being considered do not fulfill the claim that hydrogen fuel cell technology will end the use of fossil fuels or eliminate greenhouse gases. The problem is not with the fuel cells themselves but with the processes needed to produce hydrogen fuel. I am not arguing that research and development should be abandoned, and I hope some day that the hydrogen economy will take off. But what I have discovered in my research is that hydrogen power is not as clean and green as I thought.

Hydrogen Fuel-Cell Cars   9

References

California. Executive Department. (2004, April
    20). Executive order S-7-04. Retrieved May
    24, 2004, from http://www.its.ucdavis.edu/
    hydrogenhighway/Executive-Order.pdf

CNN. (2004). The issues/George Bush. *CNN.com*.
    Retrieved May 23, 2004 from http://www.cnn.com/
    ELECTION/2004/special/president/issues/
    index.bush.html

General Motors. (2004, July 28). Who's driving
    the hydrogen economy? [Advertisement]. *New
    York Times*, A19.

Hydrogen Fuel Cell Institute. (2001). Retrieved May
    27, 2004, from http://www.h2fuelcells.org

Nice, K. (n.d.). How fuel cells work.
    Howstuffworks. Retrieved May 27, 2004, from
    http://science.howstuffworks.com/
    fuel-cell.htm

Ohio University aims to use coal to power fuel cells.
    (2003, November 24). *Fuel Cell Today*. Retrieved
    June 3, 2004, from http://www.fuelcelltoday.com/
    FuelCellToday/IndustryInformation/
    IndustryInformationExternal/NewsDisplayArticle/
    0%2C1602%2C3678%2C00.html

Hydrogen Fuel-Cell Cars   10

Roberts, P. (2004, March 6). *Los Angeles Times*.

Retrieved March 23, 2004, from

http://www.commondreams.org/views04/

0307-02.htm

Wald, M. L. (2003, November 12). Will hydrogen

clear the air? Maybe not, some say. *New York*

Times, C1.

Thinking Critically about "How Clean and Green Are Hydrogen Fuel-Cell Cars?"

1. Explain how Shannon King's essay uses the surprising-reversal strategy. What question does Shannon pose? What is the common or popular answer to her question? What is Shannon's surprising answer?
2. Whereas Cheryl Carp's essay "Behind Stone Walls" (pp. 184–185) depends on personal experience for its details, Shannon's essay depends on research data. How effective is Shannon in using the surprising-reversal strategy to create an effective research paper?
3. The line between information and persuasion is often blurred. Some persons might argue that Shannon's essay has a persuasive aim that argues against hydrogen fuel cell cars rather than an informative aim that simply presents surprising information about how hydrogen is produced. To what extent do you agree with our decision to classify Shannon's aim as primarily informative rather than persuasive? Can it be both?

Our final essay, by professional writer Jonathan Rauch, appeared in the July/August 2003 issue of *The Atlantic Monthly*. Although this article focuses largely on the immigrant experience of one Chinese family, Rauch's purpose is to contrast his surprising view of Washington, D.C., as a "post-racial America" with the commonly held view of our nation's capital as a "black urban core locked in uneasy truce with it rootless white suburbs."

Jonathan Rauch
Coming to America

1   The Au family, immigrants from Hong Kong, arrived at Washington's Reagan National Airport on a sticky night late last July. I will never forget the sight of them: parents bustling after the long flight, children—three girls and a boy, ranging in age from eight to thirteen—heaped sleepily atop sixteen suitcases, as if the whole bunch had tumbled off the baggage belt.

2   They settled into a little townhouse in Arlington, Virginia, two Aus per bedroom and two more in the basement: spacious, by Hong Kong standards. The place belongs to my partner, Michael, who is brother to Mrs. Au, uncle to the children, and sponsor, for immigration purposes, of the entire family. He had applied for green cards for the Aus more than ten years ago, when he became a citizen himself. When permission to immigrate finally came, the Aus, a middle-class family headed by a recently retired civil servant, seized the chance.

3   For newcomers America is full of footholds. The Aus, Christians, immediately found a Chinese church only a couple of miles from home. Every Sunday they attend services in Cantonese. If they want bok choy or fried dace or duck's blood, they can walk to an Asian grocery just down the block.

4   In Hong Kong—where, because of its history as a British colony, many people use English names—the girls were called Queenie, Amanda, and Cassandra, the boy Bryan. In America, Bryan has become Chi-hang. That is the name in the official records, so that is what his school calls him—and anyway, isn't it more interesting than boring old "Bryan"? Asked which he prefers, the boy says that in Hong Kong he liked Bryan and in America he likes Chi-hang. This seems to him a perfectly natural arrangement. Clearly, the melting pot has changed since my grandmother passed through Ellis Island, in 1910.

5   Still, the mysterious process known as Americanization carries on. In the public schools, the Au children struggle with English but steadily improve. True to stereotype, they are whizzes at math. Last September, when I asked Bryan, who is ten, what he thought of life in the United States, he exclaimed, "I like!" (the first English sentence I heard from him). His older

sister Amanda, a seventh-grader, was soon tying up the phone talking with her American friends.

6   When I moved to the northern-Virginia suburbs from central Washington, D.C., a couple of years ago, I expected to find Confederate flags and cured hams. Instead I found the Eden Center, where the flag that flies next to Old Glory is Vietnam's, and where you can have your pho with bible tripe and soft tendon. Eden Center is an all-Vietnamese shopping mall: Vietnamese restaurants, video stores, hair salons, travel agencies, jewelers, grocers, music shops, bakeries. Even the Muzak is Vietnamese. The place is packed every day, and not much English is heard there. For a long time, though, a red banner hung beneath its gate: "Soul and heart of the Vietnamese community always with the 9-11 tragedy."

7   The long-standing meta-narrative of Washington is that of a black urban core locked in uneasy truce with its rootless white suburbs. A 2001 study by the Brookings Institution's Center on Urban and Metropolitan Policy, however, contains surprising news for people who still see the city and its environs in those terms. "Unlike some other major immigrant destinations such as Miami or Los Angeles, where one or two immigrant groups tend to predominate," says the study, "Washington's flow is diverse." Nearly two hundred countries are represented, with the top ten spanning Central America (El Salvador), South America (Peru), Asia (Vietnam, China, South Korea), Africa (Ethiopia), the Middle East (Iran), Oceania (the Philippines), and the Subcontinent (India and Pakistan).

8   Moreover, each of the ten metropolitan Washington zip codes with the most new immigrants draws from more than a hundred countries. In other words, instead of settling into separate ethnic neighborhoods, as Italians and Irish and Jews and Chinese did a century ago, the new arrivals scatter. In yet other words, they integrate. They work beside native-born Americans, they live beside them, and they suffer beside them. The third victim of the Washington-area sniper last year was a taxi driver named Premkumar Walekar, originally from Pune, India. He was shot while pumping gas, the *Los Angeles Times* reported, "moments after buying a newspaper, a lottery ticket and a pack of gum."

9   Washington, for so long a lagging indicator of American social life—far behind edgy New York and buzzy L.A. and brazen Chicago and even upstart Atlanta and Houston—is now, of all things, a harbinger. Increasingly, the Washington area is the post-racial America that we have all been told to expect. A member of Congress who wonders what a genuinely multicultural country might look like need only rustle up taxi fare to Arlington and walk around. My immediate neighbors include a black-white couple, a Filipino psychiatrist, a Korean accountant, and two Indian families, whose kids' names I can't pronounce. I have never lived in a more neighborly neighborhood. If this is the future, it seems to work.

10   When spring finally sprang this year, I came home one Sunday afternoon to find our place aswarm with Aus, the four children bantering in

Cantonese with an occasional aside to me in shy English. Under Michael's direction this Chinese task force had descended on the yard to plant flowers. Thus does new growth take root in northern Virginia, rejuvenating the soil. This Independence Day will be the Au children's first in America. Through their eyes I will see the fireworks afresh.

Thinking Critically about "Coming to America"

1. Rauch begins his article with a long anecdote about the Au family. What is the function of this anecdote within the whole article? At what point in the article do you begin to see where Rauch is going—that is, where you begin to understand his purpose and thesis?
2. What is Rauch's point in explaining that the Au son likes to be called "Chi-hang" in America but "Bryan" in Hong Kong?
3. Where in this article does Rauch explain the popular or common view of Washington, D.C.? What is that common view?
4. What is the new, surprising view of Washington, D.C., that Rauch presents? Besides the personal example of the Au family, what other data does Rauch use to support his surprising view?
5. If you had to pick out one sentence from the article as its thesis statement, what would that sentence be? Why does Rauch locate the sentence where he does?

Composing Your Essay—Option A: Informative Report

The assignment for Option A requires you to gather your own information to answer an empirical question about an observable phenomenon or about public attitudes or behaviors. For example, you might observe the number of persons who buy impulse items at a grocery checkout line or who jaywalk at a certain intersection. Or you might investigate students' usage patterns or levels of satisfaction with some aspect of student services on your campus (computer labs, security escorting service, recreational facilities, study skills workshops) or the way students spend their time during a typical week (studying, watching television, playing videogames, doing recreational sports, working).

Generating and Exploring Ideas

The key to this assignment is to ask an empirical question that you can answer through observation, interviews, or a questionnaire.

Observation

One approach is to ask a question that can be answered through observation. For example, a student wanting to know how often people violated a "Do Not Walk on the Grass" sign on her campus observed a posted lawn for one week during mornings between classes and counted persons who took a shortcut across the grass rather than follow the sidewalks. Another student hypothesized that upscale shoppers at a local Whole Foods store would drive more fuel-efficient cars than shoppers at a Wal-Mart store several miles away. The student categorized cars by size ranging from large pickups or SUVs to subcompacts. Then on several different occasions he counted the number of cars in each category at the parking lots of each store.

Interviews

Interviews can range from formal sessions lasting thirty or more minutes to informal interviews in which the researcher hopes only for brief answers to a few key questions. The researcher might even conduct an interview over the telephone, without a face-to-face meeting. As an example of informal interviews, consider the hypothetical case of a student investigating why customers at a local grocery store choose to buy or not buy organic vegetables. This student researcher might ask persons buying vegetables if they would be willing to be briefly interviewed. In a more formal setting, a student might arrange to interview several professors about how they graded students on "class participation" or about the writing process they used for their own research.

Questionnaires

Another powerful way to gather information is to construct a brief questionnaire and then give it to a random sample of the population you wish to investigate. In constructing a questionnaire, your goal is to elicit responses that are directly related to your research question and that will give you the data you need to answer it. The construction of a questionnaire—both its wording and its arrangement on the page—is crucial to its success. As you design your questionnaire, imagine respondents with only limited patience and time. Keep your questionnaire clear, easy to complete, and as short as possible, taking care to avoid ambiguous sentences. Proofread it carefully, and pilot it on a few volunteer respondents so that you can eliminate confusing spots. Figure 8.1 (which imagines a student investigating alcohol usage on her campus) gives some specific examples of types of questions often found on questionnaires.

Shaping and Drafting

An informative report for a popular audience typically follows the structure of a scientific report (which has a four-part sequence of "Introduction," "Method," "Findings," and "Discussion") except that its style is more informal. You will note

FIGURE 8.1   Types of Questions Used in Questionnaires

Fixed-choice question
Compared to other campuses with which you are familiar, this campus's use of alcohol is (mark one):
—— greater than other campuses'
—— less than other campuses'
—— about the same as other campuses'

Open-ended question
How would you say alcohol use on this campus compares to other campuses?
Comment: Fixed-choice questions are easier to tabulate and report statistically; open-ended questions can yield a wider variety of insights but are impractical for large numbers of respondents.

Question with operationally defined rather than undefined term
Undefined term: Think back over the last two weeks. How many times did you engage in binge drinking?
Operationally defined term: Think back over the last two weeks. How many times have you had four or more drinks in a row?
Comment: An "operational definition" states empirically measurable criteria for a term. In the first version of the question, the term "binge drinking" might mean different things to different persons. Moreover, respondents are apt to deny being binge drinkers given that it is an unflattering categorization. In the revised question, the term "binge drinking" is replaced with an observable and measurable behavior; respondents are more apt to give an honest response.

Category question
What is your current class standing?
—— freshman
—— sophomore
—— junior
—— senior
—— other (please specify)
Comment: In category questions, it is often helpful to have an "Other" category for respondents who do not fit neatly into any of the other categories.

Scaled-answer question
This campus has a serious drinking problem (circle one):

strongly agree	agree	neither agree nor disagree	disagree	strongly disagree
5	4	3	2	1

How much drinking goes on in your dormitory on Friday or Saturday nights?

a lot	some	not much	none

Comment: Although scaled-answer questions are easy to tabulate and are widely used, the data can be skewed by the subjective definitions of each respondent (one person's "a lot" may be another person's "not much").

that Kerri Ann Matsumoto's essay on the cost of organic food follows this structure. It poses a research question (How much extra does it cost to buy organic food over non-organic food?); explains her process or method for investigating the question (she investigated the price for organic and nonorganic vegetables and chicken to determine the cost of organic versus nonorganic chicken stir-fry for a family of four); presents her findings in both words and graphics (organic foods cost more); and suggests the significance of her research (the benefits of organic foods versus the advantages of spending the extra money in other ways).

If your instructor asks you to format your paper to look like a magazine article, you will get some practice in using your word processing program to form columns and import graphics. It is also possible to format the paper using scissors and paste.

Revising

As you revise, make sure that your graphics (if you used them) and your words tell the same story and reinforce each other. As you edit, try to achieve a popular "easy reading" voice appropriate for a magazine article. When you have a near final draft, exchange it with a classmate for a peer review following the guidelines on pages 206–208.

Composing Your Essay—Option B: Informative Writing Using Surprising Reversal

The Option B assignment asks for an informative essay that surprises the reader with new information. Your new information can come either from your own personal experience (as Cheryl Carp uses her personal experience to reverse the common view of prison inmates) or from research (as Shannon King uses her research on fuel cells to complicate, if not reverse, the common view that fuel cell technology will produce pollution-free energy).

As you write your essay, keep in mind that *surprise* is a relative term based on the relationship between you and your intended audience. You don't have to surprise everyone in the world, just those who hold a mistaken or narrow view of your topic. With its emphasis on enlarging your audience's view through something unexpected or surprising, the Option B assignment teaches you to imagine an audience as you consider possible topics. The key for this task is to imagine an audience less informed about your topic than you are. Suppose, as an illustration, that you have just completed an introductory economics course. You are less informed about economics than your professor, but more informed about economics than persons who have never had an econ class. You might therefore write a surprising-reversal paper to the less informed audience:

> The average airplane traveler thinks that the widely varying ticket pricing for the same flight is chaotic and silly, but I can show how this pricing scheme makes per-

fect sense economically. [written to the "average airplane traveler," who hasn't taken an economics course]

This paper would be surprising to your intended audience, but not to the economics professor. From a different perspective, however, you could also write about economics to your professor because you might know more than your professor about, say, how students struggle with some concepts:

> Many economics professors assume that students can easily learn the concept of "elasticity of demand," but I can show why this concept was particularly confusing for me and my classmates. [written to economics professors who aren't aware of student difficulties with particular concepts]

Additionally, your surprising view doesn't necessarily have to be diametrically opposed to the common view. Perhaps you think the common view is *incomplete* or *insufficient* rather than *dead wrong*. Instead of saying, "View X is wrong, whereas my view, Y, is correct," you can say, "View X is correct and good as far as it goes, but my view, Y, adds a new perspective." In other words, you can also create surprise by going a step beyond the common view to show readers something new.

Generating and Exploring Ideas

Your goal for the Option B assignment is to find a topic where you possess knowledge or experience that will give your targeted audience a new perspective. As you search for a subject, the key is to consider both a topic (something that you care about and that you have quite a bit of information about through personal experience or recent reading and research) and an audience (persons who have a mistaken or overly narrow view of your topic because they lack the information that you can provide).

If you do the Option B assignment as a mini-research project, start by posing a research question. As you begin doing initial research on your topic area, you will soon know more about your topic than most members of the general public. Ask yourself, "What has surprised me about my research so far? What have I learned that I didn't know before?" Your answers to these questions can suggest possible approaches to your paper. Shannon King, for example, began her research believing that fuel cell technology produced totally pollution-free energy. She didn't realize that one needed to burn fossil fuels in order to produce the hydrogen. This initial surprise shaped her paper. She decided that if this information surprised her, it should surprise others also.

What follows are two exercises you can try to generate ideas for your paper.

Small-Group Task to Generate Ideas
Form small groups. Assign a group recorder to make a two-column list, with the left column titled "Mistaken or Narrow View of X" and the right column titled "Groupmate's Surprising View." Brainstorm ideas for surprising-reversal essay topics until every group member has generated at least one entry for the right-hand column. Here is a sample list entry:

Mistaken or Narrow View of X	Groupmate's Surprising View
Football offensive lineman is a no-brain, repetitive job requiring size, strength, and only enough brains and athletic ability to push people out of the way.	Jeff can show that being an offensive lineman is an interesting job that requires mental smarts as well as size, strength, and athletic ability.

To help stimulate ideas, you might consider topic areas such as the following:

- *People:* computer programmers, homeless people, cheerleaders, skateboarders, gang members, priests or rabbis, feminists, house-spouses, mentally ill or developmentally disabled persons.
- *Activities:* washing dishes, climbing mountains, wrestling, modeling, gardening, living with a chronic disease or disability, owning a certain breed of dog, riding a subway at night, entering a dangerous part of a city.
- *Places:* particular neighborhoods, particular buildings or parts of buildings, local attractions, junkyards, places of entertainment, summer camps.
- *Other similar categories:* groups, animals and plants, and so forth; the list is endless.

Next, go around the room, sharing with the entire class the topics you have generated. Remember that you are not yet committed to writing about any of these topics.

Here are some examples from recent students:

A common misconception about Native Americans is that they lived in simple harmony with the earth, but my research reveals that they often "controlled" nature by setting fire to forests to make farming easier or to improve hunting.

To the average person, pawnshops are disreputable places, but my experience shows that pawnshops can be honest, wholesome businesses that perform a valuable social service.

Most of my straight friends think of the film *Frankenstein* as a monster movie about science gone amuck, but to the gay community it holds a special and quite different meaning.

Individual Task to Generate Ideas

Here are two templates that can help you generate ideas by asking you to think specifically about differences in knowledge levels between you and various audiences. Try this template:

I know more about X than [specific person or persons]

Try the exercise first by naming topics that interest you and then thinking of less informed audiences:

I know more about cars/computer games/the energy crisis than [specific persons]

Then try the exercise by naming specific audiences and then thinking of topics about which you know more than they:

I know more about X than [my mother/the college registrar/students who don't commute/my boss at work]

Shaping and Drafting

The surprising-reversal pattern requires two main writing moves: an exposition of the common or expected answers to a question, and the development of your own surprising answer to that question. In addition, your essay needs an introduction that presents the question to be addressed and a separate conclusion that finishes it off.

As a way of helping you generate ideas, we offer the following five questions. Questions 1, 2, and 4 are planning questions that will help you create broad point sentences to form your essay's skeletal framework. These questions call for one-sentence generalizations. Questions 3 and 5 are freewriting prompts to help you generate supporting details. For these questions, freewrite rapidly, either on paper or at your computer. Following each question, we speculate what Carp, King, and Rauch might have written if they had used the same questions to help them get started on their essays.

1. ***What question does your essay address?*** (Carp might have asked, "What is it like to visit inmates in a maximum-security prison?" King might have asked, "Are hydrogen fuel cell automobiles really clean and green?" Rauch might have asked, "What is Washington, D.C., really like in terms of ethnic diversity?")

2. ***What is the common, expected, or popular answer to this question held by your imagined audience?*** (Carp might have said, "Visiting these prisons will be scary because prisoners are sex-starved, dangerous people." King might have said, "Most people believe that hydrogen fuel cell cars are totally pollution free." Rauch might have said, "Most people believe that Washington, D.C., is like many other American cities with a black urban core surrounded by white suburbs.")

3. ***What examples and details support your audience's view?*** Expand on these views by developing them with supporting examples and details. (Carp might have brainstormed details about concealed razor blades, drugs, prison violence, the fear of her friends, and so on. King might have noted her research examples praising fuel cell technology such as the General Motors advertisement or California Governor Arnold Schwarzenegger's desire to build hydrogen fuel stations across the state. Rauch might have brainstormed his experiences with other American cities. His essay provides the least development for the common view, which he encapsulates in his academic-sounding phrase "the long-standing meta-narrative of Washington.")

4. ***What is your own surprising view?*** (Carp might have answered, "Visiting the prison is uplifting because prisoners can be kind, creative, and generous." King might have said, "Although hydrogen fuel cell cars are pollution free, getting the hydrogen in the first place requires burning fossil fuels." Rauch might have said, "Many suburbs of Washington, D.C., have hundreds of different ethnic groups all intermixed together with native-born Americans.")

5. ***What examples and details support this view? Why do you hold this view? Why should a reader believe you?*** Writing rapidly, spell out the evidence that supports your point. (Carp would have done a freewrite on all the

experiences she had that changed her views about prisoners. Later she would have selected the most powerful ones and refined them for her readers. King would have done a freewrite about her research discoveries that hydrogen has to be recovered from carbon-based fossils or from electrolysis of water—all of which mean continued use of pollution-causing fossil fuels. Rauch would have done a freewrite on his observation of the Au family, his experiences living in a Washington, D.C., suburb, and his memory of the 2001 study done by the Brookings Institute.)

After you finish exploring your responses to these five trigger questions, you will be well on your way to composing a first draft of your Option B essay. Now, finish writing your draft fairly rapidly without worrying about perfection.

Revising

Once you have your first draft on paper, the goal is to make it work better, first for yourself and then for your readers. If you discovered ideas as you wrote, you may need to do some major restructuring. Check to see that the question you are addressing is clear. Do you state it directly, as do Carp and King, or simply imply it, as does Rauch? Make sure that you distinguish between your audience's common view and your own surprising view. Do you put your meanings up front, with point sentences at the head of each section and near the beginning of every paragraph? Carp's and King's essays are more closed form than is Rauch's essay, but all three clearly contrast a surprising view with a common view.

We conclude this chapter with peer review guidelines that sum up the features to look for in your essay and remind you of the criteria your instructor will use in evaluating your work.

GUIDELINES FOR PEER REVIEWS

Instructions for peer reviews are provided in Chapter 11 (pp. 293–294).

For the Writer
Prepare two or three questions you would like your peer reviewer to address while responding to your draft. The questions can focus on some aspect of your draft that you are uncertain about, on one or more sections where you particularly seek help or advice, on some feature that you particularly like about your draft, or on some part you especially wrestled with. Write out your questions and give them to your peer reviewer along with your draft.

For the Reviewer

   I. Read the draft at a normal reading speed from beginning to end. As you read, do the following:

A. Place a wavy line in the margin next to any passages that you find confusing, that contain something that doesn't seem to fit, or that otherwise slow down your reading.

B. Place a "Good!" in the margin next to any passages where you think the writing is particularly strong or interesting.

II. Read the draft again slowly and answer the following questions by writing down brief explanations for your answers.

A. Option A—Short Informative Report

1. Identify on the draft where the writer does each of the following: (a) explains the problem or question to be addressed; (b) explains the process for gathering information; (c) reports the findings; and (d) suggests the significance of the findings.

2. Is the draft written in a popular easy-reading style? Is the draft clear and easy to follow? Is the draft interesting? How might the writer improve the style, clarity, or interest level of the draft?

3. If the draft includes visual graphics, are they effective? Do the words and the visuals tell the same story? Are the visuals properly titled and labeled? How might the use of visuals be improved?

4. If the instructor asks writers to "desktop publish" their papers to look like popular magazine articles, is the document design effective? Are the graphics readable? How might the visual design of the paper be improved?

B. Option B—Informative Writing with Surprising Reversal

1. Do the title and introduction hook your interest? If not, how might the title and introduction be improved?

2. Where does the writer pose the question that the paper will address? Could this section of the paper be made clearer or more effective?

3. Where does the writer explain the common or popular view of the topic? Do you agree that this is the common view? How does the writer develop or support this view? What additional supporting examples, illustrations, or details might make the common view more vivid or compelling?

4. What is the writer's surprising view? Were you surprised? Identify the writer's thesis statement. Where does the writer locate the thesis? Would it be more effective to locate it elsewhere?

5. What details does the writer use to develop the surprising view? What additional supporting examples, illustrations, or details might help make the surprising view more vivid and compelling?

6. How might the writer improve the overall structure and clarity of this draft?

III. Rhetorical considerations

A. *Purpose, audience,* and *genre:* To what extent does the tone, style, and document design of the draft fit the assigned rhetorical context? How does the draft meet the demands of its genre and the needs of its audience while fulfilling the writer's purpose?

B. *Logos, ethos,* and *pathos:* How convincing or effective is the logical or conceptual part of this draft? What strategies does the writer use to construct a persona that inspires the reader's trust or confidence? How does the writer connect this study to the interests and values of the audience?

IV. Sum up what you see as the chief strengths and problem areas of this draft:
   A. Strengths
   B. Problem areas

V. Read the draft one more time. Place a check mark in the margin wherever you notice problems in grammar, spelling, or mechanics (one check mark per problem).

Analyzing Images

About Analyzing Images

This chapter asks you to analyze images in order to understand their persuasive power—a skill often called "visual literacy." By *visual literacy*, we mean your awareness of the importance of visual communication and your ability to interpret or make meaning out of images and graphics (photos, pictures, illustrations, icons, charts, graphs, and other visual displays of data). In this chapter, we seek to enhance your visual literacy by focusing on the way that images influence our conceptual and emotional understanding of a phenomenon and the way that they validate, reveal, and construct the world.

As you may recall from Chapter 3, when you write to analyze and synthesize, you apply your own critical thinking to a puzzling object or to puzzling data and offer your own new ideas to a conversation. Your goal is to raise interesting questions about the object or data being analyzed—questions that perhaps your reader hasn't thought to ask—and then to provide tentative answers to those questions, supported by points and particulars derived from your own close examination of the object or data. The word *analysis* derives from a Greek word meaning "to dissolve, loosen, undo." Metaphorically, analysis means to divide or dissolve the whole into its constituent parts, to examine these parts carefully, to look at the relationships among them, and then to use this understanding of the parts to better understand the whole—how it functions, what it means. Synonyms for writing to analyze might be *writing to interpret, clarify,* or *explain.* In this chapter, the objects being analyzed are photographs or other images as they appear in a rhetorical context—for example, as part of a news story, a television documentary, a public relations brochure, or an advertisement.

See Table 3.1, pp. 49–50 for an explanation of the aims of writing.

To appreciate the cultural importance of images, consider how British cultural critic John Berger, in his book *About Looking,* sketches the pervasive use of photographs shortly after the invention of the camera.

> The camera was invented by Fox Talbot in 1839. Within a mere 30 years of its invention as a gadget for an elite, photography was being used for police filing, war reporting, military reconnaissance, pornography, encyclopedic documentation, family albums, postcards, anthropological records (often, as with the Indians in the United States, accompanied by genocide), sentimental moralizing, inquisitive probing (the wrongly named "candid camera"), aesthetic effects, news reporting and formal portraiture. The speed with which the possible uses of photography were seized upon is surely an indication of photography's profound, central applicability to industrial capitalism.

One of photography's purposes—as Berger hints—is to create images that "have designs on" us, that urge us to believe ideas, buy things, go places, or otherwise alter our views or behaviors. Information brochures use carefully selected photographs to enhance a product's image (consider how the photographs in your college's catalog or view book have been selected); news photographs editorialize their content (during the Vietnam War a newspaper photograph of a naked Vietnamese child running screaming toward the photographer while a napalm bomb explodes behind her turned many Americans against the war; and recently, the images of weeping Iraqi mothers and houses reduced to rubble shown in newspapers and documentary films have raised questions about U.S. tactics in Iraq); social issue posters urge us to protest capital punishment or contribute money to save the salmon or sponsor a child in a third world country; and advertisements urge us not only to buy a certain product but to be a certain kind of person with certain values.

Visual literacy is so important in our world that we have already introduced it elsewhere in this text. In Chapter 4, we showed how stakeholders in the current controversy over medical care enlist competing images of doctors such as Norman Rockwell's image of the family doctor who makes house calls versus images of physicians in lab coats surrounded by high technology equipment. In Chapter 5, we showed how specially selected photographs of the Arctic National Wildlife Refuge (ANWR) could be used to advance arguments for or against opening the ANWR to oil exploration (pp. 96–98). And for the Part Openers in this text, we have chosen examples of striking visual texts that grew out of particular rhetorical contexts and were created to have a specific rhetorical effect.

For the images in this chapter, we have selected those directly related to Berger's assertion that photographs often have a "profound, central applicability to industrial capitalism." We look specifically at how photographs and other images are used in "corporate image" advertisements and in product advertisements. We focus on advertisements because they are a wonderful source of images for analysis and because they raise important questions about how our own lives intersect with the processes of a free market economy. In addition to enhancing your visual literacy, studying advertising has other values as well. We suggest four benefits you will gain from your study of advertisements:

- You will appreciate more fully the fun, pleasure, and creativity of advertisements.
- You will become a more savvy consumer, better able to critique ads and make wise buying decisions.
- You will learn rhetorical strategies that you can use in your own career and civic life. (Your understanding of the relationship between words and images in advertising can be readily transferred to other rhetorical settings— for example, when you design a brochure or Web site or write any kind of document that incorporates images and depends on document design.)
- You will become a more perceptive cultural critic who understands how ads both convey and help construct our cultural values, our self-image, our sense of what is normal or ideal, and our ideas about gender, race, and class. A study of advertisements can raise viewers' consciousness to counter prejudice, injustice, and discrimination.

Exploring Image Analysis

To introduce you to the concept of image analysis, we provide two exercises to stimulate your thinking and discussion.

Task 1: Working on your own, freewrite your responses to the following questions:

1. Can you recall a time when a magazine or TV advertisement directly influenced you to buy a product? Describe the occasion and try to recall the specifics of how the ad influenced you.
2. Have the images in a magazine or TV advertisement ever caused you to desire a certain experience or style of life? For example, an ad might not have influenced you to buy a particular product, but it may have sparked a desire to ride a horse through a pounding surf, have a romantic encounter in a European café, or live in a certain kind of house or apartment. To what extent have the images of advertising shaped any of your values, longings, or desires?

In small groups or as a whole class, share your freewrites. From the ensuing discussion, create a list of specific ways in which magazine or TV advertisements have been successful in persuading members of your class to buy a product or to desire certain experiences or lifestyles.

Task 2: For further exploration, we invite you to imagine that you are an advertising consultant hired by the United States Army. Your mission is to create an advertisement recruiting women. Working in small groups, brainstorm ideas for the design of an advertisement that would cause women to consider enlisting in the Army. What photograph or drawing might be placed on your ad? What would the words say? Each group should propose one or two possible design ideas and explain why you think they might appeal to women.

Then look closely at an actual advertisement designed for this purpose. (See the Part Opener on page 93.) As a class, analyze this advertisement by responding to the following questions:

1. To what extent do you think this is an effective ad? Why or why not?
2. Why do you think the ad designers aimed the ad at fathers as well as daughters instead of directly at women? Why did the ad designers write the verbal part of the ad focusing on respect, honor, and courage rather than, say, on adventure or career?
3. Try playing the "what if they changed . . . ?" game. Try looking at specific details of the ad and asking how the effect of the ad would be different if the ad designers had made slight changes. For example:
   a. What if the girl in the picture were blonde rather than brunette? (Why did the ad designers decide against a blonde?)
   b. What if her hair style, makeup, or clothing were different in some way?
   c. What if the father were dressed differently—say wearing a suit—or had a different physical appearance—say the rugged, handsome type? Why is he wearing a plaid flannel shirt? Why is he clean-shaven rather than bearded?

How would the impact be different if the father and daughter were black or Asian rather than white?

d. Why did they frame the father and daughter in a window and pose them as they did with the daughter in front looking out the window instead of toward her father? How would the impact be different if the father and daughter were walking in the woods, sitting beside a tennis court, or going for a drive?

e. What if they had used a mother and daughter instead of a father and daughter?

4. Finally, do you think questions like these are worth asking? Why or why not? Do you think ad designers make choices as consciously and purposefully as we have suggested?

WRITING PROJECT

Choose two print advertisements—or use the two sport-utility ads shown in the For Writing and Discussion exercise on pages 217–218—that sell the same kind of product but appeal to different audiences (for example, a car advertisement aimed at men and one aimed at women; a cigarette ad aimed at upper-middle-class consumers and one aimed at working-class consumers; a clothing ad from *The New Yorker* and one from *Rolling Stone*). Describe the ads in detail so that an audience can easily visualize them without actually seeing them. Analyze the advertisements and explain how each appeals to its target audience. To what values does each ad appeal? How is each ad constructed to appeal to those values? In addition to analyzing the rhetorical appeals made by each ad, you may also wish to evaluate or criticize the ads, commenting on the images of our culture that they convey.

This writing assignment asks you to analyze how advertisers use words and images together to appeal to different audiences. By comparing ads for the same product targeted at different demographic groups, you learn how every aspect of an ad is chosen for an audience-specific rhetorical effect. You will discover, for example, that advertisers often vary their ads for female versus male audiences and that certain products or services are targeted at a specific socioeconomic class. Similarly, advertisers often vary their appeals to reach African-American, Hispanic, or Asian markets. This assignment asks you to explain how these appeals are targeted and created.

As a variation of this assignment, your instructor might ask you to analyze two photographs of a politician from magazines with different political biases; two news photographs from articles addressing the same story from different angles of vision; the images on the home pages of two Web sites presenting different perspectives on heated topics such as global warming, medical research using animals, and environmental protection; or two advocacy ads for corporations or political causes that represent opposing views. Although these images, articles, and Web sites are not selling you a product per se, they are "selling" you a viewpoint on an issue, and thus this chapter's explanations of how to analyze camera techniques and the use of details, props, and the posing of human figures in photographs can also be applied to visual images other than commercial advertisements.

Understanding Image Analysis

Before we turn directly to advertising, let's look at some strategies you can use to analyze any image intended to have a specific rhetorical effect.

How Images Create a Rhetorical Effect

An image can be said to have a rhetorical effect whenever it moves us emotionally or intellectually. We might identify with the image or be repelled by it; the image might evoke our sympathies, trigger our fears, or call forth a web of interconnected ideas, memories, and associations. When the image is a photograph, its rhetorical effect derives from both the camera techniques that produced it and the composition of the image itself. Let's look at each in turn.

Analyzing Camera Techniques

The rhetorical effect of a photographic image often derives from skillful use of the camera and from the way the film is developed or the digital image is manipulated.* To analyze a photograph, begin by considering the photographer's choices about the camera's relationship to the subject:

- *Distance of camera from subject:* Note whether the photograph is a close-up, medium shot, or long shot. Close-ups tend to increase the intensity of the photograph and suggest the importance of the subject; long shots tend to blend the subject into the environment.
- *Orientation of the image and camera angle:* Note whether the camera is positioned in front of or behind the subject; note also whether the camera is positioned below the subject, looking up (a low-angle shot), or above the subject, looking down (a high-angle shot). Front-view shots tend to emphasize the persons being photographed; rear-view shots often emphasize the scene or setting. A low-angle camera tends to grant superiority, status, and power to the subject, while a high-angle camera can comically reduce the subject to childlike status. A level angle tends to imply equality.
- *Eye gaze:* Note which persons in the photograph, if any, gaze directly at the camera or look away. Looking directly at the camera implies power; looking away can imply deference or shyness.

*Our ideas in this section are indebted to Paul Messaris, *Visual Persuasion: The Role of Images in Advertising* (Thousand Oaks, CA: Sage, 1997).

- *Point of view:* Note whether the photographer strives for an "objective effect," in which the camera stands outside the scene and observes it, or a "subjective effect," in which the camera seems to be the eyes of someone inside the scene. Subjective shots tend to involve the viewer as an actor in the scene.

In addition, photographers often use other highly artistic film or digital techniques: making parts of an image crisp and in focus and others slightly blurred; using camera filters for special effects; distorting or merging images (a city that blends into a desert; a woman who blends into a tree); and creating visual parodies (a Greek statue wearing jeans).

There are also various ways that a photographic image can be manipulated or falsified. Be aware of the following devices used to create visual deception: staging images (scenes that appear to be documentaries but are really staged); altering images (for example, airbrushing, reshaping body parts, or constructing a composite image such as putting the head of one person on the body of another); selecting images or parts of images (such as cropping photographs so that only parts of the body or only parts of a scene are shown); and mislabeling (putting a caption on a photograph that misrepresents what it actually is).

For Writing and Discussion

Look at three photographic images of bears: Figure 5.1 (Chapter 5, p. 96), Figure 5.2 (Chapter 5, p. 97), and the Nikon camera advertisement (p. 215). Then, working in small groups or as a whole class, analyze the camera techniques of each photograph, and explain how these techniques are rhetorically effective for the purpose of the message to which each is attached.

Analyzing the Compositional Features of the Image

In addition to analyzing camera and film or digital techniques, you need to analyze the compositional features of the photograph's subject. When photographs are used in ads, every detail down to the props in the photograph or the placement of a model's hands are consciously chosen.

1. ***Examine the settings, furnishings, and props.***
   a. List all furnishings and props. If the photograph pictures a room, look carefully at such details as the kind and color of the rug; the subject matter of the paintings on the walls; furniture styles; objects on tables; and the general arrangement of the room. (Is it neat and tidy, or does it have a lived-in look? Is it formal or casual?) If the photograph is outdoors, observe the exact features of the landscape. (Why a mountain rather than a meadow? Why a robin rather than a crow or pigeon?)
   b. What social meanings are attached to the objects you listed? In a den, for example, duck decoys and fishing rods create a different emotional effect than computers and fax machines do. The choice of a breed of dog can signal differences in values, social class, or lifestyle—a Labrador retriever ver-

FIGURE 9.1 Nikon Ad

The camera for those who look at this picture and think, "Gosh, how'd they open up the shadows without blowing out the highlights?"

When staring into the mouth of a 10 ft. grizzly bear, you tend to think about life. Limbs. And how handy legs are. Not the fill-flash ratio needed to expose teeth about to rip your leg off.

Nikon created the N90 specifically for complicated situations like this. When you have no time to think. A brown bear on brown earth, about to mangle a brown shoe. So instead of overexposing this picture like other cameras might, the N90™ works for you, properly analyzing the situation and delivering an accurate exposure.

Here's how it does it. The 3D Matrix Meter divides the scene into eight segments. It measures the brightness in each one of the segments and then compares them for contrast. D-type lenses incorporate the subject's distance which allows the N90 to calculate the proper ambient light exposure.

The SB-25 Speedlight fires a rapid series of imperceptible pre-flashes to determine the bear's reflectance. And then provides the precise amount of fill-flash needed to lighten the bear's dark brown fur, without overexposing his slightly yellow teeth.

The N90 can give you near-perfect exposures when other cameras would be fooled. Or, for that matter, eaten.

Professionals trust the N90. So you can too. Because it works just as well on children eating ice cream as it does on bears eating people.

The N90 System

Nikon.
We take the world's greatest pictures.®

See the Nikon N90 at authorized dealers where you see this symbol. Nikon Data Link System available Winter '93. For more on our MasterCard, call 1-800-NIKON-35.

sus a groomed poodle; an English sheepdog versus a generic mutt. Even choice of flowers can have symbolic significance: A single rose connotes romance or elegance, a bouquet of daisies suggests freshness, and a hanging fuchsia suggests earthy naturalness.

2. ***Consider the characters, roles, and actions.***
   a. Create the story behind the image. Who are these people in the photograph? Why are they here? What are they doing? In advertisements, models can be either *instrumental,* in which case they are acting out real-life

roles, or *decorative,* in which case they are eye candy. A female model working on a car engine in grungy mechanics clothes would be instrumental; a female model in a bikini draped over the hood would be decorative.

b. Note every detail about how models are posed, clothed, and accessorized. Note facial expressions, eye contact, gestures, activities, posed relationships among actors and among actors and objects, and relative sizes. (Who is looking at whom? Who is above or below whom? Who or what is in the foreground or background?) Pay special attention to hairstyles because popular culture endows hair with great significance.

c. Ask what social roles are being played and what values appealed to. Are the gender roles traditional or nontraditional? Are the relationships romantic, erotic, friendly, formal, uncertain? What are the power relationships among characters?

3. ***Analyze the rhetorical context of the image.***

a. Images are always encountered in a rhetorical context: They accompany a news story, are part of a poster or Web site, or are used in an advertisement. Consider how the image functions within that context and how it contributes to the rhetorical effect of the whole to which it is a part.

b. In advertisements, consider carefully the relationship between the image and the words in the copy. The words in advertisements are chosen with the same care as the details in the image. Pay special attention to the document design of the copy, the style of the language, and the connotations, double entendres, and puns. Also note the kind of product information that is included or excluded from the ad.

See Chapter 3, pp. 62–68, for a discussion of document design.

For Writing and Discussion

This exercise asks you to consider both the camera and film techniques and the compositional features of two Jeep advertisements. Figure 9.2 shows an ad for Jeep Grand Cherokee that appeared in the March 2004 edition of *Brio,* an upscale, elegant, glamorous Japanese magazine. Figure 9.3 shows an ad for the Jeep Wrangler from the May 2004 edition of *Spin,* an American magazine about the contemporary rock music scene. An examination of these ads will help you see how an automobile company with a global reputation targets very different audiences through different publications.

Working individually or in groups, study these ads and answer the following questions:

1. Analysis of the composition of the ads

a. Describe the Jeep Grand Cherokee ad. In the full-size version of this ad, two shadowy figures are visible—the driver and the woman looking down on the Jeep from the lighted window high up in the building. How would you describe the building and the strange effect with water on the right side of the picture? Is the water coming from a fountain, or is the effect the result of composite trick photography? Then describe the Jeep Wrangler ad. Describe the setting and note the contents of the hiker's "backpack."

FIGURE 9.2 Jeep Grand Cherokee Ad

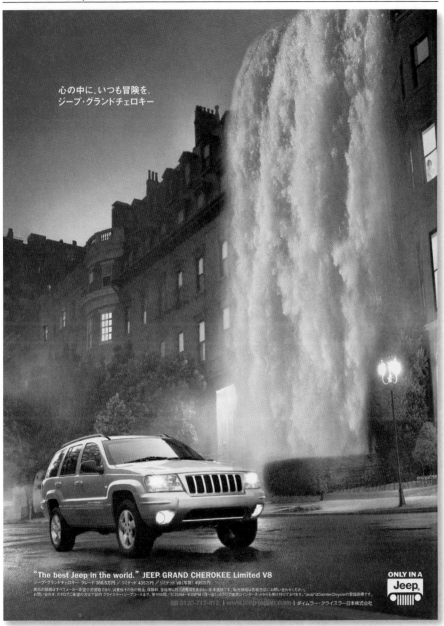

b. How is each ad composed? Note how the vehicle is positioned with regard to the viewer; also note the vehicle's size in relation to the setting. What is the relative importance of image versus verbal text in these ads?

(*continued*)

FIGURE 9.3 Jeep Wrangler Ad

c. What story does each ad tell? What roles do persons and vehicle play in each story? (In the Japanese ad, the words in the upper left part of the ad can be translated as "Always have adventure in your heart. Jeep Grand Cherokee.")

2. Analysis of the appeal of the ads
   a. To what values does each ad appeal?
   b. What connections do you see between the images and appeals of the ads and the nationality, age, class, and economic status of the audiences? How do these ads illustrate the concept of targeting different audiences?
   c. How do the features of each ad create their appeals? How would you explain the function of the setting in the Grand Cherokee ad, particularly the blended effect of an elegant building in a courtyard and an apparent waterfall? What effect is created by the woman looking down on the driver from a lighted window? Why is she behind the waterfall? Why is it a night scene rather than a day scene? In the Jeep Wrangler ad, why did the ad designers opt for humor? Why do they have the hiker carrying all the "stuff" rather than showing it packed in the Wrangler? Why is the setting a dry desert rather than a mountaintop or beach?
3. Sport-utility vehicles are at the center of the public controversy over global warming, pollution of the environment, and the growing shortage of fossil fuel. Critics of SUVs commonly point out two ironies: (1) these vehicles, which are designed to take people out into nature, are contributing disproportionately to the destruction of nature; and (2) these all-terrain vehicles are often used in urban driving that does not call for the size, power, or features of SUVs. How do these ads work to deflect these criticisms and "hide" these ironies?

How to Analyze an Advertisement

It is now time to examine advertising in more detail. In the previous section, we said that you should always analyze images within their specific rhetorical context. To analyze ads, you need to understand the context in which advertisers work—their specific goals and strategies.

Understanding an Advertiser's Goals and Strategies

Although some advertisements are primarily informational—explaining why the company believes its product is superior—most advertisements involve parity products such as soft drinks, deodorants, breakfast cereals, toothpaste, and jeans. (*Parity* products are products that are roughly equal in quality to their competitors and so can't be promoted through any rational or scientific proof of superiority.)

Advertisements for parity products usually use psychological and motivational strategies to associate a product with a target audience's (often subconscious) dreams, hopes, fears, desires, and wishes, suggesting that the product will magically dispel these fears and anxieties or magically deliver on values, desires, and dreams. Using sophisticated research techniques, advertisers study how people's fears, dreams, and values differ according to their ethnicity, gender, educational level, socioeconomic class, age, and so forth; this research allows advertisers to tailor their appeals precisely to the target audience.

Furthermore, advertisers often focus on long-range advertising campaigns rather than on just a single ad. Their goal is not simply to sell a product but to build brand loyalty or a relationship with consumers that will be long lasting. (Think of how the brand Marlboro has a different image from the brand Winston, or how Calvin Klein's "heroin chic" of the late 1990s differed from Tommy Hilfiger's "American freedom" image.) Advertisers try to convert a brand name from a label on a can or on the inside of a sweater to a field of qualities, values, and imagery that lives inside the heads of its targeted consumers. An ad campaign, therefore, uses subtle repetition of themes through a variety of individual ads aimed at building up a psychological link between the product and the consumer. Advertisers don't just want you to buy Nikes rather than Reeboks, but also to see yourself as a Nike kind of person who attributes part of your identity to Nikes. Some ad campaigns have been brilliant at turning whole segments of a population into loyal devotees of a brand. Among the most famous campaigns are the Volkswagen ads of the 1950s and early 1960s, the long-lived Marlboro cowboy ads, the independent female theme of Virginia Slims ads, and more recently, the dairy farmers and milk processors' "Got Milk?" ads in magazines and on billboards that feature all kinds of celebrities with milk mustaches, making it "cool" to drink milk.

How Advertisers Target Specific Audiences

When advertisers produce an ad, they create images and copy intended to appeal to the values, hopes, and desires of a specific audience. How do they know the psychological attributes of a specific audience? Much of the market research on which advertisers rely is based on an influential demographic tool developed by SRI Research called the "VALS" (Values And Lifestyle System).* This system divides consumers into three basic categories with further subdivision:

1. ***Needs-driven consumers.*** Poor, with little disposable income, these consumers generally spend their money only on basic necessities.
   - *Survivors:* Live on fixed incomes or have no disposable income. Advertising seldom targets this group.
   - *Sustainers:* Have very little disposable income, but often spend what they have impulsively on low-end, mass-market items.
2. ***Outer-directed consumers.*** These consumers want to identify with certain in-groups, to "keep up with the Joneses," or to surpass them.
   - *Belongers:* Believe in traditional family values and are conforming, nonexperimental, nostalgic, and sentimental. They are typically blue-collar or

---

*Our discussion of VALS is adapted from Harold W. Berkman and Christopher Gibson, *Advertising,* 2nd ed. (New York: Random House, 1987), pp. 134–137.

lower middle class, and they buy products associated with Mom, apple pie, and the American flag.

- *Emulators:* Are ambitious and status conscious. They have a tremendous desire to associate with currently popular in-groups. They are typically young, have at least moderate disposable income, are urban and upwardly mobile, and buy conspicuous items that are considered "in."
- *Achievers:* Have reached the top in a competitive environment. They buy to show off their status and wealth and to reward themselves for their hard climb up the ladder. They have high incomes and buy top-of-the-line luxury items that say "success." They regard themselves as leaders and persons of stature.

3. ***Inner-directed consumers.*** These consumers are individualistic and buy items to suit their own tastes rather than to symbolize their status.

- *I-am-me types:* Are young, independent, and often from affluent backgrounds. They typically buy expensive items associated with their individual interests (such as mountain bikes, stereo equipment, or high-end camping gear), but may spend very little on clothes, cars, or furniture.
- *Experiential types:* Are process-oriented and often reject the values of corporate America in favor of alternative lifestyles. They buy organic foods, make their own bread, do crafts and music, value holistic medicine, and send their children to alternative kindergartens.
- *Socially conscious types:* Believe in simple living and are concerned about the environment and the poor. They emphasize the social responsibility of corporations, take on community service, and actively promote their favorite causes. They have middle to high incomes and are usually very well educated.

No one fits exactly into any one category, and most people exhibit traits of several categories, but advertisers are interested in statistical averages, not individuals. When a company markets an item, it enlists advertising specialists to help target the item to a particular market segment. Budweiser is aimed at belongers, while upscale microbeers are aimed at emulators or achievers. To understand more precisely the fears and values of a target group, researchers can analyze subgroups within each of these VALS segments by focusing specifically on women, men, children, teenagers, young adults, or retirees or on specified ethnic or regional minorities. Researchers also determine what kinds of families and relationships are valued in each of the VALS segments, who in a family initiates demand for a product, and who in a family makes the actual purchasing decisions. Thus, ads aimed at belongers depict traditional families; ads aimed at I-am-me types may depict more ambiguous sexual or family relationships. Advertisements aimed at women can be particularly complex because of women's conflicting social roles in our society. When advertisers target the broader category of gender, they sometimes sweep away VALS distinctions and try to evoke more deeply embedded emotional and psychological responses.

For Writing and Discussion

You own a successful futon factory that has marketed its product primarily to experiential types. Your advertisements have associated futons with holistic health, spiritualism (transcendental meditation, yoga), and organic whole-someness (all-natural materials, gentle people working in the factory, incense and sitar music in your retail stores, and so forth). You have recently expanded your factory and now produce twice as many futons as you did six months ago. Unfortunately, demand hasn't increased correspondingly. Your market research suggests that if you are going to increase demand for futons, you have to reach other VALS segments.

Working in small groups, develop ideas for a magazine or TV advertisement that might sell futons to one or more of the other target segments in the VALS system. Your instructor can assign a different target segment to each group, or each group can decide for itself which target segment constitutes the likeliest new market for futons.

Groups should then share their ideas with the whole class.

Sample Analysis of an Advertisement

With an understanding of possible photographic effects and the compositional features of ads, you now have all the background knowledge needed to begin doing your own analysis of ads. To illustrate how an analysis of an ad can reveal the ad's persuasive strategies, we show you our analysis of an ad for Coors Light (Figure 9.4) that ran in a variety of women's magazines. First, consider the contrast between the typical beer ads that are aimed at men (showing women in bikinis fulfilling adolescent male sexual fantasies or men on fishing trips or in sports bars, representing male comradeship and bonding) and this Coors Light ad with its "Sam and Me" theme.

Rather than associating beer drinking with a wild party, this ad associates beer drinking with the warm friendship of a man and a woman, with just a hint of potential romance. The ad shows a man and a woman, probably in their early- to mid-twenties, in relaxed conversation; they are sitting casually on a tabletop, with their legs resting on chair seats. The woman is wearing casual pants, a summery cotton top, and informal shoes. Her braided, shoulder-length hair has a healthy, mussed appearance, and one braid comes across the front of her shoulder. She is turned away from the man, leans on her knees, and holds a bottle of Coors Light. Her sparkling eyes are looking up, and she smiles happily, as if reliving a pleasant memory. The man is wearing slacks, a cotton shirt with the sleeves rolled up, and scuffed tennis shoes with white socks. He also has a reminiscing smile on his face, and he leans on the woman's shoulder. The words "Coors Light. Just between friends." appear immediately below the picture next to a Coors Light can.

This ad appeals to women's desire for close friendships and relationships. Everything about the picture signifies long-established closeness and intimacy—

FIGURE 9.4 Beer Ad Aimed at Women

old friends rather than lovers. The way the man leans on the woman shows her strength and independence. Additionally, the way they pose, with the woman slightly forward and sitting up more than the man, results in their taking up equal space in the picture. In many ads featuring male-female couples, and man appears larger and taller than the woman; this picture signifies mutuality and equality.

The words of the ad help interpret the relationship. Sam and the woman have been friends since the first grade, and they are reminiscing about old times. The relationship is thoroughly mutual. Sometimes he brings the Coors Light and sometimes she brings it; sometimes she does the listening and sometimes he does; sometimes she leans on his shoulder and sometimes he leans on hers. Sometimes the ad says, "Sam and me"; sometimes it says, "me and Sam." Even the "bad grammar" of "Sam and me" (rather than "Sam and I") suggests the lazy, relaxed absence of pretense or formality.

These two are reliable, old buddies. But the last three lines of the copy give just a hint of potential romance: "Me and Sam? Together? I've never even thought about it. Okay, so I've thought about it." Whereas beer ads targeting men portray women as sex objects, this ad appeals to many women's desire for relationships and for romance that is rooted in friendship rather than sex.

And why the name "Sam"? Students in our classes have hypothesized that Sam is a "buddy" kind of name rather than a romantic-hero name. Yet it is more modern and more interesting than other buddy names such as "Bob" or "Bill" or "Dave." "A 'Sam,'" said one of our students, "is more mysterious than a 'Bill.'" Whatever associations the name strikes in you, be assured that the admakers spent hours debating possible names until they hit on this one. For an additional example of an ad analysis, see the sample student essay (pp. 230–233).

For Writing and Discussion

1. Examine any of the ads reprinted in this chapter or magazine ads brought to class by students or your instructor, and analyze them in detail, paying particular attention to setting, furnishings, and props; characters, roles, and actions; photographic effects; and words and copy. Prior to discussion, freewrite your own analysis of the chosen ad.

2. An excellent way to learn how to analyze ads is to create your own advertisement. Read the following introduction to a brief article with the headline "Attention Advertisers: Real Men Do Laundry." This article appeared in an issue of *American Demographics,* a magazine that helps advertisers target particular audiences based on demographic analysis of the population.

   > Commercials almost never show men doing the laundry, but nearly one-fifth of men do at least seven loads a week. Men don't do as much laundry as women, but the washday gap may be closing. In the dual-career 1990's laundry is going unisex.
   >
   > Forty-three percent of women wash at least seven loads of laundry a week, compared with 19 percent of men, according to a survey conducted for Lever Brothers Company, manufacturers of Wisk detergent. Men do 29 percent of the 419 million loads of laundry Americans wash each week. Yet virtually all laundry-detergent advertising is aimed at women.

   Working in small groups, create an idea for a laundry-detergent ad to be placed in a men's magazine such as *Men's Health, Sports Illustrated, Field and Stream,* or *Esquire.* Draw a rough sketch of your ad that includes the picture, the placement of words, and a rough idea of the content of the words. Pay particular attention to the visual features of your ad—the models, their ages, ethnicity, social status or class, and dress; the setting, such as a self-service laundry or a home laundry room; and other features. When you have designed a possible approach, explain why you think your ad will be successful.

Cultural Perspectives on Advertisements

There isn't space here to examine in depth the numerous cultural issues raised by advertisements, but we can introduce you to a few of them and provide some thought-provoking tasks for exploratory writing and talking. The key issue we want you to think about in this section is how advertisements not only reflect the cultural values and the economic and political structures of the society that produces them but also actively construct and reproduce that society.

For example, look at the 1924 advertisement for the Hoover vacuum cleaner shown in Figure 9.5. This ad appealed to a middle class that was becoming more dependent on household inventions as the use of domestic help became less common. In this ad, a well-dressed wife with carefully-styled hair embraces her well-dressed husband as he returns from a day of work in the business world. Notice that the image and the words reinforce the idea of distinct gender roles while promoting pride in a comfortable, clean, and aesthetically pleasing home. The ad sells more than Hoover vacuum cleaners; it sells a vision of middle class domestic harmony in which the wife's "natural" role is housecleaning.

In its depiction of gender roles, the Hoover ad now strikes us as very old-fashioned. However, cultural critics often argue that contemporary advertisements continue to depict women in culturally subordinate ways. In 1979, the influential sociologist and semiotician* Erving Goffman published a book called *Gender Advertising,* arguing that the way in which women are pictured in advertisements removes them from serious power. In many cases, Goffman's point seems self-evident. Women in advertisements are often depicted in frivolous, childlike, exhibitionistic, sexual, or silly poses that would be considered undignified for a man, such as the "Of Sound Body" Zenith Ad (Figure 9.6). Women in advertisements are often fun to look at or enthralling to "gaze" at, but are seldom portrayed in positions of power. What distinguishes Goffman's work is his analysis of apparently positive portrayals of women in advertisements. He points out tiny details that differentiate the treatment of men from that of women. For example, when men hold umbrellas in an ad, it is usually raining, but women often hold umbrellas for decoration; men grip objects tightly, but women often caress objects or cup them in a gathering in or nurturing way. Female models dance and jump and wiggle in front of the camera (like children playing), whereas male models generally stand or sit in a dignified manner. Even when trying to portray a powerful and independent woman, ads reveal cultural signs that the woman is subordinate.

---

*A *semiotician* is a person who studies the meanings of signs in a culture. A *sign* is any human-produced artifact or gesture that conveys meaning. It can be anything from a word to a facial expression to the arrangement of silverware at a dinner table.

FIGURE 9.5 Hoover Ad

you darling!

ANOTHER year has slipped by since you last thought of giving her a Hoover.

But *she* has thought of it many times.

As cleaning days come and go she struggles resolutely with the only "tools" she has in her "workshop," your home.

And they are woefully inadequate, wasteful of time and strength.

As she wields her broom foot by foot across the dusty, dirty rugs her arms rebel and her back seems near to breaking.

Yet she tries to greet you with a smile when you come home at night.

In your heart you pay her tribute. "She's a brave little woman," you say.

But why put her courage to such an unfair test?

Why ask her to bear her burdens patiently when they can so easily be lifted?

The Hoover will save her strength.

The Hoover will speed her work.

The Hoover will safeguard her pride in a clean home.

You cannot afford to deny her these things for the small monthly payments which The Hoover costs.

Don't disappoint her again this Christmas!

Show her that you really do care, and throughout her lifetime your thoughtfulness will be ever in her mind.

A decade later, another cultural critic, researcher Jean Kilbourne, made a more explicit argument against the way advertisements negatively construct women. In her films *Still Killing Us Softly* (1987) and *Slim Hopes: Advertising and the Obsession with Thinness* (1995), Kilbourne argues that our culture's fear of powerful women is embodied in advertisements that entrap women in futile

FIGURE 9.6 Zenith Audio Products Ad

pursuit of an impossible, flawless standard of beauty. Advertisements help construct the social values that pressure women (particularly middle-class white women) to stay thin, frail, and little-girlish and thus become perfect objects. In *Slim Hopes,* she claims that basically only one body type is preferred (the waif look or the waif-made-voluptuous-with-reconstructed-breasts look). Further, the dismemberment of women in ads—the focus on individual body parts—both objectifies women and intensifies women's anxious concentration on trying to perfect each part of their bodies. Kilbourne asserts that ads distort women's attitudes toward food through harmful and contradictory messages that encourage binging while equating moral goodness with thinness and control over eating. Ads convert women into lifelong consumers of beauty and diet products while undermining their self-esteem.

FIGURE 9.7 Adidas "Adrenaline" Ad

To what extent do the criticisms of Goffman or Kilbourne still apply to the most current advertisements? To what extent has advertising made gains in portraying women as strong, independent, intelligent, and equal with men in their potential for professional status? The picture painted by Goffman and Kilbourne is complicated by some new ads—for example, the new genre of physical fitness ads that emphasize women's physical strength and capabilities as well as their sexuality and femininity. Ads for athletic products feature models with beautiful hair and faces and strong, trim, and shapely bodies. These ads strike different balances between female athleticism and sexuality, perhaps creating a more powerful view of women. (See the ad for Adidas "Adrenaline" in Figure 9.7.) It is also more common today to find ads picturing women in professional "business executive" roles. For example, how much cultural power is possessed by the woman in the AT&T calling card ad in Figure 9.8?

FIGURE 9.8 AT&T Calling Card Ad

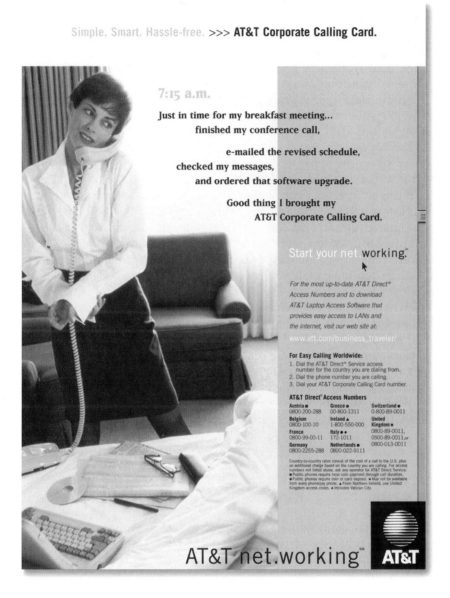

For Writing and Discussion

To test for yourself the extent to which Goffman and Kilbourne's claims about ads still apply, we invite you to explore this issue in the following sequence of activities, which combine class discussion with invitations for exploratory writing.

(continued)

1. Examine again the four ads discussed in the previous section: the Hoover ad (Figure 9.5); the "Of Sound Body" Zenith ad (Figure 9.6); the Adidas "Adrenaline" ad (Figure 9.7); and the AT&T Calling Card ad (Figure 9.8). To what extent does each of these ads construct women as lacking in power in the economic, political, and professional structures of our culture? Which ads, if any, treat women as powerful? Using these ads as your evidence, draw some conclusions about how the social roles for women have changed in the last eighty years. Freewrite your responses to the way women are constructed in these ads as preparation for class discussion.

2. Consider again the AT&T Calling Card ad (Figure 9.8). To what extent would you call the woman in this ad an empowered professional? How might Goffman or Kilbourne argue that this ad subtly subordinates women? Try playing the "What if they changed . . . .?" game with this ad. What would be different if this ad featured a man rather than a woman to advertise the calling card? How would the image change? How would the verbal text change?

The "What if they changed . . . ?" game is explained earlier in this chapter on pp. 211–212.

3. Bring to class advertisements for women's clothing, perfumes, or accessories from recent fashion and beauty magazines such as *Glamour, Elle, InStyle,* and *Vogue.* Study the ways that female models are typically posed in these ads. Then have male students assume the postures of the female models. How many of the postures, which look natural for women, seem ludicrous when adopted by men? To what extent are these postures really natural for women? To what extent do these postures illustrate Goffman's point that advertisements don't take women seriously?

4. Bring to class some examples of recent advertisements that you think portray women in a particularly positive and empowered way—ads that you think neither Goffman nor Kilbourne could deconstruct to show the subordination of women in our culture. Share your examples with the class and see whether your classmates agree with your assessment of these ads.

READINGS

Our reading is a student essay written in response to the assignment in this chapter. It contrasts the strategies of two different cigarette ads to make smoking appear socially desirable despite public sentiment to the contrary.

Stephen Bean (Student)
How Cigarette Advertisers Address the Stigma Against Smoking:
A Tale of Two Ads

1   Any smoker can tell you there's a social stigma attached to smoking in this country. With smokers being pushed out of restaurants, airports, and

many office buildings, how could anyone not feel like a pariah lighting up? While never associated with the churchgoing crowd, smoking is increasingly viewed as lower class or as a symbol of rebellion. Smoking has significantly decreased among adults while increasing among teenagers and young adults in recent years—a testament to its growing status as an affront to middle- and upper-class values. Cigarette advertisers are sharply tuned into this cultural attitude. They must decide whether to overcome the working-class/rebellious image of smoking in their advertisements or use it to their advantage. The answer to this question lies in what type of people they want an ad to target—the young? the rich? the poor?—and in what values, insecurities, and desires they think this group shares. Two contrasting answers to these questions are apparent in recent magazine ads for *Benson & Hedges* cigarettes and for *Richland* cigarettes.

2   The ad for Benson & Hedges consists of a main picture and a small insert picture below the main one. The main picture shows five women (perhaps thirty years old) sitting around, talking, and laughing in the living room of a comfortable and urbane home or upscale apartment. The room is filled with natural light and is tastefully decorated with antique lamps and Persian rugs. The women have opened a bottle of wine, and a couple of glasses have been poured. They are dressed casually but fashionably, ranging from slightly hip to slightly conservative. One woman wears a loose, black, sleeveless dress; another wears grungesque boots with a sweater and skirt. One of the women, apparently the hostess, sits on a sofa a bit apart from the others, smiles with pleasure at the conversation and laughter of her friends, and knits. Two of the women are smoking, and three aren't. No smoke is visible coming from the cigarettes. Underneath the main picture is a small insert photograph of the hostess—the one knitting in the main picture—in a different pose. She is now leaning back in pleasure, apparently after the party, and this time she is smoking a cigarette. Underneath the photos reads the slogan "For people who like to smoke."

3   The ad for Richland cigarettes shows a couple in their late twenties sitting in a diner or perhaps a tavern off the freeway. The remains of their lunch— empty burger and fries baskets, a couple of beer bottles—lie on the table. They seem to be talking leisurely, sharing an after-meal smoke. The man is wearing black jeans and a black T-shirt. The woman is wearing a pinkish skirt and tank top. Learning back with her legs apart she sits in a position that signals sexuality. The slogan reads, "It's all right here." And at the bottom of the ad, "Classic taste. Right price." Outside the window of the diner you can see a freeway sign slightly blurred as if from heated air currents.

4   Whom do these different advertisements target? What about them might people find appealing? Clearly the Benson & Hedges ad is aimed at women, especially upper-middle-class women who wish to appear successful. As the media have noted lately, the social stigma against smoking is strongest among middle- and upper-class adults. My sense of the B&H ad is that it is targeting younger, college-educated women who feel social pressure to quit smoking. To them the ad is saying, "Smoking makes you no less

sophisticated; it only shows that you have a fun side too. Be comfortable doing whatever makes you happy."

5   What choices did the advertisers make in constructing this scene to create this message? The living room—with its antique lamps and vases, its Persian rugs and hardcover books, and its wall hanging thrown over what appears to be an old trunk—creates a sense of comfortable, tasteful, upscale living. But figuring out the people in the room is more difficult. Who are these women? What is their story? What brought them together this afternoon? Where did their money come from? Are these professional women with high-paying jobs, or are they the wives of young bankers, attorneys, and stockbrokers? One woman has a strong business look—short hair feathered back, black sleeveless dress—but why is she dressed this way on what is apparently a Saturday afternoon? In contrast, another woman has a more hip, almost grunge look—slightly spiky hair that's long in the back, a loose sweater, a black skirt, and heavy black boots. Only one woman wears a wedding ring. It seems everything about these women resists easy definition or categorization. The most striking image in the ad is the hostess knitting. She looks remarkably domestic, almost motherly, with her knees drawn close, leaning over her knitting and smiling to herself as others laugh out loud. Her presence gives the scene a feeling of safety and old-fashioned values amidst the images of independence. Interestingly, we get a much different image of the hostess in the insert picture placed just above the B&H logo. This picture shows the hostess leaning back pleasurably on the couch and smoking. The image is undeniably sexual. Her arms are back; she's deeply relaxed; the two top buttons of her blouse are open; her hair is slightly mussed; she smokes languidly, taking full pleasure in the cigarette, basking in the party's afterglow.

6   The opposing images in the advertisement (knitting/smoking, conservative/hip, wife/career, safe/independent, domestic/sexual) mean that these women can't easily be defined—as smokers or as anything else. For an ad promoting smoking, the cigarettes themselves take a back seat. In the main picture the cigarettes are hardly noticeable; the two women holding cigarettes do so inconspicuously and there is no visible smoke. The ad doesn't say so much that it is good to smoke, but that it is okay to smoke. Smoking will not make you less sophisticated. If anything, it only shows that you have an element of youth and fun. The slogan, "For people who like to smoke," targets nonsmokers as much as it does smokers—not so much to take up smoking but to be more tolerant of those who choose to smoke. The emphasis is on choice, independence, and acceptance of others' choices. The ad attacks the social stigma against smoking; it eases the conscience of "people who like to smoke."

7   While the B&H ad hopes to remove the stigma attached to smoking, the Richland ad feasts on it. Richland cigarettes aren't for those cultivating the upper-class look. The ad goes for a rebellious, gritty image, for beer drinkers, not wine sippers. While the story of the women in the B&H ad is difficult to

figure out, the Richland ad gives us a classic image: a couple on the road who have stopped at a diner or tavern. Here the story is simpler: a man and woman being cool. They are going down the freeway to the big city. I picture a heavy American cruising car parked out front. Everything about the ad has a gritty, blue-collar feel. They sit at a booth with a Formica tabletop; the walls are bare, green-painted wood. The man is dressed in black with a combed-back, James Dean haircut. The woman wears a pink skirt with a tank top; her shoulder-length hair hasn't been fussed over, and she wears a touch of makeup. Empty baskets and bottles cluttering the table indicate they had a classic American meal—hamburgers, fries, and a beer—eaten for pleasure without politically correct worries about calories, polyunsaturated fats, cruelty to animals, or cancer. While the sexual imagery in the B&H ad is subtle, in the Richland ad it is blatant. The man is leaning forward with his elbows on the table; the woman is leaning back with her legs spread and her skirt pushed up slightly. Her eyes are closed. They smoke leisurely, and the woman holds the cigarette a couple of inches from her expecting lips. The slogan, "It's all right here," is centered beneath the woman's skirt. Smoking, like sex, is about pure pleasure—something to be done slowly. Far from avoiding working-class associations with smoking, this ad aims to reinforce them. The cigarettes are clearly visible, and, unlike the cigarettes in the B&H ad, show rings of rising smoke. This ad promotes living for the moment. The more rebellious, the better.

8   So we see, then, two different ways that cigarette companies address the stigma against smoking. The B&H ad tries to eliminate it by targeting middle-class, college-educated women. It appeals to upscale values, associating cigarette smoking with choice, and showing that "people who like to smoke" can also knit (evoking warm, safe images of domestic life) or lean back in postparty pleasure (evoking a somewhat wilder, more sexual image). In contrast, the Richland ad exploits the stigma. It associates smoking with on-the-road freedom, rebellion, sexuality, and enjoyment of the moment. The smoke visibly rising from the cigarettes in the Richland ad and noticeably absent from the Benson & Hedges ad tells the difference.

Thinking Critically about "How Cigarette Advertisers Address the Stigma Against Smoking"

1. Stephen Bean argues that the Benson & Hedges and the Richland ads use very different appeals to encourage their target audiences to smoke. What are the appeals he cites? Do you agree with Stephen's analysis?
2. Collect a variety of cigarette ads from current magazines, and analyze their various appeals. How do the ads vary according to their intended audiences? Consider ads targeted at men versus women or at audiences from different VALS segments.
3. What do you see as the strengths and weaknesses of Stephen's essay?

Composing Your Essay

Generating and Exploring Ideas

Your first task is to find two ads that sell the same general product to different target audiences or that make appeals to noticeably different value systems. Look for ads that are complex enough to invite detailed analysis. Then, analyze the ads carefully, using the strategies suggested earlier in this chapter. The sample student essay (pp. 230–233) provides an example of the kind of approach you can take.

  If you get stuck, try freewriting your responses to the following questions: (a) What attracted your attention to this ad? (b) Whom do you think this ad targets? Why? (c) What photographic techniques, visual devices, and camera angles are used in this ad? (d) What props and furnishings are in this ad, and what values or meanings are attached to them? (e) What are the characters like, what are they doing, and why are they wearing what they are wearing and posed the way they are posed? (f) How do the words of the ad interplay with the picture? (g) How would the ad be less effective if its key features were changed in some way? (h) Overall, to what fears, values, hopes, or dreams is this ad appealing?

Shaping and Drafting

Your essay should be fairly easy to organize at the big-picture level, but each part will require its own organic organization depending on the main points of your analysis. At the big-picture level, you can generally follow a structure like this:

  I. Introduction (hooks readers' interest, gives background on how ads vary their appeals, asks the question your paper will address, and ends with initial mapping in the form of a purpose or thesis statement)
 II. General description of the two ads
    A. Description of ad 1
    B. Description of ad 2
III. Analysis of the two ads
    A. Analysis of ad 1
    B. Analysis of ad 2
 IV. Conclusion (returns to the big picture for a sense of closure; makes final comments about the significance of your analysis or touches in some way on larger issues raised by the analysis)

We recommend that you write your rough draft rapidly, without worrying about gracefulness, correctness, or even getting all your ideas said at once. Many people like to begin with the description of the ads and then write the analysis before writing the introduction and the conclusion. After you have written your draft, put it aside for a while before you begin revising. We recommend that you ask classmates for a peer review of your draft early in the revising process.

Revising

Most experienced writers make global changes in their final drafts when they revise, especially when they are doing analytical writing. The act of writing a rough draft generally leads to the discovery of more ideas. You may also realize that many of your original ideas aren't clearly developed or that the draft feels scattered and unorganized.

GUIDELINES FOR PEER REVIEWS

Instructions for peer reviews are provided in Chapter 11 (pp. 293–294).

For the Writer

Prepare two or three questions you would like your peer reviewer to address while responding to your draft. The questions can focus on some aspect of your draft that you are uncertain about, on one or more sections where you particularly seek help or advice, on some feature that you particularly like about your draft, or on some part you especially wrestled with. Write out your questions and give them to your peer reviewer along with your draft.

For the Reviewer

I. Read the draft at a normal reading speed from beginning to end. As you read, do the following:
  A. Place a wavy line in the margin next to any passages that you find confusing, that contain something that doesn't seem to fit, or that otherwise slow down your reading.
  B. Place a "Good!" in the margin next to any passages where you think the writing is particularly strong or interesting.
II. Read the draft again slowly and answer the following questions by writing brief explanations of your answers.
  A. Introduction:
    1. Is the title appropriate for an academic analysis? Does it suggest the thesis and focus of the paper and pique your interest? How might the title be improved?
    2. What does the writer do to capture your interest, provide needed background, and set up the question to be addressed?
    3. How does the thesis statement, purpose statement, or forecasting statement provide the big picture for both the description and the analysis of the two ads? How might the writer improve the introduction?
  B. Description of the ads:
    1. Does the writer describe the ads in an interesting and vivid manner? How could this description help you "see" the ads more clearly?

2. In what ways do the ads appeal to different audiences or have different value systems? What makes the ads complex enough to justify an analysis?

C. Analysis of the ads:

1. How does the analysis of the ads shed light on and build on the description of the ads?

2. How many of the following features does the writer discuss? Which could be added to deepen and complicate the analysis?

a. Setting, props, and furnishings: how they indicate lifestyle and socioeconomic status; appeal to certain values; carry certain cultural associations or meanings; serve as symbols.

b. Characters, roles, and actions: the story of the ad; power relationships and status of the characters; gender, age, or ethnic roles followed or violated; the significance of clothing and accessories, of hair and facial expressions, and of posing, positioning, and gestures.

c. Photographic effects: lighting, camera angle, cropping, focus.

d. Language and wording of the ad's copy: its overt message; feelings, mood, and values communicated through connotations, double entendres, and so forth; visual layout of copy.

3. What portions of the analysis are convincing? Which details of the ads contradict the analysis? Do you disagree with the writer's view of these ads?

4. How could the body of the paper be made clearer, better organized, or easier to follow? Where might the writer better apply the principles of clarity from Chapter 12 (starting with the big picture; putting points before particulars; using transitions; following the old/new contract)?

III. Rhetorical considerations

A. *Purpose, audience,* and *genre:* The writer's purpose is to write an academic paper analyzing two advertisements for an audience who hasn't seen them. How effectively does this paper describe and analyze these ads for this audience? How effectively does it meet the genre expectations for an academic paper?

B. *Logos, ethos,* and *pathos:* How convincing or effective is the logical or conceptual part of this draft? How does the writer build an *ethos* that readers will find reliable, fair, and authoritative? How does the writer connect this analysis to the interests and values of the audience?

IV. If the writer has prepared questions for you, respond to his or her inquiries.

V. Sum up what you see as the chief strengths and problem areas of this draft:

A. Strengths

B. Problem areas

VI. Read the draft one more time. Place a check mark in the margin wherever you notice problems in grammar, spelling, or mechanics (one check mark per problem).

Writing a Classical Argument

About Classical Argument

The assignment for this chapter introduces you to a classical way of arguing in which you take a stand on an issue, offer reasons and evidence in support of your position, and summarize and respond to alternative views. Your goal is to persuade your audience, who can be initially perceived as either opposed to your position or undecided about it, to adopt your position or at least to regard it more openly or favorably.

The need for argument arises whenever members of a community disagree on an issue. Classical rhetoricians believed that the art of arguing was essential for good citizenship. If disputes can be resolved through exchange of perspectives, negotiation of differences, and flexible seeking of the best solutions to a problem, then nations won't have to resort to war or individuals to fisticuffs.

The study of argumentation involves two components: truth seeking and persuasion. By *truth seeking,* we mean a diligent, open-minded, and responsible search for the best course of action or solution to a problem, taking into account all the available information and alternative points of view. By *persuasion,* we mean the art of making a claim* on an issue and justifying it convincingly so that the audience's initial resistance to your position is overcome and they are moved toward your position.

These two components of argument seem paradoxically at odds: Truth seeking asks us to relax our certainties and be willing to change our views; persuasion asks us to be certain, to be committed to our claims, and to get others to change their views. We can overcome this paradox if we dispel two common but misleading views of argument. The most common view is that argument is a fight as in "I just got into a horrible argument with my roommate." This view of argument as a fist-waving, shouting match in which you ridicule anyone who disagrees with you (popularized by radio and television talk shows) entirely disregards argument as truth seeking, but it also misrepresents argument as persuasion because it polarizes people, rather than promoting understanding, new ways of seeing, and change.

Another common but misleading view is that argument is a pro/con debate modeled after high school or college debate matches or presidential debates. Although debating can be an excellent way to develop critical thinking skills, it misrepresents argument as a two-sided contest with winners and losers. Because controversial issues involve many different points of view, not just two, reducing

---

*By longstanding tradition, the thesis statement of an argument is often called its "claim."

an issue to pro/con positions distorts the complexity of the disagreement. Instead of thinking of *both* sides of an issue, we need to think of *all* sides. Equally troublesome, the debate image invites us to ask, "Who won the debate?" rather than "What is the best solution to the question that divides us?" The best solution might be a compromise between the two debaters or an undiscovered third position. The debate image tends to privilege the confident extremes in a controversy rather than the complex and muddled middle.

From our perspective, the best image for understanding argument is neither "fight" nor "debate" but the deliberations of a committee representing a wide spectrum of community voices charged with finding the best solution to a problem. From this perspective, argument is both a *process* and a *product.* As a process, argument is an act of inquiry characterized by fact finding, information gathering, and consideration of alternative points of view. As a product, it is someone's contribution to the conversation at any one moment—a turn taking in a conversation, a formal speech, or a written position paper such as the one you will write for this chapter. The goal of argument as process is truth seeking; the goal of argument as product is persuasion. When members of a diverse committee are willing to argue persuasively for their respective points of view but are simultaneously willing to listen to other points of view and to change or modify their positions in light of new information or better arguments, then both components of argument are fully in play.

We cannot overemphasize the importance of both truth seeking and persuasion to your professional and civic life. Truth seeking makes you an informed and judicious employee and a citizen who delays decisions until a full range of evidence and alternative views are aired and examined. Persuasion gives you the power to influence the world around you, whether through letters to the editor on political issues or through convincing position papers for professional life. Whenever an organization needs to make a major decision, those who can think flexibly and write persuasively can wield great influence.

Exploring Classical Argument

An effective way to appreciate argument as both truth seeking and persuasion is to address an issue that is new to you and then watch how your own views evolve. Your initial position will probably reflect what social scientists sometimes call your personal *ideology*—that is, a network of basic values, beliefs, and assumptions that tend to guide your view of the world. However, if you adopt a truth-seeking attitude, your initial position may evolve as the conversation progresses. In fact, the conversation may even cause changes in some of your basic beliefs, since ideologies aren't set in stone and since many of us have unresolved allegiance to competing ideologies that may be logically inconsistent (for example, a belief in freedom of speech combined with a belief that hate speech should be banned). In this exercise we ask you to keep track of how your views change and to note what causes the change.

The case we present for discussion involves ethical treatment of animals.

Situation: A bunch of starlings build nests in the attic of a family's house, gaining access to the attic through a torn vent screen. Soon the eggs hatch, and every morning at sunrise the family is awakened by the sound of birds squawking and wings beating against rafters as the starlings fly in and out of the house to feed the hatchlings. After losing considerable early morning sleep, the family repairs the screen. Unable to get in and out, the parent birds are unable to feed their young. The birds die within a day. Is this cruelty to animals?

1. Freewrite your initial response to this question. Was the family's act an instance of cruelty to animals (that is, was their act ethically justifiable or not)?

2. Working in small groups or as a whole class, share your freewrites and then try to reach a group consensus on the issue. During this conversation (argument as process), listen carefully to your classmates' views and note places where your own initial views begin to evolve.

3. So far we have framed this issue as an after-the-fact yes/no question: Is the family guilty of cruelty to animals? But we can also frame it as an open-ended, before-the-fact question: "What should the family have done about the starlings in the attic?" Suppose you are a family member discussing the starlings at dinner, prior to the decision to fix the vent screen. Make a list of your family's other options and try to reach class consensus on the two or three best alternative solutions.

4. At the end of the discussion, do another freewrite exploring how your ideas evolved during the discussion. What insights did you get about the twin components of argument, truth seeking and persuasion?

WRITING PROJECT

Write a position paper that takes a stand on a controversial issue. Your introduction should present your issue, provide background, and state the claim you intend to support. The body of your argument will summarize and respond to opposing views as well as present reasons and evidence in support of your own position. You need to choose whether to summarize and refute opposing views before or after you have made your own case. Try to end your essay with your strongest arguments.

We sometimes call this assignment an argument in the *classical style* because it is patterned after the persuasive speeches of ancient Greek and Roman orators. In the terms of ancient rhetoricians, the main parts of a persuasive speech are the *exordium,* in which the speaker gets the audience's attention; the *narratio,* which provides needed background; the *propositio,* the speaker's proposition or thesis; the *partitio,* a forecast of the main parts of the speech, equivalent to a blueprint statement; the *confirmatio,* the speaker's arguments in favor of the proposition; the *confutatio,* the refutation of opposing views; and the *peroratio,* the conclusion that sums up the argument, calls for action, and leaves a strong, lasting impression.

We cite these tongue-twisting Latin terms only to assure you that in writing a classical argument you are joining a time-honored tradition that links you to Roman senators on the capitol steps. From their discourse arose the ideal of a democratic society based on superior arguments rather than on superior weaponry. Although there are many other ways to persuade audiences, the classical approach is a particularly effective introduction to persuasive writing.

Understanding Classical Argument

Having introduced you to argument as both process and product, we now turn to the details of effective argumentation. To help orient you, we begin by describing the typical stages that mark students' growth as arguers.

Stages of Development: Your Growth as an Arguer

We have found that when we teach argument in our classes, students typically proceed through identifiable stages as their argumentative skills increase. While these stages may or may not describe your own development, they suggest the skills you should strive to acquire.

- *Stage 1: Argument as personal opinion.* At the beginning of instruction in argument, students typically express strong personal opinions but have trouble justifying their opinions with reasons and evidence and often create short, undeveloped arguments that are circular, lacking in evidence, and insulting to those who disagree. The following freewrite, written by a student first confronting the starling case (p. 239), illustrates this stage:

  > The family shouldn't have killed the starlings because that is really wrong! I mean that act was disgusting. It makes me sick to think how so many people are just willing to kill something for no reason at all. How are these parents going to teach their children values if they just go out and kill little birds for no good reason?!! This whole family is what's wrong with America!

  This writer's opinion is passionate and heartfelt, but it provides neither reasons nor evidence why someone else should hold the same opinion.

- *Stage 2: Argument structured as claim supported by one or more reasons.* This stage represents a quantum leap in argumentative skill because the writer can now produce a rational plan containing point sentences (the reasons) and particulars (the evidence). The writer who produced the previous freewrite later developed a structure like this:

The family's act constituted cruelty to animals

- because the starlings were doing minimal harm.
- because other options were available.
- because the way they killed the birds caused needless suffering.

- *Stage 3: Increased attention to truth seeking.* In stage 3 students become increasingly engaged with the complexity of the issue as they listen to their classmates' views, conduct research, and evaluate alternative perspectives and stances. They are often willing to change their positions when they see the power of other arguments.
- *Stage 4: Ability to articulate the unstated assumptions underlying their arguments.* As we show later in this chapter, each reason in a writer's argument is based on an assumption, value, or belief (often unstated) that the audience must accept if the argument is to be persuasive. Often the writer needs to state these assumptions explicitly and support them. At this stage students identify and analyze their own assumptions and those of their intended audiences. Students gain increased skill at accommodating alternative views through refutation or concession.
- *Stage 5: Ability to link an argument to the values and beliefs of the intended audience.* In this stage writers are increasingly able to link their arguments to their audience's values and beliefs and to adapt structure and tone to the resistance level of their audience. Writers also appreciate how delayed-thesis arguments or other psychological strategies can be more effective than closed-form arguments when addressing hostile audiences.

The rest of this chapter helps you progress through these stages. Although you can read the remainder in one sitting, we recommend that you break your reading into sections, going over the material slowly and applying it to your own ideas in progress. Let the chapter's concepts and explanations sink in gradually, and return to them periodically for review. This section on "Understanding Classical Argument" contains the chapter's key instructional material and comprises a compact but comprehensive course in argumentation.

Creating an Argument Frame: A Claim with Reasons

Somewhere in the writing process, whether early or late, you need to create a frame for your argument. This frame includes a clear question that focuses the argument, your claim, and one or more supporting reasons. Often your reasons, stated as *because* clauses, can be attached to your claim to provide a working thesis statement.

Finding an Arguable Issue
At the heart of any argument is an issue, which we can define as a question that invites more than one reasonable answer and thus leads to perplexity or disagreement. This requirement excludes disagreements based on personal tastes, where no shared criteria could be developed ("Baseball is more fun than soccer"). It also

excludes purely private questions because issues arise out of disagreements in communities. When you are thinking of issues, ask what questions are currently being contested in one of the communities to which you belong (your family, neighborhood, religious or social group, workplace, classroom, dormitory, campus, hometown, state, region, nation, and so forth).

Issue questions are often framed as yes/no choices, especially when they appear on ballots or in courtrooms: Should gay marriage be legalized? Should the city pass the new school bond proposal? Is this defendant guilty of armed robbery? Just as frequently, they can be framed openly, inviting many different possible answers: What should our city do about skateboarders in downtown pedestrian areas? How can children be kept from pornography on the Internet?

It is important to remember that framing an issue as a yes/no question does not mean that all points of view fall neatly into pro/con categories. Although citizens may be forced to vote yes or no on a proposed ballot initiative, they can support or oppose the initiative for a variety of reasons. Some may vote happily for the initiative, others vote for it only by holding their noses, and still others oppose it vehemently but for entirely different reasons. To argue effectively, you need to appreciate the wide range of perspectives from which people approach the yes/no choice.

How you frame your question necessarily affects the scope and shape of your argument itself. In our exploratory exercise we framed the starling question in two ways: (1) Was the family guilty of cruelty to animals? and (2) What should the family do about the starlings? Framed in the first way, your argument would have to develop criteria for "cruelty to animals" and then argue whether the family's actions met those criteria. Framed in the second way, you could argue for your own solution to the problem, ranging from doing nothing (waiting for the birds to grow up and leave, then fixing the screen) to climbing into the attic and drowning the birds so that their deaths are quick and painless. Or you could word the question in a broader, more philosophical way: When are humans justified in killing animals? Or you could focus on a subissue: When can an animal be labeled a "pest"?

For Writing and Discussion

1. Working individually, make a list of several communities that you belong to and then identify one or more questions currently being contested within those communities. (If you have trouble, get a copy of your local campus and city newspapers or an organizational newsletter; you'll quickly discover a wealth of contested issues.) Then share your list with classmates.
2. Pick two or three issues of particular interest to you, and try framing them in different ways: as broad or narrow questions, as open-ended or yes/no questions. Place several examples on the chalkboard for class discussion.

Stating a Claim

Your claim is the position you take on the issue. It is your brief, one-sentence answer to your issue question:

> The family was not ethically justified in killing the starlings.

> The city should build skateboarding areas with ramps in all city parks.

You will appreciate argument as truth seeking if you find that your claim evolves as you think more deeply about your issue and listen to alternative views. Be willing to rephrase your claim to soften it or refocus it or even to reverse it as you progress through the writing process.

Articulating Reasons

Your claim, which is the position you take on an issue, needs to be supported by reasons and evidence. A *reason* (sometimes called a "premise") is a subclaim that supports your main claim. In speaking or writing, a reason is usually linked to the claim with such connecting words as *because, therefore, so, consequently,* and *thus.* In planning your argument, a powerful strategy for developing reasons is to harness the grammatical power of the conjunction *because;* think of your reasons as *because* clauses attached to your claim. Formulating your reasons in this way allows you to create a thesis statement that breaks your argument into smaller parts, each part devoted to one of the reasons.*

Suppose, for example, that you are examining the issue "Should the government legalize hard drugs such as heroin and cocaine?" Here are several different points of view on this issue, each expressed as a claim with *because* clauses:

ONE VIEW

Cocaine and heroin should be legalized

- because legalizing drugs will keep the government out of people's private lives.
- because keeping these drugs illegal has the same negative effects on our society that alcohol prohibition did in the 1920s.

ANOTHER VIEW

Cocaine and heroin should be legalized

- because the subsequent elimination of the black market would cut down on muggings and robberies.

---

*The thesis statement for your essay could be your claim by itself or you could include in your thesis statement your main supporting reasons. For advice on how much of your supporting argument you should summarize in your thesis statement, see Chapter 12, pp. 319–320.

- because decriminalization would cut down on prison overcrowding and free police to concentrate on dangerous crime rather than on finding drug dealers.
- because elimination of underworld profits would change the economic structure of the underclass and promote shifts to socially productive jobs and careers.

STILL ANOTHER VIEW

The government should not legalize heroin and cocaine

- because doing so will lead to an increase in drug users.
- because doing so will send the message that it is okay to use hard drugs.

Although the yes/no framing of this question seems to reduce the issue to a two-position debate, many different value systems are at work here. The first pro-legalization argument, libertarian in perspective, values maximum individual freedom. The second argument—although it too supports legalization—takes a community perspective valuing the social benefits of eliminating the black market. In the same way, individuals could oppose legalization for a variety of reasons.

For Writing and Discussion

Working in small groups or as a whole class, generate a list of reasons for and against one or more of the following yes/no claims. State your reasons as *because* clauses. Think of as many *because* clauses as possible by imagining a wide variety of perspectives on the issue.

1. The school year for grades 1 through 12 should be lengthened to eleven months.
2. The war against terrorism requires Americans to relinquish some of their freedoms.
3. Women's fashion and style magazines (such as *Glamour* and *Seventeen*) are harmful influences on teenage females.
4. The United States should replace its income tax with a national sales tax.
5. Medical insurance should cover alternative medicine (massage therapy, acupuncture, herbal treatments, and so forth).

Articulating Unstated Assumptions

So far, we have focused on the frame of an argument as a claim supported with one or more reasons. Shortly, we will proceed to the flesh and muscle of an argument, which is the evidence you use to support your reasons. But before turning to evidence, we need to look at another crucial part of an argument's frame: its *unstated assumptions*.

What Do We Mean by an Unstated Assumption?

Every time you link together a claim with a reason, you make a silent assumption that may need to be articulated and examined. Consider this argument:

The family was justified in killing the starlings because starlings are pests.

To support this argument, the writer would first need to provide evidence that starlings are pests (examples of the damage they do and so forth). But the persuasiveness of the argument rests on the unstated assumption that it is okay to kill pests. If an audience doesn't agree with that assumption, then the argument flounders unless the writer articulates the assumption and defends it. The complete frame of the argument must therefore include the unstated assumption.

Claim: The family was justified in killing the starlings.

Reason: Because starlings are pests.

Unstated assumption: It is ethically justifiable to kill pests.

It is important to examine the unstated assumption behind any claim with reason *because you must determine whether your audience will accept that assumption. If not, you need to make it explicit and support it.* Think of the unstated assumption as a general principle, rule, belief, or value that connects the reason to the claim. It answers your reader's question, "Why, if I accept your reason, should I accept your claim?"

Here are a few more examples:

Claim with reason: Women should be allowed to join combat units because the image of women as combat soldiers would help society overcome gender stereotyping.

Unstated assumption: It is good to overcome gender stereotyping.

Claim with reason: The government should not legalize heroin and cocaine because doing so will lead to an increase in drug users.

Unstated assumption: It is bad to increase the number of drug users.

Claim with reason: The family was guilty of cruelty to animals in the starling case because less drastic means of solving the problem were available.

Unstated assumption: A person should choose the least drastic means to solve a problem.

For Writing and Discussion

Identify the unstated assumptions for each of the following claims with reasons.

1. Cocaine and heroin should be legalized because legalizing drugs will keep the government out of people's private lives.
2. The government should eliminate welfare payments to unwed mothers because doing so will reduce the illegitimacy rate.
3. The government is justified in detaining suspected terrorists indefinitely without charging them with a crime because doing so may prevent another terrorist attack.
4. We should strengthen the Endangered Species Act because doing so will preserve genetic diversity on the planet.

(continued)

5. The Endangered Species Act is too stringent because it severely damages the economy.

Using Toulmin Terminology to Describe an Argument's Structure

Our explanation of argument structure is influenced by the work of philosopher Stephen Toulmin, who viewed argumentation as a dynamic courtroom drama where opposing attorneys exchange arguments and cross-examinations before a judge and jury. The terms used by Toulmin to describe the structure of argument are widely accepted in rhetoric and composition studies and provide a handy vocabulary for discussing arguments. Toulmin called the unstated assumption behind a claim with reason the argument's *warrant*, based on our common word *warranty* for guarantee. If the audience accepts your warrant—that is, if they agree with your unstated assumption—then your argument is sound, or guaranteed. To put it another way, if your audience accepts your warrant, and if you can convince them that your reason is true, then they will accept your claim.

Besides the term *warrant*, Toulmin also uses the terms *grounds, backing, conditions of rebuttal,* and *qualifier.* We will explain these terms to you at the appropriate moments as we proceed.

Using Evidence Effectively

In Chapter 2 we showed you that the majority of words in a closed-form essay are particulars used to support points. If you think of reasons and warrants as the main points of your argument, then think of evidence as the supporting particulars. Each of your reasons needs to be supported by evidence. Toulmin's term for evidence in support of a reason is *grounds,* which we can think of as all the facts, data, testimony, statistics, subarguments, and other details a writer can find to support a reason. Toulmin calls the evidence and arguments used to support a warrant its *backing.* In this section we survey different kinds of evidence and show you how to incorporate that evidence into an argument, either as grounds to support a reason or as backing to support a warrant. Some arguments can be fleshed out with evidence based on your personal experience and observations. But most arguments require more formal evidence—the kind you gather from library or field research.

Kinds of Evidence

The kinds of evidence most often used for the grounds and backing are the following:

Examples.   An example from personal experience can often be used to support a reason. Here is how one student writer, arguing that her church building needs to be remodeled, used a personal example to support a reason.

> Finally, Sacred Heart Church must be renovated immediately because the terrazzo floor that covers the entire church is very dangerous. Four Sundays ago, during 11:00 Mass, nine Eucharistic Ministers went up to the altar to prepare for distribut-

ing communion. As they carefully walked to their assigned post on the recently buffed terrazzo floor, a loud crash of crystal echoed through the church. A woman moving to her post slipped on the recently buffed floor, fell to the ground, hit her head on the marble, and was knocked unconscious. People rushed to her aid, thinking she was dead. Fortunately she was alive, only badly hurt. This woman was my mother.

Besides specific examples like this, writers sometimes invent hypothetical examples, or *scenarios,* to illustrate an issue or hypothesize about the consequences of an event. (Of course, you must tell your reader that the example or scenario is hypothetical.)

Summaries of Research.   Another common way to support an argument is to summarize research articles. Here is how a student writer, investigating whether menopausal women should use hormone replacement therapy to combat menopausal symptoms, used one of several research articles in her paper. The student began by summarizing research studies showing possible dangers of hormone replacement therapy. She then made the following argument:

> Another reason not to use hormone replacement therapy is that other means are available to ease menopausal symptoms such as hot flashes, irritability, mood changes, and sleep disturbance. One possible alternative treatment is acupuncture. One study (Cohen, Rousseau, & Carey, 2003) revealed that a randomly selected group of menopausal women receiving specially designed acupuncture treatment showed substantial decreases in menopausal symptoms as compared to a control group. What was particularly persuasive about this study was that both the experimental group and the control group received acupuncture, but the needle insertion sites for the experimental group were specifically targeted to relieve menopausal symptoms whereas the control group received acupuncture at sites used to promote general well-being. The researchers concluded that "acupuncture may be recommended as a safe and effective therapy for reducing menopausal hot flushes as well as contributing to the reduction in sleep disruptions" (p. 299).*

Statistics.   Another common form of evidence is statistics. Here is how one writer uses statistics to argue that the federal government should raise fuel-efficiency standards placed on auto manufacturers:

> There is very little need for most Americans to drive huge SUVs. One recent survey found that 87 percent of four-wheel-drive SUV owners had never taken their SUVs off-road (Yacobucci). . . . By raising fuel-efficiency standards, the government would force vehicle manufacturers to find a way to create more earth-friendly vehicles that would lower vehicle emissions and pollution. An article entitled "Update:

---

*This student is using the APA (American Psychological Association) style for documenting sources. At first mention of the article, the writer names the authors and the date of publication in parentheses. The page number for the quotation is placed in parentheses immediately after the closing quotation mark. Full bibliographic information about the article will be found in the "References" list at the end of the essay, alphabetized under the first author, "Cohen." See Chapter 14 for full explanations of how to use both the APA and the MLA (Modern Language Association) systems for citing and documenting sources.

What You Should Know Before Purchasing a New Vehicle" states that for every gallon of gasoline used by a vehicle, 20 to 28 pounds of carbon dioxide are released into the environment. This article further states that carbon dioxide emissions from automobiles are responsible for 20 percent of all carbon dioxide released into the atmosphere from human causes.*

Testimony.   Writers can also use expert testimony to bolster a case. The following passage from a student essay arguing in favor of therapeutic cloning uses testimony from a prominent physician and medical researcher. Part of the paragraph quotes this expert directly; another part paraphrases the expert's argument.

> As Dr. Gerald Fischbach, Executive Vice President for Health and Biomedical Sciences and Dean of Medicine at Columbia University, said in front of a United States Senate subcommittee: "New embryonic stem cell procedures could be vital in solving the persistent problem of a lack of genetically matched, qualified donors of organs and tissues that we face today." Along with organ regeneration, therapeutic cloning could potentially cure many diseases that currently have no cure. Fischbach goes on to say that this type of cloning could lead to the discovery of cures for diseases such as ALS, Parkinson's disease, Alzheimer's disease, diabetes, heart disease, cancer, and possibly others.†

Subarguments.   Sometimes writers support reasons not directly through data but through sequences of subarguments. Sometimes these subarguments develop a persuasive analogy, hypothesize about consequences, or simply advance the argument through a chain of connected points. In the following passage, taken from a philosophic article justifying torture under certain conditions, the author uses a subargument to support one of his main points—that a terrorist holding victims hostage has no "rights":

> There is an important difference between terrorists and their victims that should mute talk of the terrorist's "rights." The terrorist's victims are at risk unintentionally, not having asked to be endangered. But the terrorist knowingly initiated his actions. Unlike his victims, he volunteered for the risks of his deed. By threatening to kill for profit or idealism, he renounces civilized standards, and he can have no complaint if civilization tries to thwart him by whatever means necessary.

Rather than using direct empirical evidence, the author supports his point with a subargument showing how terrorists differ from victims and thus relinquish their claim to rights.

---

*This writer is using the MLA (Modern Language Association) style for documenting sources. The full bibliographic information about the off-road usage statistic will be found in the "Works Cited" list at the end of the paper alphabetized under "Yacobucci," the last name of the author of the article. The bibliographic information for the source of the carbon dioxide statistics will also be found in "Works Cited" alphabetized under "Update"—the first word of the article title. The writer cites the title rather than an author because the author is anonymous. See Chapter 14.

†This writer is also using the MLA style for documenting sources. Because there is no page number cited in parentheses for the direct quotation, the source is probably from a Web site. Readers will find an entry under "Fischbach" in the "Works Cited" list at the end of the essay. See Chapter 14.

Reliability of Evidence

When you use empirical evidence, you can increase its persuasiveness by monitoring its recency, relevance, impartiality, and sufficiency.

Recency. As much as possible, and especially if you are addressing current issues in science, technology, politics, or social trends, use the most recent evidence you can find.

Relevance. Ensure that the evidence you cite is relevant to the point you are making. For example, for many decades the medical profession offered advice about heart disease to their female patients based on studies of male patients. No matter how extensive or how recent those studies, some of their conclusions were bound to be irrelevant for female patients.

Impartiality. While all data must be interpreted and hence are never completely impartial, careful readers are aware of how easily data can be skewed. Newspapers, magazines, and journals often have political biases and different levels of respectability. Generally, evidence from peer-reviewed scholarly journals is more highly regarded than evidence from secondhand sources. Particularly problematic is information gathered from Internet Web sites, which can vary wildly in reliability and degree of bias.

See pp. 343–355 for help on evaluating Web sites.

Sufficiency. One of the most common reasoning fallacies is to make a sweeping generalization based on only one or two instances. The criterion of sufficiency (which means having enough examples to justify your point) helps you guard against hasty generalizations.

Addressing Objections and Counterarguments

Having looked at the frame of an argument (claim, reasons, and warrants) and at the kinds of evidence used to flesh out the frame, let's turn now to the important concern of anticipating and responding to objections and counterarguments. In this section, we show you an extended example of a student's anticipating and responding to a reader's objection. We then describe a planning schema that can help you anticipate objections and show you how to respond to counterarguments, either through refutation or concession. Finally, we show how your active imagining of alternative views can lead you to qualify your claim.

Anticipating Objections: An Extended Example

In our earlier discussions of the starling case, we saw how readers might object to the argument "The family was justified in killing the starlings because starlings are pests." What rankles these readers is the unstated assumption (warrant) that it is okay to kill pests. Imagine an objecting reader saying something like this:

It is *not* okay to get annoyed with a living creature, label it a "pest," and then kill it. This whole use of the term *pest* suggests that humans have the right to dominate nature. We need to have more reverence for nature. The ease with which the family solved their problem by killing living things sets a bad example for children. The family could have waited until fall and then fixed the screen.

Imagining such an objection might lead a writer to modify his or her claim. But if the writer remains committed to that claim, then he or she must develop a response. In the following example in which a student writer argues that it is okay to kill the starlings, note (1) how the writer uses evidence to show that starlings are pests; (2) how he summarizes a possible objection to his warrant; and (3) how he supports his warrant with backing.

STUDENT ARGUMENT DEFENDING REASON AND WARRANT

Claim with reason

The family was justified in killing the starlings because starlings are pests. Starlings are nonindigenous birds that drive out native species and multiply rapidly. When I searched "starlings and pests" on the Alta Vista search engine, I discovered 161 Web sites dealing with starlings as pests. Starlings are hated by farmers and gardeners because huge flocks of them devour newly planted seeds in spring as well as fruits and berries at harvest. A flock of starlings can devastate a cherry orchard in a few days. As invasive nesters, starlings can also damage attics by tearing up insulation and defecating on stored items. Many of the Web site articles focused on ways to kill off starling populations. In killing the starlings, the family was protecting its own property and reducing the population of these pests.

Evidence that starlings are pests

Summary of a possible objection

Many readers might object to my argument, saying that humans should have a reverence for nature and not quickly try to kill off any creature they label a pest. Further, these readers might say that even if starlings are pests, the family could have waited until fall to repair the attic or found some other means of protecting their property without having to kill the baby starlings. I too would have waited until fall if the birds in the attic had been swallows or some other native species without starlings' destructiveness and propensity for unchecked population growth. But starlings should be compared to rats or mice. We set traps for rodents because we know the damage they cause when they nest in walls and attics. We don't get sentimental trying to save the orphaned rat babies. In the same way, we are justified in eliminating starlings as soon as they begin infesting our houses. Think of them not as chirpy little songsters but as rats of the bird world.

Response to the objection

In the preceding example, we see how the writer uses grounds to support his reason and then, anticipating his readers' objection to his warrant, summarizes that objection and offers backing. One might not be convinced by the argument, but the writer has done a good job trying to support both the reason and the warrant.

Using a Planning Schema to Anticipate Objections

The arguing strategy used by the previous writer was triggered by his anticipation of objections—what Toulmin calls *conditions of rebuttal*. Under conditions of rebuttal, Toulmin asks arguers to imagine various ways skeptical readers might object to a writer's argument or specific conditions under which the argument might not hold. The Toulmin system lets us create a planning schema that can help writers develop a persuasive argument.

This schema encourages writers to articulate their argument frame (reason and warrant) and then to imagine what could be used for grounds (to support the reason) and backing (to support the warrant). Equally important, the schema encourages writers to anticipate counterarguments by imagining how skeptical readers might object to the writer's reason or warrant or both. To create the schema, simply make a chart headed by your claim with reason and then make slots for grounds, warrant, backing, and conditions of rebuttal. Then brainstorm ideas to put into each slot. Here is how another student writer used this schema to plan an argument on the starling case:

CLAIM WITH REASON

The family showed cruelty to animals because the way they killed the birds caused needless suffering.

GROUNDS

I've got to show how the birds suffered and also how the suffering was needless. The way of killing the birds caused the birds to suffer. The hatchlings starved to death, as did the parent birds if they were trapped inside the attic. Starvation is very slow and agonizing. The suffering was also needless since other means were available such as calling an exterminator who would remove the birds and either relocate them or kill them painlessly. If no other alternative was available, someone should have crawled into the attic and found a painless way to kill the birds.

WARRANT

If it is not necessary to kill an animal, then don't; if it is necessary, then the killing should be done in the least painful way possible.

BACKING

I've got to convince readers it is wrong to make an animal suffer if you don't have to. Humans have a natural antipathy to needless suffering—our feeling of unease if we imagine cattle or chickens caused to suffer for our food rather than being cleanly and quickly killed. If a horse is incurably wounded, we put it to sleep rather then let it suffer. We are morally obligated to cause the least pain possible.

CONDITIONS OF REBUTTAL

How could a reader object to my reason? A reader could say that killing the starlings did not cause suffering. Perhaps hatchling starlings don't feel pain of starvation and die very quickly. Perhaps a reader could object to my claim that other means were available: There is no other way to kill the starlings—impossibility of catching a bunch of adult starlings flying around an attic. Poison may cause just as much suffering. Cost of exterminator is prohibitive.

How could a reader object to my warrant? Perhaps the reader would say that my rule to cause the least pain possible does not apply to animal pests. In class, someone said that worrying about the baby starlings was sentimental. Laws of nature condemn millions of animals each year to death by starvation or by being eaten alive by other animals. Humans occasionally have to take their place within this tooth-and-claw natural system.

How many of the ideas from this schema would the writer use in her actual paper? That is a judgment call based on the writer's analysis of the audience. In

every case, the writer should support the reason with evidence because supporting a claim with reasons and evidence is the minimal requirement of argument.
But it is not necessary to state the warrant explicitly or provide backing for it
unless the writer anticipates readers who doubt it.

The same rule of thumb applies to the need for summarizing and responding
to objections and counterarguments: Let your analysis of audience be your
guide. If we imagined the preceding argument aimed at readers who thought it
was sentimental to worry about the suffering of animal pests, the writer should
make her warrant explicit and back it up. Her task would be to convince readers
that humans have ethical responsibilities that exclude them from tooth-and-
claw morality.

For Writing and Discussion

Working individually or in small groups, create a planning schema for the following arguments. For each claim with reason: (a) imagine the kinds of evidence needed as grounds to support the reason; (b) identify the warrant; (c)
imagine a strategy for supporting the warrant (backing); and (d) anticipate possible objections to the reason and to the warrant (conditions of rebuttal).

1. *Claim with reason*: We should buy a hybrid car rather than an SUV with a
   HEMI engine because doing so will help the world save oil. (Imagine this
   argument aimed at your significant other, who has his or her heart set on a
   huge HEMI-powered SUV.)
2. *Claim with reason*: Gay marriage should be legalized because doing so will
   promote faithful, monogamous relationships among lesbians and gay
   men. (Aim this argument at supporters of traditional marriage.)
3. *Claim with reason*: The government should eliminate welfare payments
   for unwed mothers because doing so would reduce the illegitimacy rate.
   (Imagine this argument aimed at liberals who support welfare payments to
   single mothers.)
4. *Claim with reason*: The war in Iraq was justified because it rid the world of
   a hideous and brutal dictator. (Aim this argument at a critic of the war.)

Responding to Objections, Counterarguments, and Alternative Views Through Refutation or Concession

We have seen how a writer needs to anticipate alternative views that give rise to
objections and counterarguments. Surprisingly, one of the best ways to
approach counterarguments is to summarize them fairly. Make your imagined
reader's best case against your argument. By resisting the temptation to distort a
counterargument, you demonstrate a willingness to consider the issue from all
sides. Moreover, summarizing a counterargument reduces your reader's tendency to say, "Yes, but have you thought of . . .?" After you have summarized an

objection or counterargument fairly and charitably, you must then decide how to respond to it. Your two main choices are to rebut it or concede to it.

Rebutting Opposing Views

When rebutting or refuting an argument, you can question the argument's reasons/grounds or warrant or both. In the following student example, the writer summarizes her classmates' objections to abstract art and then analyzes shortcomings in their reasons and grounds.

> Some of my classmates object to abstract art because it apparently takes no technical drawing talent. They feel that historically artists turned to abstract art because they lacked the technical drafting skills exhibited by Remington, Russell, and Rockwell. Therefore these abstract artists created an art form that anyone was capable of and that was less time consuming, and then they paraded it as artistic progress. But I object to the notion that these artists turned to abstraction because they could not do representative drawing. Many abstract artists, such as Picasso, were excellent draftsmen, and their early pieces show very realistic drawing skill. As his work matured, Picasso became more abstract in order to increase the expressive quality of his work. *Guernica* was meant as a protest against the bombing of that city by the Germans. To express the terror and suffering of the victims more vividly, he distorted the figures and presented them in a black and white journalistic manner. If he had used representational images and color—which he had the skill to do—much of the emotional content would have been lost and the piece probably would not have caused the demand for justice that it did.

Conceding to Counterarguments

In some cases, an alternative view can be very strong. If so, don't hide that view from your readers; summarize it and concede to it.

Making concessions to opposing views is not necessarily a sign of weakness; in many cases, a concession simply acknowledges that the issue is complex and that your position is tentative. In turn, a concession can enhance a reader's respect for you and invite the reader to follow your example and weigh the strengths of your own argument charitably. Writers typically concede to opposing views with transitional expressions such as the following:

admittedly	I must admit that	I agree that	granted
even though	I concede that	while it is true that	

After conceding to an opposing view, you should shift to a different field of values where your position is strong and then argue for those new values. For example, adversaries of drug legalization argue plausibly that legalizing drugs would increase the number of users and addicts. If you support legalization, here is how you might deal with this point without fatally damaging your own argument:

> Opponents of legalization claim—and rightly so—that legalization will lead to an increase in drug users and addicts. I wish this weren't so, but it is. Nevertheless, the other benefits of legalizing drugs—eliminating the black market, reducing street crime, and freeing up thousands of police from fighting the war on drugs—more than outweigh the social costs of increased drug use and addiction, especially if tax revenues from drug sales are plowed back into drug education and rehabilitation programs.

The writer concedes that legalization will increase addiction (one reason for opposing legalization) and that drug addiction is bad (the warrant for that reason). But then the writer redeems the case for legalization by shifting the argument to another field of values (the benefits of eliminating the black market, reducing crime, and so forth).

Qualifying Your Claim

The need to summarize and respond to alternative views lets the writer see an issue's complexity and appreciate that no one position has a total monopoly on the truth. Consequently, in the argument schema that we have adapted from Toulmin, there is one final term that is important to know: the *qualifier*. This term refers to words that limit the scope or force of a claim to make it less sweeping and therefore less vulnerable. Consider the difference between the sentences "After-school jobs are bad for teenagers" and "After-school jobs are often bad for teenagers." The first claim can be refuted by one counterexample of a teenager who benefited from an after-school job. Because the second claim admits exceptions, it is much harder to refute. Unless your argument is airtight, you will want to limit your claim with qualifiers such as the following:

perhaps	maybe
in many cases	generally
tentatively	sometimes
often	usually
probably	likely
may *or* might (*rather than* is)	

You can also qualify a claim with an opening *unless* clause ("*Unless* your apartment is well soundproofed, you should not buy such a powerful stereo system").

Appealing to *Ethos* and *Pathos*

When the classical rhetoricians examined ways that orators could persuade listeners, they focused on three kinds of proofs: *logos*, the appeal to reason; *ethos*, the appeal to the speaker's character; and *pathos*, the appeal to the emotions and the sympathetic imagination. We introduced you to these appeals in Chapter 4 (pp. 78–80) because they are important rhetorical considerations in any kind of writing. Understanding how arguments persuade through *logos*, *ethos*, and *pathos* is particularly helpful when your aim is persuasion. So far in this chapter we have focused on *logos*. In this section we examine *ethos* and *pathos*.

Appeal to *Ethos*

A powerful way to increase the persuasiveness of an argument is to gain your readers' trust. You appeal to *ethos* whenever you present yourself as credible and trustworthy. In Chapter 3 we discussed how readers develop an image of the writer—the writer's *persona*—based on features of the writer's prose. For most readers to accept your argument, they must perceive a persona that's knowledgeable, trust-worthy, and fair. We suggest three ways to enhance your argument's *ethos:*

1. Demonstrate that you know your subject well. If you have personal experi-ence with the subject, cite that experience. Reflect thoughtfully on your sub-ject, citing research as well as personal experience, and accurately and careful-ly summarize a range of viewpoints.
2. Be fair to alternative points of view. Scorning an opposing view may occa-sionally win you favor with an audience predisposed toward your position, but it will offend others and hinder critical analysis. As a general rule, treating opposing views respectfully is the best strategy.
3. Build bridges toward your audience by grounding your argument in shared values and assumptions. Doing so will demonstrate your concern for your audience and enhance your trustworthiness. Moreover, rooting your argu-ment in the audience's values and assumptions has a strong emotional appeal, as we explain in the next section.

Appeals to Pathos

Besides basing your argument on appeals to *logos* and *ethos*, you might also base it on an appeal to what the Greeks called *pathos.* Sometimes *pathos* is interpreted narrowly as an appeal to the emotions. This interpretation effectively devalues *pathos* because popular culture generally values reason above emotion. Although appeals to *pathos* can sometimes be irrational and irrelevant ("You can't give me a C! I need a B to get into medical school, and if I don't it'll break my ill grand-mother's heart"), they can also arouse audience interest and deepen understand-ing of an argument's human dimensions. Here are some ways to use *pathos* in your arguments:

Use Vivid Language and Examples.   One way to create *pathos* is to use vivid lan-guage and powerful examples. If you are arguing in favor of homeless shelters, for example, you can humanize your appeal by describing one homeless person:

> He is huddled over the sewer grate, his feet wrapped in newspapers. He blows on his hands, then tucks them under his armpits and lies down on the sidewalk with his shoulders over the grate, his bed for the night.

But if you are arguing for tougher laws against panhandling, you might let your reader see the issue through the eyes of downtown shoppers intimidated by "rat-ty, urine-soaked derelicts drinking fortified wine from a shared sack."

Find Audience-Based Reasons.   The best way to think of *pathos* is not as an appeal to emotions but rather as an appeal to the audience's values and beliefs. With its emphasis on warrants, Toulmin's system of analysis naturally encourages this kind of appeal. For example, in engineer David Rockwood's argument against wind-generated power, Rockwood's final reason is that constructing wind-generation facilities will damage the environment. To environmentalists, this reason has

Rockwood's argument appears in Chapter 1, pp. 17–18.

emotional as well as rational power because its warrant ("Preserving the environment is good") appeals to their values. It is an example of an audience-based reason, which we can define simply as any reason whose warrant the audience already accepts and endorses. Such reasons, because they hook into the beliefs and values of the audience, appeal to *pathos.*

When you plan your argument, seek audience-based reasons whenever possible. Suppose, for example, that you are advocating the legalization of heroin and cocaine. If you know that your audience is concerned about their own safety in the streets, then you can argue that legalization of drugs will cut down on crime:

> We should legalize drugs because doing so will make our streets safer: It will cut down radically on street criminals seeking drug money, and it will free up narcotics police to focus on other kinds of crime.

If your audience is concerned about improving the quality of life for youths in inner cities, you might argue that legalization of drugs will lead to better lives for the current underclass:

> We should legalize drugs because doing so will eliminate the lure of drug trafficking that tempts so many inner-city youth away from honest jobs and into crime.

Or if your audience is concerned about high taxes and government debt, you might say:

> We should legalize drugs because doing so will help us balance federal and state budgets: It will decrease police and prison costs by decriminalizing narcotics; and it will eliminate the black market in drugs, allowing us to collect taxes on drug sales.

In each case, you move people toward your position by connecting your argument to their beliefs and values.

Some Advanced Considerations

You have now finished reading what we might call a "basic course in argumentation." In this final section, we briefly discuss some more advanced ideas about argumentation. Your instructor may want to expand on these in class, simply ask you to read them, or not assign this section at all. The three concepts we explore briefly are argument types, delayed-thesis and Rogerian arguments, and informal fallacies.

Argument Types

The advice we have given you so far in this chapter applies to any type of argument. However, scholars of argumentation have categorized arguments into several different types, each of which uses its own characteristic structures and ways of development. One way to talk about argument types is to divide them into truth issues and values issues.

Truth issues stem from questions about the way reality is (or was or will be). Unlike questions of fact, which can be proved or disproved by agreed-on empirical measures, issues of truth require interpretation of the facts. "Does Linda smoke an average of twenty or more cigarettes per day?" is a question of fact, answerable with a yes or a no. But "Why did Linda start smoking when she was fifteen?" is a question of truth with many possible answers. Was it because of cigarette advertising? Peer pressure? The dynamics of Linda's family? Dynamics in the culture (for example, white American youths are seven times more likely to smoke than are African-American youths)? Truth issues generally take one of the three following forms:

1. *Definitional issues.* Does this particular case fit into a particular category? (Is bungee jumping a "carnival ride" for purposes of state safety regulations? Is tobacco a "drug" and therefore under the jurisdiction of the Federal Drug Administration?)
2. *Causal issues.* What are the causes or consequences of this phenomenon? (Does the current welfare system encourage teenage pregnancy? Has the war in Iraq made America safer against terrorists?)
3. *Resemblance or precedence issues.* Is this phenomenon like or analogous to some other phenomenon? (Is U.S. involvement in Iraq like U.S. involvement in Vietnam? Is killing a starling like killing a rat?)

Rational arguments can involve disputes about values as well as truth. Family disagreements about what car to buy typically revolve around competing values: What is most important? Looks? Performance? Safety? Economy? Comfort? Dependability? Prestige? Similarly, many public issues ask people to choose among competing value systems: Whose values should be adopted in a given situation: Those of corporations or environmentalists? Of the fetus or the pregnant woman? Of owners or laborers? Of the individual or the state? Values issues usually fall in one of the following two categories:

1. *Evaluation issues.* How good is this particular member of its class? Is this action morally good or bad? (Was Ronald Reagan a great president? Which computer system best meets the company's needs? Is the death penalty morally wrong?)
2. *Policy issues.* Should we take this action? (Should Congress pass stricter gun control laws? Should health insurance policies cover eating disorders?)

Delayed-Thesis and Rogerian Arguments

Classical arguments are usually closed form with the writer's thesis stated prominently at the end of the introduction. Classical argument works best for neutral audiences weighing all sides of an issue or for somewhat-opposed audiences who are willing to listen to other views. However, when you address a highly resistant audience, one where your point of view seems especially threatening to your audience's values and beliefs, classical argument can seem too blunt and aggressive. In such cases, a *delayed-thesis argument* works best. In such an argument you don't state your actual thesis until the conclusion. The body of the paper extends your sympathy to the reader's views, shows how troubling the issue is to you, and leads the reader gradually toward your position.

A special kind of delayed-thesis argument is called *Rogerian argument,* named after psychologist Carl Rogers, who specialized in helping people with widely divergent views learn to talk to each other. The principle of Rogerian communication is that listeners must show empathy toward each other's worldviews and make every attempt to build bridges toward each other. In planning a Rogerian argument, instead of asking, "What reasons and evidence will convince my reader to adopt my claim?", you ask, "What is it about my view that especially threatens my reader? How can I reduce this threat?" Using a Rogerian strategy, the writer summarizes the audience's point of view fairly and charitably, demonstrating the ability to listen and understand the audience's views. The writer then reduces the threat of his or her own position by showing how both writer and resistant audience share many basic values. The key to successful Rogerian argument, besides the art of listening, is the ability to point out areas of agreement between the writer's and the reader's positions. Then the writer seeks a compromise between the two views.

As an example, if you support a woman's right to choose abortion and you are arguing with someone completely opposed to abortion, you're unlikely to convert your reader, but you may reduce the level of resistance. You begin this process by summarizing your reader's position sympathetically, stressing your shared values. You might say, for example, that you also value babies; that you also are appalled by people who treat abortion as a form of birth control; that you also worry that the easy acceptance of abortion diminishes the value society places on human life; and that you also agree that accepting abortion lightly can lead to lack of sexual responsibility. Building bridges like these between you and your readers makes it more likely that they will listen to you when you present your own position.

Avoiding Informal Fallacies

Informal fallacies are instances of murky reasoning that can cloud an argument and lead to unsound conclusions. Because they can crop up unintentionally in anyone's writing, and because advertisers and hucksters often use them intentionally to deceive, it is a good idea to learn to recognize the more common fallacies.

Post Hoc, Ergo Propter Hoc (After This, Therefore Because of This).   This fallacy involves mistaking sequence for cause. Just because one event happens before another event doesn't mean the first event caused the second. The connection may be coincidental, or some unknown third event may have caused both of these events.

> **Example**   For years I suffered from agonizing abdominal itching. Then I tried Smith's pills. Almost overnight my abdominal itching ceased. Smith's pills work wonders.

Hasty Generalization.   Closely related to the *post hoc* fallacy is the hasty generalization, which refers to claims based on insufficient or unrepresentative data.

> **Example**   The food stamp program supports mostly freeloaders. Let me tell you about my worthless neighbor.

False Analogy.   Analogical arguments are tricky because there are, almost always, significant differences between the two things being compared. If the two things differ greatly, the analogy can mislead rather than clarify.

> **Example**   You can't force a kid to become a musician any more than you can force a tulip to become a rose.

Either/Or Reasoning.   This fallacy occurs when a complex, multisided issue is reduced to two positions without acknowledging the possibility of other alternatives.

Example   Either you are pro-choice on abortion or you are against the advancement of women in our culture.

Ad Hominem ("Against the Person").   When people can't find fault with an argument, they sometimes attack the arguer, substituting irrelevant assertions about that person's character for an analysis of the argument itself.

Example   Don't pay any attention to Fulke's views on sexual harassment in the workplace. I just learned that he subscribes to *Playboy.*

Appeals to False Authority and Bandwagon Appeals.   These fallacies offer as support the fact that a famous person or "many people" already support it. Unless the supporters are themselves authorities in the field, their support is irrelevant.

Example   Buy Freeble oil because Joe Quarterback always uses it in his fleet of cars.

Example   How can abortion be wrong if millions of people support a woman's right to choose?

Non Sequitur ("It Does Not Follow").   This fallacy occurs when there is no evident connection between a claim and its reason. Sometimes a *non sequitur* can be repaired by filling in gaps in the reasoning; at other times, the reasoning is simply fallacious.

Example   I don't deserve a B for this course because I am a straight-A student.

Circular Reasoning.   This fallacy occurs when you state your claim and then, usually after rewording it, you state it again as your reason.

Example   Marijuana is injurious to your health because it harms your body.

Red Herring.   This fallacy refers to the practice of raising an unrelated or irrelevant point deliberately to throw an audience off the track. Politicians often employ this fallacy when they field questions from the public or press.

Example   You raise a good question about my support of companies' outsourcing jobs to find cheaper labor. Let me tell you about my admiration for the productivity of the American worker.

Slippery Slope.   The slippery slope fallacy is based on the fear that one step in a direction we don't like inevitably leads to the next step with no stopping place.

Example   If we allow embryonic stem cells to be used for medical research, we will open the door for full-scale reproductive cloning.

READINGS

Our first reading, by student writer Ross Taylor, aims to increase appreciation of paintball as a healthy sport. An avid paintballer, Ross was frustrated by how many of his friends and acquaintances didn't appreciate paintball and had numerous misconceptions about it. The following argument is aimed at those who don't understand the sport or condemn it for being dangerous and violent.

Ross Taylor (Student)
Paintball:
Promoter of Violence or Healthy Fun?

1   Glancing out from behind some cover, I see an enemy soldier on the move. I level my gun and start pinching off rounds. Hearing the incoming fire, he turns and starts to fire, but it is far too late. His entire body flinches when I land two torso shots, and he falls when I hit his leg. I duck back satisfied with another good kill on my record. I pop up this time again to scan for more enemy forces. Out of the corner of my eye I see some movement and turn to see two soldiers peeking out from behind a sewer pipe. I move to take cover again, but it's futile. I feel the hits come one by one hitting me three times in the chest and once on the right bicep before I fall behind the cover. I'm hit. It's all over—for me at least. The paintball battle rages on as I carefully leave the field to nurse my welts, which are already showing. Luckily, I watch my three remaining teammates trample the two enemy soldiers who shot me to win the game. This is paintball in all its splendor and glory.

2   Paintball is one of the most misunderstood and generally looked down upon recreational activities. People see it as rewarding violence and lacking the true characteristics of a healthy team sport like ultimate Frisbee, soccer, or pickup basketball. Largely the accusations directed at paintball are false because it is a positive recreational activity. Paintball is a fun, athletic, mentally challenging recreational activity that builds teamwork and releases tension.

3   Paintball was invented in the early 1980s as a casual activity for survival enthusiasts, but it has grown into a several hundred million dollar industry. It is, quite simply, an expanded version of tag. Players use a range of CO_2 powered guns that fire small biodegradable marbles of paint at approximately 250–300 feet per second. The result of a hit is a small splatter of oily paint and a nice dark bruise. Paintball is now played nationwide in indoor and outdoor arenas. Quite often variants are played such as "Capture the Flag" or "Assassination." In "Capture the Flag" the point is to retrieve the heavily guarded flag from the other team and return it to your base. The game of "Assassination" pits one team of "assassins" against the "secret service." The secret service men guard an unarmed player dubbed the "president." Their goal is get from point A to point B without the president's getting tagged.

Contrary to popular belief, the games are highly officiated and organized. There is always a referee present. Barrel plugs are required until just before a game begins and must be reinserted as soon as the game ends. No hostages may be taken. A player catching another off guard at close range must first give the player the opportunity to surrender. Most importantly there is no physical contact between players. Punching, pushing, or butt-ending with the gun is strictly prohibited. The result is an intense game that is relatively safe for all involved.

4   The activity of paintball is athletically challenging. There are numerous sprint and dives to avoid being hit. At the end of a game, typically lasting around 20 minutes, all the players are winded, sweaty, and ultimately exhilarated. The beginning of the game includes a mad dash for cover by both teams with heavy amounts of fire being exchanged. During the game, players execute numerous strategic moves to gain a tactical advantage, often including quick jumps, dives, rolls, and runs. While under cover, players crawl across broad stretches of playing field often still feeling their bruises from previous games. These physical feats culminate in an invigorating and physically challenging activity good for building muscles and coordination.

5   In addition to the athletic challenge, paintball provides strong mental challenge, mainly the need for constant strategizing. There are many strategic positioning methods. For example, the classic pincer move involves your team's outflanking an opponent from each side to eliminate his or her mobility and shelter. In the more sophisticated ladder technique, teammates take turns covering each other as the others move onward from cover to cover. Throughout the game, players' minds are constantly reeling as they calculate their positions and cover, their teammates' positions and cover, and their opponents' positions and strength. Finally, there is the strong competitive pull of the individual. It never fails to amaze me how much thought goes into one game.

6   Teamwork is also involved. Paintball takes a lot of cooperation. You need special hand signals to communicate with your teammates, and you have to coordinate, under rapidly changing situations, who is going to flank left or right, who is going to charge, and who is going to stay back to guard the flag station. The importance of teamwork in paintball explains why more and more businesses are taking their employees for a day of action with the intent of creating a closer knit and smooth-functioning workplace. The value of teamwork is highlighted on the Web site of a British Columbia facility, Action and Adventure Paintball, Ltd, which says that in paintball,

> as in any team sport, the team that communicates best usually wins. It's about thinking, not shooting. This is why Fortune 500 companies around the world take their employees to play paintball together.

An advantage of paintball for building company team spirit is that paintball teams, unlike teams in many other recreational sports, can blend very skilled and totally unskilled players. Women like paintball as much as men, and the game is open to people of any size, body type, and strength level. Since a game usually takes no more than seven to ten minutes, teams can run a series of different games with different players to have lots of different match-ups. Also families like to play paintball together.

7   People who object to paintball criticize its danger and violence. The game's supposed danger gets mentioned a lot. The public seems to have received the impression that paintball guns are simply eye-removing hardware. It is true that paintball can lead to eye injuries. An article by medical writer Cheryl Guttman in a trade magazine for ophthalmologists warns that eye injuries from paintball are on the rise. But the fact is that Guttman's article says that only 102 cases of eye injuries from paintballs were reported from 1985 to 2000 and that 85 percent of those injured were not wearing the required safety goggles. This is not to say that accidents don't happen. I personally had a friend lose an eye after inadvertently shooting himself in the eye from a very close range. The fact of the matter is that he made a mistake by looking down the barrel of a loaded gun and the trigger malfunctioned. Had he been more careful or worn the proper equipment, he most likely would have been fine. During my first organized paintball experience I was hit in the goggles by a very powerful gun and felt no pain. The only discomfort came from having to clean all the paint off my goggles after the game. When played properly, paintball is an incredibly safe sport.

8   The most powerful argument against paintball is that it is inherently violent and thus unhealthy. Critics claim paintball is simply an accepted form of promoting violence against other people. I have anti-war friends who think that paintball glorifies war. Many new parents today try to keep their kids from playing cops and robbers and won't buy them toy guns. These people see paintball as an upgraded and more violent version of the same antisocial games they don't want their children to play. Some people also point to the connections between paintball and violent video games where participants get their fun from "killing" other people. They link paintball to all the other violent activities that they think lead to such things as gangs or school shootings. But there is no connection between school shootings and paintball. As seen in Michael Moore's Bowling for Columbine, the killers involved there went bowling before the massacre; they didn't practice their aim by playing paintball.

9   What I am trying to say is that, yes, paintball is violent to a degree. After all, its whole point is to "kill" each other with guns. But I object to paintball's being considered a promotion of violence. Rather, I feel that it is a healthy release of tension. From my own personal experience, when playing the game, the players aren't focused on hurting the other players; they are focused on winning the game. At the end of the day, players are not full of violent urges, but just the opposite. They want to celebrate together as a team, just as do softball or soccer teams after a game. Therefore I don't think paintball is an unhealthy activity for adults. (The only reason I wouldn't include children is because I believe the pain is too intense for

them. I have seen some younger players cry after being shot.) Paintball is simply a game, a sport, that produces intense exhilaration and fun. Admittedly, paintball guns can be used in irresponsible manners. Recently there have been some drive-by paintballings, suggesting that paintball players are irresponsible and violent. However, the percentage of people who do this sort of prank is very small and those are the bad apples of the group. There will always be those who misuse equipment. For example, baseball bats have been used in atrocious beatings, but that doesn't make baseball a violent sport. So despite the bad apples, paintball is still a worthwhile activity when properly practiced.

10   Athletic and mentally challenging, team-building and fun—the game of paintball seems perfectly legitimate to me. It is admittedly violent, but it is not the evil activity that critics portray. Injuries can occur, but usually only when the proper safety equipment is not being used and proper precautions are ignored. As a great recreational activity, paintball deserves the same respect as other sports. It is a great way to get physical exercise, make friends, and have fun.

Thinking Critically about "Paintball: Promoter of Violence or Healthy Fun?"

1. Before reading this essay, what was your own view of paintball? To what extent did this argument create for you a more positive view of paintball? What aspects of the argument did you find particularly effective or ineffective?

2. How effective are Ross's appeals to *ethos* in this argument? Does he create a persona that you find trustworthy and compelling? How does he do so or fail to do so?

3. How effective are Ross's appeals to *pathos*? How does he appeal to his readers' values, interests, and emotions in trying to make paintball seem like an exhilarating team sport? To what extent does he show empathy with readers when he summarizes objections to paintball?

4. How effective are Ross's appeals to *logos*? How effective are Ross's reasons and evidence in support of his claim? How effective are Ross's responses to opposing views?

5. What are the main strengths and weaknesses of Ross's argument?

Our next reading, "Spare the Rod, Spoil the Parenting," is an op-ed piece by *Miami Herald* columnist Leonard Pitts, Jr., that appeared in newspapers across the country in September 2001. In this editorial, Pitts jumps into the ongoing controversy over corporal punishment, children's rights, child-rearing practices, and spanking.

Leonard Pitts, one of the nation's foremost African-American opinion writers, won the Pulitzer Prize for commentary in 2004. He is the author of *Becoming Dad: Black Men and the Journey to Fatherhood.*

Leonard Pitts, Jr.
Spare the Rod, Spoil the Parenting

1 I hate to tell you this, but your kid is spoiled. Mine aren't much better.

2 That, in essence, is the finding of a recent Time/CNN poll. Most of us think most of our kids are overindulged, materialistic brats.

3 If you're waiting for me to argue the point, you're in the wrong column.

4 No, I only bring it up as context to talk about a controversial study released late last month. It deals with corporal punishment—spanking—and it has outraged those who oppose the practice while rearming those who support it.

5 It seems that Dr. Diana Baumrind, a psychologist at the University of California at Berkeley, followed 164 middle-class families from the time their children were in preschool until they reached their 20s. She found that most used some form of corporal punishment. She further found that, contrary to what we've been told for years, giving a child a mild spanking (defined as open-handed swats on the backside, arm or legs) does not leave the child scarred for life.

6 Baumrind, by the way, opposes spanking. Still, it's to her credit as an academic that her research draws a distinction other opponents refuse to. That is, a distinction between the minor punishments practiced by most parents who spank and the harsher variants practiced by a tiny minority (shaking and blows to the head or face, for example).

7 Yes, children whose parents treat them that severely are, indeed, more likely to be maladjusted by the time they reach adolescence. And, yes, the parents themselves are teetering dangerously close to child abuse.

8 But does the same hold true in cases where corporal punishment means little more than swatting a misbehaving backside?

9 For years, the official consensus from the nation's child-rearing experts was that it did. Maybe that's about to change. We can only hope.

10 For my money, there was always something spurious about the orthodoxy that assured us all corporal punishment, regardless of severity, was defacto abuse. Nevertheless, we bought into it, with the result being that parents who admitted to spanking were treated as primitive dolts and heaped with scorn. They were encouraged to negotiate with misbehaving children in order to nurture their self-esteem.

11 But the orthodoxy was wrong on several fronts.

12 In the first place, it's plainly ridiculous—and offensive—to equate a child who has been swatted on the butt with one who has been stomped, scalded or punched. In the second, the argument that reasonable corporal punishment leads inevitably to mental instability always seemed insupportable and

has just been proven so by Baumrind's study. And in the third, have you ever tried to "negotiate" with a screaming 5-year-old? It may do wonders for the child's self-esteem, but, I promise, it's going to kill yours. Your sanity, too.

13 Don't get me wrong, contrary to what its proponents sometimes claim, corporal punishment is not a panacea for misbehavior. Rearing a child requires not just discipline, but also humor, love and some luck.

14 Yet the very fact that spanking must be exonerated by a university study suggests how far afield we've wandered from what used to be the central tenet of family life: parents in charge. Ultimately, it probably doesn't matter whether that tenet is enforced by spanking or other corrective measures, so long as it is enforced.

15 I've seen too many children behave with too grand a sense of entitlement to believe that it is. Heard too many teachers tell horror stories of dealing with kids from households where parents are not sovereign, adult authority not respected. As a culture, we seem to have forgotten that the family is not a democracy, but a benign dictatorship.

16 Small wonder our kids are brats.

17 So the pertinent question isn't: To spank or not to spank? Rather, it's: Who's in charge here? Who is teaching whom? Who is guiding whom?

18 The answer used to be obvious. It's obvious no more. And is it so difficult to see where that road leads? To understand that it is possible to be poisoned by self-esteem, and that a spoiled child becomes a self-centered adult ill-equipped to deal with the vagaries and reversals of life?

19 Some folks think it's abuse when you swat a child's backside. But maybe, sometimes, it's abuse when you don't.

Thinking Critically about "Spare the Rod, Spoil the Parenting"

1. In the introductory paragraphs of this op-ed piece, Leonard Pitts, Jr., mentions the rhetorical situation that has called forth his argument. What contemporary research is prompting Pitts's column?
2. Pitts's argument takes a stand on the issue question, "Is spanking a good child-rearing practice?" What claim does he make in this argument? What reasons and evidence does he offer to support this claim?
3. Where does Pitts acknowledge and respond to opposing views?
4. To understand the intensity of the social controversy on this issue, we suggest that you search the key words "spanking" and "corporal punishment" using an online database and the Web. What different positions do you find represented in articles and by advocacy Web sites such as the site for the Center for Effective Discipline? How would these sources challenge Pitts's position and evidence?

The last reading is by student writer A. J. Chavez, who wrote this paper for the classical argument assignment in this chapter. In proposing the legalization of gay marriage, A. J. Chavez draws on personal knowledge and experience, some Internet research, and information from an anthropology course he was taking simultaneously with first-year composition.

A. J. Chavez (Student)
The Case for (Gay) Marriage

1   "What if it was a gay world? And you were straight?" a recent TV spot asks (the ad can be viewed at commercialcloset.org—see "What If" in Works Cited). The camera pans across a hospital waiting room, filled with gay and lesbian couples. There, a middle-aged man sits, waiting. "Your partner's in a coma. She's not responding," a young male doctor says to him. "Unfortunately, since the state doesn't recognize your marriage, I can't grant you spousal visitation. If she were to wake, or a family member gave consent—I wish there was more I could do. I'm sorry." After that, the camera quickly zooms out from the man's heartbroken face. The scene blurs, and a female voiceover reads the fact that appears on the screen: "hospital visitation: just one of over 1000 rights granted to a legally married couple." Next, the scene fades into a black screen with a blue rectangle that has a yellow equal sign on it. The female voiceover continues, "Support equality for all Americans. Millionformarriage.org." This spot, sponsored by the Human Rights Campaign, the largest queer political organization in the United States, shows a scenario that undoubtedly happens every day in America, just with the tables turned. According to a report from the United States General Accounting Office, released after the passage of the federal Defense of Marriage Act of 1996, there are at least 1,049 federal laws in the U.S. code that relate to rights specific to marriage (2). Some are obvious, like Social Security or Veterans' Administration benefits upon the death of a spouse for the surviving spouse and children. Others are not so obvious, but equally important, such as the federally guaranteed right of an employee to take time off from work to care for an ill spouse or the so-called "spousal privilege" of not having to testify against a husband or wife in court. Currently, marriage rights are denied to a small, but still significant group in America—gays and lesbians, a group of which I am a part. We are denied the same rights enjoyed by straight people, simply because we are attracted to and love members of our own sex and have chosen to live open, honest lives, instead of closeted ones.

2   In opposition to the current Congressional proposal to amend the Constitution by defining marriage as a union between a man and a woman, I am proposing the nationwide legalization of same-sex marriage. First of all, gay marriage is the easiest way to ensure equality for all. Civil unions can only go part of the way. Secondly, the government must define marriage

through a secular framework that respects the spirit of laws already in place, not a religious one that would violate separation between church and state. Third, the costs to taxpayers for legalizing gay marriage would be negligible. Some studies even suggest it would save taxpayer money. Finally, anthropological evidence exists for the existence of what we would refer to today as "gay marriage" across a long time span and wide range of cultures, demonstrating that it is not abnormal or perverted.

3   There are many arguments against gay marriage. Some are definitional, such as "Marriage is between a man and a woman." Other claims against gay marriage stem from concern for the well-being of children raised by gay or lesbian couples from previous straight marriages, adoption, or reproductive assistance. Still others arise out of respect for the Hebrew and Christian scriptures, the moral code from which most of Western civilization has lived by for thousands of years—certain passages in them prohibit homosexual relations. Another objection is that marriage is reserved for procreation, and that gay marriage, obviously, cannot serve this end. Additionally, there is the argument that legal options already exist for gay couples that offer some of the benefits of marriage, such as power of attorney or living will. Some politicians claim that marriage is something that should be left to the states to decide how to define and deal with individually. Furthermore, there is the argument that the legalization of gay marriage will open the doors to the legalization of more radical unions, such as adult-child unions or polygamy. Last, some members of America's queer community oppose gay marriage because they see it as just an attempt to copy and live a hetero lifestyle.

4   My first reason for legalizing gay marriage is that it is the easiest and most effective way to ensure equal rights for all in this country. Currently, sexual minorities receive no explicit protection from federal anti-discrimination acts, such as Title VII from the Civil Rights Act of 1964, which only prohibits discrimination in employment based on "race, color, religion, sex, or national origin." Employers are not required to offer the same benefits to the significant others of gay employees as they do to straight employees. With gay marriage, they would be obliged under laws that protect the rights of married couples to do so. Civil unions relegate gays and lesbians to second-class status. Civil unions or domestic partnerships are offered only by a few states, but can be disregarded by neighboring anti-gay states because of the federal Defense of Marriage Act. Civil unions can guarantee protections only at the state level, and at that, only the state they were issued in. Gay marriage, with its protections, would help prevent discrimination toward sexual minorities from prejudiced individuals. Here, it becomes clear that marriage laws should not just be left to the states, as some politicians who would rather not take a stand on the issue suggest, because if they are, patchwork laws will continue to develop across the nation. Some states will prohibit same-sex marriages and civil unions, while others will provide civil unions, and, perhaps in the future, gay marriage. A clear, federal standard

for the inclusion of gay marriage will also prevent possible loopholes in marriage or civil union laws for inappropriate unions between adults and children or among more than two partners.

5   Second, for public policy, marriage, like all other things, needs to be defined through a non-religious, secular framework. The separation of church and state has always been an important tenet in American government. Allowing religious dogma to define marriage violates this tenet, setting up a dangerous precedent for further unification of church and state. If gay marriage were legalized, religions would still be allowed to distinguish what they do and do not see as "marriage." The Human Rights Campaign Web site provides the example of the Catholic church, which does not bless second marriages after divorce. Yet people can still file for divorce and then remarry if they see fit. In this case, the state recognizes a legal marriage that is not officially sanctioned by the church ("I Believe God Meant"). Also, while certain passages of the Bible prohibit sexual relationships between members of the same sex, others condone slavery and polygamy—both practices that would not be approved in American society today. Clearly, appeals to the Bible cannot be used to determine public policy. We would not only violate the important principle of separation between church and state, but by strict Biblical interpretation of morality, we could theoretically have a polygamous, slave-owning society.

6   Another compelling reason for legalizing same-sex marriage is the money that could actually be *saved* in state budgets every year. The FAQ section on marriage on the Human Rights Campaign Web site explains how government savings could add up through increased reliance between gay and lesbian couples on each other, reducing reliance on government assistance programs such as Temporary Assistance to Needy Families (welfare), Supplemental Security Income (disability), food stamps and Medicaid. The Web site cites two economic studies by professors at UCLA and the University of Massachusetts, Amherst, who examined possible savings to state governments in California and New Jersey if domestic benefits were extended to same-sex couples. According to these studies, the savings were projected to be $10.6 million in California and $61 million in New Jersey ("Won't This Cost"). Additionally, the legalization of gay marriage would provide medical insurance benefits for thousands of currently uninsured children. While gay and lesbian couples obviously cannot conceive children on their own, plenty raise children from previous, heterosexual marriages, adopt children, or use reproductive assistance such as surrogate mothers or assisted insemination to bear their own children. The fact that many gay and lesbian partners are raising children shows the fallacy in claiming that gays should not be allowed to marry because they can't procreate. If we used the logic of procreation in determining whether to grant marriage rights, we would have to ban marriage between elderly couples, between sterile straight couples, and between those who plan to use birth control to pre-

vent pregnancy. Of course, we would never ban such marriages because we recognize the value of having a life partner. Extending marriage benefits to gay partners brings the same benefits to them, with the additional benefit to the states of reducing reliance on state assistance programs and bringing medical insurance to many children.

7   My final reason for the legalization of gay marriage is that same-sex unions have existed across all cultures and time. This is important to recognize, because Judeo-Christian societies like ours tend to discount the legitimacy or even existence of such unions, and of so-called "sexual minorities." Such disregard can be explained by the histories of Judaism and Christianity, says Ted Fortier, Ph.D., a cultural anthropologist at Seattle University. In early Jewish societies, largely due to problems with underpopulation, he notes, any sexual activity without procreative power was considered taboo. Also, in Christian medieval Europe, disease and famine required that the people have all the labor possible to produce food. Again, all non-procreative sex was labeled taboo. For anthropological purposes, Fortier defines marriage as "a union between a woman and another person." This definition, however, can be quite broad, he says. The "woman" can actually be a man playing a feminine role. He explains that in our culture, we look at gender as a biological concept, instead of a socially determined one. He gives examples of different cultures that distinguish certain men who take on womanly roles as being a third gender, such as that of Tahiti, where every village has a man that takes on the role of a woman, or the Native American *berdache* role, another womanly role played by a man. These men raise children just like the other adults. For the most part, Fortier claims, throughout all societies and cultures marriage has always been about securing resources and property—known as "alliance theory" in anthropology. Looking at our own society with this concept in mind, we see that marriage is utilized in the same way—as a stabilizing combination of tangible and intangible resources that leads to benefits to society, often including the raising of children. Law professor Mark Strasser, in an essay entitled "State Interests in Recognizing Same-Sex Marriage," mentions that "there is no evidence that children will not thrive when raised by same-sex parents and, indeed, some evidence that children may be better off in certain ways when they are raised by same-sex parents than when they are raised by different-sex parents" (37). Strasser refers to the increased tolerance and appreciation of differences that children of gays and lesbians typically have and the innumerable studies over the years that show these children grow up just as well-adjusted and are no more likely to be homosexual than children living with straight parents. The government, therefore, should recognize and extend marriage protections to same-sex couples as well. While there are some gay/lesbian/bisexual/transgender people who think gay marriage is just a futile attempt to copy mainstream, straight society, and that the government should not bother legalizing it, entering into any union is based on

the mutual choice of two individuals. GLBT persons who find the institution of marriage unsavory would still not be forced by the government to marry if gay marriage were legalized.

8   The case for gay marriage is a strong one indeed, similar to earlier struggles for interracial marriage, which was legalized only relatively recently in American history. Gay marriage will result in an unprecedented addition of formal protections to America's last marginalized minority—the queer community. Studies suggest that it will save individual states millions of dollars in revenue on an annual basis. Gay marriage is not sick or a perversion—it exists across all cultures and times in one form or another and was stigmatized in Judeo-Christian traditions for the practical purpose of achieving as high of a population as possible. It is impossible to turn on a television set or open a newspaper now without seeing a reference to gay marriage. Legalizing gay marriage affirms both the "liberal" ideal of equality and the "conservative" value of community stability and individual rights. It also affirms the dignity of all of mankind.

Works Cited

Fortier, Ted. Personal interview. 26 Feb. 2004.

"I Believe God Meant Marriage for Men and Women." Human Rights Campaign 20 Feb. 2004. 15 Mar. 2004 <http://www.hrc.org>. Path: marriage; "I Believe God Meant."

Strasser, Mark. "State Interests in Recognizing Same-Sex Marriage." Marriage and Same Sex Unions: A Debate. Ed. Lynn D. Wardle, et al. Westport, CT: Praeger, 2003.

United States. General Accounting Office. Categories of Laws Involving Marital Status. Letter of transmittal. By Barry R. Bedrick. 31 Jan. 1997. 16 Mar. 2004 <http://www.gao.gov/archive/1997/og97016.pdf>.

"What If It Were a Gay World?" Advertisement. Human Rights Campaign. The Commercial Closet 2004. 2 Mar. 2004 <http://www.commercialcloset.org/cgi-bin/iowa/portrayals.html?record=1817>.

"Won't This Cost Taxpayers Too Much Money?" Human Rights Campaign 2004. 15 Mar. 2004 <http://www.hrc.org>. Path: marriage; "Won't This Cost."

Thinking Critically about "The Case for (Gay) Marriage"

1. In classical arguments there is often an overlap between the reasons used to support one's own claim and the reasons used to rebut opposing views. In such cases the distinction between support and rebuttal can become blurred (not a problem so long as the argument remains clear). In this essay, where does A. J. Chavez summarize the arguments opposing the legalization of gay marriage? How many of these arguments does he respond to as the argument proceeds? Where does he add supporting reasons in favor of gay marriage that aren't initially framed as rebuttals?

2. How effectively does A. J. create appeals to *ethos* in this argument? How would you characterize his persona based on tone, reasonableness, and empathy for opposing views?

3. On the gay marriage issue, opponents of gay marriage can range from conservative audiences with strong religious arguments against same-sex marriage to very liberal gay audiences who believe that gays shouldn't imitate heterosexual relationships. How well does A. J. use appeals to *pathos* to connect with his imagined readers at both ends of this spectrum? How does he appeal to the values, beliefs, and emotions of his audiences? Point out specific passages where you think he is successful or unsuccessful.

4. How would you assess the appeals to *logos* in this argument? Are A. J.'s use of reasons and evidence persuasive?

5. What do you see as the major strengths and weaknesses of this argument?

Composing Your Essay

Writing arguments deepens our thinking by forcing us to consider alternative views and to question the assumptions underlying our reasons and claims. Consequently, it is not unusual for a writer's position on an issue to shift—and even to reverse itself—during the writing process. If this happens to you, take it as a healthy sign of your openness to change, complexity, and alternative points of view. If writing a draft causes you to modify your views, it will be an act of discovery, not a concession of defeat.

Generating and Exploring Ideas

The tasks that follow are intended to help you generate ideas for your argument. Our goal is to help you build up a storehouse of possible issues, explore several of these possibilities, and then choose one for deeper exploration before you write your initial draft.

Make an Inventory of Issues That Interest You

Following the lead of the For Writing and Discussion exercise on page 242, make a list of various communities that you belong to and then brainstorm contested issues in those communities. You might try a trigger question like this: "When members of [X community] get together, what contested questions cause disagreements?" What decisions need to be made? What values are in conflict? What problems need to be solved?

Explore Several Issues

For this task, choose two or three possible issues from your previous list and explore them through freewriting or idea mapping. Try responding quickly to the following questions:

1. What is my position on this issue and why?
2. What are alternative points of view on this issue?
3. Why do people disagree about this issue? (Do people disagree about the facts of the case? About key definitions? About underlying values, assumptions, and beliefs?)
4. If I were to argue my position on this issue, what evidence would I need to gather and what research might I need to do?

Brainstorm Claims and Reasons

For *because* clauses, see pp. 243–244.

Choose one issue that particularly interests you and work with classmates to brainstorm possible claims that you could make on the issue. Imagining different perspectives, brainstorm possible reasons to support each claim, stating them as *because* clauses.

Conduct and Respond to Initial Research

If your issue requires research, do a quick bibliographic survey of what is available and do enough initial reading to get a good sense of the kinds of arguments that surround your issue and of the alternative views that people have taken. Then freewrite your responses to the following questions:

1. What are the different points of view on this issue? Why do people disagree with each other?
2. Explore the evolution of your thinking as you did this initial reading. What new questions have the readings raised for you? What changes have occurred in your own thinking?

Conduct an In-Depth Exploration Prior to Drafting

The following set of tasks is designed to help you explore your issue in depth. Most students take one or two hours to complete these tasks; the time will pay off, however, because most of the ideas that you need for your rough draft will be on paper.

See the discussion of issue questions on pp. 241–242.

1. Write out the issue your argument will address. Try phrasing your issue in several different ways, perhaps as a yes/no question and as an open-ended question. Try making the question broader, then narrower. Finally, frame the question in the way that most appeals to you.
2. Now write out your tentative answer to the question. This will be your beginning thesis statement or claim. Put a box around this answer. Next, write out one or more different answers to your question. These will be alternative claims that a neutral audience might consider.
3. Why is this a controversial issue? Is there insufficient evidence to resolve the issue, or is the evidence ambiguous or contradictory? Are definitions in dispute? Do the parties disagree about basic values, assumptions, or beliefs?
4. What personal interest do you have in this issue? How does the issue affect you? Why do you care about it? (Knowing why you care about it might help you get your audience to care about it.)

5. What reasons and evidence support your position on this issue? Freewrite everything that comes to mind that might help you support your case. This freewrite will eventually provide the bulk of your argument. For now, freewrite rapidly without worrying whether your argument makes sense. Just get ideas on paper.

6. Imagine all the counterarguments your audience might make. Summarize the main arguments against your position and then freewrite your response to each of the counterarguments. What are the flaws in the alternative points of view?

7. What kinds of appeals to *ethos* and *pathos* might you use to support your argument? How can you increase your audience's perception of your credibility and trustworthiness? How can you tie your argument to your audience's beliefs and values?

8. Why is this an important issue? What are the broader implications and consequences? What other issues does it relate to? Thinking of possible answers to these questions may prove useful when you write your introduction or conclusion.

Shaping and Drafting

Once you have explored your ideas, create a plan. Here is a suggested procedure:
Begin your planning by analyzing your intended audience. You could imagine an audience deeply resistant to your views or a more neutral, undecided audience acting like a jury. In some cases, your audience might be a single person, as when you petition your department chair to take an upper-division course when you are a sophomore. At other times, your audience might be the general readership of a newspaper, church bulletin, or magazine. When the audience is a general readership, you need to imagine from the start the kinds of readers you particularly want to sway. Here are some questions you can ask:

- *How much does your audience know or care about your issue?* Will you need to provide background? Will you need to convince them that your issue is important? Do you need to hook their interest? Your answers to these questions will particularly influence your introduction and conclusion.

- *What is your audience's current attitude toward your issue?* Are they deeply opposed to your position? If so, why? Are they neutral and undecided? If so, what other views will they be listening to? Classical argument works best with neutral or moderately dissenting audiences. Deeply skeptical audiences are best addressed with delayed-thesis or Rogerian approaches. For Rogerian approaches, see pp. 257–258.

- *How do your audience's values, assumptions, and beliefs differ from your own?* What aspects of your position will be threatening to your audience? Why? How does your position on the issue challenge your imagined reader's worldview or identity? What objections will your audience raise toward your argument? Your answers to these questions will help determine the content of your argument and alert you to the extra research you may have to do to respond to audience objections.

- *What values, beliefs, or assumptions about the world do you and your audience share?* Despite your differences with your audience, where can you find common links? How might you use these links to build bridges to your audience?

Your next step is to plan out an audience-based argument by seeking audience-based reasons or reasons whose warrants you can defend. Here is a process you can use:

1. Create a skeleton, tree diagram, outline, or flowchart for your argument by stating your reasons as one or more *because* clauses attached to your claim. Each *because* clause will become the head of a main section or *line of reasoning* in your argument.
2. Use the planning schema on pages 250–252 to plan each line of reasoning. If your audience accepts your warrant, concentrate on supporting your reason with grounds. If your warrant is doubtful, support it with backing. Try to anticipate audience objections by exploring conditions for rebuttal, and brainstorm ways of addressing those objections.
3. Using the skeleton you created, finish developing an outline or tree diagram for your argument. Although the organization for each part of your argument will grow organically from its content, the main parts of a classical argument are as follows:
   a. *An introduction,* in which you engage your reader's attention, introduce your issue, and state your own position.
   b. *Background and preliminary material,* in which you place your issue in a current context and provide whatever background knowledge and definitions of key terms or concepts that your reader will need. (If this background is short, it can often be incorporated into the introduction.)
   c. *Arguments supporting your own position,* in which you make the best case possible for your views by developing your claim with reasons and evidence. This is usually the longest part of your argument, with a separate section for each line of reasoning.
   d. *Anticipation of objections and counterarguments,* in which you summarize fairly key arguments against your position. This section not only helps the reader understand the issue more clearly, but also establishes your *ethos* as a fair-minded writer willing to acknowledge complexity.
   e. *Response to objections through refutation or concession,* in which you point out weaknesses in opposing arguments or concede to their strengths.
   f. *A conclusion,* in which you place your argument in a larger context, perhaps by summarizing your main points and showing why this issue is an important one or by issuing a call to action.

This classical model can be modified in numerous ways. A question that often arises is where to summarize and respond to objections and counterarguments. Writers generally have three choices: One option is to handle opposing positions before you present your own argument. The rationale for this approach is that skeptical audiences may be more inclined to listen attentively to your argument if they have been assured that you understand their point of view. A second option is to place this material after you have presented your argument. This approach is effective for neutral audiences who don't start off with strong opposing views. A final option is to intersperse opposing views throughout your argument at appropriate moments. Any of these possibilities, or a combination of all of them, can be effective.

Another question often asked is, "What is the best way to order one's reasons?" A general rule of thumb when ordering your own argument is to put your strongest reason last and your second-strongest reason first. The idea here is to start and end with your most powerful arguments. If you imagine a quite skeptical audience, build bridges to your audience by summarizing alternative views early in the paper and concede to those that are especially strong. If your audience is neutral or undecided, you can summarize and respond to possible objections after you have presented your own case.

Revising

As you revise your argument, you need to attend both to the clarity of your writing (all the principles of closed-form prose described in Chapter 12) and also to the persuasiveness of your argument. As always, peer reviews are valuable, and especially so in argumentation if you ask your peer reviewers to role-play an opposing audience. The following Guidelines for Peer Reviews can both assist your peer reviewers and help you with revision.

GUIDELINES FOR PEER REVIEWS

Instructions for peer reviews are provided in Chapter 11 (pp. 293–294).

For the Writer
Prepare two or three questions you would like your peer reviewer to address while responding to your draft. The questions can focus on some aspect of your draft that you are uncertain about, on one or more sections where you particularly seek help or advice, on some feature that you particularly like about your draft, or on some part you especially wrestled with. Write out your questions and give them to your peer reviewer along with your draft.

For the Reviewer

I. Read the draft at a normal reading speed from beginning to end. As you read, do the following:
   A. Place a wavy line in the margin next to any passages that you find confusing, that contain something that doesn't seem to fit, or that otherwise slow down your reading.

B. Place a "Good!" in the margin next to any passages where you think the writing is particularly strong or interesting.

II. Read the draft again slowly and answer the following questions by writing brief explanations of your answers.

A. Introduction

1. How could the title be improved so that it announces the issue, reveals the writer's claim, or otherwise focuses your expectations and piques interest?

2. What strategies does the writer use to introduce the issue, engage your interest, and convince you that the issue is significant and problematic? What would add clarity and appeal?

3. How could the introduction more effectively forecast the argument and present the writer's claim? What would make the statement of the claim more focused, clear, or risky?

B. Arguing for the claim

1. Consider the overall structure: What strategies does the writer use to make the structure of the paper clear and easy to follow? How could the structure of the argument be improved?

2. Consider the support for the reasons: Where could the writer provide better evidence or support for each line of reasoning? Look for the grounds in each line of reasoning by noting the writer's use of facts, examples, statistics, testimony, or other evidence. Where could the writer supply more evidence or use existing evidence more effectively?

3. Consider the support for the warrants: For each line of reasoning, determine the assumptions (warrants) that the audience needs to grant for the argument to be effective. Are there places where these warrants need to be stated directly and supported with backing? How could the use of backing be improved?

4. Consider the writer's summary of and response to alternative viewpoints: Where does the writer treat alternative views? Are there additional alternative views that the writer should consider? What strategies does the writer use to respond to alternative views? How could the writer's treatment of alternative views be improved?

C. Conclusion: How might the conclusion more effectively bring completeness or closure to the argument?

III. Rhetorical considerations

A. *Purpose, audience,* and *genre:* How well has the writer achieved his or her persuasive purpose? Were you persuaded by this argument? Why or why not? How effective is the writer at imagining a neutral or skeptical audience (as opposed to preaching to the choir)? How effective is this writer at meeting the constraints of the classical argument genre?

B. *Logos, ethos,* and *pathos:* Overall, how could the writer improve the reasoning of this argument? How effective is the writer at gaining the reader's confidence and trust? How effective is the writer at appealing to the audience's values, beliefs, and emotions? How could the argument be made more vivid or gripping?

IV. If the writer has prepared questions for you, respond to his or her inquiries.

V. Sum up what you see as the main strengths and problem areas of the draft.
   A. Strengths
   B. Problem areas

VI. Read the draft one more time. Place a check mark in the margin wherever you notice problems in grammar, spelling, or mechanics (one check mark per problem).

A Guide to Composing and Revising

This energy poster is part of a series produced by Energy Conservation Awareness Products (www.energyconservationposters .com). These posters are intended to make people conscious of how they use and waste energy and of alternative energy sources that can lessen the use of fossil fuels. Consider how the poster's words, the features of this image, and the use of color all work together to attract viewers and make them think about their energy habits. This poster relates to various readings on energy and various For Writing and Discussion exercises throughout Parts One and Two of this text.

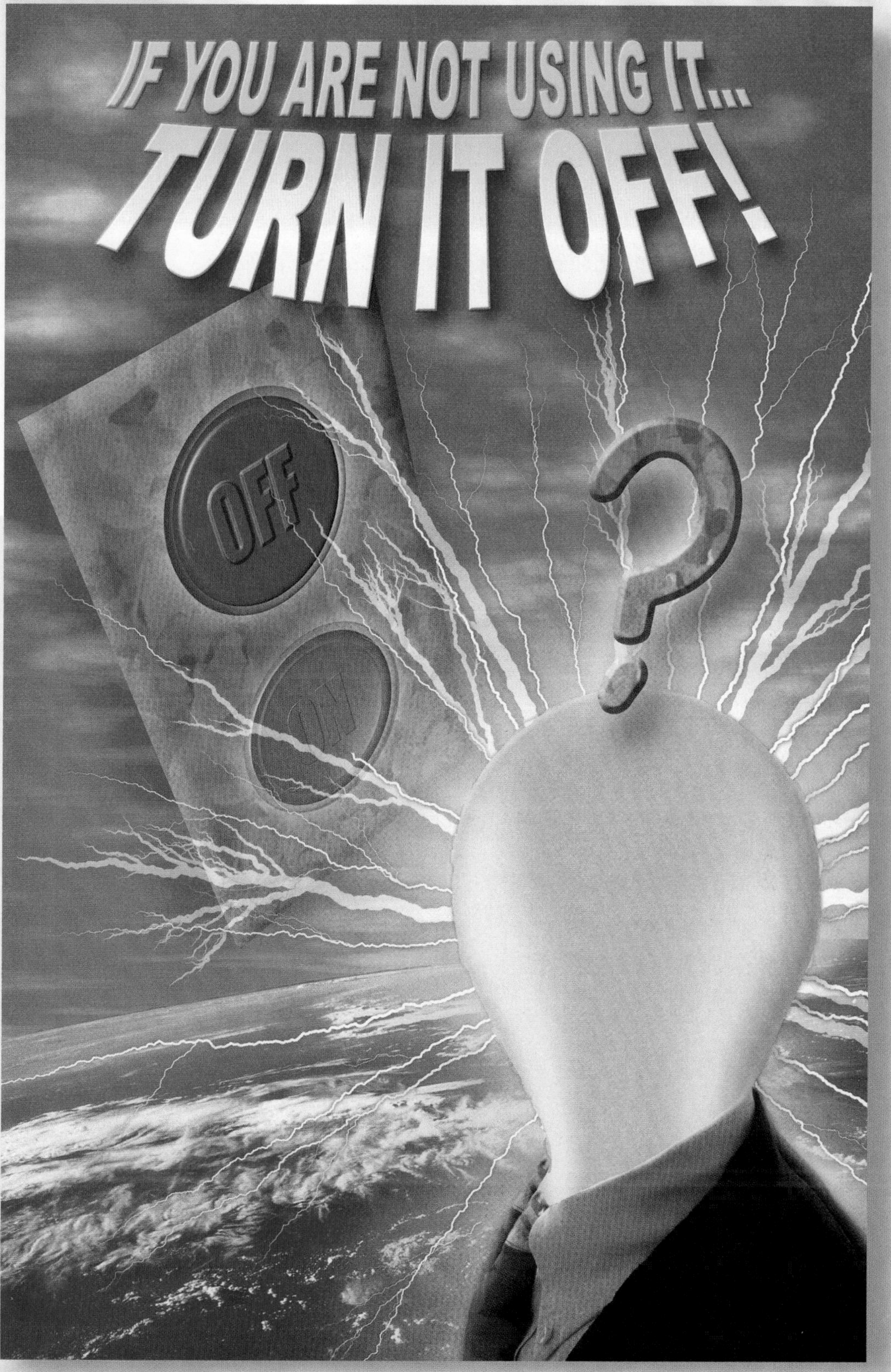
IF YOU ARE NOT USING IT...
TURN IT OFF!
OFF

Part 3 A Guide to Composing and Revising

Writing as a Problem-Solving Process

I rewrite as I write. It is hard to tell what is a first draft because it is not determined by time. In one draft, I might cross out three pages, write two, cross out a fourth, rewrite it, and call it a draft. I am constantly writing and rewriting. I can only conceptualize so much in my first draft—only so much information can be held in my head at one time; my rewriting efforts are a reflection of how much information I can encompass at one time. There are levels and agenda which I have to attend to in each draft.*

> —DESCRIPTION OF REVISION BY AN EXPERIENCED WRITER

I read what I have written and I cross out a word and put another word in; a more decent word or a better word. Then if there is somewhere to use a sentence that I have crossed out, I will put it there.*

> —DESCRIPTION OF REVISION BY AN INEXPERIENCED WRITER

Blot out, correct, insert, refine,
Enlarge, diminish, interline;
Be mindful, when invention fails,
To scratch your head, and bite your nails.

> —JONATHAN SWIFT

In Part One of this text we focused on writing as a problem-solving process in which writers pose and solve both subject-matter problems and rhetorical problems. Part Three shows you how to translate these basic principles into effective strategies for composing and revising your writing. The two self-contained chapters, which can be read in whatever sequence best fits your instructor's course plan, will help you compose and revise the essays you write for the assignments in Part Two.

This chapter explains how experienced writers use multiple drafts to manage the complexities of writing and suggests ways for you to improve your own writing processes. Chapter 12, which takes the form of eight self-contained lessons, focuses on key strategies for composing and revising closed-form prose.

*From Nancy Sommers, "Revision Strategies of Student Writers and Experienced Adult Writers," *College Composition and Communication* 31 (October 1980): 291–300.

Understanding How Experts Compose and Revise

We begin this chapter with a close look at how experienced writers compose, explaining what they think about when they write and why they often need multiple drafts. Composition theorist Peter Elbow has asserted that "meaning is not what you start out with" but "what you end up with." Thus composing is a discovery process. In the early stages of writing, experienced writers typically discover what they are trying to say, often deepening and complicating their ideas rather than clarifying them. Only in the last drafts will such writers be in sufficient control of their ideas to shape them elegantly for readers.

It's important not to overgeneralize, however, because no two writers compose exactly the same way; moreover, the same writer may use different processes for different kinds of prose. Some writers outline their ideas before they write; others need to write extensively before they can outline. Some write their first drafts very slowly, devoting extensive thought and planning to each emerging paragraph; others write first drafts rapidly, to be sure to get all their ideas on paper, and then rework the material part by part. Some prefer to work independently, without discussing or sharing their ideas; others seek out classmates or colleagues to help them hash out ideas and rehearse their arguments before writing them down. Some seek out the stillness of a library or private room; others do their best writing in noisy cafeterias or coffee shops.

The actual mechanics of composing differ from writer to writer as well. Some writers create first drafts directly at a keyboard, whereas others require the reassuring heft of a pen or pencil. Among writers who begin by planning the structure of their work, some make traditional outlines (perhaps using the flexible outline feature on their word processors), whereas others prefer tree diagrams or flowcharts. Some of those who use word processors revise directly at the computer, whereas others print out a hard copy, revise with pen, and then type the changes into the computer.

Also, writers often vary their composing processes from project to project. A writer might complete one project with a single draft and a quick editing job, but produce a half dozen or more drafts for another project.

What experienced writers do have in common is a willingness to keep revising their work until they feel it is ready to go public. They typically work much harder at drafting and revising than do inexperienced writers, taking more runs at their subject. And experienced writers generally make more substantial alterations in their drafts during revision. (Compare the first two quotations that open this chapter—one from an experienced and one from an inexperienced writer.) An experienced writer will sometimes throw away a first draft and start over; a beginning writer tends to be more satisfied with early drafts and to think of revision as primarily cleaning up errors. Figure 11.1 shows the first page of a first draft for a magazine article written by an experienced writer.

FIGURE 11.1 Draft Page of Experienced Writer

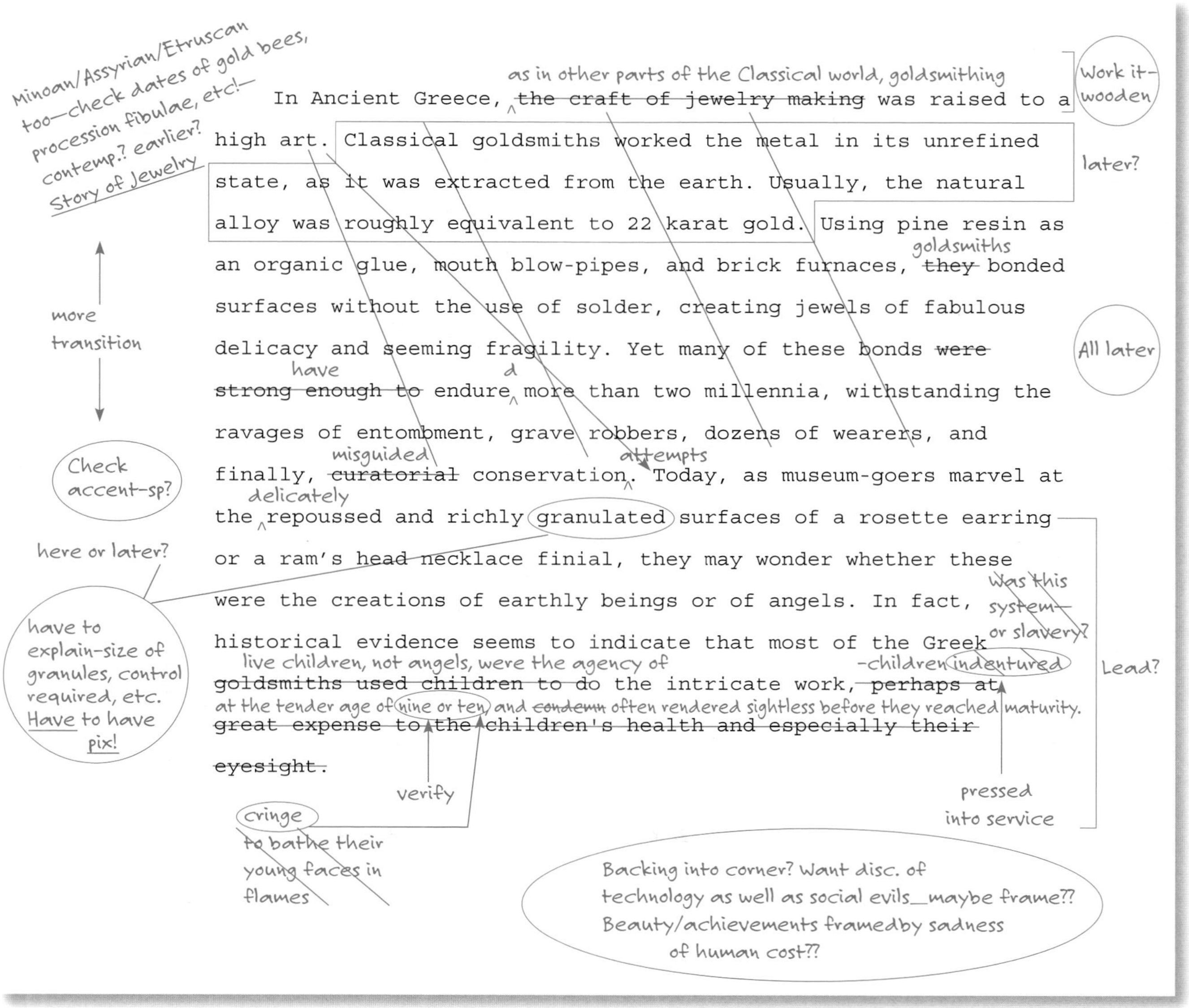

In Ancient Greece, the craft of jewelry making was raised to a high art. Classical goldsmiths worked the metal in its unrefined state, as it was extracted from the earth. Usually, the natural alloy was roughly equivalent to 22 karat gold. Using pine resin as an organic glue, mouth blow-pipes, and brick furnaces, they bonded surfaces without the use of solder, creating jewels of fabulous delicacy and seeming fragility. Yet many of these bonds were strong enough to endure more than two millennia, withstanding the ravages of entombment, grave robbers, dozens of wearers, and finally, curatorial conservation. Today, as museum-goers marvel at the repoussed and richly granulated surfaces of a rosette earring or a ram's head necklace finial, they may wonder whether these were the creations of earthly beings or of angels. In fact, historical evidence seems to indicate that most of the Greek goldsmiths used children to do the intricate work, perhaps at great expense to the children's health and especially their eyesight.

Handwritten annotations:

as in other parts of the Classical world, goldsmithing

Work it in wooden later?

All later

Lead?

Minoan/Assyrian/Etruscan too—check dates of gold bees, procession fibulae? earlier? contemp.? Story of jewelry

move transition

Check accent-sp?

here or later?

have to explain-size of granules, control required, etc. Have to have pix!

goldsmiths

have

misguided attempts / delicately

granulated

Was this system— / children indentured or slavery?

live children, not angels, were the agency of

at the tender age of nine or ten / and condemn often rendered sightless before they reached maturity.

pressed into service

verify

Cringe / to bathe their young faces in flames

Backing into corner? Want disc. of technology as well as social evils...maybe frame?? Beauty/achievements framed by sadness of human cost??

A Working Description of the Writing Process

The writing process we have just described may be considerably different from what you have previously been taught. For many years—before researchers began studying the composing processes of experienced writers—writing teachers typically taught a model something like this:

OLD MODEL OF THE WRITING PROCESS

1. Choose a topic
2. Narrow it
3. Write a thesis
4. Make an outline
5. Write a draft
6. Revise
7. Edit

The major problem with this model is that hardly anyone writes this way. We know of no writers who being by choosing a topic and narrowing it. Rather, as we explained in Part One, writers begin with a sense of a problem or of a conversation that isn't quite satisfactory. Writers identify questions that impel them to add their own voice to a conversation. Nor is the process neatly linear, as the old model implies. Sometimes writers settle on a thesis early in the writing process. But just as frequently they formulate a thesis during an "Aha!" moment of discovery later in the process, perhaps after several drafts. (So *this* is my point! Here is my argument in a nutshell!) Even very late in the process, while checking spelling and punctuation, experienced writers are apt to think of new ideas, thus triggering more revision.

Rather than dividing the writing process into distinct, sequential steps, let's review the kinds of things experienced writers are likely to do early, midway, and late in the process of writing an essay.

More Accurate View of the Writing Process

Early in the process	• *Writers become aware of a question or problem.* Initially the question may not be well defined, but writers identify something unknown about the topic, feel dissatisfied with someone else's view of it, or wish to add something new or different to the conversation.
	• *Writers explore the problem.* Through research, critical thinking, and exploratory writing and talking, writers search for an effective response to the problem. They consider what different audiences might already know about the problem, what these audiences believe, and how they might be surprised by the writer's view. Writers might take time off from the problem and let ideas cook in the subconscious.

More Accurate View of the Writing Process *continued*

- *Writers begin conceptualizing the paper in terms of purpose, audience, and genre.* As ideas for a paper take shape—through outlining or early drafting—writers try to imagine a purpose for writing in terms of the change they want to bring about in the audience. They also consider the conventions and constraints of their intended genre.

- *Writers complete a first draft.* At some point writers put ideas on paper in a whole or partial draft. Some writers make an informal outline prior to writing. Others discover direction as they write, putting aside concerns about form and coherence until later. One of the major causes of writer's block among less experienced writers is the desire to make the paper perfect the first time. Experienced writers know their first drafts are often messy and unfocused, and they lower their expectations accordingly. Some writers even like to call their first drafts "zero drafts" or "garbage drafts" to emphasize these lower expectations.

Midway through the process
- *Writers begin to revise and reformulate.* The real work of actual composing now begins. Once they have written a first draft, writers can start to see the whole territory. The second draft may be quite different from the first. Some writers actually discard the first draft, reshaping their initial insights into a different structure. Others go slowly through the first draft, adding, deleting, reordering, or completely rewriting passages.

- *Writers increasingly consider the needs and expectations of readers.* As writers clarify their ideas for themselves, they increasingly reorganize for readers. Using knowledge of "reader expectation theory," which we describe in detail in Chapter 12, writers build into their text mapping statements, transitions, and structural cues. They also create unity and coherence by following the "old/new contract" explained in Chapter 12.

- *Writers seek feedback from readers.* Experienced writers regularly ask trusted colleagues to read their drafts and offer feedback. Composition instructors often try to create the same experience for students by organizing peer review workshops.

- *Writers often go through many additional drafts.* It is not unusual for an experienced writer to go through numerous drafts, making both large-scale "global revisions" (different structure, complete rewriting of sections, revised purpose) as well as small-scale "local revisions" (unifying or developing paragraphs, rewriting sentences).

Late in the process
- *Writers edit for style and correctness.* Eventually the writer's sense of purpose and audience stabilizes, and the ideas become increasingly clear, well organized, and developed. At this point writers begin shifting their attention to the craft of writing—getting each word, phrase, sentence, and paragraph just right so that the prose is clear, graceful, and correct.

- *Writers edit for manuscript form and genre considerations.* Writers also edit to meet the genre conventions of document design, citation style, and so forth. The professional appearance of a manuscript creates the audience's first impression of the writer's *ethos*.

We should emphasize again that the writing process is recursive, rather than linear. A writer might be "early in the process" for one part of a draft and "late in the process" for another. Frequently, a writer can also reconceptualize the argument late in the process and seemingly "start over"—but the time has not been wasted since the whole process has led to the writer's new ideas.

For Writing and Discussion

When you write, do you follow a process resembling the one we just described? Have you ever

- had a writing project grow out of your engagement with a problem or question?
- explored ideas by talking with others or by doing exploratory writing?
- made major changes to a draft because you changed your mind or otherwise discovered new ideas?
- revised a draft from a reader's perspective by consciously trying to imagine and respond to a reader's questions, confusions, and other reactions?
- road-tested a draft by trying it out on readers and then revising it as a result of what they told you?

Working in groups or as a whole class, share stories about previous writing experiences that match or do not match the description of experienced writers' processes. To the extent that your present process differs, what strategies of experienced writers might you like to try?

Improving Your Own Writing Processes

The previous section describes the many ways in which experienced writers compose. In this section we'll show you how to use this knowledge to improve your own writing processes. We'll begin with an overview list of expert composing strategies that you can start to practice right away. We'll then explain techniques for exploratory writing followed by some advice on drafting and global revision.

Practice the Composing Strategies of Experienced Writers

One of the best ways to improve your composing processes is to practice strategies used by experienced writers.

- *Use exploratory writing and talking to discover and clarify ideas.* Don't let your first draft be the first time you put your ideas into written words. Use exploratory writing to generate ideas and deepen thinking. (Later in this section we explain the techniques of freewriting, focused freewriting, and idea mapping.) Also seek out opportunities to talk about your ideas with classmates or friends in order to clarify your own thinking and appreciate alternative points of view. Whenever possible, talk through your draft with a friend; rehearse your argument in conversation as practice for putting it in writing.

- *Schedule your time.* Plan for exploration, drafting, revision, and editing. Don't begin your paper the night before it is due. Give ideas time to ruminate in your mind. Recognize that your ideas will shift, branch out, even turn around as you write. Allow some time off between writing the first draft and beginning revision. Experienced writers build in time for revision.

- *Discover what methods of drafting work best for you.* Some people compose rough drafts directly on the computer; others write longhand. Some make outlines first; others plunge directly into drafting and make outlines later. Some revise extensively on the computer as they are drafting; others plough ahead until they have a complete draft before they start revising. Some people sit at their desk for hours at a time; others need to get up and walk around every couple of minutes. Some people need a quiet room; others work best in a coffee shop. Discover the methods that work best for you.

- *Occasionally revise on double- or triple-spaced hard copy.* Because many experienced writers revise on the screen without going through paper drafts, it is hard to say when one draft ends and another begins. Nevertheless, there are powerful advantages in printing off occasional paper drafts. Research suggests that writers are apt to make more large-scale changes in a draft if they work from hard copy. Because they can see the whole draft at once without having to scroll through a file, they can see more easily how the parts connect to the whole. They can look back at page two while revising page six. We suggest that you occasionally print out a double- or triple-spaced hard copy of your draft and then mark it up aggressively. Cross out text to be changed and write new text in the blank spaces between the lines. Make inserts. Draw arrows. (See again Figure 11.1, which shows how a professional writer marks up a draft.) When your draft gets too messy, type your changes in your computer and begin another round of revision.

- *Exchange drafts with others.* Get other people's reactions to your work in exchange for your reactions to theirs. Experienced writers regularly seek critiques of their drafts from trusted readers. Later in this chapter we explain procedures for peer review of drafts.

- *Save correctness for last.* To revise productively, concentrate first on the big questions: Do I have good ideas in this draft? Am I responding appropriately to the assignment? Are my ideas adequately organized and developed? Save questions about exact wording, grammar, and mechanics for later. These concerns are important, but they cannot be efficiently attended to until after higher-order concerns are met. Your first goal is to create a thoughtful, richly developed draft.

Explore Ideas through Freewriting, Idea Mapping, and Dialectic Discussion

Another way to improve your writing processes is to explore ideas through informal writing and talking. Composition theorists sometimes refer to this stage of writing as *prewriting* or *invention*. When you use exploratory writing, such as writing in a journal or doing regular "thinking pieces," you'll have a record of your thinking that you can draw on later. Moreover, the very act of recording your thoughts on paper—or articulating them to others orally—stimulates more ideas. In this section, we will briefly describe four exploratory strategies that will help you learn to think like an experienced writer: freewriting, focused freewriting, idea mapping, and dialectic discussion.

Freewriting

Freewriting, also sometimes called *nonstop writing* or *silent, sustained writing*, asks you to record your thinking directly. To freewrite, put pen to paper (or sit at your computer screen, perhaps turning *off* the monitor so that you can't see what you are writing) and write rapidly, *nonstop*, for ten to fifteen minutes at a stretch. Don't worry about grammar, spelling, organization, transitions, or other features of edited writing. The object is to think of as many ideas as possible. Some freewriting looks like stream of consciousness. Some is more organized and focused, although it lacks the logical connections and development that would make it suitable for an audience of strangers.

Many freewriters find that their initial reservoir of ideas runs out in three to five minutes. If this happens, force yourself to keep your fingers moving. If you can't think of anything to say, write, "Relax" over and over (or "This is stupid" or "I'm stuck") until new ideas emerge.

What do you write about? The answer varies according to your situation. Often you will freewrite in response to a question or problem posed by your instructor. Sometimes you will pose your own questions and use freewriting to explore possible answers or simply generate ideas. Here is an example of a student's freewrite in response to the prompt "What puzzles you about homelessness?"

> Let's see, what puzzles me about homelessness? Homeless homeless. Today on my way to work I passed a homeless guy who smiled at me and I smiled back though he smelled bad. What are the reasons he was out on the street? Perhaps an extraordinary string of bad luck. Perhaps he was pushed out onto the street. Not a background of work ethic, no place to go, no way to get someplace to live that could be afforded, alcoholism. To what extent do government assistance, social spending, etc, keep people off the street? What benefits could a person get that stops "the cycle"? How does welfare affect homelessness, drug abuse programs, family planning? To what extent does the individual have control over homelessness? This question of course goes to the depth of the question of how community affects the individual. Relax, relax. What about the signs that I see on the way to work posted on the windows of businesses that read, "please don't give to panhandlers it only promotes

drug abuse etc" a cheap way of getting homeless out of the way of business? Are homeless the natural end of unrestricted capitalism? What about the homeless people who are mentally ill? How can you maintain a living when haunted by paranoia? How do you decide if someone is mentally ill or just laughs at society? If one can't function obviously. How many mentally ill are out on the street? If you are mentally ill and have lost the connections to others who might take care of you I can see how you might end up on the street. What would it take to get treatment? To what extent can mentally ill be treated? When I see a homeless person I want to ask, How do you feel about the rest of society? When you see "us" walk by how do you think of us? Do you possibly care how we avoid you?

Note how this freewrite rambles, moving associatively from one topic or question to the next. Freewrites often have this kind of loose, associative structure. The value of such freewrites is that they help writers discover areas of interest or rudimentary beginnings of ideas. When you read back over one of your freewrites, try to find places that seem worth pursuing. Freewriters call these places "hot spots," "centers of interest," "centers of gravity," or simply "nuggets" or "seeds." The student who wrote the preceding freewrite discovered that he was particularly interested in the cluster of questions beginning "What about the homeless people who are mentally ill?" and he eventually wrote a research paper proposing a public policy for helping the mentally ill homeless. Because we believe this technique is of great value to writers, we suggest that you use it to generate ideas for class discussions and essays.

Focused Freewriting

Freewriting, as we have just described it, can be quick and associational, like brainstorming aloud on paper. Focused freewriting, in contrast, is less associational and aimed more at developing a line of thought. You wrestle with a specific problem or question, trying to think and write your way into its complexity and multiple points of view. Because the writing is still informal, with the emphasis on your ideas and not on making your writing grammatically or stylistically polished, you don't have to worry about spelling, punctuation, grammar, or organizational structure. Your purpose is to deepen and extend your thinking on the problem. Some instructors will create prompts or give you specific questions to ponder, and they may call this kind of exploratory writing "focused freewriting," "learning log responses," "writer's notebook entries," or "thinking pieces."

Idea Mapping

Another good technique for exploring ideas is *idea mapping*, a more visual method than freewriting. To make an idea map, draw a circle in the center of a page and write down your broad topic area (or a triggering question or your thesis) inside the circle. Then record your ideas on branches and subbranches that extend out from the center circle. As long as you pursue one train of thought, keep recording your ideas on subbranches off the main branch. But as soon as that chain of ideas runs dry, go back and start a new branch.

Often your thoughts will jump back and forth between one branch and another. This technique will help you see them as part of an emerging design rather than as strings of unrelated ideas. Additionally, idea mapping establishes at an early stage a sense of hierarchy in your ideas. If you enter an idea on a subbranch, you can see that you are more fully developing a previous idea. If you return to the hub and start a new branch, you can see that you are beginning a new train of thought.

An idea map usually records more ideas than a freewrite, but the ideas are not as fully developed. Writers who practice both techniques report that they can vary the kinds of ideas they generate depending on which technique they choose. Figure 11.2 shows a student's idea map made while he was exploring issues related to the grading system.

Dialectic Discussion

Another effective way to explore the complexity of a topic is through face-to-face discussions with others, whether in class, over coffee in the student union, or late at night in bull sessions. Not all discussions are productive; some are too superficial and scattered, others too heated. Good ones are *dialectic*—participants with differing views on a topic try to understand each other and resolve their differences by examining contradictions in each person's position. The key to dialectic conversation is careful listening, made possible by an openness to each other's views. A dialectic discussion differs from a talk show shouting match or a pro/con debate in which proponents of opposing positions, their views set in stone, attempt to win the argument. In a dialectic discussion, participants assume that each position has strengths and weaknesses and that even the strongest position contains inconsistencies, which should be exposed and examined. When dialectic conversation works well, participants scrutinize their own positions more critically and deeply, and often alter their views. True dialectic conversation implies growth and change, not a hardening of positions.

For more discussion of dialectic conversation, see the criteria for class discussions in Chapter 4, p. 77.

Draft Purposefully

When you sit down to compose your first draft, write purposefully by thinking of your rhetorical context: What is the question or problem you are addressing? Who is your audience? What change do you want to bring about in your audience's thinking? Sometimes you will know the answers to these questions before you start drafting. At other times, the act of drafting helps you discover ideas. Have confidence that the revising process will help you eventually make your ideas well structured, clear, and surprising to your readers. When writing your first draft, lower your expectations. (We said earlier that many experienced writers think of the first draft as their *zero draft* or *garbage draft*.) For more specific advice on drafting and revising, see Chapter 12 on composing and revising closed-form prose. Pay particular attention at the drafting stage to Chapter 12's advice on planning and visualizing your structure (Lesson 3, pp. 309–315) and on writing

FIGURE 11.2 Idea Map on Problems with the Grading System

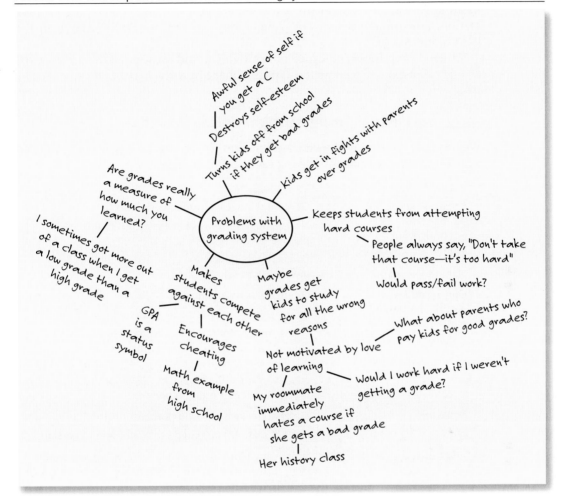

introductions (Lesson 4, pp. 316–322). We have found that these lessons particularly help writers get started on a draft.

After Drafting, Revise Globally

As we explained at the start of this chapter, experienced writers revise their drafts much more extensively than do inexperienced writers. Inexperienced writers tend to revise *locally*; experienced writers revise *globally*. By *local revision*, we mean small-scale revisions at the level of the sentence—correcting spelling, finding a different word, perhaps adding a short example. By *global revision*, we mean large-scale revision at the level of ideas and structure—reshaping a whole section, crossing out a series of paragraphs, and rewriting from scratch in the light of new ideas.

To appreciate the significance of both global and local revision, consider the changes that experienced writers typically make in their drafts.

Recognize Kinds of Changes Typically Made in Drafts

We begin by classifying the kinds of changes writers typically make in drafts and explaining their reasons for making each sort of change.

Kinds of Changes	Reasons for Change
Crossing out whole passage and rewriting from scratch	Original passage was unfocused; ideas have changed.
	New sense of purpose or point meant that whole passage needed reshaping.
	Original passage was too confused or jumbled for mere editing.
Cutting and pasting; moving parts around	Original was disorganized.
	Points weren't connected to particulars.
	Conclusion was clearer than introduction; part of conclusion had to be moved to introduction.
	Rewriting introduction led to discovery of more effective plan of development; new forecasting required different order in body.
Deletions	Material not needed or irrelevant.
	Deleted material was good but went off on a tangent.
Additions	Supporting particulars needed to be added: examples, facts, illustrations, statistics evidence (usually added to bodies of paragraphs).
	Points and transitions needed to be supplied (often added to openings of paragraphs).
	New section needed to be added or a brief point expanded.
Recasting of sentences (crossing out and rewriting portions of sentences; combining sentences; rephrasing; starting sentences with a different grammatical structure)	Passage violated old/new contract (see pp. 330–336).
	Passage was wordy or choppy.
	Passage lacked rhythm and voice.
	Grammar was tangled, diction odd, meaning confused.
Editing sentences to correct mistakes	Words were misspelled or mistyped.
	Comma splices, fragments, dangling participles, other grammatical errors were found.

For Writing and Discussion

Choose an important paragraph in the body of a draft you are currently working on. Then write out your answers to these questions about that paragraph.

1. Why is this an important paragraph?
2. What is its main point?
3. Where is that main point stated?

Now—as an exercise only—write the main point at the top of a blank sheet of paper, put away your original draft, and, without looking at the original, write a new paragraph with the sole purpose of developing the point you wrote at the top of the page.

When you are finished, compare your new paragraph to the original. What have you learned that might help you revise your original?

Here are some typical responses of writers who have tried this exercise:

I recognized that my original paragraph was unfocused. I couldn't find a main point.

I recognized that my original paragraph was underdeveloped. I had a main point but not enough particulars supporting it.

I began to see that my draft was scattered and that I had too many short paragraphs.

I recognized that I was making a couple of different points in my original paragraph and that I needed to break it into separate paragraphs.

I recognized that I hadn't stated my main point (or that I had buried it in the middle of the paragraph).

I recognized that there was a big difference in style between my two versions and that I had to choose which version I liked best. (It's not always the "new" version!)

Using Peer Reviews to Stimulate Revision

One of the best ways to become a better reviser is to see your draft from a *reader's* rather than a *writer's* perspective. As a writer, you know what you mean; you are already inside your own head. But you need to see what your draft looks like to someone outside your head.

The best way to learn this skill is to practice reading your classmates' drafts and have them read yours. In this section we offer advice on how to respond candidly to your classmates' drafts and how to participate in peer reviews.

Becoming a Helpful Reader of Classmates' Drafts

When you respond to a writer's draft, learn to make readerly rather than writerly comments; describe your mental experience in trying to understand the draft rather than pointing out problems or errors in the draft. For example, instead of saying, "Your draft is disorganized," say, "I got lost when. . . ." Instead of saying,

"This paragraph needs a topic sentence," say, "I had trouble seeing the point of this paragraph."

When you help a writer with a draft, your goal is both to point out where the draft needs more work and to brainstorm with the writer possible ways to improve the draft. Begin by reading the draft all the way through at a normal reading speed. As you read, take mental notes to help focus your feedback. We suggest that you make wavy lines in the margin next to passages that you find confusing; write "Good!" in the margin where you like something; and write "?" in the margin where you want to ask questions.

After you have read the draft, use the following strategies for making helpful responses:

IF THE IDEAS IN THE DRAFT SEEM THIN OR UNDEVELOPED, OR IF THE DRAFT IS TOO SHORT:

- help the writer brainstorm for more ideas.
- help the writer add more examples, better details, more supporting data or arguments.

IF YOU GET CONFUSED OR LOST:

- have the writer talk through ideas to clear up confusing spots.
- help the writer sharpen the thesis: suggest that the writer view the thesis as the answer to a controversial or problematic question; ask the writer to articulate the question that the thesis answers.
- help the writer create an outline, tree diagram, or flowchart.
- help the writer clarify the focus by asking him or her to complete these statements about purpose:
  My purpose in this paper is _____.
  My purpose in this section (paragraph) is _____.
  Before reading my paper, the reader will have this view of my topic: _____; after reading my paper, my reader will have this different view of my topic: _____.
- show the writer where you got confused or miscued in reading the draft ("I started getting lost here because I couldn't see why you were giving me this information" or "I thought you were going to say X, but then you said Y").

See Chapter 12 for a detailed explanation of these revision strategies.

IF YOU CAN UNDERSTAND THE SENTENCES BUT CAN'T SEE THE POINT:

- help the writer articulate the meaning by asking "So what?" questions, making the writer bring the point to the surface by stating it directly. ("I can understand what you are saying here but I don't quite understand why you are saying it. I read all these facts, and I say, 'So what?' What do these facts have to do with your thesis?")

IF YOU DISAGREE WITH THE IDEAS OR THINK THE WRITER HAS AVOIDED ALTERNATIVE POINTS OF VIEW:

- play devil's advocate to help the writer deepen and complicate ideas.
- show the writer specific places where you had queries or doubts.

For Writing and Discussion

In the following exercise, we ask you to respond to a student's draft ("Should the University Carpet the Dorm Rooms?" below). The assignment asked students to take a stand on a local campus issue. Imagine that you have exchanged drafts with this student and that your task is to help this student improve the draft.

Read the draft carefully; make wavy lines in the margins where you get confused, write "Good!" for something you like, and write "?" where you want to ask questions.

On your own, complete the following tasks:

1. Identify one specific place in the draft where you got confused. Freewrite a brief explanation for why you got confused. Make readerly rather than writerly comments.
2. Identify one place in the draft where you think the ideas are thin or need more development.
3. Identify one place where you might write "So what?" in the margins. These are places where you understand the sentences but don't see the point the writer is getting at.
4. Identify at least one place where you could play devil's advocate or otherwise object to the writer's ideas. Freewrite your objections.

In groups or as a whole class, share your responses. Then turn to the following tasks:

1. With the instructor serving as a guide, practice explaining to the writer where or how you got confused while reading the draft. Readers often have difficulty explaining their reading experience to a writer. Let several class members role-play being the reader. Practice using language such as "I like the way this draft started because . . . ." "I got confused when . . . ." "I had to back up and reread when . . . ." "I saw your point here, but then I got lost again because . . . ." Writing theorist Peter Elbow calls such language a "movie of your mind."
2. Have several class members role-play being devil's advocates by arguing against the writer's thesis. Where are the ideas thin or weak?

Should the University Carpet the Dorm Rooms?

Tricia, a university student, came home exhausted from her work-study job. She took a blueberry pie from the refrigerator to satisfy her hunger and a tall glass of milk to quench her thirst. While trying to get comfortable on her bed, she tipped her snack over onto the floor. She cleaned the mess, but the blueberry and milk stains on her brand-new carpet could not be removed.

Tricia didn't realize how hard it was to clean up stains on a carpet. Luckily this was her own carpet.

A lot of students don't want carpets. Students constantly change rooms. The next person may not want carpet.

Some students say that since they pay to live on campus, the rooms should reflect a comfortable home atmosphere. Carpets will make the dorm more comfortable. The carpet will act as insulation and as a soundproofing system.

Paint stains cannot be removed from carpets. If the university carpets the rooms, the students will lose the privilege they have of painting their rooms any color. This would limit students' self-expression.

The carpets would be an institutional brown or gray. This would be ugly. With tile floors, the students can choose and purchase their own carpets to match their taste. You can't be an individual if you can't decorate your room to fit your personality.

According to Rachel Jones, Assistant Director of Housing Services, the cost will be $300 per room for the carpet and installation. Also the university will have to buy more vacuum cleaners. But will vacuum cleaners be all that is necessary to keep the carpets clean? We'll need shampoo machines too.

What about those stains that won't come off even with a shampoo machine? That's where the student will have to pay damage deposit costs.

There will be many stains on the carpet due to shaving cream fights, food fights, beverage parties, and smoking, all of which can damage the carpets.

Students don't take care of the dorms now. They don't follow the rules of maintaining their rooms. They drill holes into the walls, break mirrors, beds, and closet doors, and leave their food trays all over the floor.

```
     If the university buys carpets our room rates will skyrocket.

In conclusion, it is a bad idea for the university to buy carpets.
```

Conducting a Peer Review Workshop

If you are willing to respond candidly to a classmate's draft—in a readerly rather than a writerly way—you will be a valuable participant in peer review workshops. In a typical workshop, classmates work in groups of two to six to respond to each other's rough drafts and offer suggestions for revisions. These workshops are most helpful when group members have developed sufficient levels of professionalism and trust to exchange candid responses. A frequent problem in peer review workshops is that classmates try so hard to avoid hurting each other's feelings that they provide vague, meaningless feedback. Saying, "Your paper's great. I really liked it. Maybe you could make it flow a little better" is much less helpful than saying, "Your issue about environmental pollution in the Antarctic is well defined in the first paragraph, but I got lost in the second paragraph when you began discussing penguin coloration."

Responsibilities of Peer Reviewers and Writers

Learning to respond conscientiously and carefully to others' work may be the single most important thing you can do to improve your own writing. When you review a classmate's draft, you should prepare as follows:

1. ***Understand how experienced writers revise their drafts.*** Prior to reviewing a classmate's draft, review the material in this chapter. Pay particular attention to pages 293–294, which provide general guidelines about what to look for when reading a draft, and to page 292, which summarizes the kinds of changes writers often make in response to reviews: additions, deletions, reordering, complete refocusing and rewriting, and so forth.

2. ***Understand the assignment and the guidelines for peer reviewers.*** For assignments in Part Two of this text, carefully read both the assignment itself and the Guidelines for Peer Reviews at the end of the chapter in which the assignment appears. These guidelines will help both the writer and you, as peer reviewer, to understand the demands of the assignment and the criteria on which it should be evaluated.

3. ***Understand that you are not acting as a teacher.*** A peer reviewer's role is that of a fresh reader. You can help the writer appreciate what it's like to encounter his or her text for the first time. Your primary responsibility is to articulate your understanding of what the writer's words say to you and to identify places where you get confused, where you need more details, where you have doubts or queries, and so on. Although the specific kinds of evaluations called for in the Guidelines for Peer Reviews will be helpful, you don't need to be an expert offering solutions to every problem.

When you play the role of writer during a workshop session, your responsibilities parallel those of your peer reviewers. You need to provide a legible rough draft, preferably typed and double-spaced, that doesn't baffle the reader with illegible handwriting, crossouts, arrows, and confusing pagination. Your instructor may ask you to bring photocopies of your draft for all group members. During the workshop, your primary responsibility is to *listen*, taking in how others respond to your draft without becoming defensive. Many instructors also ask writers to formulate two or three specific questions about their drafts—questions they particularly want their reviewers to address. These questions might focus on something writers particularly like about their drafts or on specific problem areas or concerns.

Exchanging Drafts

An excellent system for exchanging drafts is to have each writer read his or her draft aloud while group members follow along in their own photocopies. We value reading drafts aloud when time allows. Reading expressively, with appropriate emphasis, helps writers distance themselves from their work and hear it anew. When you read your work silently to yourself, it's all too easy to patch up bits of broken prose in your head or to slide through confusing passages. But if you stumble over a passage while reading aloud, you can place a check mark in the margin to indicate where further attention is needed. Another benefit to reading aloud is perhaps more symbolic than pragmatic: Reading your work to others means that you are claiming responsibility for it, displaying your intention to reach a range of readers other than the teacher. And knowing that you will have to read your work aloud will encourage you to have that work in the best possible shape before bringing it to class.

Types of Peer Review Workshops

After you've read your draft aloud, the next stage of your peer review may take one of several forms, depending on your instructor's preference. We describe here two basic strategies: response-centered workshops, and advice-centered workshops. Additional strategies often build on these approaches.

Response-Centered Workshops

This process-oriented, non-intrusive approach places maximum responsibility on the writer for making decisions about what to change in a draft. After the writer reads the draft aloud, group members follow this procedure:

1. All participants take several minutes to make notes on their copies of the manuscript. We recommend using the wavy line, "Good!", "?" system described in the Guidelines for Peer Reviews.
2. Group members take turns describing to the writer their responses to the piece—where they agreed or disagreed with the writer's ideas, where they got confused, where they wanted more development, and so forth. Group members do not give advice; they simply describe their own personal response to the draft as written.
3. The writer takes notes during each response but does not enter into a discussion. The writer listens without trying to defend the piece or explain what he or she intended.

No one gives the writer explicit advice. Group members simply describe their reactions to the piece and leave it to the writer to make appropriate changes.

Advice-Centered Workshops

In this more product-oriented and directive approach, peer reviewers typically work in pairs. Each writer exchanges drafts with a partner, reviews the draft carefully, and then writes specific advice on how to improve the draft. This method works best when peer reviewers use the Guidelines for Peer Reviews that conclude each chapter in Part Two, either addressing all the questions in the guidelines or focusing on specific questions identified by the instructor.

A variation on this approach, which allows peer reviewers to collaborate in pairs when analyzing a draft, uses the following process:

1. The instructor divides the class into initial groups of four.
2. Each group then divides into pairs; each pair exchanges drafts with the other pair.
3. The members of each pair collaborate to compose jointly written reviews of the two drafts they have received.
4. The drafts and the collaboratively written reviews are then returned to the original writers. If time remains, the two pairs meet to discuss their reviews.

When two students collaborate to review a draft, they often produce more useful and insightful reviews than when working individually. In sharing observations and negotiating their responses, they can write their reviews with more confidence and reduce the chances of idiosyncratic advice.

However, because each pair has received two drafts and has to write two peer reviews, this approach takes more class time. Instructors can speed this process by setting up the groups of four in advance and asking pairs to exchange and read drafts prior to the class meeting. Class time can then be focused on collaborative writing of the reviews.

Responding to Peer Reviews

After you and your classmates have gone over each other's papers and walked each other through the responses, everyone should identify two or three things about his or her draft that particularly need work. Before you leave the session, you should have some notion about how you want to revise your paper.

You may get mixed or contradictory responses from different reviewers. One reviewer may praise a passage that another finds confusing or illogical. Conflicting advice is a frustrating fact of life for all writers, whether students or professionals. Such disagreements reveal how readers cocreate a text with a writer: Each brings to the text a different background, set of values, and way of reading.

It is important to remember that you are in charge of your own writing. If several readers offer the same critique of a passage, then no matter how much you love that passage, you probably need to follow their advice. But when readers disagree, you have to make your own best judgment about whom to heed.

Once you have received advice from others, reread your draft again slowly and then develop a revision plan, allowing yourself time to make sweeping, global changes if needed. You also need to remember that you can never make your draft perfect. Plan when you will bring the process to a close so that you can turn in a finished product on time and get on with your other classes and your life.

Composing and Revising Closed-Form Prose

[Form is] an arousing and fulfillment of desires. A work has form insofar as one part of it leads a reader to anticipate another part, to be gratified by the sequence.

—KENNETH BURKE, *RHETORICIAN*

I think the writer ought to help the reader as much as he can without damaging what he wants to say; and I don't think it ever hurts the writer to sort of stand back now and then and look at his stuff as if he were reading it instead of writing it.

—JAMES JONES, *WRITER*

Chapter 11 explained the composing processes of experienced writers and suggested ways that you can improve your own writing processes. In this chapter we present eight lessons in composing and revising closed-form prose. This chapter is not intended to be read in one sitting, lest you suffer from information overload. To help you learn the material efficiently, we have made each lesson a self-contained unit that can be read comfortably in half an hour or less and discussed in class as part of a day's session. You will benefit most from these lessons if you focus on one lesson at a time and then return to the lessons periodically as you progress through the term. Each lesson's advice will become increasingly meaningful and relevant as you gain experience as a writer.

The first lesson—on reader expectations—is intended as a theoretical overview to the rest of the chapter. The remaining lessons can then be assigned and read in any order your instructor desires. You will learn how to convert loose structures into thesis/support structures (Lesson 2); how to plan and visualize your structure (Lesson 3); how to create effective titles and introductions (Lesson 4); how to use topic sentences, transitions, and the old/new contract to guide your readers through the twists and turns of your prose (Lessons 5–7); and finally, how to write good conclusions (Lesson 8). Together these lessons will teach you strategies for making your closed-form prose reader-friendly, well structured, clear, and persuasive.

Lesson 1: Understanding Reader Expectations

In this opening lesson, we show you how to think like a reader. Imagine for a moment that your readers have only so much *reader energy,* which they can use either to follow and respond to your ideas (the result you want) or to puzzle over what you are trying to say (the result you don't want).* Skilled readers make predictions about where a text is heading based on clues provided by the writer. When readers get lost, the writer has often failed to give clues about where the text is going or has failed to do what the reader predicted. "Whoa, you lost me on the turn," a reader might say. "How does this passage relate to what you just said?" To write effective closed-form prose, you need to help readers see how each part of your text is related to what came before. (Sometimes with open-form prose, surprise or puzzlement may be the very effect you want to create. But with closed-form prose this kind of puzzlement is fatal.)

In this lesson we explain what readers of closed-form prose need in order to predict where a text is heading. Specifically we show you that readers need three things in a closed-form text:

- They need unity and coherence.
- They need old information before new information.
- They need forecasting and fulfillment.

Let's look at each in turn.

Unity and Coherence

Together the terms *unity* and *coherence* are defining characteristics of closed-form prose. *Unity* refers to the relationship between each part of an essay and the larger whole. *Coherence* refers to the relationship between adjacent sentences, paragraphs, and parts. The following thought exercise will illustrate your own expectations for unity and coherence:

THOUGHT EXERCISE 1

Read the following two passages and try to explain why each fails to satisfy your expectations as a reader:

A. Recent research has given us much deeper—and more surprising—insights into the father's role in childrearing. My family is typical of the east side in that we never had much money. Their tongues became black and hung out of their mouths. The back-to-basics movement got a lot of press, fueled as it was by fears of growing illiteracy and cultural demise.

B. Recent research has given us much deeper—and more surprising—insights into the father's role in childrearing. Childrearing is a complex process that is frequently

---

*For the useful term *reader energy,* we are indebted to George Gopen and Judith Swan, "The Science of Scientific Writing," *American Scientist* 78 (1990): 550–559. In addition, much of our discussion of writing in this chapter is indebted to the work of Joseph Williams, George Gopen, and Gregory Colomb. See especially Gregory G. Colomb and Joseph M. Williams, "Perceiving Structure in Professional Prose: A Multiply Determined Experience," in Lee Odell and Dixie Goswamie (eds.), *Writing in Nonacademic Settings* (New York: The Guilford Press, 1985), pp. 87–128.

investigated by psychologists. Psychologists have also investigated sleep patterns and dreams. When we are dreaming, psychologists have shown, we are often reviewing recent events in our lives.

If you are like most readers, Passage A comically frustrates your expectations because it is a string of random sentences. Because the sentences don't relate either to each other or to a larger point, Passage A is neither unified nor coherent.

Passage B frustrates expectations in a subtler way. If you aren't paying attention, Passage B may seem to make sense because each sentence is linked to the one before it. But the individual sentences don't develop a larger whole: the topics switch from a father's role in childrearing to psychology to sleep patterns to the function of dreams. This passage has coherence without unity.

To fulfill a reader's expectations, then, a closed-form passage must be both unified and coherent:

> C. (*Unified and coherent*) Recent research has given us much deeper—and more surprising—insights into the father's role in childrearing. It shows that in almost all of their interactions with children, fathers do things a little differently from mothers. What fathers do—their special parenting style—is not only highly complementary to what mothers do but is by all indications important in its own right. [The passage continues by showing the special ways that fathers contribute to childrearing.]

This passage makes a unified point—that fathers have an important role in childrearing. Because all the parts relate to that whole (unity) and because the connections from sentence to sentence are clear (coherence), the passage satisfies our expectations: It makes sense.

Because achieving unity and coherence is a major goal in revising closed-form prose, we'll refer frequently to these concepts in later lessons.

Old before New

One dominant way that readers process information and register ideas is by moving from already known (old) information to new information. In a nutshell, this concept means that new material is meaningful to a reader only if it is linked to old material that is already meaningful. To illustrate this concept, consider the arrangement of names and numbers in a telephone directory. Because we read from left to right, we want people's names in the left column and the telephone numbers in the right column. A person's name is the old, familiar information we already know and the number is the new, unknown information that we seek. If the numbers were in the left column and the names in the right, we would have to read backward.

You can see the same old-before-new principle at work in the following thought exercise:

THOUGHT EXERCISE 2

You are a passenger on an airplane flight into Chicago and need to transfer to Flight 29 to Memphis. As you descend into Chicago, the flight attendant announces transfer gates. Which of the following formats is easier for you to process? Why?

Option A	Option B
To Atlanta on Flight 29 Gate C12	Gate C12 Flight 29 to Atlanta
To Dallas on Flight 35 Gate C25	Gate C25 Flight 35 to Dallas
To Memphis on Flight 16 Gate B20	Gate B20 Flight 16 to Memphis

If you are like most readers, you prefer Option A, which puts old information before new. In this case, the old/known information is our destination (cities arranged alphabetically) and perhaps our flight number (To Memphis on Flight 16). The new/unknown information is Gate B20. Option B causes us to expend more energy than does Option A because it forces us to hold the number of each gate in memory until we hear its corresponding city and flight number. Whereas Option A allows us to relax until we hear the word "Memphis," Option B forces us to concentrate intensely on each gate number until we find the meaningful one.

The principle of old before new has great explanatory power for writers. At the level of the whole essay, this principle helps writers establish the main structural frame and ordering principle of their argument. An argument's frame derives from the writer's purpose to change some aspect of the reader's view of the topic. The reader's original view of the topic—what we might call the common, expected, or ordinary view—constitutes old/known/familiar material. The writer's surprising view constitutes the new/unknown/unfamiliar material. The writer's hope is to move readers from their original view to the writer's new and different view. By understanding what constitutes old/familiar information to readers, the writer can determine how much background to provide, how to anticipate readers' objections, and how to structure material by moving from the old to the new. We discuss these matters in more depth in Lesson 4, on writing effective introductions.

At the sentence level, the principle of old before new also helps writers create coherence between adjacent parts and sentences. Most sentences in an essay should contain both an old element and a new element. To create coherence, the writer begins with the old material, which links back to something earlier, and then puts the new material at the end of the sentence. (See the discussion of the old/new contract in Lesson 7.)

Forecasting and Fulfillment

Finally, readers of closed-form prose expect writers to forecast what is coming and then to fulfill those forecasts. To appreciate what we mean by forecasting and fulfillment, try one more thought exercise:

THOUGHT EXERCISE 3

Although the following paragraph describes a simple procedure in easy-to-follow sentences, most readers still scratch their heads in bewilderment. Why? What makes the passage difficult to understand?

The procedure is actually quite simple. First, you arrange things into different groups. Of course, one pile may be sufficient depending on how much there is to do. If you have to go somewhere else due to lack of facilities, that is the next step; otherwise, you are pretty well set. Next you operate the machines according to the instructions. After the procedure is completed, one arranges the materials into differ-ent groups again. Then they can be put in their appropriate places. Eventually, they will be used once more and the whole cycle will have to be repeated. However, that is part of life.

Most readers report being puzzled about the paragraph's topic. Because the opening sentence doesn't provide enough context to tell them what to expect, the paragraph makes no forecast that can be fulfilled. Now try rereading the para-graph, but this time substitute the following opening sentence:

> The procedure for washing clothes is actually quite simple.

With the addition of "for washing clothes," the sentence provides a context that allows you to predict and understand what's coming. In the language of cog-nitive psychologists, this new opening sentence provides a schema for interpreta-tion. A *schema* is the reader's mental picture of a structure for upcoming material. The new opening sentence allows you as reader to say mentally, "This paragraph will describe a procedure for washing clothes and argue that it is simple." When the schema proves accurate, you experience the pleasure of prediction and fulfill-ment. In the language of rhetorician Kenneth Burke, the reader's experience of form is "an arousing and fulfillment of desires."

What readers expect from a closed-form text, then, is an ability to predict what is coming as well as regular fulfillment of those predictions. Writers forecast what is coming in a variety of ways: by writing effective titles and introductions, by putting points at the beginning of paragraphs, by creating effective transitions and mapping statements, and by using effective headings and subheadings if appropriate for the genre. To meet their readers' needs for predictions and fulfill-ment, closed-form writers start and end with the big picture. They tell readers where they are going before they start the journey, they refer to this big picture at key transition points, and they refocus on the big picture in their conclusion.

Lesson 2: Converting Loose Structures into Thesis/Support Structures

In Lesson 1 we described readers' expectations for unity and coherence, old infor-mation before new, and forecasting and fulfillment. In academic contexts, readers also expect closed-form prose to have a thesis/support structure. As we explained in Chapter 2, most closed-form academic writing—especially writing with the aim of analysis or persuasion—is governed by a contestable or risky thesis state-ment. Because developing and supporting a thesis is complex work requiring much critical thought, writers sometimes retreat into loose structures that are eas-ier to compose than a thesis-based argument with points and particulars.

In this lesson we help you better understand thesis-based writing by contrast-ing it with prose that looks like thesis-based writing but isn't. We show you three common ways in which inexperienced writers give the appearance of writing thesis-based prose while actually retreating from the rigors of making and developing an argument. Avoiding the pitfalls of these loose structures can go a long way toward improving your performance on most college writing assignments.

And Then Writing, or Chronological Structure

Chronological structure, often called "narrative," is the most common organizing principle of open-form prose. It may also be used selectively in closed-form prose to support a point. But sometimes the writer begins recounting the details of a story until chronological order takes over, driving out the thesis-based structure of points and particulars.

To a large degree, chronological order is the default mode we fall into when we aren't sure how to organize material. For example, if you were asked to analyze a fictional character, you might slip into a plot summary instead. In much the same way, you might substitute historical chronology ("First A happened, then B happened . . .") for historical analysis ("B happened because A happened . . ."); or you might give a chronological recounting of your research ("First I discovered A, then I discovered B . . .") instead of organizing your material into an argument ("I question A's account of this phenomenon on the grounds of B's recent findings . . .").

The tendency toward loose chronological structure is revealed in the following example from a student's essay on Shakespeare's *The Tempest.* This excerpt is from the introduction of the student's first draft:

PLOT SUMMARY—*AND THEN* WRITING

Prospero cares deeply for his daughter. In the middle of the play Prospero acts like a gruff father and makes Ferdinand carry logs in order to test his love for Miranda and Miranda's love for him. In the end, though, Prospero is a loving father who rejoices in his daughter's marriage to a good man.

Here the student seems simply to retell the play's plot without any apparent thesis. (The body of her rough draft primarily retold the same story in more detail.) However, during an office conference, the instructor discovered that the student regarded her sentence about Prospero's being a loving father as her thesis. In fact, the student had gotten in an argument with a classmate over whether Prospero was a good person or an evil one. The instructor helped her convert her draft into a thesis/support structure:

REVISED INTRODUCTION—THESIS/SUPPORT STRUCTURE

Many persons believe that Prospero is an evil person in the play. They claim that Prospero exhibits a harsh, destructive control over Miranda and also, like Faust, seeks superhuman knowledge through his magic. However, I contend that Prospero is a kind and loving father.

This revised version implies a problem (What kind of father is Prospero?), presents a view that the writer wishes to change (Prospero is harsh and hateful), and asserts a contestable thesis (Prospero is a loving father). The body of her paper can now be converted from plot summary to an argument with reasons and evidence supporting her claim that Prospero is loving.

This student's revision from an *and then* to a thesis/support structure is typical of many writers' experience. Because recounting events chronologically is a natural way to organize, many writers—even very experienced ones—lapse into long stretches of *and then* writing in their rough drafts. However, experienced writers have learned to recognize these *and then* sections in their drafts and to rework this material into a closed-form, thesis-based structure.

All About Writing, or Encyclopedic Structure

Whereas *and then* writing turns essays into stories by organizing details chronologically, *all about* writing turns essays into encyclopedia articles by piling up details in heaps. When *all about* writing organizes these heaps into categories, it can appear to be well organized: "Having told you everything I learned about educational opportunities in Cleveland, I will now tell you everything I learned about the Rock and Roll Hall of Fame." But the categories do not function as points and particulars in support of a thesis. Rather, like the shelving system in a library, they are simply ways of arranging information for convenient retrieval, not a means of building a hierarchical structure.

To illustrate the differences between *all about* writing and thesis-based writing, consider the case of two students choosing to write term papers on the subject of female police officers. One student is asked simply to write "all about" the topic; the other is asked to pose and investigate some problem related to female police officers and to support a thesis addressing that problem. In all likelihood, the first student would produce an initial outline with headings such as the following:

I. History of women in police roles
   A. Female police or soldiers in ancient times
   B. 19th century (Calamity Jane)
   C. 1900s–1960
   D. 1960–present
II. How female police officers are selected and trained
III. A typical day in the life of a female police officer
IV. Achievements and acts of heroism of female police officers
V. What the future holds for female police officers

Such a paper is a data dump that places into categories all the information the writer has uncovered. It is riskless, and, except for occasional new information, surpriseless. In contrast, when a student focuses on a significant question—one that grows out of the writer's own interests and demands engagement—the writing can be quite compelling.

Consider the case of a student, Lynnea, who wrote a research paper entitled "Women Police Officers: Should Size and Strength Be Criteria for Patrol Duty?" Her essay begins with a group of male police officers complaining about being assigned to patrol duty with a new female officer, Connie Jones (not her real name), who is four feet ten inches tall and weighs ninety pounds. Here is the rest of the introduction to Lynnea's essay.

> Connie Jones has just completed police academy training and has been assigned to patrol duty in _____. Because she is so small, she has to have a booster seat in her patrol car and has been given a special gun, since she can barely manage to pull the trigger of a standard police-issue .38 revolver. Although she passed the physical requirements at the academy, which involved speed and endurance running, situps, and monkey bar tests, most of the officers in her department doubt her ability to perform competently as a patrol officer. But nevertheless she is on patrol because men and women receive equal assignments in most of today's police forces. But is this a good policy? Can a person who is significantly smaller and weaker than her peers make an effective patrol officer?

Lynnea examined all the evidence she could find—through library and field research (interviewing police officers) and arrived at the following thesis: "Because concern for public safety overrides all other concerns, police departments should set stringent size and strength requirements for patrol officers, even if these criteria exclude many women." This thesis has plenty of tension because it sets limits on equal rights for women. Because Lynnea considers herself a feminist, it caused her considerable distress to advocate setting these limits and placing public safety ahead of gender equity. The resulting essay is engaging precisely because of the tension it creates and the controversy it engenders.

Engfish Writing, or Structure without Surprise

Unlike the chronological story and the *all about* paper, the *engfish* essay has a thesis.* But the thesis is a riskless truism supported with predictable reasons—often structured as the three body paragraphs in a traditional five-paragraph theme. It is fill-in-the-blank writing: "The food service is bad for three reasons. First, it is bad because the food is not tasty. Blah, blah, blah about tasteless food. Second, it is bad because it is too expensive. Blah, blah, blah about the expense." And so on. The writer is on autopilot and is not contributing to a real conversation about a real question. In some situations, writers use *engfish* intentionally: bureaucrats and politicians may want to avoid saying something risky; students may want to avoid writing about complex matters that they fear they do not fully understand. In the end, using *engfish* is bad not because what you say is *wrong,* but because what you say couldn't *possibly be* wrong. To avoid *engfish,* stay focused on the need to surprise your reader.

---

*The term *engfish* was coined by the textbook writer Ken Macrorie to describe a fishy kind of canned prose that bright but bored students mechanically produce to please their teachers. See Ken Macrorie, *Telling Writing* (Rochelle Park, NJ: Hayden Press, 1970).

For Writing and Discussion

As a class, choose a topic from popular culture such as TV talk shows, tattooing, eating disorders, rock lyrics, or something similar.

1. Working as a whole class or in small groups, give examples of how you might write about this topic in an *and then* way, an *all about* way, and an *engfish* way.
2. Then develop one or more questions about the topic that could lead to thesis/support writing. What contestable theses can your class create?

Lesson 3: Planning and Visualizing Your Structure

As we explained in Lesson 2, closed-form writing supports a contestable thesis through a hierarchical network of points and particulars. One way to visualize this structure is to outline its skeleton, an exercise that makes visually clear that not all points are on equal levels. The highest-level point is an essay's thesis statement, which is usually supported by several main points that are in turn supported by subpoints and sub-subpoints, all of which are supported by their own particulars. In this lesson we show you how to create such a hierarchical structure for your own papers and how to visualize this structure through an outline, tree diagram, or flowchart.

At the outset, we want to emphasize two important points. First, structural diagrams are not rigid molds, but flexible planning devices that evolve as your thinking shifts and changes. The structure of your final draft may be substantially different from your initial scratch outline. In fact, we want to show you how your outlines or diagrams can help you generate more ideas and reshape your structure.

Second, outlines or diagrams organize *meanings,* not topics. Note that in all our examples of outlines, diagrams, and flowcharts, we write *complete sentences* rather than phrases in the high-level slots. We do so because sentences can make a point, which conveys meaning, unlike a phrase, which identifies a topic but doesn't make an assertion about it. Any point—whether a thesis, a main point, or a subpoint—is a contestable assertion that requires its own particulars for support. By using complete sentences rather than phrases in an outline, the writer is forced to articulate the point of each section of the emerging argument.

With this background, we now proceed to a sequence of steps you can take to plan and visualize a structure.

Use Scratch Outlines Early in the Writing Process

Many writers can't make a detailed outline of their arguments until they have written exploratory drafts. At these early stages, writers often make brief scratch outlines that list the main ideas they want to develop initially or they make a list of points that emerged from a freewrite or a very early draft. Here is student writer Christopher Leigh's initial scratch outline for his argument against metal detectors in schools:

We first introduced Christopher's research problem in Chapter 1, p. 9. Christopher's final paper is shown in Chapter 14, pp. 363–374.

Schools should not use metal detectors as a way of reducing violence.

- Media have created a panic.
- Metal detectors are easily defeated.
- Students hate them.
- Should I put in a section on whether they violate rights???
- Poland article shows we should put the money into creating better school atmosphere.

Before Making a Detailed Outline, "Nutshell" Your Argument

As you explore your topic and begin drafting, your ideas will gradually become clearer and more structured. You can accelerate this process through a series of short exercises that will help you "nutshell" your argument (see Figure 12.1).

The six exercises in this figure cause you to look at your argument from different perspectives, helping you clarify the question you are addressing, articulate

FIGURE 12.1 Exercises for Nutshelling Your Argument

Exercise 1	What puzzle or problem initiated your thinking about X?
Exercise 2	*(Paradigm: Many people think X, but I am going to argue Y.)*

Before reading my paper, my readers will think this about my topic:

_____ .

But after reading my paper, my readers will think this new way about my topic:

_____ .

Exercise 3	The purpose of my paper is _____ .
Exercise 4	My paper addresses the following question: _____
Exercise 5	My one-sentence summary answer to the above question is this:

_____ .

Exercise 6	A tentative title for my paper is this: _____

_____ .

the kind of change you want to make in your audience's view of your topic, and directly state your purpose, thesis, and tentative title. The authors of this text often use this exercise in one-on-one writing conferences to help students create an initial focus from a swirl of ideas. We recommend that you write out your responses to each exercise as a preliminary step in helping you visualize your structure. Here are Christopher Leigh's responses to these questions:

> Exercise 1: I was initially puzzled by how best to reduce school violence. When I found that many schools were using metal detectors, I wondered whether this was a good approach.
>
> Exercise 2: Before reading my paper, my readers will believe that metal detectors are a good way to reduce school violence. After reading my paper, my readers will realize that there are many problems with metal detectors and will want to put money instead into improving the school environment.
>
> Exercise 3: The purpose of my paper is to argue against metal detectors and to argue for a better school environment.
>
> Exercise 4: Should schools use metal detectors? Are metal detectors a good way to reduce school violence?
>
> Exercise 5: Metal detectors should not be used in schools because there are other, more effective, and less costly alternatives for violence prevention.
>
> Exercise 6: The Case Against Metal Detectors in Schools.

Articulate a Working Thesis and Main Points

Once you have nutshelled your argument, you are ready to visualize a structure containing several sections, parts, or chunks, each of which is headed by a main point and supported with particulars. Try answering these questions:

1. My working thesis statement is:
2. The main sections or chunks needed in my paper are:

Here are Christopher Leigh's answers to these questions:

> 1. Metal detectors should not be used in schools because there is no basis for panic about violence and because there are other, more effective, and less costly alternatives for violence prevention.
> 2. (a) A section on the media's having created a panic; (b) a big section on the arguments against metal detectors; (c) a section on my solution, which is to improve the school atmosphere.

Sketch Your Structure Using an Outline, Tree Diagram, or Flowchart

At this point you can make an initial structural sketch of your argument and use the sketch to plan out the subpoints and particulars necessary to support the main points. We offer you three different ways to visualize your argument: outlines, tree diagrams, and flowcharts. Use whichever strategy best fits your way of thinking and perceiving.

Outlines

The most common way of visualizing structure is the traditional outline, which uses letters and numerals to indicate levels of points, subpoints, and particulars. If you prefer outlines, we recommend that you use the outlining feature of your word processing program, which allows you to move and insert material and change heading levels with great flexibility. What follows is Christopher Leigh's detailed outline of his argument. Note that Chris uses complete sentences rather than phrases for each level.

The importance of complete sentences is explained at the beginning of this lesson, p. 309.

Thesis: Except for schools with severe threats of danger, metal detectors should not be used because there is no basis for panic and because there are other, more effective, and less costly alternatives for violence prevention in schools.

I. Media have created panic over school violence.
   A. School violence is actually quite rare.
   B. Frequency of weapons being brought to school has declined since 1993.
II. There are many strong arguments against use of metal detectors.
   A. Metal detectors may violate student rights.
      1. Quotations from students reveal belief that metal detectors violate their rights.
      2. Court rulings leave gray areas.
   B. Metal detectors are easily defeated.
      1. They can't close off all entrances.
      2. A shooter can always find a way to get guns inside.
   C. Metal detectors are costly.
   D. Metal detectors have bad psychological consequences for students.
      1. Quotations from students show students' dislike of prison atmosphere.
      2. Metal detectors create feeling of distrust and humiliation.
III. A better solution is to use the money spent on metal detectors to provide a better school atmosphere.
   A. Quotation from high school senior Malik Barry-Buchanan shows need to create respect and caring in the schools.
   B. Article by Poland shows need to make schools more personal and to provide more counseling.
      1. Teachers should make efforts to know each student as an individual.
      2. Extracurricular activities should not be cut.
      3. Schools should provide more counseling.
IV. Conclusion

Tree Diagrams

A tree diagram displays a hierarchical structure visually, using horizontal and vertical space instead of letters and numbers. Figure 12.2 shows Christopher's argument as a tree diagram. His thesis is at the top of the tree. His main reasons, written as point sentences, appear as branches beneath his claim. Supporting evidence and arguments are displayed as subbranches beneath each reason.

FIGURE 12.2 Christopher's Tree Diagram

FIGURE 12.2 Christopher's Tree Diagram

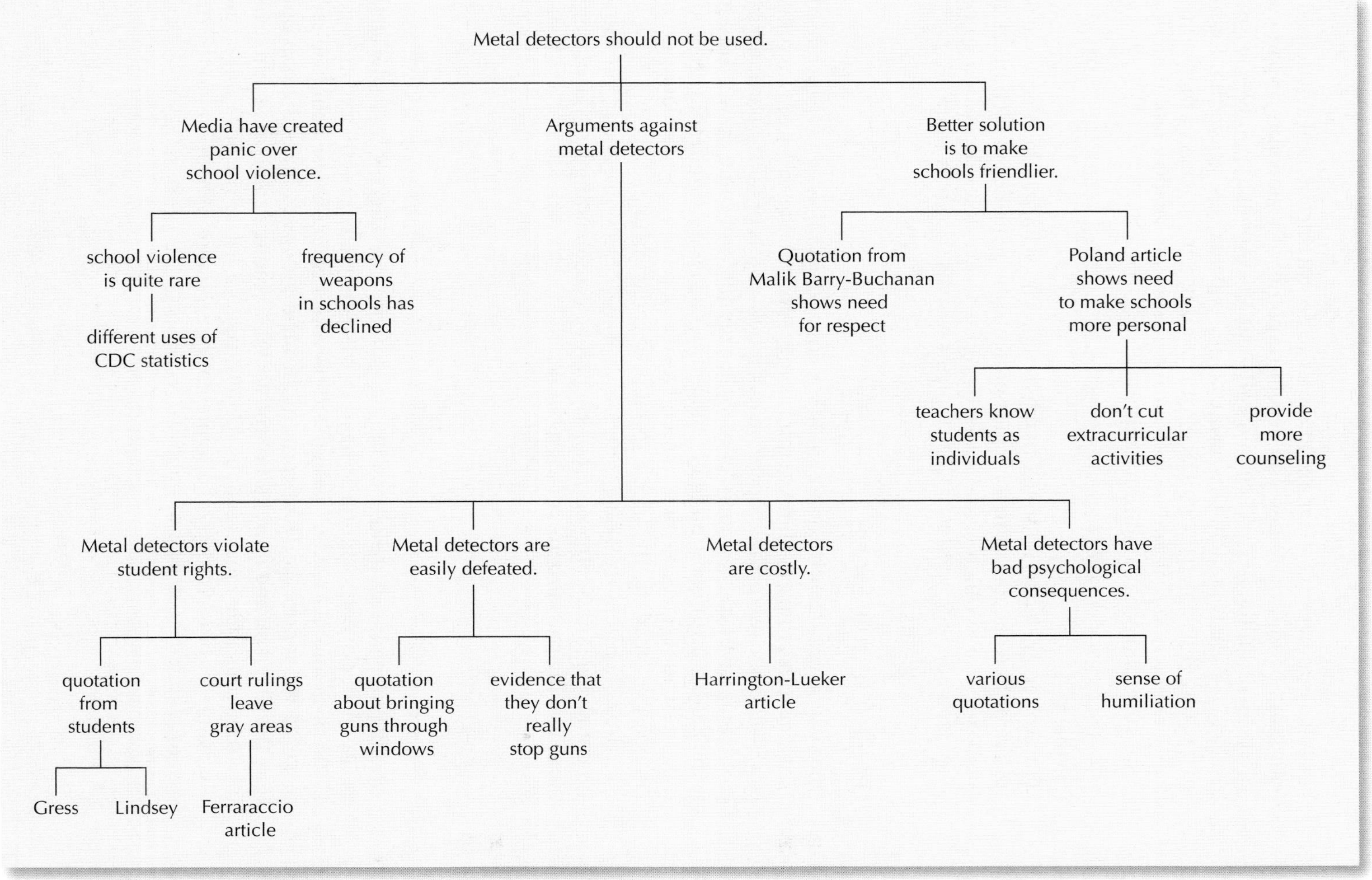

Unlike outlines, tree diagrams allow us to *see* the hierarchical relationship of points and particulars. When you develop a point with subpoints or particulars, you move down the tree. When you switch to a new point, you move across the tree to make a new branch. Our own teaching experience suggests that for many writers, this visual/spatial technique, which engages more areas of the brain than the more purely verbal outline, produces fuller, more detailed, and more logical arguments than does a traditional outline.

Flowcharts

Many writers prefer an informal, hand-sketched flowchart as an alternative to an outline or tree diagram. The flowchart presents the sequence of sections as separate boxes, inside which (or next to which) the writer notes the material needed to fill each box. A flowchart of Christopher's essay is shown in Figure 12.3.

Let the Structure Evolve

Once you have sketched out an initial structural diagram, use it to generate ideas. Tree diagrams are particularly helpful because they invite you to place question marks on branches to "hold open" spots for new points or for supporting particulars. If you have only two main points, for example, you could draw a third main branch and place a question mark under it to encourage you to think of another supporting idea. Likewise, if a branch has few supporting particulars, add question marks beneath it. The trick is to think of your structural diagrams as evolving sketches rather than rigid blueprints. As your ideas grow and change, revise your structural diagram, adding or removing points, consolidating and refocusing sections, moving parts around, or filling in details.

For Writing and Discussion

Working individually, make a traditional outline, tree diagram, and flow chart of David Rockwood's argument against wind-generated electricity on pages 17–18 or of another reading designated by your instructor. Use complete sentences at the top levels. Then convene in small groups to make a group outline, tree diagram, and flowchart of the assigned reading, combining and revising from your individual versions. Finally, make a list of the advantages and disadvantages of each method of representing structure. Which methods work best for different members of the class?

FIGURE 12.3 Christopher's Flowchart

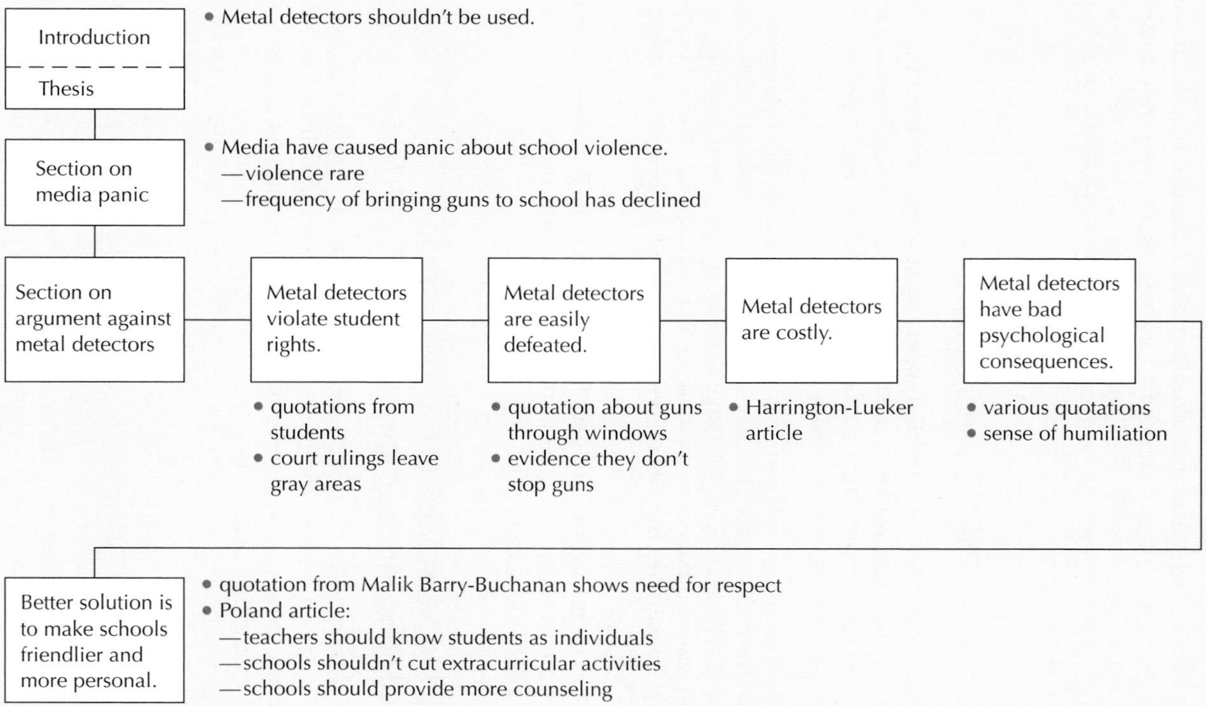

Introduction / **Thesis**	• Metal detectors shouldn't be used.			
Section on media panic	• Media have caused panic about school violence. —violence rare —frequency of bringing guns to school has declined			
Section on argument against metal detectors	**Metal detectors violate student rights.** • quotations from students • court rulings leave gray areas	**Metal detectors are easily defeated.** • quotation about guns through windows • evidence they don't stop guns	**Metal detectors are costly.** • Harrington-Lueker article	**Metal detectors have bad psychological consequences.** • various quotations • sense of humiliation
Better solution is to make schools friendlier and more personal.	• quotation from Malik Barry-Buchanan shows need for respect • Poland article: —teachers should know students as individuals —schools shouldn't cut extracurricular activities —schools should provide more counseling			

Lesson 4: Writing Effective Titles and Introductions

Because effective titles and introductions give readers a big-picture overview of a paper's argument, writers often can't compose them until they have finished one or more exploratory drafts. But as soon as you know your essay's big picture, you'll find that writing titles and introductions follows some general principles that are easy to learn.

What Not to Do: The "Funnel Introduction"

Some students have been taught an opening strategy, sometimes called the "funnel," that encourages students to start with broad generalizations and then narrow down to their topics. This strategy often leads to vapid generalizations in the opening sentences, as the following example shows:

> Since time immemorial people have pondered the question of freedom. What it means to be free was asked by the great philosophers of ancient Greece and Rome, and the question has echoed through the ages up until the present day. One modern psychologist who asked this question was B. F. Skinner, who wanted to study whether humans had free will or were programmed by their environment to act the way they did. . . .

Here the writer eventually gets to his subject, B. F. Skinner. But the opening sentences are snoozers. A better approach, as we will show, is to hook immediately into your readers' interests.

From Old to New: The General Principle of Closed-Form Introductions

We introduced the principle of old before new in Lesson 1. See pp. 303–304.

Whereas the broad-to-narrow strategy is mechanical, the strategy we show you in this lesson, based on the principle of old information before new information, is dynamic and powerful. Old information is something your readers already know and find interesting before they start reading your essay. New information is the surprise of your argument, the unfamiliar material that you add to your readers' understanding.

See the explanation of a prototypical academic introduction in Chapter 2, pp. 32–34.

Because the writer's thesis statement forecasts the new information the paper will present, a thesis statement for a closed-form essay typically comes *at the end of the introduction*. What precedes the thesis is typically the old, familiar information that the reader needs in order to understand the conversation that the thesis joins. In most closed-form prose, particularly in academic prose, this old information is the problem or question that the thesis addresses. A typical closed-form introduction has the following shape:

PROBLEM
[old information]
↓
THESIS
[new information]

The length and complexity of your introduction is a function of how much your reader already knows and cares about the question or problem your paper addresses. The function of an introduction is to capture the reader's interest in the first few sentences, to identify and explain the question or problem that the essay addresses, to provide any needed background information, and to present the thesis. You can leave out any of the first three elements if the reader is already hooked on your topic and already knows the question you are addressing. For example, in an essay exam you can usually start with your thesis statement because you can assume the instructor already knows the question and finds it interesting.

To illustrate how an effective closed-form introduction takes the reader from the question to the thesis, consider how the following student writer revised his introduction to a paper on Napster.com:

ORIGINAL INTRODUCTION (CONFUSING)

Napster is all about sharing, not stealing, as record companies and some musicians would like us to think. Napster is an online program that was released in October of '99. Napster lets users easily search for and trade mp3s—compressed, high-quality music files that can be produced from a CD. Napster is the leading file sharing community; it allows users to locate and share music. It also provides instant messaging, chat rooms, an outlet for fans to identify new artists, and a forum to communicate their interests.

Thesis statement

Background on Napster

Most readers find this introduction confusing. The writer begins with his thesis statement before the reader is introduced to the question that the thesis addresses. He seems to assume that his reader is already a part of the Napster conversation, and yet in the next sentences, he gives background on Napster. If the reader needs background on Napster, then the reader also needs background on the Napster controversy. In rethinking his assumptions about old-versus-new information for his audience, this writer decides he wants to reach general newspaper readers who may have heard about a lawsuit against Napster and are interested in the issue but aren't sure of what Napster is or how it works. Here is his revised introduction:

REVISED INTRODUCTION (CLEARER)

Several months ago the rock band Metallica filed a lawsuit against Napster.com, an online program that lets users easily search for and trade mp3s—compressed, high-quality music files that can be produced from a CD. Napster.com has been wildly popular among music lovers because it creates a virtual community where users can locate and share music. It also provides instant messaging, chat rooms, an outlet for fans to identify new artists, and a forum to communicate their interests. But big-name bands like Metallica, alarmed at what they see as lost revenues, claim that Napster.com is stealing their royalties. However, Napster is all about sharing, not stealing, as some musicians would like us to think.

Triggers readers' memory of lawsuit

Background on Napster

Clarification of problem (Implied question: Should Napster be shut down?)

Thesis

This revised introduction fills in the old information the reader needs in order to recall and understand the problem; then it presents the thesis.

Typical Elements of a Closed-Form Introduction

Now that you understand the general principle of closed-form introductions, let's look more closely at its four typical features or elements:

An Opening Attention-Grabber.   The first few sentences in an introduction have to capture your reader's interest. If you aren't sure your reader is already interested in your problem, you can begin with an attention-grabber (what journalists call the "hook" or "lead"), which is typically a dramatic vignette, a startling fact or statistic, an arresting quotation, an interesting scene, or something else that taps into your reader's interests. Attention-grabbers are uncommon in academic prose (where you assume your reader will be initially engaged by the problem itself) but frequently used in popular prose. The student writer of the Napster paper initially toyed with the following attention-grabber to begin his essay:

> How many times have you liked one or two songs on a CD but thought the rest of it was garbage? How many times have you burned your own customized CDs by finding your favorite music on Napster.com? Well, that opportunity is about to be lost if Metallica wins its lawsuit against Napster.

He decided not to use this attention-grabber, however, because he wanted to reach audiences who weren't already users of Napster. He decided that these general readers were already interested in the lawsuit and didn't need the extra zing of an attention-grabber.

The brief writing project in Chapter 1 teaches you how to show that a question is problematic and significant. See pp. 24–25.

Explanation of the Question to Be Investigated.   If you assume that your reader already knows about the problem and cares about it, then you need merely to summarize it. This problem or question is the starting point of your argument. Closed-form writers often state the question directly in a single sentence ending with a question mark, but sometimes they imply it, letting the reader formulate it from context. If you aren't sure whether your audience fully understands the question or fully cares about it, then you need to explain it in more detail, showing why it is both problematic and significant.

Background Information.   In order to understand the conversation you are joining, readers sometimes need background information—perhaps a definition of key terms, a summary of events leading up to the problem you're presenting, factual details needed for basic understanding of the problem, and so forth. In scientific papers, this background often includes a review of the preexisting literature on the problem. In the Napster introduction, the writer devotes several sentences to background on Napster.com.

A Preview of the Whole.   The final element of a closed-form introduction sketches the big picture of your essay by giving readers a sense of the whole. This preview is initially new information for your readers (this is why it comes at the end of the introduction). Once stated, however, it becomes old information that readers will use to locate their position in their journey through your argument. By predicting what's coming, this preview initiates the pleasurable process of forecasting/fulfillment that we discussed in Lesson 1. Writers typically forecast the whole by stating their thesis, but they can also use a purpose statement or a blueprint statement to accomplish the same end. These strategies are the subject of the next section.

See this chapter's opening epigraph from rhetorician Kenneth Burke, p. 301.

Forecasting the Whole with a Thesis Statement, Purpose Statement, or Blueprint Statement

The most succinct way to forecast the whole is to state your thesis directly. Student writers often ask how detailed their thesis statements should be and whether it is permissible, sometimes, to delay revealing the thesis until the conclusion—an open-form move that gives papers a more exploratory, mystery-novel feel. It is useful, then, to outline briefly some of your choices as a writer. To illustrate a writer's options for forecasting the whole, we use Christopher Leigh's essay on metal detectors in schools that we discussed in Lesson 3.

To see the choices Christopher Leigh actually made, see his complete essay on pp. 363–374.

Options for Forecasting the Whole

Option	Explanation	Example
Short thesis	State claim without summarizing your supporting argument or forecasting your structure.	Schools should not use metal detectors to reduce school violence.
Detailed thesis	Summarize whole argument; may begin with an *although* clause that summarizes the view you are trying to change.	Although metal detectors may be justified in schools with severe threats of danger, they should generally not be used because there is no basis for panic and because there are other, more effective, and less costly alternatives for violence prevention in schools.
Purpose statement	State your purpose or intention without summarizing the argument. A purpose statement typically begins with a phrase such as "My purpose is to . . ." or "In the following paragraphs I wish to . . .:"	My purpose in this essay is to make a case against using metal detectors in schools.
Blueprint or mapping statement	Describe the structure of your essay by announcing the number of main parts and describing the function or purpose of each one.	First I show that the media have created a false panic about school violence. Next I present four reasons metal detectors have bad consequences. Finally I outline a better approach—making schools friendlier and more personal.

In addition you have at least two other options:

- *Multisentence summary.* In long articles, academic writers often use all three kinds of statements—a purpose statement, a thesis statement, and a blueprint statement. While this sort of extensive forecasting is common in academic and business writing, it occurs less frequently in informal or popular essays. Christopher decided that his paper wasn't complex enough to justify an extensive multisentence overview.
- *Thesis question.* When writers wish to delay their thesis until the middle or the end of their essays, letting their arguments slowly unfold and keeping their stance a mystery, they often end the introduction with a question. This open-form strategy invites readers to join the writer in a mutual search for the answer.

> Although I would prefer having no metal detectors in schools, I am strongly in favor of making schools safer. So the question of whether metal detectors are justified leaves me baffled and puzzled. Should schools use them or not? [This approach would have required a very different structure from the paper Christopher actually wrote.]

Which of these options should a writer choose? There are no firm rules to help you answer this question. How much you forecast in the introduction and where you reveal your thesis is a function of your purpose, audience, and genre. The more you forecast, the clearer your argument is and the easier it is to read quickly. You minimize the demands on readers' time by giving them the gist of your argument in the introduction, making it easier to skim your essay if they don't have time for a thorough reading. The less you forecast, the more demands you make on readers' time: You invite them, in effect, to accompany you through the twists and turns of your own thinking process, and you risk losing them if they become confused, lost, or bored. For these reasons, academic writing is generally closed form and aims at maximum clarity. In many rhetorical contexts, however, more open forms are appropriate.

Chapter 3, pp. 56–57, gives more advice on when to choose closed or open forms.

If you choose a closed-form structure, we can offer some advice on how much to forecast. Readers sometimes feel insulted by too much forecasting, so include only what is needed for clarity. For short papers, readers usually don't need to have the complete supporting argument forecast in the introduction. In longer papers, however, or in especially complex ones, readers appreciate having the whole argument forecast at the outset. Academic writing in particular tends to favor explicit and often detailed forecasting.

Writing Effective Titles

The strategies we have suggested for a closed-form introduction apply equally well to a closed-form title. A good title needs to have something old (a word or phrase that hooks into a reader's existing interests) and something new (a hint of the writer's thesis or purpose). Here is an example of an academic title:

"Style as Politics: A Feminist Approach to the Teaching of Writing" [This title attracts scholars interested either in style or in feminist issues in writing (old); it promises to analyze the political implications of style (new).]

As this example shows, your title should provide a brief but detailed overview of what your paper is about. Academic titles are typically longer and more detailed than are titles in popular magazines. They usually follow one of four conventions:

1. Some titles simply state the question that the essay addresses:

   "Will Patriarchal Management Survive Beyond the Decade?"

2. Some titles state, often in abbreviated form, the essay's thesis:

   "The Writer's Audience Is Always a Fiction"

3. Very often the title is the last part of the essay's purpose statement:

   "The Relationship between Client Expectation of Improvement and Psychotherapy Outcome"

4. Many titles consist of two parts separated by a colon. To the left of the colon the writer presents key words from the essay's issue or problem or a "mystery phrase" that arouses interest; to the right the author places the essay's question, thesis, or summary of purpose:

   "Money and Growth: An Alternative Approach"
   "Deep Play: Notes on a Balinese Cockfight"
   "Fine Cloth, Cut Carefully: Cooperative Learning in British Columbia"

Although such titles might seem overly formal to you, they indicate how much a closed-form writer wishes to preview an article's big picture. Although their titles may be more informal, popular magazines often use these same strategies. Here are some titles from *Redbook* and the business magazine *Forbes*:

   "Is the Coffee Bar Trend About to Peak?" (question)
   "A Man *Can* Take Maternity Leave—And Love It" (abbreviated thesis)
   "Why the Department of Education Shouldn't Take Over the Student Loan Program" (last part of purpose statement)
   "Feed Your Face: Why Your Complexion Needs Vitamins" (two parts linked by colon)

Composing a title for your essay can help you find your focus when you get bogged down in the middle of a draft. Thinking about your title forces you to *nutshell* your ideas by seeing your project's big picture. It causes you to reconsider your purpose and to think about what's old and what's new for your audience.

For Writing and Discussion

Individual task: Choose an essay you are currently working on or have recently completed and examine your title and introduction based on the advice in this lesson. Ask yourself these questions:

- What audience am I imagining? What do I assume are my readers' initial interests that will lead them to read my essay (the old information I must hook into)? What is new in my essay?
- Do I have an attention-grabber? Why or why not?
- Where do I state or imply the question or problem that my essay addresses?
- Do I explain why the question is problematic and significant? Why or why not?
- For my audience to understand the problem, do I provide too much background information, not enough, or just the right amount?
- What strategies do I use to forecast the whole?

Based on your analysis of your present title and introduction, revise as appropriate.

Group task: Working with a partner or in small groups, share the changes you made in your title or introduction and explain why you made the changes.

Lesson 5: Placing Points before Particulars

In our lesson on outlining (Lesson 3), we suggested that you write complete sentences rather than phrases for the high-level slots of the outline in order to articulate the *meaning* or *point* of each section of your argument. In this lesson we show you how to place these points where readers expect them: near the beginning of the sections or paragraphs they govern.

When you place points before particulars, you follow the same principle illustrated in Lesson 1 with the flight attendant announcing the name of the city before the departure gate (the city is the old information, the departure gate the new information). When you first state the point, it is the new information that the next paragraph or section will develop. Once you have stated it, it becomes old information that helps readers understand the meaning of the particulars that follow. If you withhold the point until later, the reader has to keep all the particulars in short-term memory until you finally reveal the point that the particulars are supposed to support or develop.

Place Topic Sentences at the Beginning of Paragraphs

Readers of closed-form prose need to have point sentences (usually called "topic sentences") at the beginnings of paragraphs. However, writers of rough drafts often don't fulfill this need because, as we explained in Chapter 11, drafting is an exploratory process in which writers are often still searching for their points as they compose. Consequently, in their rough drafts writers often omit topic sentences entirely or place them at the ends of paragraphs, or they write topic sentences that misrepresent what the paragraphs actually say. During revision, then, you should check your body paragraphs carefully to be sure you have placed accurate topic sentences near the beginning.

What follow are examples of the kinds of revisions writers typically make. We have annotated the examples to explain the changes the writer has made to make the paragraphs unified and clear to readers. The first example is from a later draft of the essay on dorm room carpets from Chapter 11 (pp. 295–297).

Revision—Topic Sentence First

Another reason for the university not to buy carpets is the cost.
ʌAccording to Rachel Jones, Assistant Director of Housing   *Topic sentence placed first*

Services, the initial purchase and installation of carpeting would

cost $300 per room. Considering the number of rooms in the three

residence halls, carpeting amounts to a substantial investment.

Additionally, once the carpets are installed, the university would

need to maintain them through the purchase of more vacuum cleaners

and shampoo machines. This money would be better spent on other

dorm improvements that would benefit more residents, such as

expanded kitchen facilities and improved recreational space. ~~Thus~~

~~carpets would be too expensive.~~

In the original draft, the writer states the point at the end of the paragraph. In his revision he states the point in an opening topic sentence that links back to the thesis statement, which promises "several reasons" that the university should not buy carpets for the dorms. The words "another reason" thus link the topic sentence to the argument's big picture.

Revise Paragraphs for Unity

In addition to placing topic sentences at the heads of paragraphs, writers often need to revise topic sentences to better match what the paragraph actually says, or revise the paragraph to better match the topic sentence. Paragraphs have unity when all their sentences develop the point stated in the topic sentence. Paragraphs in rough drafts are often not unified because they reflect the writer's shifting, evolving, thinking-while-writing process. Consider the following paragraph from an early draft of an argument against euthanasia by student writer Dao Do. Her peer reviewer labeled it "confusing." What makes it confusing?

We look at more examples from Dao's essay later in this chapter.

Early Draft—Confusing

First, euthanasia is wrong because no one has the right to take the life of another person. Some people say that euthanasia or suicide will end suffering and pain. But what proofs do they have for such a claim? Death is still mysterious to us; therefore, we do not know whether death will end suffering and pain or not. What seems to be the real claim is that death to those with illnesses will end <u>our</u> pain. Such pain involves worrying over them, paying their medical bills, and giving up so much of our time. Their deaths end our pain rather than theirs. And for that reason, euthanasia is a selfish act, for the outcome of euthanasia benefits us, the nonsufferers, more. Once the sufferers pass away, we can go back to our normal lives.

The paragraph opens with an apparent topic sentence: "Euthanasia is wrong because no one has the right to take the life of another person." But the rest of the paragraph doesn't focus on that point. Instead, it focuses on how euthanasia benefits the survivors more than the sick person. Dao had two choices: to revise the paragraph to fit the topic sentence or to revise the topic sentence to fit the paragraph. Here is her revision, which includes a different topic sentence and an additional sentence midparagraph to keep particulars focused on the opening point. Dao unifies this paragraph by keeping all its parts focused on her main point: "Euthanasia . . . benefits the survivors more than the sick person."

Revision for Unity

First, euthanasia is wrong because it benefits the survivors more than the sick person.
~~First, euthanasia is wrong because no one has the right to~~

~~take the life of another person~~. Some people say that euthanasia
            the sick person's ◄───────────────────
or suicide will end ₍suffering and pain. But what proofs do they

have for such a claim? Death is still mysterious to us;

therefore, we do not know whether death will end suffering and
Moreover, modern pain killers can relieve most of the pain a sick person has to endure. ◄───────
pain or not. ₍What seems to be the real claim is that death to

those with illnesses will end <u>our</u> pain. Such pain involves

worrying over them, paying their medical bills, and giving up so

much of our time. Their deaths end our pain rather than theirs.

And for that reason, euthanasia is a selfish act, for the outcome

of euthanasia benefits us, the nonsufferers, more. Once the

sufferers pass away, we can go back to our normal lives.

Revised topic sentence better forecasts focus of paragraph

Keeps focus on "sick person"

Concludes subpoint about sick person

Supports subpoint about how euthanasia benefits survivors

A paragraph may lack unity for a variety of reasons. It may shift to a new direction in the middle, or one or two sentences may simply be irrelevant to the point. The key is to make sure that all the sentences in the paragraph fulfill the reader's expectations based on the topic sentence.

Add Particulars to Support Points

Just as writers of rough drafts often omit point sentences from paragraphs, they also sometimes leave out the particulars needed to support a point. In such cases, the writer needs to add particulars such as facts, statistics, quotations, research summaries, examples, or further subpoints. Consider how adding additional particulars to the following draft paragraph strengthens student writer Tiffany Linder's argument opposing the logging of old-growth forests.

DRAFT PARAGRAPH: PARTICULARS MISSING

One reason that it is not necessary to log old-growth forests is that the timber industry can supply the world's lumber needs without doing so. For example, we have plenty of new-growth forest from which timber can be taken (Sagoff 89). We could also reduce the amount of trees used for paper products by using other materials besides wood for paper pulp. In light of the fact that we have plenty of trees and ways of reducing our wood demands, there is no need to harvest old-growth forests.

REVISED PARAGRAPH: PARTICULARS ADDED

One reason that it is not necessary to log old-growth forests is that the timber industry can supply the world's lumber needs without doing so. For example, we have plenty of new-growth forest from which timber can be taken as a result of major reforestation efforts all over the United States (Sagoff 89). In the Northwest, for instance, Oregon law requires every acre of timber harvested to be replanted. According to Robert Sedjo, a forestry expert, the world's demand for industrial wood could be met by a widely implemented tree farming system (Sagoff 90). We could also reduce the amount of trees used for paper products by using a promising new innovation called Kenaf, a fast-growing annual herb which is fifteen feet tall and is native to Africa. It has been used for making rope for many years, but recently it was found to work just as well for paper pulp. In light of the fact that we have plenty of trees and ways of reducing our wood demands, there is no need to harvest old-growth forests.

Added particulars support subpoint that we have plenty of new-growth forest

Added particulars support second subpoint that wood alternatives are available

For Writing and Discussion

Individual Task: Bring to class a draft-in-progress for a closed-form essay. Pick out several paragraphs in the body of your essay and analyze them for "points-first" structure. For each paragraph, ask the following questions:

- Does my paragraph have a topic sentence near the beginning?
- If so, does my topic sentence accurately forecast what the paragraph says?
- Does my topic sentence link to my thesis statement or to a higher-order point that my paragraph develops?
- Does my paragraph have enough particulars to develop and support my topic sentence?

Group Task: Then exchange your draft with a partner and do a similar analysis of your partner's selected paragraphs. Discuss your analyses of each other's paragraphs and then help each other plan appropriate revision strategies. If time permits, revise your paragraphs and show your results to your partner. [Note: Sometimes you can revise simply by adding a topic sentence to a paragraph, rewording a topic sentence, or making other kinds of local revisions. At other times, you may need to cross out whole paragraphs and start over, rewriting from scratch after you rethink your ideas.]

Lesson 6: Signaling Relationships with Transitions

As we have explained in previous lessons, when readers read closed-form prose, they expect each new sentence, paragraph, and section to link clearly to what they have already read. They need a well-marked trail with signposts signaling the twists and turns along the way. They also need resting spots at major junctions where they can review where they've been and survey what's coming. In this lesson, we show you how transition words as well as summary and forecasting passages can keep your readers securely on the trail.

Use Common Transition Words to Signal Relationships

Transitions are like signposts that signal where the road is turning and limit the possible directions that an unfolding argument might take. Consider how the use of "therefore" and "nevertheless" limits the range of possibilities in the following examples:

> While on vacation, Suzie caught the chicken pox. Therefore, _____.
> While on vacation, Suzie caught the chicken pox. Nevertheless, _____.

"Therefore" signals to the reader that what follows is a consequence. Most readers will imagine a sentence similar to this one:

> Therefore, she spent her vacation lying in bed itching, feverish, and miserable.

In contrast, "nevertheless" signals an unexpected or denied consequence, so the reader might anticipate a sentence such as this:

> Nevertheless, she enjoyed her two weeks off, thanks to a couple of bottles of calamine lotion, some good books, and a big easy chair overlooking the ocean.

Here is a list of the most common transition words and phrases and what they signal to the reader:*

Words or Phrases	What They Signal
first, second, third, next, finally, earlier, later, meanwhile, afterward	*sequence*—First we went to dinner; then we went to the movies.
that is, in other words, to put it another way,—(dash), :(colon)	*restatement*—He's so hypocritical that you can't trust a word he says. To put it another way, he's a complete phony.
rather, instead	*replacement*—We shouldn't use the money to buy opera tickets; rather, we should use it for a nice gift.
for example, for instance, a case in point	*example*—Mr. Carlysle is very generous. For example, he gave the janitors a special holiday gift.

---

*Although all the words on the list serve as transitions or connectives, grammatically they are not all equivalent, nor are they all punctuated the same way.

Words or Phrases	What They Signal
because, since, for	*reason*—Taxes on cigarettes are unfair because they place a higher tax burden on the working class.
therefore, hence, so, consequently, thus, then, as a result, accordingly, as a consequence	*consequences*—I failed to turn in the essay; therefore I flunked the course.
still, nevertheless	*denied consequence*—The teacher always seemed grumpy in class; nevertheless, I really enjoyed the course.
although, even though, granted that (*with* still)	*concession*—Even though the teacher was always grumpy, I still enjoyed the course.
in comparison, likewise, similarly	*similarity*—Teaching engineering takes a lot of patience. Likewise, so does teaching accounting.
however, in contrast, conversely, on the other hand, but	*contrast*—I disliked my old backpack immensely; however, I really like this new one.
in addition, also, too, moreover, furthermore	*addition*—Today's cars are much safer than those of ten years ago. In addition, they get better gas mileage.
in brief, in sum, in conclusion, finally, to sum up, to conclude	*conclusion or summary*—In sum, the plan presented by Mary is the best choice.

For Writing and Discussion

This exercise is designed to show you how transition words govern relationships between ideas. Working in groups or on your own, finish each of the following statements using ideas of your own invention. Make sure what you add fits the logic of the transition word.

1. Writing is difficult; therefore _____.
2. Writing is difficult; however, _____.
3. Writing is difficult because _____.
4. Writing is difficult. For example, _____.
5. Writing is difficult. To put it another way, _____.
6. Writing is difficult. Likewise, _____.
7. Although writing is difficult, _____.
8. _____. In sum, writing is difficult.

In the following paragraph, various kinds of linking devices have been omitted. Fill in the blanks with words or phrases that would make the paragraph coherent. Clues are provided in brackets.

> Writing an essay is a difficult process for most people. _____ [contrast] the process can be made easier if you learn to practice three simple techniques. _____ [sequence] learn the technique of nonstop writing. When you are first trying to think of ideas for an essay, put your pen to your paper and write nonstop for ten or fifteen minutes without letting your pen leave the paper. Stay loose and free. Let your pen follow the waves of thought. Don't worry about grammar or spelling. _____ [concession] this technique won't work for everyone, it helps many people get a good cache of ideas to draw on. A _____ [sequence] technique is to write your rough draft rapidly without worrying about being perfect. Too many writers try to get their drafts right the first time. _____ [contrast] by learning to live with imperfection, you will save yourself headaches and a wastepaper basket full of crumpled paper. Think of your first rough draft as a path hacked out of the jungle—as part of an exploration, not as a completed highway. As a _____ [sequence] technique, try printing out a triple-spaced copy to allow space for revision. Many beginning writers don't leave enough space to revise. _____ [consequence] these writers never get in the habit of crossing out chunks of their rough draft and writing revisions in the blank spaces. After you have revised your rough draft until it is too messy to work from anymore, you can _____ [sequence] enter your changes into your word processor and print out a fresh draft, again setting your text on triple-space. The resulting blank space invites you to revise.

Write Major Transitions between Parts

In long closed-form pieces, writers often put *resting places* between major parts—transitional passages that allow readers to shift their attention momentarily away from the matter at hand to a sense of where they've been and where they're going. Often such passages sum up the preceding major section, refer back to the essay's thesis statement or opening blueprint plan, and then preview the next major section. Here are three typical examples:

> So far I have looked at a number of techniques that can help people identify debilitating assumptions that block their self-growth. In the next section, I examine ways to question and overcome these assumptions.

> Now that the difficulty of the problem is fully apparent, our next step is to examine some of the solutions that have been proposed.

> These, then, are the major theories explaining why Hamlet delays. But let's see what happens to Hamlet if we ask the question in a slightly different way. In this next section, we shift our critical focus, looking not at Hamlet's actions, but at his language.

Signal Transitions with Headings and Subheadings

In many genres, particularly scientific and technical reports, government documents, business proposals, textbooks, and long articles in magazines or scholarly journals, writers conventionally break up long stretches of text with headings and subheadings. Headings are often set in different type sizes and fonts and mark transition points between major parts and subparts of the argument.

Lesson 7: Binding Sentences Together by Following the Old/New Contract

In the previous lesson we showed you how to mark the reader's trail with transitions. In this lesson we show you how to build a smooth trail without potholes or washed-out bridges.

An Explanation of the Old/New Contract

A powerful way to prevent gaps is to follow the old/new contract—a writing strategy derived from the principle of old before new that we explained and illustrated in Lesson 1. Simply put, the old/new contract asks writers to begin sentences with something old—something that links to what has gone before—and then to end sentences with new information.

To understand the old/new contract more fully, try the following thought exercise. We'll show you two passages, both of which explain the old/new contract. One of them, however, follows the principle it describes; the other violates it.

THOUGHT EXERCISE

Which of these passages follows the old/new contract?

VERSION 1

The old/new contract is another principle for writing clear closed-form prose. Beginning your sentences with something old—something that links to what has gone before—and then ending your sentences with new information that advances the argument is what the old/new contract asks writers to do. An effect called *coherence,* which is closely related to *unity,* is created by following this principle. Whereas the clear relationship between the topic sentence and the body of the paragraph and between the parts and the whole is what *unity* refers to, the clear relationship between one sentence and the next is what *coherence* relates to.

VERSION 2

Another principle for writing clear closed-form prose is the old/new contract. The old/new contract asks writers to begin sentences with something old—something that links to what has gone before—and then to end sentences with new information that advances the argument. Following this principle creates an effect called *coherence,* which is closely related to unity. Whereas *unity* refers to the clear relationship between the body of a paragraph and its topic sentence and between the parts and the whole, *coherence* refers to the clear relationship between one sentence and the next, between part and part.

If you are like most readers, you have to concentrate much harder to understand Version 1 than Version 2 because it violates the old-before-new way that our minds normally process information. When a writer doesn't begin a sentence with old material, readers have to hold the new material in suspension until they have figured out how it connects to what has gone before. They can stay on the trail, but they have to keep jumping over the potholes between sentences.

To follow the old/new contract, place old information near the beginning of sentences in what we call the *topic position* and new information that advances the argument in the predicate or *stress position* at the end of the sentence. We associate topics with the beginnings of sentences simply because in the standard English sentence, the topic (or subject) comes before the predicate—hence the notion of a "contract" by which we agree not to fool or frustrate our readers by breaking with the "normal" order of things. The contract says that the old, backward-linking material comes at the beginning of the sentence and that the new, argument-advancing material comes at the end.

For Writing and Discussion

What follow are two more passages, one of which obeys the old/new contract while the other violates it. Working in small groups or as a whole class, reach consensus on which of these passages follows the old/new contract. Explain your reasoning by showing how the beginning of each sentence links to something old.

PASSAGE A

Play is an often-overlooked dimension of fathering. From the time a child is born until its adolescence, fathers emphasize caretaking less than play. Egalitarian feminists may be troubled by this, and spending more time in caretaking may be wise for fathers. There seems to be unusual significance in the father's style of play. Physical excitement and stimulation are likely to be part of it. With older children more physical games and teamwork that require the competitive testing of physical and mental skills are also what it involves. Resemblance to an apprenticeship or teaching relationship is also a characteristic of fathers' play: Come on, let me show you how.

PASSAGE B

An often-overlooked dimension of fathering is play. From their children's birth through adolescence, fathers tend to emphasize play more than caretaking. This may be troubling to egalitarian feminists, and it would indeed be wise for most fathers to spend more time in caretaking. Yet the fathers' style of play seems

(*continued*)

to have unusual significance. It is likely to be both physically stimulating and exciting. With older children it involves more physical games and teamwork that require the competitive testing of physical and mental skills. It frequently resembles an apprenticeship or teaching relationship: Come on, let me show you how.

How to Make Links to the "Old"

To understand how to link to "old information," you need to understand more fully what we mean by "old" or "familiar." In the context of sentence-level coherence, we mean everything in the text that the reader has read so far. Any upcoming sentence is new information, but once the reader has read it, it becomes old information. For example, when a reader is halfway through a text, everything previously read—the title, the introduction, half the body—is old information to which you can link to meet your readers' expectations for unity and coherence.

In making these backward links, writers have three targets:

1. They can link to a key word or concept in the immediately preceding sentence (creating coherence).
2. They can link to a key word or concept in a preceding point sentence (creating unity).
3. They can link to a preceding forecasting statement about structure (helping readers map their location in the text).

Writers have a number of textual strategies for making these links. In Figure 12.4 our annotations show how a professional writer links to old information within the first five or six words of each sentence. What follows is a compendium of these strategies:

- *Repeat a key word.* The most common way to open with something old is to repeat a key word from the preceding sentence or an earlier point sentence. In our example, note the number of sentences that open with "father," "father's," or "fathering." Note also the frequent repetitions of "play."
- *Use a pronoun to substitute for a key word.* In our example, the second sentence opens with the pronouns "it," referring to "research," and "their," referring to "fathers." The last three sentences open with the pronoun "It," referring to "father's style of play."
- *Summarize, rephrase, or restate earlier concepts.* Writers can link to a preceding sentence by using a word or phrase that summarizes or restates a key concept. In the second sentence, "interactions with children" restates the concept of childrearing. Similarly, the phrase "an often-overlooked dimension" refers to a concept implied in the preceding paragraph—that recent

FIGURE 12.4 How a Professional Writer Follows the Old/New Contract

Recent research has given us much deeper—and more surprising—insights into the father's role in childrearing. It shows that in almost all of their interactions with children, fathers do things a little differently from mothers. What fathers do—their special parenting style—is not only highly complementary to what mothers do but is by all indications important in its own right.

For example, an often-overlooked dimension of fathering is play. From their children's birth through adolescence, fathers tend to emphasize play more than caretaking. This may be troubling to egalitarian feminists, and it would indeed be wise for most fathers to spend more time in caretaking. Yet the fathers' style of play seems to have unusual significance. It is likely to be both physically stimulating and exciting. With older children it involves more physical games and teamwork that require the competitive testing of physical and mental skills. It frequently resembles an apprenticeship or teaching relationship: Come on, let me show you how.

David Popenoe, "Where's Papa?" from *Life Without Father: Compelling New Evidence that Fatherhood and Marriage Are Indispensable for the Good of Children and Society.*

Annotations (left margin):
- *Refers to "fathers" in previous sentence*
- *Transition tells us new paragraph will be an example of previous concept*
- *Refers to fathers*
- *New information that becomes topic of this paragraph*
- *Repeats words "father" and "play" from the topic sentence of the paragraph*

Annotations (right margin):
- *Refers to "research" in previous sentence*
- *Rephrases idea of "childrearing"*
- *Repeats "fathers" from previous sentence*
- *Rephrases concept in previous paragraph*
- *Pronoun sums up previous concept*
- *"It" refers to fathers' style of play*

research reveals something significant and not widely known about a father's role in childrearing. An "often-overlooked dimension" sums up this idea. Finally, note that the pronoun "this" in the second paragraph sums up the main concept of the previous two sentences. (But see our warning on page 334 about the overuse of "this" as a pronoun.)

- *Use a transition word.* Writers can also use transition words such as *first . . . , second . . . , third . . .* or *therefore* or *however* to cue the reader about the logical relationship between an upcoming sentence and the preceding ones. Note how the second paragraph opens with "For example," indicating that the upcoming paragraph will illustrate the concept identified in the preceding paragraph.

These strategies give you a powerful way to check and revise your prose. Comb your drafts for gaps between sentences where you have violated the old/new contract. If the opening of a new sentence doesn't refer back to an earlier word, phrase, or concept, your readers could derail, so use what you have learned to repair the tracks.

For Writing and Discussion

Individual Task: Bring to class a draft-in-progress for a closed-form essay. On a selected page, examine the opening of each sentence. Place a vertical slash in front of any sentence that doesn't contain near the beginning some backward-looking element that links to old, familiar material. Then revise these sentences to follow the old/new contract.

Group Task: Working with a partner, share the changes you each made on your drafts. Then on each other's pages, work together to identify the kinds of links made at the beginning of each sentence. (For example, does the opening of a sentence repeat a key word, use a pronoun to substitute for a key word, rephrase or restate an earlier concept, or use a transition word?)

As we discussed in Lesson 1, the principle of old before new has great explanatory power in helping writers understand their choices when they compose. In this last section, we give you some further insights into the old/new contract.

Avoid Ambiguous Use of "This" to Fulfill the Old/New Contract

Some writers try to fulfill the old/new contract by frequent use of the pronoun *this* to sum up a preceding concept. Occasionally such usage is effective, as in our example passage on fathers' style of play when the writer says: "*This* may be troubling to egalitarian feminists." But frequent use of *this* as a pronoun creates lazy and often ambiguous prose. Consider how our example passage might read if many of the explicit links were replaced by *this:*

LAZY USE OF *THIS* AS PRONOUN

Recent research has given us much deeper—and more surprising—insights into **this.** It shows that in doing **this,** fathers do things a little differently from mothers. **This** is not only highly complementary to what mothers do but is by all indications important in its own right.

For example, an often-overlooked dimension of **this** is play.

Perhaps this passage helps you see why we refer to *this* (used by itself as a pronoun) as "the lazy person's all-purpose noun-slot filler."*

---

*It's acceptable to use *this* as an adjective, as in "this usage"; we refer only to *this* used by itself as a pronoun.

How the Old/New Contract Modifies the Rule "Avoid Weak Repetition"

Many students have been warned against repetition of the same word (or *weak repetition,* as your teacher may have called it). Consequently, you may not be aware that repetition of key words is a vital aspect of unity and coherence. The repeated words create what linguists call "lexical strings" that keep a passage focused on a particular point. Note in our passage about the importance of fathers' style of play the frequent repetitions of the words *father* and *play.* What if the writer worried about repeating *father* too much and reached for his thesaurus?

UNNECESSARY ATTEMPT TO AVOID REPETITION

Recent research has given us much deeper—and more surprising—insights into the **male parent's** role in childrearing. It shows that in almost all of their interactions with children, **patriarchs** do things a little differently from mothers. What **sires** do. . . .

For example, an often-overlooked dimension of **male gender parenting** is. . . .

You get the picture. Keep your reader on familiar ground through repetition of key words.

How the Old/New Contract Modifies the Rule "Prefer Active over Passive Voice"

Another rule that you may have learned is to use the active voice rather than the passive voice. In the active voice the doer of the action is in the subject slot of the sentence, and the receiver is in the direct object slot, as in the following examples:

The dog caught the Frisbee.
The women wrote letters of complaint to the boss.
The landlord raised the rent.

In the passive voice the receiver of the action becomes the subject and the doer of the action either becomes the object of the preposition *by* or disappears from the sentence:

The Frisbee was caught by the dog.
Letters of complaint were written (by the women) to the boss.
The rent was raised (by the landlord).

Other things being equal, the active voice is indeed preferable to the passive because it is more direct and forceful. But in some cases, other things *aren't* equal, and the passive voice is preferable. *What the old/new contract asks you to consider is whether the doer or the receiver represents the old information in a sentence.* Consider the difference between the following passages:

Second Sentence, Active Voice	My great-grandfather was a skilled cabinetmaker. He made this dining room table near the turn of the century.
Second Sentence, Passive Voice	I am pleased that you stopped to admire our dining room table. It was made by my great-grandfather near the turn of the century.

In the first passage, the opening sentence is about *my great-grandfather.* To begin the second sentence with old information ("He," referring to "great-grandfather"), the writer uses the active voice. The opening sentence of the second passage is about the *dining room table.* To begin the second sentence with old information ("It," referring to "table"), the writer must use the passive voice, since the table is the receiver of the action. In both cases, the sentences are structured to begin with old information.

Lesson 8: Writing Effective Conclusions

Conclusions can best be understood as complements to introductions. In both the introduction and the conclusion, writers are concerned with the essay as a whole more than with any given part. In a conclusion, the writer attempts to bring a sense of completeness and closure to the profusion of points and particulars laid out in the body of the essay. The writer is particularly concerned with helping the reader move from the parts back to the big picture and to understand the importance or significance of the essay.

If you are having trouble figuring out how to conclude an essay, consider the following guide questions, which are designed to stimulate thought about how to conclude and to help you determine which model best suits your situation.

1. How long and complex is your essay? Is it long enough or complex enough that readers might benefit from a summary of your main points?
2. What's the most important point (or points) you want your readers to remember about your essay? How long ago in the essay did you state that point? Would it be useful to restate that point as succinctly and powerfully as possible?
3. Do you know of an actual instance, illustration, or example of your main point that would give it added weight?
4. What larger principle stands behind your main point? Or what must your audience accept as true in order to accept your main point? How would you defend that assumption if someone were to call it into question?
5. Why is your main point significant? Why are the ideas in your paper important and worth your audience's consideration? What larger issues does your

topic relate to or touch on? Could you show how your topic relates to a larger and more significant topic? What might that topic be?

6. If your audience accepts your thesis, where do you go next? What is the next issue or question to be examined? What further research is needed? Conversely, do you have any major reservations, unexpressed doubts, or "All bets are off if X is the case" provisos you'd like to admit? What do you *not* know about your topic that reduces your certainty in your thesis?

7. How much antagonism or skepticism toward your position do you anticipate? If it's a great deal, would it be feasible to delay your thesis, solution, or proposal until the very end of the paper?

Because many writers find conclusions challenging to write, we offer the following six possible models:

The *Simple Summary* Conclusion

The most common, though often not the most effective, kind of conclusion is a simple summary, in which the writer recaps what has just been said. This approach is useful in a long or complex essay or in an instructional text that focuses on concepts to be learned. We use *summary* conclusions for several chapters in this text. In a short, easy-to-follow essay, however, a *summary* conclusion can be dull and may even annoy readers who are expecting something more significant, but a brief summary followed by a more artful concluding strategy can often be effective.

The *Larger Significance* Conclusion

A particularly effective concluding strategy is to draw the reader's attention to the *larger significance* of your argument. In our discussion of academic problems (see Chapter 1), we explained that a good academic question needs to be significant (worth pursuing). Although readers need to be convinced from the outset that the problem investigated in your paper is significant, the conclusion is a good place to elaborate on that significance by showing how your argument now leads to additional benefits for the reader. For example, you might explain how your proposed solution to a question leads to potential understanding of a larger, more significant question or brings practical benefits to individuals or society. If you posed a question about values or about the interpretation of a confusing text or phenomenon, you might show how your argument could be applied to related questions or to related texts or phenomena. Your goal in writing this kind of conclusion is to show how your answer to the question posed in your paper has larger applications or significance.

The *Proposal* Conclusion

Another option, often used in analyses and arguments, is the *proposal* conclusion, which calls for action. A *proposal* conclusion states the action that the writer believes needs to be taken and briefly demonstrates the advantages of this action over alternative actions or describes its beneficial consequences. If your paper analyzes the negative consequences of shifting from a graduated to a flat-rate income tax, your conclusion may recommend an action such as modifying or opposing the flat tax. A slight variation is the *call-for-future-study* conclusion, which indicates what else needs to be known or resolved before a proposal can be offered. Such conclusions are especially common in scientific writing.

The *Scenic* or *Anecdotal* Conclusion

Popular writers often use a *scenic* or *anecdotal* conclusion, in which a scene or brief story illustrates the theme's significance without stating it explicitly. A paper opposing the current trend against involuntary hospitalization of the homeless mentally ill might end by describing a former mental patient, now an itinerant homeless person, collecting bottles in a park. Such scenes can help the reader experience directly the emotional significance of the topic analyzed in the body of the paper.

The *Hook and Return* Conclusion

A related variety of conclusion is the *hook and return,* in which the ending of the essay returns to something introduced in the opening hook or lead. If the lead of your essay is a vivid illustration of a problem—perhaps a scene or an anecdote—then your conclusion might return to the same scene or story, but with some variation to illustrate the significance of the essay. This sense of return can give your essay a strong feeling of unity.

The *Delayed-Thesis* Conclusion

This type of conclusion delays the thesis until the end of the essay. Rather than stating the thesis, the introduction merely states the problem, giving the body of the essay an open, exploratory, "let's think through this together" feel. Typically, the body of the paper examines alternative solutions or approaches to the problem and leaves the writer's own answer—the thesis—unstated until the end. This approach is especially effective when writing about highly complex or divisive issues on which you want to avoid taking a stand until all sides have been fairly presented.

For Writing and Discussion

Choose a paper you have just written and write an alternative conclusion using one of the strategies discussed in this lesson. Then share your original and revised conclusions in groups. Have group members discuss which one they consider most effective and why.

A Rhetorical Guide to Research

This screen capture shows the home page of Women Against Gun Control (www.wagc.com), a grassroots organization dedicated to supporting women's right to defend themselves. This organization participates in pro-gun political activism, legislative research, media awareness, distribution of print resources, and gun-related education. The Web site itself uses color, images, other design features, and bold text to stake out its position in the complex controversy over women's role in the hotly contested, larger issue of gun control. This Web site home page is featured in a class discussion exercise in Chapter 13.

Ladies of
High-Caliber

**Protect Your
Rights!**

Join Now!

Click Here
for the 10
Commandments
of gun safety!

Home

WAGC
Information

WAGC
Features

WAGC
Boycotts

WAGC
Links

WAGC
Site map

WAGC
Contact

Get your pin in
honor of WAGC!

Women Against Gun Control

"The Second Amendment IS the Equal

Click here to sign and read our new forum board!

WAGC sends amicus brief to the U. S. Supreme Court!

Click Here (Opens New Window)

Click here to read a press release regarding this hearing.

Click here
for a
special
message
from
WAGC
President,
Janalee
Tobias

Contact Us

Postal Address

- WAGC

  PO Box 95357
  South Jordan, UT
  84095

Telephone

- 801-328-9660

E-Mail

- info@wagc.com
- State and Local Chapters
- webmaster

It's a Fact:

*RECENT RESEARCH INDICATES
THAT GUNS ARE USED
DEFENSIVELY 2.5 MILLION
TIMES PER YEAR.*

It's not surprising then, that more women
than ever want to keep their rights to own
and carry a gun.
The reason is simple: Women **are**
concerned about becoming victims of
crime. Guns give women a fighting chance
against crime.

Join Women Against Gun Control.
Take the Women Against Gun Control
Pledge and you qualify for a membership in
Women Against Gun Control, a grass roots
volunteer organization dedicated to
preserving our gun rights.

Join thousands of women (and men) in
sending a powerful message throughout the
world.

"Guns **SAVE** Lives. We do **NOT** support
gun control. Gun Control does **NOT**
control crime!"

2nd Amendment
A well regulated Militia being necessary to
the security of a free State, the right of the
people to keep and bear Arms shall not be
infringed.

"The Second Amendment IS
Homeland Security."

Special Article
Have gun, will not fear it anymore

Rosie
O' Donnel

Hillary
Clinton

Janet
Reno

Diane
Feinstein

Want Americans
to believe all
women support
gun control...

Let's BLOW
HOLES
in this MYTH!

If women are
disarmed, a
rapist will
never hear...

"STOP OR
I'LL
SHOOT!"

Looking for
Pro-Second
Amendment and
Pro-Freedom
Books? Check
Out These Book
Reviews and
Help Support
This Site!

Support WAGC
Efforts with the
Utah GIRAFFE
Society!

Part 4　A Rhetorical Guide to Research

The Rhetoric of Web Sites

The ability to do college-level research requires a variety of skills including the ability to use your college library to locate books, reference works, multimedia materials, and periodical sources such as scholarly journals, magazines, and newspapers. Most college handbooks explain how to conduct library searches, with particular emphasis on using licensed databases to search periodicals. To be in charge of your writing, you need to know how to read these sources rhetorically (as explained in Chapter 6) and to integrate them effectively into your own argument.

Today researchers also rely on the World Wide Web to supplement the kinds of research they do in libraries. But because the Web contains so much transient and dubious material, skilled researchers develop special skills for understanding the rhetoric of Web sites. In this chapter, we pass on to you some of these expert skills:

- Reading the Web as a unique rhetorical environment.
- Analyzing the purpose of a site and connecting it to your own research purpose. (We'll illustrate this skill by looking at sites related to women and gun control.)
- Evaluating a Web source by applying specific criteria.

The Web as a Unique Rhetorical Environment

The resources available on the World Wide Web are mind-boggling. Some Web sites are historical archives, functioning like major research libraries. For example, a professional association of medieval historians has created a site that gives scholars access to thousands of rare historical documents, enabling a scholar to do research without traveling to Paris or Madrid. Or, consider a site created by the Federal Bureau of Investigation that gives detailed information about its latest investigations, posts pictures of its "most wanted" criminals and terrorists, solicits public help on unsolved cases, and provides a series of children's detective games.

The sites just mentioned are highly professional and expensive to produce. But the Web is also a great vehicle for democracy, giving voice to the otherwise voiceless. Anyone with a cause and a rudimentary knowledge of Web page design can create a Web site. Before the invention of the Web, people with a message had to stand on street corners passing out flyers or put money into newsletters or advocacy advertisements. The Web, in contrast, is cheap. The result is a rhetorical medium that differs in significant ways from print.

Consider, for example, the difference in the way writers attract readers. Magazines displayed on racks attract readers through interest-grabbing covers and teaser headlines inviting readers to look inside. Web sites, however, can't begin attracting readers until the readers have found them through links from another site or through a "hit" on a Web search. Research suggests that Web surfers stay connected to a site for no more than thirty seconds unless something immediately attracts their interest; moreover they seldom scroll down to see the bottom of a page. The design of the home page—the arrangement and size of the print, the use of images and colors, the locations and labels of navigational buttons—must hook readers immediately and send a clear message about the purpose and contents of the site. If the home page is a confused jumble or simply a long, printed text, the average surfer will take one look and leave.

The biggest difference between the Web and print is the Web's hypertext structure. Users click from link to link rather than read linearly down the page. Users often "read" a Web page as a configuration of images and strategically arranged text that is frequently bulleted or enclosed in boxes. Long stretches of straight text are effective only deep within a site where a user purposively chooses to read something in a conventional, linear way.

Analyzing the Purpose of a Site

As a researcher, your first question when you arrive at a potentially useful Web site should be, Who placed this piece on the Web and why? You can begin answering this question by analyzing the site's home page, where you will often find navigational buttons linking to "Mission," "About Us," or other identifying information about the site's sponsors. You can also get hints about the site's purpose by asking, What kind of Web site is it? Different kinds of Web sites have different purposes, often revealed by the domain identifier following the server name (for example, .com, .net, .org, .edu, .gov, or .mil). Table 13.1, "A Rhetorical Overview of Web Sites," describes key rhetorical elements of different types of sites. Knowing who sponsors a site and analyzing the sponsor's purpose for creating the site will prepare you to read the site rhetorically. In the next section, we illustrate this process by examining the rhetoric of Web sites that address the issue of gun control and are aimed at women.

Reading Web Sites Rhetorically: An Illustration

To illustrate the rhetorical analysis of Web sites, we imagined ourselves as student researchers exploring the following research question: How are women represented and involved in the public controversy over gun control and Second Amendment rights? We launched our search by typing *"gun control" women* into Google. As we clicked on links from the first screen of our Google results, we began encountering a vigorous national conversation on gun control by women's groups and by traditionally male-dominated groups seeking support or membership from women.

TABLE 13.1 A Rhetorical Overview of Web Sites

Type of Site	Author/Sponsor and Angle of Vision	Characteristics
.COM OR .BIZ (A COMMERCIAL SITE CREATED BY A BUSINESS OR CORPORATION)		
• Either of these suffixes signals a for-profit operation; this group includes major periodicals and publishers of reference materials • Purpose is to enhance image, attract customers, market products and services, provide customer service • Creators are paid by salary or fees and often motivated by desire to design innovative sites • Also in the business category: specialized suffixes .aero (for sites related to air travel), .pro (for professionals—doctors, lawyers, accountants)	**Author:** Difficult to identify individual writers; sponsoring company often considered the author **Angle of vision:** Purpose is to promote the point of view of the corporation or business; links are to sites that promote same values	• Links are often to other products and services provided by company • Photographs and other visuals used to enhance corporate image
.ORG (NONPROFIT ORGANIZATIONS OR ADVOCACY GROUPS)		
• Note: Sites with the ".museum" suffix have similar purposes and feel. • Sometimes purpose is to provide accurate, balanced information (for example, the American Red Cross site) • May function as a major information portal, such as NPR.org, PBS.org, a think tank, or a museum (for example, the Heritage Foundation, the Art Institute of Chicago, or the Museum of Modern Art) • Frequently, purpose is to advocate for or explain the organization (for example, the Ford Foundation or local charity sites); thus, advocacy for fund-raising or political views is likely (for example, Persons for the Ethical Treatment of Animals [PETA] site or blog portals [Cursor.org])	**Author:** Often hard to identify individual writers; sponsoring organization often considered the author; some sites produced by amateurs with passionate views; others produced by well-paid professionals **Angle of vision:** Purpose is to promote views of sponsoring organization and influence public opinion and policy; many encourage donations through the site	• Advocacy sites sometimes don't announce purpose on home page • You may enter a node of an advocacy site through a link from another site and not realize the political slant • Facts/data selected and filtered by site's angle of vision • Often uses visuals for emotional appeal
.EDU (AN EDUCATIONAL SITE ASSOCIATED WITH A COLLEGE OR UNIVERSITY)		
• Wide range of purposes • Home page aimed at attracting prospective students and donors • Inside the site are numerous subsites devoted to research, pedagogy, libraries, student employment, and so forth	**Author:** Professors, staff, students **Angle of vision:** Varies enormously from personal sites of professors and students to organizational sites of research centers and libraries; can vary from scholarly and objective to strong advocacy on issues	• Often an .edu site has numerous "subsites" sponsored by the university library, art programs, research units • Links to .pdf documents may make it difficult to determine where you are in the site—e.g., professor's course site, student site, administrative site

(*continued*)

TABLE 13.1 continued

Type of Site	Author/Sponsor and Angle of Vision	Characteristics
.GOV OR .MIL (SPONSORED BY GOVERNMENT AGENCIES OR MILITARY UNITS)		
• Provides enormous range of basic data about government policy, bills in Congress, economic forecasts, and so forth • Aims to create good public relations for agency or military unit	**Author:** Development teams employed by the agency; sponsoring agency is usually considered the author **Angle of vision:** Varies—informational sites publish data and government documents with an objective point of view; agency sites also promote agency's agenda—e.g., Dept. of Energy, Dept. of Labor	• Typical sites (for example, www.energy.gov, the site of the U.S. Dept. of Energy) are extremely layered and complex and provide hundreds of links to other sites • Valuable for research • Sites often promote values/assumptions of sponsoring agency
PERSONAL WEB SITES (.NAME OR .NET)		
• An individual contracts with server to publish the site; many personal Web sites have .edu affiliation • Promotes hobbies, politics; provides links according to personal preferences	**Author:** Anyone can create a personal Web site **Angle of vision:** Varies from person to person	• Credentials/bias of author often hard to determine • Irresponsible sites might have links to excellent sites; tracing links is complicated • Probably not designed for fast download
.INFO (INFORMATION PROVIDERS—UNRESTRICTED, SO BECOMING A CATCHALL)		
• Libraries and library information materials • Regulations, hours, procedures, resources from local governments (e.g., www.lowermanhattan.info) • Publicity brochures for local organizations (e.g., Celtic Heritage Society, hobby groups) • Consumer alerts • Lodging, restaurants, bike rental, hiking trails, or other travel advice from tourist bureaus • Privately authored materials	**Author:** Varies widely from small public and private offices with an information mandate to individuals or groups with an ax to grind **Angle of vision:** Varies from genuinely helpful (Where can bicycles be loaded onto the ferry?) to business motives (Where can you find books or movies about bicycles?) to thinly disguised advocacy (e.g., "Debunking the Myths about Gun Control")	• Makes some information easier to find through advanced searches that specify the domain type • If author is identified, credentials difficult to determine • Information will be filtered through author(s) and sponsor(s) • Quality of editing and fact-checking will vary

Our next step was to analyze these sites rhetorically to understand the ways that women frame their interests and represent themselves on sites for or against gun control. We discovered that the angle of vision of each kind of site—whether pro–gun control or anti–gun control—filters evidence in distinctive ways. For example, women's groups advocating gun control emphasize accidental deaths from guns (particularly of children), suicides from easy access to guns, domestic violence turned deadly, guns in schools, and gun-related crime (particularly juvenile crime). In contrast, women's groups opposing gun control emphasize armed resistance to assaults and rapes, inadequate police responses to crime, the right of individuals to protect themselves and their families, and the Second Amendment right to keep and bear arms. (Women's anti–gun control sites often frame the gun control issue as pro-self-defense versus anti-self-defense.) We also noted that most of these sites make powerful use of visual elements—icons, colors (bright pink in particular), and well-known symbols—to enhance their emotional appeals. For instance, anti–gun control sites often have patriotic themes with images of waving American flags, stern-eyed eagles, and colonial patriots with muskets. Pro–gun control sites often have pictures of children about to find a gun in Mommy's or Daddy's dresser drawer.

Most of the sites we examined tailor their appeals directly to women. We started our analysis with the site of the most well-known women's group advocating gun control—the Million Mom March (Figure 13.1). This page, like many others on both sides of the issue at the time, drew attention to the 1994 ban on assault weapons, which was set to expire on September 13, 2004, unless Congress renewed it. (Politically oriented Web sites change quickly, so as you read this, the current page undoubtedly emphasizes a different issue.) We were initially struck by the site's heavy use of pink, a perennially feminine color. As we considered the diverse but eye-catching images strewn across the busy page, we noted that they created an *ethos* of grassroots action, of women working together to protect children. From the verbal image of moms seeking "to halt the assault" by traveling cross-country in a "big pink rig" (a twenty-six-foot pink RV, we learned from the news clips) to the many opportunities for making the page interactive, this Web site was working harder at promoting specific action, and more types of action, than the others we studied. As you examine the page, note how the theme of grassroots action becomes explicit in the lower half. Note, too, how a change in color brings a change in mood in the bottom boxes, which link to more aggressive sites sponsored by "StoptheNRA.com."

A careful look at the list of links in the purple box near the bottom of the page reveals how the Million Mom March (MMM) has branded itself with connotations of motherhood. "Meet a mom," reads one of the links; "a million stories . . . ," offers another. In this homespun spirit, the organization gives a monthly award called "Mom's Apple Pie Award" to a person or organization that advances the cause of gun legislation. It also gives a "Time Out" award to individuals who set

FIGURE 13.1 Million Mom March home page

millionmommarch

united with the Brady Campaign to Prevent Gun Violence

Save the Assault Weapons Ban

Moms on the road to

Upcoming Stops:
• Portland, ME
  July 18-20
• New Hampshire:
  July 22-23
• Boston, MA
  (Democratic
  Convention)
  July 25-28

Sign this Petition!
Before the end of summer, assault weapons will be readily available in your neighborhood. Do you want the police to be outgunned?

Click here to send this petition to Congress and the President!

DONATE
Tell A Friend

Help Us Save the Assault Weapons Ban before it expires on September 13, 2004

Congress Has 5 Working Days to Renew the Assault Weapons Ban

Tell President Bush to keep his promise:
TELL CONGRESS TO RENEW THE ASSAULT WEAPONS BAN
CLICK HERE

| News Coverage | Tour Blog | Local Tour Events | Support the Tour! |

Media Coverage of the Big Pink Rig...
06/24/04 - Columbus, OH: NBC Channel 4
6/19/04 - Chicago, IL: Chicago Sun Times
6/10/04 - Duluth, MN: Duluth Superior

Click here for more headlines

a million stories of why we march

Posted by Judy (GA):

"My son's death was preventable, all the gun owner had to do was lock up the gun...seems pretty simple to me."

Judy's story »

 Add your story  Read More Stories

Read about our previous stops in the Tour Blog.

| Richmond, VA | ▾ | Go » |

JULY	
July 5-7	Pittsburgh, PA
July 9-13	Philadelphia, PA
July 14-16	New Jersey Tour
July 18-20	Portland, ME
July 22-23	New Hampshire
July 25-28	Boston, MA
AUGUST	
August 1-2	Detroit, MI
August 9-10	Seattle, WA
August 11-12	Portland, OR
August 14-16	Northern California
August 17	Los Angeles, CA
August 18-19	Phoenix, AZ
August 22-23	Denver, CO
August 29-31	New York City
SEPTEMBER	
September 1	New York City
September 13	Assault Weapons Ban Expires

Schedule subject to change, please check back often

Grassroots in Action   Updated: Jul. 22, 2004

Utah: State Supreme Court Upholds Business Right To Restrict Guns on Property
Minnesota: Judge Strikes Down NRA's Dangerous Concealed Handgun Law (CCW)
State Polls: Key State Voters Support Renewing and Strengthening Assault Weapons Ban

register to vote
your vote matters

JOIN TOGETHER Online
Gun Violence
www.jointogether.org/gv

LOOKING FOR A FEW GOOD MOMS
Buy Million Mom March Founder Donna Dees-Thomases' New Book At Amazon.com!

Help Spread the Word!
Download our new print and radio ads!

back the cause. (Note that these moms have time-outs rather than spankings.) A click on "About Us" took us to a history of the organization, which describes itself as "the nation's largest national, non-partisan, grassroots organization leading the fight to prevent gun violence . . . dedicated to creating an America free from gun violence." Its mission statement lists specific legislative actions that the MMM advocates and then closes with this memorable sentence: "With one loud voice, we will continue to cry out that we love our children more than the gun lobby loves its guns!"

At this point, we wondered: How do women who oppose gun control represent themselves? Do they also portray themselves as nurturing mothers or as something else? We invite you now to consider the Web sites of Women Against Gun Control (see p. 341) and the Northern Colorado Chapter of the Second Amendment Sisters (Fig. 13.2).

FIGURE 13.2 Home Page of Northern Colorado Chapter of Second Amendment Sisters

Second Amendment Sisters, Inc.
Self Defense is a Basic Human Right®

Northern Colorado Chapter

Women's Personal Safety Training
September 13, 2002
Click Here!

Family Day at the Range Report
June 15, 2002
Click Here!

Click on the Calendar

Teach someone
How to change a tire
How to connect to the Internet
How to play chess

HOW TO HANDLE A GUN.

WHO WE ARE   CONTACT US

NEWS   EDUCATION

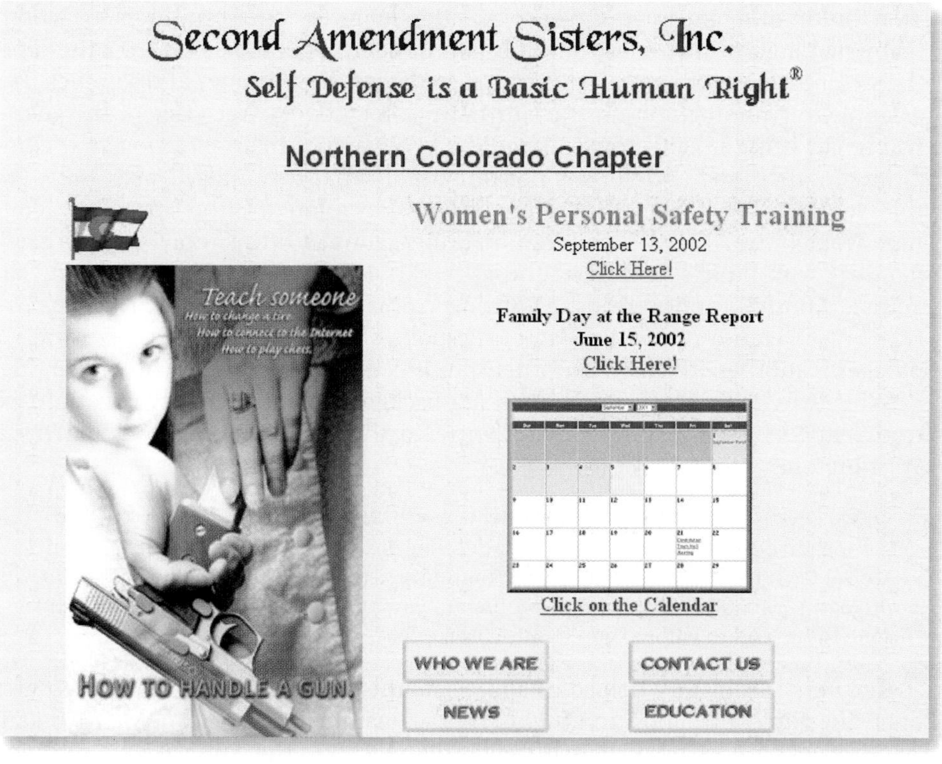

For Writing and Discussion

Working in small groups or as a whole class, try to reach consensus answers to the following questions about how these Web sites seek to draw in readers.

1. How are the visual images of women in each of these home pages different from that evoked by the Million Mom March page?
2. What images of women are conveyed in the "Teach someone . . . How to handle a gun" poster in the Second Amendment Sisters (SAS) page or the phrases "Ladies of High-Caliber" and "Let's Blow Holes in the Myth!" in the Women Against Gun Control page?
3. In the Women Against Gun Control (WAGC) page, what seems to be the Web designer's intention in the use of color, curved background lines, and images?
4. How do these pages use appeals to *ethos* and *pathos* as part of the argument they are making?

Appeals to *ethos* and *pathos* are discussed in Chapter 4, p. 79, and Chapter 10, pp. 254–256.

Now that you have had an opportunity to consider these sites, we offer our own rhetorical analysis. We were struck by the fact that both the Million Mom March and Northern Colorado SAS pages portray women as protectors of children, but in different ways. One projects the image of activist mothers for whom lobbying for gun control legislation is part of being a good parent. The other portrays combative mothers using firearms to defend their homes and families. For example, the photograph on the Northern Colorado SAS Web page of the gentle young girl being taught how to handle a pistol argues by implication that combining motherhood and guns is not unnatural—that it is, indeed, necessary. On the Web site itself, this picture is one of four that rotate to show attractive, feminine women, usually with children, handling guns. A fifth simply shows a sleek handbag with bullets next to it, and asks, "My Mother Can Protect Herself. Can Yours?" Another caption reads, "A Strong Woman and Well-Armed. Her Kids Are Safe." "In Defense of Family Values. Responsible People Protect Their Family," proclaims another, in which a mother stands behind a teenage son holding a rifle.

When we clicked on "Who We Are" for background about the organization, we read that SAS was organized in response to the first Million Mom March on Washington:

> SECOND AMENDMENT SISTERS Inc. was founded in 1999 by five women who got together on the internet. . . . [because] they didn't want the anti-rights Million Mom March to speak for them. [These founding sisters made] a powerful statement on May 12, 2000—that there were women to whom the Second Amendment meant something, and to whom "gun control" was a false promise.

Knowing this history helped us appreciate the extent to which many Web sites opposing gun control position themselves against the Million Mom March organization with competing images as well as messages. On the days we were studying these pages, for example, we were not surprised to see that the national SAS page was advocating for the expiration of the assault weapons ban as strenuously as the Million Mom March page was advocating for its renewal.

When we looked at the Women Against Gun Control home page, we noticed that it, too, talks back to the Million Mom March activists and takes ironic delight in antagonizing feminists. Its bold, pink colors and provocatively curved lines use traditional symbols of coy seductiveness to create an in-your-face, Annie Oakley-style message: This gun-toting cowgirl won't take any guff. The messages are complex: Women can be sexy and feminine while simultaneously being powerful and independent if they own and carry a gun. The language in the home page is vigorous and powerful, associating women with self-defense and protection of Second Amendment rights. This home page purports to "BLOW HOLES" in the myth that all women support gun control. Instead, these women seek, through guns, "a fighting chance against crime" and yell "STOP OR I'LL SHOOT" at burglars. The statistic next to the Annie Oakley figure says that "guns are used defensively 2.5 million times per year"—a factoid evidently meant to startle the reader into getting a gun for self-defense. The gritty realism of these no-nonsense women is brought out in the caption at the bottom of the home page:

> Gun Control: The theory that a woman found dead in an alley, raped and stran-
> gled with her panty hose, is somehow morally superior to a woman explaining to
> police how her attacker got that fatal bullet wound.

Whereas the home page of the Million Mom March site ends with defiant links to "Stop the NRA" Web sites, the WAGC home page ends with the verbal image of a raped woman dead in the street (an implied consequence of gun control) versus the image of a heroic woman shooting an assailant dead (the implied consequence of empowering women with guns). These sites are in conversation both with gun control sites and with feminist sites—redefining the gun-carrying woman as defiant, sexy, and independent, and yet protective of the family.

Just as we have done here, when you conduct your own research on the Web, you need to be aware that you might be stepping into a heated controversy. To read a site rhetorically, you've got to understand its position within the larger social conversation in order to interpret its use of both visual and textual elements.

Evaluating a Web Source

Once you've considered your reasons for using a source and the rhetorical context of your issue on the Web, you are ready to evaluate a site's reliability, credibility, angle of vision, and degree of advocacy. As we show, part of evaluating a source is evaluating the site in which it is posted. In Table 13.2 we offer five criteria developed by scholars and librarians as points to consider when you are evaluating Web sites.

An Example: Applying Evaluation Criteria

In this section we offer a brief example of the thinking processes used to evaluate a potential Web source. Suppose, for illustrative purposes, that you are trying to determine your own stance on gun control from a woman's perspective. In doing a Web search, you click on a link that takes you to the following site: http://www.

TABLE 13.2 Criteria for Evaluating Web Sites

Criteria	Questions to Ask
1. Authority	• Is the document author or site sponsor clearly identified? • Does the site identify the occupation, position, education, experience, or other credentials of the author? • Does the home page or a clear link from the home page reveal the author's or sponsor's motivation for establishing the site? • Does the site provide contact information for the author or sponsor such as an e-mail or organization address?
2. Objectivity or Clear Disclosure of Advocacy	• Is the site's purpose clear (for example, to inform, entertain, or persuade)? • Is the site explicit about declaring its point of view? • Does the site indicate whether the author is affiliated with a specific organization, institution, or association? • Does the site indicate whether it is directed toward a specific audience?
3. Coverage	• Are the topics covered by the site clear? • Does the site exhibit a suitable depth and comprehensiveness for its purpose? • Is sufficient evidence provided to support the ideas and opinions presented?
4. Accuracy	• Are the sources of information stated? • Do the facts appear to be accurate? • Can you verify this information by comparing this source with other sources in the field?
5. Currency	• Are dates included in the Web site? • Do the dates apply to the material itself, to its placement on the Web, or to the time the site was last revised and updated? • Is the information current, or at least still relevant, for the site's purpose? For your purpose?

armedandsafe.com/women.htm. What appears on your screen is an article entitled "Women Are the Real Victims of Handgun Control" by Kelly Ann Connolly, who is identified as the director of the Nevada State Rifle and Pistol Association. (See Figure 13.3, which shows the first screen of this article.) The site includes a biographical note indicating that she is a public school teacher with a master's degree and that her husband is a former California Deputy Sheriff and police officer.

Connolly argues that a woman can walk confidently down any street in America if she is carrying a concealed weapon and is skilled in using it. She offers as support anecdotal cases of women who fought off rapists and cites numerous statistics, attributing the sources to "Bureau of Justice Statistics (1999)." Here are some examples from later screens in the article:

- "3 out of 4 American women *will* be a victim of violent crime at least once in their lifetime."
- 2 million women are raped each year, one every 15 seconds.

FIGURE 13.3 First Screen of "Women Are the Real Victims of Handgun Control"

Women are the Real Victims of Handgun Control

By Kelly Ann Connolly
Director, Nevada State Rifle and Pistol Assoc.

Women are 100 times more likely to be raped than men and 3 out of 4 American women <u>will</u> be a victim of violent crime at least once in their lifetime.* Women, by far, have the greatest need for self-defense.

Handgun control, laws designed to limit legal access to handguns, are also more likely to limit women's access to guns, as a group, than men or criminals because women are less likely to knowingly break laws.

And the most effective form of self-defense is a handgun. Ask any law enforcement official if he would trade his firearm in for pepper spray alone.

Personal devices used exclusively as a safety strategy (mace, alarms and objects used to jab or poke) offer little resistance to an attacker who usually outweighs and has greater strength than most women. Traditional self-defense techniques, while increasing strength and confidence, are ineffective for most women in hand-to-hand street fighting.

Developing and practicing Personal Safety Strategies* to avoid falling prey to an attack and learning a trained counterattack, such as Model Mugging *are excellent ways to help women. Those who use them have a better shot at being that 1 in 4 who remain free of personal tragedy, but we need access to handguns for a real fighting chance if we hope to really change the odds that are stacked against women. Even the originator of Model Mugging, Matthew Thomas agrees, "Firearms are our most efficient tool for defending life and freedom."

Highlighting a well-known case, albeit dated, illustrates the effectiveness of armed women in reducing crime. In Orlando, Florida in 1966, a series of brutal rapes caused a dramatic increase in handgun purchases by female residents. The local newspaper (as usual) had an anti-gun editorial policy and some of its staff tried to persuade the chief of police to halt the sale of handguns to women. Since Orlando law protected the right to buy handguns, the newspaper and police department sponsored a
one day gun-training course. With an overwhelming response of over 2,500 women, they organized classes over a five-month period resulting in the training of more than 6,000 women. For the next five years, Orlando's incidents of rape, violent assault and burglary decreased dramatically while it sky-rocketed in every other city in the country. Additionally, there hadn't been a single accidental shooting, misuse of handguns against family or intimates nor even reported use of a firearm for defense by any of the women. Experts who have studied this situation attribute the decrease in crime to the media publicity of women who were armed and trained.

Criminals prefer easy targets.

- Rapists know they have only a 1 in 605 chance of being caught, charged, convicted, and sentenced to serving time.

The effect of these statistics is to inform women about the prevalence of rape and to reduce women's confidence in the police or justice system to protect them. The implied solution is to buy a pistol and learn how to use it.

How might you evaluate such an article for your own research purposes? A first step is to evaluate the site itself. We found the home page by deleting "/women.htm" from the URL and looking directly at www.armedandsafe.com. The screen that appeared is shown in Figure 13.4. This is the commercial site of a husband-and-wife team who run a firing range and give lessons in the use of rifles, pistols, and machine guns. The site obviously advocates Second Amendment

FIGURE 13.4 Home Page of armedandsafe.com

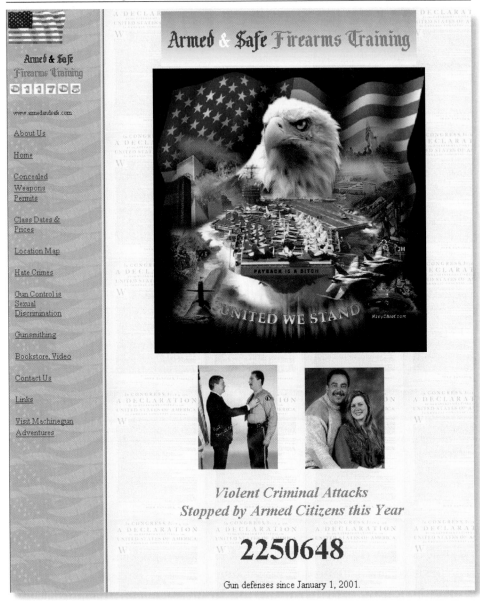

rights and promotes gun ownership as a means of domestic and personal security. The fierce eagle emerging from a collage of the American flag, the burning World Trade Center towers, and an aircraft carrier appeals to the patriotic sentiments that tend to dominate pro-gun Web sites. (On the day we accessed it, the site also played a John Wayne rendition of "America the Beautiful.") It is easy to evaluate this site against the five criteria:

1. *Authority:* You can clearly tell who created the site and is responsible for its contents.
2. *Advocacy:* The site clearly advocates Second Amendment rights and gun ownership.
3. *Coverage:* The site will not cover gun control issues in a complex way. Every aspect of the site will be filtered to support its pro-gun vision.
4. *Accuracy:* You still need to check its facts against other sources, but you can predict that the information will be rhetorically filtered and selected to promote the site's position.
5. *Currency:* Because the site supports a pro-gun stance, it will use data that are most effective in promoting its view. Dates are included in the material and the Web site. Some dates cited are not recent (1996 Florida example), but appear relevant to the issue presented.

How might you therefore use Connolly's article posted on the site? The article could be very useful to you as one point of view on the gun control controversy. It is a fairly representative example of the argument that guns can increase a woman's sense of confidence and well-being, and it clearly shows the kinds of rhetorical strategies such articles use—statistics on rape, descriptions of guns as equalizers in empowering women, and so forth.

As a source of factual data, however, the article is questionable. The sources used are not well documented, and the data appear to be filtered through the writer's pro-gun lens. As a responsible researcher, you need to find primary sources of statistics about gun usage and crime. You will also want to see how data are used in other sites, including those that support gun control.

14 Citing and Documenting Sources

In the previous chapter we explained an expert research skill you need to master—how to read Web sites rhetorically. In this chapter we look briefly at the nuts and bolts of citing and documenting sources. Particularly we explain the following skills:

- How to avoid plagiarism
- How to cite sources using both the Modern Language Association (MLA) and the American Psychological Association (APA) systems
- How to document sources in a "Works Cited" list (MLA) or in a "References" list (APA)

To help you see how students use these skills in their own writing, we also show you two student research papers—one in MLA style and one in APA style.

How to Avoid Plagiarism

Before discussing how to cite and document your sources, we need to take a brief excursion into the realm of ethics to explain plagiarism. *Plagiarism* occurs whenever you take someone else's work and pass it off as your own. Plagiarism can happen in two ways: by borrowing another person's *ideas* without giving credit through a proper citation and by borrowing another writer's *language* without giving credit through quotation marks or block indentation.

The second kind of plagiarism is far more common than the first, perhaps because inexperienced writers don't appreciate how much they need to change the wording of a source to make the writing their own. It is not enough to change the order of phrases in a sentence or to replace a few words with synonyms. In the following example, compare an acceptable rewording of a passage with unacceptable plagiarism.

ORIGINAL PASSAGE (FROM AN ARTICLE ON VIOLENCE IN THE OLD WEST BY ROGER D. MCGRATH)

There is considerable evidence that women in Bodie were rarely the victims of crime. Between 1878 and 1882 only one woman, a prostitute, was robbed, and there were no reported cases of rape. (There is no evidence that rapes occurred but were not reported.)

ACCEPTABLE REWORDING

According to Roger D. McGrath, women in Bodie rarely suffered at the hands of criminals. Between 1878 and 1882, the only female robbery victim in Bodie was a prostitute. Also rape seemed nonexistent, with no reported cases and no evidence that unreported cases occurred (20).

PLAGIARISM

According to Roger D. McGrath, there is considerable evidence that women in Bodie were seldom the victims of crime. Between 1878 and 1882 only one woman, a prostitute, was robbed, and there were no reported rapes. There is no evidence that unreported cases of rape occurred (20).

Although the writer of the plagiarized passage correctly used the MLA citation system (see next section) to indicate that his data comes from page 20 in the McGrath article, he nevertheless plagiarized his source because he copied its language directly without indicating the borrowing with quotation marks.

How to Cite Sources

When academic writers cite a source, they use the conventions appropriate to their discipline. In the sciences, citation systems often emphasize the date of a research study and refer to researchers only by last names and first initials. In the humanities, citation systems often emphasize the full names of scholars and place less emphasis on dates. Two of the most extensively used systems are those of the Modern Language Association (MLA) in the humanities and the American Psychological Association (APA) in the social sciences. In both systems, complete bibliographic information on all cited sources is placed at the end of the paper—in a Works Cited list (MLA) or a References list (APA). For in-text citations, both systems place reference information in parentheses directly in the text, not in footnotes or endnotes. However, the two systems differ somewhat in the way parenthetical reference information is selected and structured.

MLA System of In-Text Citation

In the MLA system, you place the author's last name and the page number of the cited source in parentheses. (If the author's name is mentioned in a preceding attributive tag such as "according to Michael Levin" or "says Levin," only the page number should be placed in parentheses.)

> Torture, claims one philosopher, should be applied only to those "<u>known</u> to hold innocent lives in their hands" and only if the person being tortured is clearly guilty and clearly can prevent a terrorist act from occurring (Levin 13).

or

> Torture, claims Michael Levin, should be applied only to those "<u>known</u> to hold innocent lives in their hands" and only if the person being tortured is clearly guilty and clearly can prevent a terrorist act from occurring (13).

If your readers wish to follow up on this source, they will look for the name of the Levin article in the Works Cited list at the end of your essay. If you use more than one work by Levin as a source in the essay, include in the in-text citation a shortened version of the title of the work following Levin's name:

> (Levin, "Torture" 13)

Once Levin has been cited the first time and it is clear that you are still quoting from Levin, you need put only the page number in parentheses.

APA System of In-Text Citation

In the APA system, you place the author's last name and the publication date of the cited source in parentheses. If you are quoting a particular passage or citing a particular table, include the page number where the information is found. Use a comma to separate each element in the parenthetical citation, and use the abbreviation *p.* or *pp.* before the page number. (If the author's name is mentioned in a preceding attributive tag, only the date needs to be placed in parentheses.)

> Torture, claims one philosopher, should be applied only to those "<u>known</u> to hold innocent lives in their hands" and only if the person being tortured is clearly guilty and clearly can prevent a terrorist act from occurring (Levin, 1982, p. 13).

or

> Torture, claims Michael Levin, should be applied only to those "<u>known</u> to hold innocent lives in their hands" and only if the person being tortured is clearly guilty and clearly can prevent a terrorist act from occurring (1982, p. 13).

If your readers wish to follow up on this source, they will look for the 1982 Levin article listed in the References section at the end of your essay. If you cite two works by Michael Levin published in 1982, list the works in alphabetical order by title in your References list, and add a lowercase *a* to the date of the first one and a lowercase *b* to the date of the second one. Your in-text parenthetical citation will be either

> (Levin, 1982a)

or

> (Levin, 1982b)

In APA style, if an article or book has more than one author, the word *and* is used to join the authors' names in the text, but an ampersand (&) is used to join them in the parenthetical reference:

> Smith and Peterson (1983) found that. . .
>
> More recent data (Smith & Peterson, 1983) have shown . . .

Citing a Quotation or Other Data from a Secondary Source

Occasionally, you may wish to use a quotation or other kinds of data from a secondary source. Suppose you are writing an argument that the United States should reconsider its trade policies with China. You read an article entitled "China's Gilded Age" by Xiao-huang Yin appearing in the April 1994 issue of the *Atlantic*. This article contains the following passage appearing on page 42:

> Dual ownership has in essence turned this state enterprise into a private business. Asked if such a practice is an example of China's "socialist market economy," a professor of economics at Nanjing University, where I taught in the early 1980's, replied, "Nobody knows what the concept means. It is only rhetoric, and it can mean anything but socialism."

In citing material from a secondary source, it is always best, when possible, to locate the original source and cite your data directly from it. But in the case above, no other source is likely to be available. Here is how you would cite the internal quotation in the MLA and APA systems.

> **MLA:** According to an economics professor at Nanjing University, the term "socialist market economy" has become confused under capitalistic influence. "Nobody knows what the concept means. It is only rhetoric, and it can mean anything but socialism" (qtd. in Yin 42).
>
> **APA:** According to an economics professor at Nanjing University, the term "socialist market economy" has become confused under capitalistic influence: "Nobody knows what the concept means. It is only rhetoric, and it can mean anything but socialism" (cited in Yin, 1994, p. 42).

Using either system, you would place a full citation to the Yin article in your end-of-text bibliographic list.

Documenting Sources in a "Works Cited" List (MLA)

In the MLA system, you place a complete bibliography, titled "Works Cited," at the end of the paper. The list includes all the sources that you mention in your paper. However, it does not include works you read but did not use. Entries in the Works Cited list are arranged alphabetically by author, or by title if there is no author.

Here are some general formatting guidelines for the Works Cited list:

- Begin the list on a new sheet of paper with the words "Works Cited" centered one inch from the top of the page.

To see what citations look like when typed in a manuscript, see Christopher Leigh's Works Cited list on pp. 373–374. The MLA example citations in Table 14.1 show the correct elements, sequence, and punctuation, but not typing formats.

- Sources are listed alphabetically, the first line flush with the left margin and succeeding lines indented one-half inch or five spaces. (Use the "hanging indentation" feature on your word processor.)
- MLA formatting style uses abbreviations for months of the year (except for May, June, and July) and publishers' names (for example, Random House is shortened to "Random" and "University Press" is shortened to "UP"). For a complete list of abbreviations, consult the fifth edition of the *MLA Handbook for Writers of Research Papers*.
- Author entries include the name as it appears in the article byline or on the book's title page.
- MLA style recommends underlines rather than italics for book titles and names of journals and magazines (because underlines stand out better on the page). Do not underline any punctuation marks following an underlined title.

Here is a typical example of a work, in this case a book, cited in MLA form.

> Karnow, Stanley. <u>In Our Image: America's Empire in the Philippines</u>. New York: Random, 1989.

Special Case: Two or More Listings for One Author

When two or more works by one author are cited, the works are listed alphabetically by title. For the second and all additional entries, type three hyphens and a period in place of the author's name.

> Dombrowski, Daniel A. <u>Babies and Beasts: The Argument from Marginal Cases</u>. Urbana: U of Illinois P, 1997.
> ---. <u>The Philosophy of Vegetarianism</u>. Amherst: U of Massachusetts P, 1984.

The remaining pages in this section show examples of MLA formats for different kinds of sources.

MLA Quick Reference Guide for the Most Common Citations

Table 14.1 provides MLA models for the most common kinds of citations. This table will help you distinguish the forest from the trees when you try to cite sources. All the major categories of sources are displayed in this table. For further explanation of citations, along with instructions on citing variations and sources not listed in the Quick Reference Guide, see Joseph Gibaldi, *MLA Handbook for Writers of Research Papers*, 6th ed. New York: MLA, 2003.

TABLE 14.1 Quick Reference Guide for MLA Citations

Kind of Source	Basic Citation Model
PRINT SOURCES WHEN YOU HAVE USED THE ORIGINAL PRINT VERSION	
Book	Tannen, Deborah. <u>The Argument Culture: Moving From Debate to Dialogue</u>. New York: Random, 1998.
Article in anthology with an editor	Shamoon, Linda. "International E-mail Debate." <u>Electronic Communication Across the Curriculum</u>. Ed. Donna Reiss, Dickie Self, and Art Young. Urbana: NCTE, 1998. 151–61.
Article in scholarly journal	Pollay, Richard W., Jung S. Lee, and David Carter-Whitney. "Separate, but Not Equal: Racial Segmentation in Cigarette Advertising." <u>Journal of Advertising</u> 21.1 (1992): 45–57.
Article in magazine or newspaper	Beam, Alex. "The Mad Poets Society." <u>Atlantic Monthly</u> July–Aug. 2001: 96–103.
	Lemonick, Michael D. "Teens Before Their Time." <u>Time</u> 30 Oct. 2000: 66–74.
	Cauvin, Henri E. "Political Climate Complicates Food Shortage in Zimbabwe." <u>New York Times</u> 18 July 2001: A13.
PRINT SOURCES THAT YOU HAVE DOWNLOADED FROM A DATABASE OR THE WEB	
Article downloaded from database	Barr, Bob. "Liberal Media Adored Gun-Control Marchers." <u>Insight on the News</u> 5 June 2000: 44. ProQuest. Lemieux Lib., Seattle U. 15 Aug. 2001 <http://proquest.com>.
Article downloaded from Web	Goodman, Ellen. "The Big Hole in Health Debate." <u>Boston Globe Online</u> 24 June 2001: D7. 18 July 2001 <http://www.boston.com/dailyglobe2/175/oped/The_big_hole_in_health_debate+.shtml>.
WEB SOURCES THAT HAVEN'T APPEARED IN PRINT	
Citation for an entire Web site	<u>Ducks Unlimited</u>. 14 Mar. 2002 <http://www.ducks.org/>.
Authored document within a Web site	Connolly, Kelly Ann. "Gun Control is Sexual Discrimination." <u>Armed and Safe Firearms Training</u>. 24 Jan. 2005 <http://www.armedandsafe.com/flash/discrim.htm>.
Document with unnamed author within a Web site	"Ouch! Body Piercing." <u>Menstuff</u>. 1 Feb. 2001. National Men's Resource Center. 17 July 2004 <http://www.menstuff.org/issues/byissue/fathersgeneral.html#bodypiercing>.
MISCELLANEOUS SOURCES	
Interview	Van der Peet, Rob. Personal interview. 24 June 2001.
Lecture, address, or speech	Jancoski, Loretta. "I Believe in God, and She's a Salmon." University Congregational United Church of Christ. Seattle. 30 Oct. 2001.

Formatting an Academic Paper in MLA Style

An example research paper in MLA style is shown on pages 363–374. Here are the distinctive formatting features of MLA papers.

- Double-space throughout including block quotations and the Works Cited list.
- Use one-inch margins top and bottom, left and right. Indent one-half inch or five spaces from the left margin at the beginning of each paragraph.
- Number pages consecutively throughout the manuscript including the Works Cited list, which begins on a new page. Page numbers go in the upper right-hand corner, flush with the right margin, and one-half inch from the top of the page. The page number should be preceded by your last name. The text begins one inch from the top of the page.
- Do *not* create a separate title page. Type your name, professor's name, course number, and date in the upper left-hand corner of your paper (all double-spaced), beginning one inch from the top of the page; then double-space and type your title, centered, without underlines or any distinctive fonts (capitalize the first word and important words only); then double-space and begin your text.
- Start a new page for the Works Cited list. Type "Works Cited" centered, one inch from the top of the page in the same font as the rest of the paper; do not enclose it in quotation marks. Use hanging indentation of five spaces or one half inch for each entry longer than one line. Format entries according to the instructions in Table 14.1.

Student Example of an MLA-Style Research Paper

As an illustration of a student research paper written in MLA style, we present Christopher Leigh's paper on metal detectors in schools. Christopher's process in producing this paper has been discussed in various places throughout the text.

Leigh 1

Christopher Leigh

Professor Grosshans

English 110

September 1, 2001

The Case Against Metal Detectors in Public Schools

One of the most watched news stories of the last

decade took place on April 20, 1999, when two students

walked into their suburban Colorado high school and

shot twelve students and one teacher before shooting

themselves. The brutal slayings sent shock waves around

the country, leaving everyone asking the same

questions. What drove them to commit such a horrible

crime? What can we do to prevent something like this

from happening again?

In college writing, thesis is not always found in beginning

Panic over school safety has caused school boards

from coast to coast to take action. Though their use is

far from widespread, many schools are installing metal

detectors to keep guns and knives out of school.

Unfortunately, such measures do not address the causes

of violence and are simply an ill-considered quick fix

that may do more harm than good. Except for schools

with very severe threats of danger, metal detectors

should not be used because there is no basis for panic

and because there are other more effective and less

costly alternatives for violence prevention in schools.

→ move from general questions to a narrowed focus.

An important point to realize about school violence

is that the media have created a public outcry over

school safety when in fact violent incidents are
extremely rare. The media have taken uncommon incidents
like the one at Columbine High and, according to school
psychologist Tony Del Prete, "overanalyze[d] and
sensationalize[d] them to the point of hysteria" (375).

Statistics and studies regarding school violence
are astonishingly conflicting and reported in
sensationalized ways. For example, one study conducted
by the Centers for Disease Control and Prevention
(United States) reports percentages of youths who
carried a gun or weapon to school from 1993 to 1999
(Table 1).

Table 1

Percentage of Youths Carrying Weapon or Gun to School,
1993–1999

	1993	1995	1997	1999
Carried a weapon	11.8%	9.8%	8.5%	6.9%
Carried a gun	7.9%	7.6%	5.9%	4.9%

Source: United States. Dept. of Health and Human
Services. Centers for Disease Control and Prevention.

These numbers can be cited in a frightening way ("In
1993 nearly 8 percent of teenagers reported carrying a
gun to school"). But it is also possible to display
these numbers in a graph (see Figure 1) and report them
in a more comforting way: "As shown in Figure 1,

Leigh 3

between 1993 and 1999 the number of students who carried a gun to school has dropped 38 percent from 7.9 percent to 4.9 percent." Proponents of metal detectors generally cite the figures in the most alarming way. For example, advocates of metal detectors claim that 100,000 students carry guns to school each day (Wilson and Zirkel 32), but they fail to note that these statistics are based on data before 1993. Since 1993, violence incidents in schools have declined steadily each year, and youth homicide has dropped by over 50 percent (Barr 44). Of course it is true that weapons and violence are undeniably present in schools. But the percentage of schools in which violence is a recurring problem is perceived to be exponentially larger than it actually is. As a result, metal detectors have been installed in schools that have had no problems with weapons and violence simply to appease a panicked and irrational public.

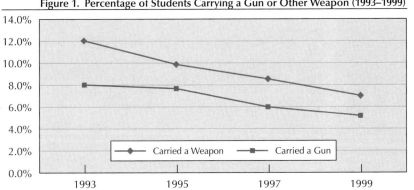

Figure 1. Percentage of Students Carrying a Gun or Other Weapon (1993–1999)

Leigh 4

Although metal detectors may seem like a quick and tangible way to fight violence in schools, there are many strong arguments against them based on students' rights, the ease of defeating metal detectors, the cost, and the psychological consequences that the devices have on the school environment.

Many students believe that metal detectors violate their rights. According to Arizona student Jon Gress, the use of metal detectors

> invades the student's personal space, permitting anyone to see into their bags and purses. And if the detector went off, they would be required to subject their bags and body to a more thorough search. This act alone seems to infringe on the Fourth Amendment right of unwarranted search and seizure.

Another student, Lindsey, in a message posted on the juvenile.net message board, says,

> [L]earning in such a threatening environment is not good for the students. . . . Does anyone else believe [besides me] that [use of metal detectors] disrupts the 'good' students and is [a] violation against student's rights . . . ?

So far the few court cases involving metal detectors have ruled in favor of the schools, saying that the benefit of public safety outweighs the right to privacy. According to Michael Ferraraccio, the Supreme

Leigh 5

Court has said metal detectors in schools are legal.
However, he says, the Supreme Court decision "seemed to
indicate that generally some level of individualized
suspicion is necessary for a search to be reasonable
under the Fourth Amendment" (215). Although this case
does not address generalized metal detector searches,
legal experts believe that minimally invasive
"administrative" searches will be permitted by the
courts (Stefkovich and O'Brien 155). Judges liken them
to searches used in airports where people are searched
for weapons without reasonable suspicion. But I think
there is a key distinction between the two situations.
People are not required to travel through airports and
may walk away from a search, but students are required
by law to attend school and do not have the option of
refusing a search. Despite court rulings so far, many
students will continue to believe their constitutional
rights are being violated.

Besides possibly violating students' rights, metal
detectors have another serious problem: they can be
easily defeated. As <u>American School Board Journal</u>
contributor Donna Harrington-Lueker points out, schools
have many entrances that can't be locked due to fire
codes, windows that can be opened, "and legions of
youngsters arriving en masse at the same time each day"
(26). As she forcefully puts it, a "permanent, full
time metal detector at the front door isn't going to

Leigh 6

stop a youngster from passing a gun to a buddy through the side window" (26).

Also, metal detectors are often used only at the beginning of the day and sometimes not every day, which creates a false sense of security. In 1992, a student in a New York school was shot and killed on a day when the metal detectors were not in use (Yarbrough 586). Other shootings have taken place in schools despite the use of metal detectors. In Los Angeles, ten shooting incidents occurred after the school district began using metal detectors in schools, and not a single gun was confiscated through the searches (Stecklow A1). Similar conditions exist in a Washington, D.C., school district, which left one security guard "convinced that the [metal] detectors were useless" (Stecklow A6). Dennis Cunningham, a spokesman for a metal detector manufacturer, notes that the devices are a " 'Band Aid' solution that 'an innovative student' could foil 'very easily' " (qtd. in Stecklow A1). Some students interviewed note that "anyone could sneak in a knife . . . or a gun" (Stecklow A6). Even organizations that strongly advocate metal detectors, such as the National School Safety and Security Services, warn on their Web site that metal detectors are "not a panacea for solving safety concerns." Yet schools continue to use the devices despite the compelling evidence that indicates that they are not working.

Leigh 7

Another major concern surrounding the use of metal detectors is cost. Airport-style units cost anywhere between four and ten thousand dollars (Harrington-Lueker 27). Handheld units are cheaper and therefore considerably more common, but they are much more time consuming and much less effective. Personnel are also required to operate the machinery, and large schools will often require upwards of fifteen officers to conduct the searches. According to Harrington-Lueker, it is not unusual for school districts to spend several million dollars to implement a comprehensive metal detector system in their schools (27). Parents and citizens argue that the safety of our children shouldn't carry a price tag, but when metal detectors prove ineffective, alternatives need to be investigated.

Perhaps the most harmful effect of metal detectors is their psychological impact on students subjected to daily searches. Student essays posted on the Web, along with dozens of postings on electronic message boards, show students' dismay at being subjected to metal detectors. "Guards, cameras, scanners, and metal detectors every day take over our schools," a Philadelphia high school senior complained to Venture Lee. Another student, using the nickname "ummm" on a message board, says:

It's not actually walking through the metal detectors that I'm against. . . . It's much

> more the principle of the thing. These damn
> things, and the people the school board has
> hired to run them, cost so much freaking money
> that could be used for useful things. Metal
> detectors will not stop a shooting in [this
> high school]. If someone wanted to kill people
> then they could just as well shoot people in
> the damn line to get through them.

Metal detectors not only reinforce the feeling that
schools are unsafe, but they also instill a sense of
humiliation in students and, as a result, a feeling of
distrust between students and school administrators.
These feelings of distrust and susceptibility erode the
atmosphere of learning that is so important to a
student's education, and schools begin to feel more
like prisons than schools.

If metal detectors are an inappropriate means to
curb violence in our schools, what is a better
approach? If we look again at student postings on the
Web, we see a consistently recurring suggestion:
friendlier schools, personal relationships, and better
counseling. As one student told Lee, "City kids get
metal detectors, suburban kids get counselors." Atlanta
high school senior Malik Barry-Buchanan was asked how
the school environment can be changed "so people don't
feel the need to bring a weapon to school." Here is his
answer:

Well, for starters, we need to find ways for
students to respect each other, have teachers
go through training to encourage them to make
even the smallest attempt at getting in touch
with the students, and have school
administrators look at students as
independent, free-thinking young adults and
not 5-year-old rug rats.

In order to combat the problem of school violence
head-on, it is essential to provide students with
better counseling and to work towards improving the
overall school environment. Scott Poland, the president
of the National Association of School Psychologists,
writes that administrators need to do more to
personalize schools and provide better counseling
services to students who may be troubled (45). He
writes that most counselors are already overworked and
are required to do things such as scheduling that take
away from their attention to the students. Poland also
emphasizes that it is important for teachers to form
strong relationships with each and every student. He
suggests that teachers set aside a small amount of time
each day to interact with students, and discourages
schools from cutting extracurricular programs that may
help students feel connected to the school (46).

In my opinion, Poland's article offers the most
encouraging and perhaps the best advice for the

Leigh 10

prevention of school violence. Teachers might complain that they do not have the time to spend getting to know every student. But getting to know each student should be part of the job requirement. If teachers know their students on a personal level, they will be able to sense when a student is in trouble, reach out to that student, and create an atmosphere of care and trust rather than suspicion and surveillance.

Violence does undoubtedly exist in schools, but the percentage of schools where the level of violence justifies metal detectors is extremely small. The problem of school violence is simply a reflection of the high level of violence in American society in general, and the problem is not the schools, but society as a whole. Metal detectors may deter some students from bringing weapons to school, but they can't prevent violence and they create an atmosphere of fear and suspicion rather than trust and community. The key to preventing school violence is to focus on improving students' relationships with teachers and, more importantly, themselves, rather than treat them like potential criminals.

Leigh 11

Works Cited

Barr, Bob. "Liberal Media Adored Gun-Control Marchers."
    <u>Insight on the News</u> 5 June 2000: 44- . <u>ProQuest</u>.
    Lemieux Lib., Seattle U. 15 Aug. 2001
    <http://proquest.umi.com>.

Barry-Buchanan, Malik. "More Rules + More Security =
    Feelings of Safety." <u>Alternet.org</u> 16 Aug. 2001
    <http://alternet.org/print.html?StoryID=9623>.

Del Prete, Tony. "Unsafe Schools: Perception or
    Reality?" <u>Professional School Counseling</u> 3 (2000):
    375-76.

Ferraraccio, Michael. "Metal Detectors in the Public
    Schools: Fourth Amendment Concerns." <u>Journal of Law
    and Education</u> 28 (1999): 209-29.

Gress, Jon. "School Violence: How to Stop the Crime of
    Today's Youth." <u>Gecko--The Student Server</u> 5 May
    2000. 16 Aug. 2001 <http://gecko.gc.maricopa.edu/
    ~jtgress/argue2.htm>.

Harrington-Lueker, Donna. "Metal Detectors." <u>American
    School Board Journal</u> 179.5 (1992): 26-27.

Lee, Venture. "Detectors Alarm Some Students." <u>Said &
    Done</u>. Urban Journalism Workshop. Summer 2000. 16
    Aug. 2001 <http://ujw.philly.com/
    2000/detector.htm>.

Lindsey. "Re: School Security." Online posting. 23 Oct.
    1999. Juvenile Information Network. 16 Aug. 2001
    <http://www.juvenilenet.org/messages/27.html>.

Leigh 12

National School Safety and Security Services. "School
    Security Equipment and Technology." 23 Aug. 2001
    <http://www.schoolsecurity.org/
    resources/security-equipment.html>.

Poland, Scott. "The Fourth R--Relationships." American
    School Board Journal 187.3 (2000): 45-46.

Stecklow, Steve. "Metal Detectors Find a Growing
    Market, But Not Many Guns." Wall Street Journal 7
    Sept. 1993: A1+.

Stefkovich, Jacqueline, and G. M. O'Brien. "Students'
    Fourth Amendment Rights and School Safety."
    Education and Urban Society 29 (1997): 149-59.

Ummm. "Alright." Online posting. 27 May 2000. ezboard.
    16 Aug. 2001 <http://pub6.ezboard.com/
    fmastermanschool.showMessage?topicID=99.topic>.

United States. Dept. of Health and Human Services. Centers
    for Disease Control and Prevention. "Youth Risk
    Behavior Trends from CDC's 1991, 1993, 1995, 1997,
    and 1999 Youth Risk Behavior Surveys." Adolescent and
    School Health 6 Aug. 2001. 11 Aug. 2001
    <http://www.cdc.gov/nccdphp/dash/yrbs/trend.htm>.

Wilson, Joseph M., and Perry Zirkel. "When Guns Come to
    School." American School Board Journal 181.1
    (1994): 32-34.

Yarbrough, Jonathan W. "Are Metal Detectors the Answer
    to Handguns in Public Schools?" Journal of Law and
    Education 22 (1993): 584-87.

Documenting Sources in a "References" List (APA)

Like the MLA system, the APA system includes a complete bibliography, called "References," at the end of the paper. Entries are listed alphabetically, with a similar kind of hanging indentation to that used in MLA style. If you list more than one item for an author, repeat the author's name each time and arrange the items in chronological order beginning with the earliest. If two works appeared in the same year, arrange them alphabetically, adding an "a" and a "b" after the year for purposes of in-text citation. Here is a hypothetical illustration:

Smith, R. (1995). *Body image in Western cultures, 1750-present.* London: Bonanza Press.

Smith, R. (1999a). *Body image in non-Western cultures.* London: Bonanza Press.

Smith, R. (1999b). Eating disorders reconsidered. *Journal of Appetite Studies, 45,* 295–300.

APA Quick Reference Guide for the Most Common Citations

Table 14.2 provides examples in APA style for the most common kinds of citations to be placed in a "References" list at the end of the paper. For a complete explanation of citations, consult the *Publication Manual of the American Psychological Association*, 5th ed., Washington, D.C.: APA, 2001.

Student Example of an APA-Style Research Paper

An example of a paper in APA style is shown on pages 187–196.

TABLE 14.2 Quick Reference Guide for APA Citations

Kind of Source	Basic Citation Model
PRINT SOURCES WHEN YOU HAVE USED THE ORIGINAL PRINT VERSION	
Book	Tannen, D. (1998). *The argument culture: Moving from debate to dialogue*. New York: Random House.
Article in anthology with an editor	Shamoon, L. (1998). International e-mail debate. In D. Reiss, D. Self, & A. Young (Eds.), *Electronic communication across the curriculum* (pp. 151–161). Urbana, IL: National Council of Teachers of English.
Article in scholarly journal	Pollay, R. W., Lee, J. S., & Carter-Whitney, D. (1992). Separate, but not equal: Racial segmentation in cigarette advertising. *Journal of Advertising, 21*(1), 45–57.
Article in magazine or newspaper	Beam, A. (2001, July–August). The mad poets society. *Atlantic Monthly, 288*, 96–103.
	Lemonick, M. D. (2000, October 30). Teens before their time. *Time, 156*, 66–74.
	Cauvin, H. E. (2001, July 18). Political climate complicates food shortage in Zimbabwe. *The New York Times*, A13.
PRINT SOURCES THAT YOU HAVE DOWNLOADED FROM A DATABASE OR THE WEB	
Article downloaded from database	Barr, B. (2000, June 5). Liberal media adored gun-control marchers. *Insight on the News*, 44. Retrieved August 15, 2001, from ProQuest database.
Article downloaded from Web	Goodman, E. (2001, June 24). The big hole in health debate. *Boston Globe Online*, p. D7. Retrieved July 18, 2001, from http://www.boston.com/dailyglobe2/175/oped/The_big_hole_in_health_debate+.shtml
WEB SOURCES THAT HAVEN'T APPEARED IN PRINT	
Authored document within a Web site	Tobin, S. (2000). Getting the word out on the human genome project: A course for physicians. Retrieved July 18, 2001, from Stanford University, Center for Biomedical Ethics Web site: http://scbe.stanford.edu/research/current_programs.html#genomics
Document with corporate or unnamed author within a Web site	National Men's Resource Center. (2001, February 1). Ouch! Body piercing. Retrieved July 17, 2001, from http://www.menstuff.org/issues/byissue/tattoo.html
MISCELLANEOUS SOURCES	
Interview, personal communication	Van der Peet (personal communication, June 24, 2001) stated that . . . [In-text citation only; not included in References]
Lecture, address, or speech	According to Jancoski (speech to University Congregational United Church of Christ, Seattle, October 30, 2001), salmon . . . [In-text citation only; not included in References; further details about speech can be included in text]

Acknowledgments

Page 5. Rodney Kilcup, "A Modest Proposal for Reluctant Writers," *Newsletter of the Pacific Northwest Writing Consortium 2*, no. 3 (September 1982): 5.

Page 5. Stephen D. Brookfield, *Developing Critical Thinkers: Challenging Adults to Explore Alternative Ways of Thinking and Acting* (San Francisco: Jossey-Bass, 1987):5.

Page 6. Andrea Lunsford and Lisa Ede, *Singular Texts/Plural Authors: Perspective on Collaborative Writing* (Carbondale and Edwardsville, IL: Southern Illinois University Press, 1992): 21, 45–48.

Pages 7–8. Excerpts from a workshop for new faculty members, Jeffrey R. Stephens (Department of Chemistry, Seattle University) and Tomas Guillen (Department of Speech Communication and Journalism, Seattle University).

Pages 9. Christopher Leigh, journal entries, student writing. Reprinted with the permission of the author.

Page 11. Paulo Freire, *Pedagogy of the Oppressed* (New York: Continuum, 1989).

Page 12. Ron Gluckman, "Shifting into High Gear," *Silk Road* (April 2004).

Page 13. "Greenpeace Responds to the Bush/Cheney National Energy Policy Task Force." Copyright © Greenpeace.

Page 13. Danny Hakim, "A Fuel-Saving Proposal from Your Automaker: Tax the Gas," *The New York Times*, April 18, 2004. Copyright © 2004 New York Times Company, Inc. Used with permission.

Page 13. Ray Darby, "Energy Issues." Copyright © 2004 Ray Darby.

Page 15. Energy Information Administration, U.S. Department of Energy, Oil consumption graph.

Page 17. David M. Rockwood, letter to editor, *The Oregonian* (January 1, 1993): E4. Copyright © 1993 David Rockwood. Used with permission.

Page 18. Thomas Merton, "A Festival of Rain," from *Raids on the Unspeakable* by Thomas Merton. Copyright © 1966 by The Abbey of Gethsemani, Inc. Reprinted by permission of New Directions Publishing Corp.

Page 23. Noel Gaudette, "Questions about Genetically Modified Foods," student writing. Reprinted with the permission of the author.

Page 23. Brittany Tinker, "Can the World Sustain an American Standard of Living?" student writing. Reprinted with the permission of the author.

Page 27. A. Kimbrough Sherman, in *Thinking and Writing in College: A Naturalistic Study of Students in Four Disciplines* by Barbara E. Walvoord and Lucille P. McCarthy (Urbana, IL: NCTE, 1990): 51.

Page 28. William G. Perry, *Forms of Intellectual and Ethical Development in the College Years* (Troy, MO: Holt, Rinehart & Winston, 1970).

Page 32. Judy Cohen and John Richardson, "Pit Bull Panic," *Journal of Popular Culture*, Fall 2002, Vol. 36, Issue 2, pp. 285-333. Copyright © 2002 Blackwell Publishing. Used with permission.

Page 34. Peter Elbow, *Writing Without Teachers* (New York: Oxford University Press, 1973): 147–190.

Page 42. Peter Elbow, *Writing Without Teachers* (New York: Oxford University Press, 1973): 14–15.

Page 42. Paul Theroux, *Sunrise with Seamonsters* (Boston: Houghton Mifflin, 1985).

Page 47. James Moffett, *Active Voice: A Writing Program Across the Curriculum* (Montclair, NJ: Boynton/Cook Publishers, 1981).

Pages 58 and 66. Dale Kunkel, Kristie M. Cope, and Erica Biely, from "Sexual Messages on Television," *The Journal of Sex Research*, Vol. 36, No. 3 (August 1999): 230. Copyright © 1999 by The Society for the Study of Sexuality. Used with permission.

Pages 58 and 67. Deborah A. Lott, from "The New Flirting Game," *Psychology Today* (January/February 1999): 42. Copyright © 1999 Sussex Publishers. Reprinted with permission.

Page 59. Lisa Sussman and Tracey Cox, from "Flirting with Disaster," *Cosmopolitan* (Australian ed.) (January 2001): 108ff.

Page 71. Penny Parker, "For Teeth, Say Cheese," from *New Scientist* (April 6, 1991). Copyright © 1991 New Scientist. Used with permission.

Page 72. Carlo Patrono, "Aspirin as an Antiplatelet Drug," *The New England Journal of Medicine* 330, (May 5, 1994): 1287–1294. Copyright © 1994 Massachusetts Medical Society. Used with permission.

Page 73. Kenneth Burke, *Permanence and Change,* 3rd rev. ed. (Berkeley: University of California Press, 1984): 49.

Page 73. Nayan Chanda, quoted in Thomas Friedman, "Think Global, Act Local," *The New York Times* (June 6, 2004): WK13.

Page 75. Kenneth Burke, *A Rhetoric of Motives* (New York: Prentice Hall, 1950): 43.

Page 76. Kenneth Burke, "Rhetoric—Old and New," *Journal of General Education* 5 (April 1951): 63.

Page 91. Marianne Means, "Bush, Cheney Will Face Wall of Opposition if They Try to Resurrect Nuclear Power," (April 12, 2001). © 2001 Hearst Newspapers. Used with permission.

Page 96. From "ANWR Information Brief" from www.anwr.org/tech-facts.pdf, accessed September 24, 2001. Reprinted by permission of Arctic Power.

Page 98. From "Which One Is the Real ANWR" from www.anwr.org/features/pdfs/realanwr.pdf, accessed September 24, 2001. Reprinted by permission of Arctic Power.

Page 98. Randal Rubini, from "A Vicious Cycle," *The Seattle Times* (August 27, 1992): G1+. Copyright © 1992 Randal Rubini.

Page 102. Lorna Marshal, *The !Kung of Nyae Nyae* (Cambridge: Harvard University Press, 1976): 177–178.

Page 103. P. Draper, "!Kung Women: Contrasts in Sexual Egalitarianism in Foraging and Sedentary Contexts," in *Toward an Anthropology of Women,* ed. R. Reiter (New York: Monthly Review Press, 1975): 82–83.

Page 106. Henry Morton Stanley, "Henry Morton Stanley's Account" from "A Classroom Laboratory for Writing History" from *Social Studies Review* 31, no. 1 (1991). Copyright © 1991. Reprinted with permission.

Page 107. Donald C. Holsinger, "A Classroom Laboratory for Writing History," *Social Studies Review* 31, no. 1 (1991): 59–64.

Pages 116 and 140. Andrés Martin, M.D., "On Teenagers and Tattoos," *Journal of the American Academy of Child and Adolescent Psychiatry* 36, no. 6 (June 1997): 860–861. Copyright © 1997. Used with permission.

Page 122. Robert B. Cullen with Sullivan, "Dangers of Disarming," *Newsweek* (October 27, 1986). Copyright © 1986. All rights reserved. Reprinted by permission.

Page 123. Carl Rogers, *On Becoming a Person: A Therapist's View of Psychotherapy,* 3rd ed. (Boston: Houghton Mifflin, 1961).

Page 130. Sean Barry, "Why Do Teenagers Get Tattoos? A Response to Andrés Martin," student essay. Reprinted with the permission of the author.

Page 142. Florence King, "I'd Rather Smoke Than Kiss," *National Review* (July 9, 1990): 32, 34–36. Copyright © 1990 by National Review, Inc., 215 Lexington Avenue, New York, NY 10016. Reprinted by permission.

Page 154. Anonymous, "Essay A/Essay B" from "Inventing the University," in *When A Writer Can't Write* by David Bartholomae. Reprinted with the permission of The Guilford Press.

Page 159. Christopher Leigh, "An Exploration of How to Prevent Violence in Schools," student essay. Reprinted with the permission of the author.

Pages 166 and 169. Stephen Bean, "Sam" journal entries and "Should Women Be Allowed to Serve in Combat Units?", student writing. Reprinted with the permission of the author.

Page 175. EnchantedLearning.com, "Tarantulas." www.enchantedlearning.com/subjects/arachnids/spider.

Page 176. Rod Crawford, "Myths About 'Dangerous' Spiders" from the Burke Museum web site. www.washington.edu/burkemuseum/spidermyth/index.html. Copyright © Burke Museum. Reprinted by permission of Burke Museum, Seattle, WA.

Page 181. Article abstract of "Reefer Madness" by Eric Schlosser (August 1994). Abstract reprinted with the permission of *The Atlantic Monthly.*

Page 181. Article abstract of "The Sex-Bias Myth in Medicine" by Andrew G. Kadar, M.D. (August 1994). Abstract reprinted with the permission of *The Atlantic Monthly.*

Page 181. Article abstract of "Midlife Myths" by Winifred Gallagher (May 1993). Abstract reprinted with the permission of *The Atlantic Monthly.*

Page 183. Kerri Ann Matsumoto, "How Much Does It Cost to Go Organic?" student essay. Reprinted with the permission of the author.

Page 184. Cheryl Carp, "Behind Stone Walls," student essay. Reprinted with the permission of the author.

Page 187. Shannon King, "Will the Hydrogen Economy Solve the Energy Crisis and Protect Our Environment?" student essay. Reprinted with the permission of the author.

Page 197. Jonathan Rauch, "Coming to America," *Atlantic Monthly* (July/Aug. 2003). Copyright © 2003 Jonathan Rauch. Used with permission.

Page 209. John Berger, *About Looking* (New York: Vintage Books, 1980), p. 52.

Page 224. "Attention Advertisers: Real Men Do Laundry," *American Demographics* (March 1994): 13–14.

Page 225. Erving Goffman, *Gender Advertisements* (New York: Harper & Row, 1979).

Page 230. Stephen Bean, "How Cigarette Advertisers Address the Stigma Against Smoking: A Tale of Two Ads," student essay. Reprinted with the permission of the author.

Page 246. Stephen Toulmin, *The Uses of Argument* (Cambridge: Cambridge University Press, 1958).

Page 248. Michael Levin, "The Case for Torture," *Newsweek* (June 7, 1982).

Page 253. Walter Wink, "Biting the Bullet: The Case for Legalizing Drugs," *The Christian Century* (August 8–15, 1990).

Page 260. Ross Taylor, "Paintball: Promoter of Violence or Healthy Fun?" student essay. Reprinted with the permission of the author.

Page 264. Leonard A. Pitts, Jr., "Spare the Rod, Spoil the Parenting," *The Seattle Times* (September 6, 2001). Copyright © 2001 by the Miami Herald. Reprinted by permission.

Page 266. A. J. Chavez, "The Case for (Gay) Marriage," student essay. Reprinted with the permission of the author.

Page 281. Jonathan Swift, "A Modest Proposal," in *The Prose Works of Jonathan Swift* (London: Bell, 1914).

Page 282. Peter Elbow, *Writing Without Teachers* (New York: Oxford University Press, 1973): 14-15.

Page 288. Stephen Bean, "What Puzzles You About Homelessness?" student writing. Reprinted with the permission of the author.

Page 301. Kenneth Burke, *The Grammar of Motives* (Berkeley: University of California Press, 1969).

Page 301. James Jones, quoted in Jon Winokur (Ed.), *Writers on Writing* (Philadelphia: Running Press, 1986).

Pages 302–303. Adapted from J. D. Bransford and M. K. Johnson, "Conceptual Prerequisites for Understanding," *Journal of Learning Behavior* 11 (1972): 717–726.

Pages 307, 308. Lynnea Clark, excerpt and outline from "Women Police Officers: Should Size and Strength Be Criteria for Patrol Duty?", student essay.

Pages 324, 325. Dao Do, "Choose Life," student essay. Reprinted with the permission of the author.

Pages 325, 326. Tiffany Linder, excerpt from "Salvaging Our Old-Growth Forests," student essay. Reprinted with the permission of the author.

Pages 331, 333. David Popenoe, "Where's Papa?" from *Life Without Father: Compelling New Evidence that Fatherhood and Marriage Are Indispensable for the Good of Children and Society.* As published in "The Decline of Fatherhood," *Wilson Quarterly* (September/October 1996).

Page 341. Women Against Gun Control home page, www.wagc.com. Used with permission.

Page 348. Million Mom March home page. © Million Mom March United with the Brady Campaign to Prevent Gun Violence. Used with permission.

Page 349. Second Amendment Sisters, Northern Colorado Chapter, home page. Used with permission.

Page 353. Kelly Ann Connolly, "Women are the Real Victims of Handgun Control," from armedandsafe.com. © 2002 Kelly Ann Connolly. Used with permission.

Page 354. Armed and Safe home page. © 2002 by armedandsafe.com. Used with permission.

Page 356. Roger D. McGrath, "The Myth of Violence in the Old West," in *Gunfighters, Highwaymen, and Vigilantes: Violence on the Frontier.* Copyright © 1984 by The Regents of the University of California.

Page 363. Christopher Leigh, "The Case Against Metal Detectors in Public Schools," student essay. Reprinted with the permission of the author.

Illustrations

Page 45. Courtesy of Shell.

Page 46. Courtesy www.adbusters.org.

Page 67. Photography by Frank Veronsky.

Page 86. Allan H. Shoemake/Taxi/Getty Images.

Page 86. Bill Bachmann/The Image Works.

Page 88. Jeff Greenberg/The Image Works.

Page 88. Leland Bobbe/Taxi/Getty Images.

Page 89. Frank Micelotta/Getty Images.

Page 93. Courtesy of the U.S. Army.

Page 96. AP/Wide World Photos.

Page 97. Chuck Dial, on behalf of photographer John Benck.

Page 98. Patrick Endres/AlaskaStock.com.

Page 148. Courtesy www.adbusters.org.

Page 177. Courtesy of Manuel J. Cabrero.

Page 177. Photo Courtesy of Ron Taylor.

Page 215. Courtesy of Nikon.

Page 217. © DaimlerChrysler Corporation. Used with permission.

Page 218. © DaimlerChrysler Corporation. Used with permission.

Page 223. Coors Brewing Co.

Page 226. Courtesy of The Hoover Company.

Page 227. Courtesy Zenith Audio Products, a Division of S.D.I. Technologies.

Page 228. Courtesy of COTY US LLC.

Page 229. Courtesy of AT&T.

Page 279. Courtesy of MarketingSolutionsAndConservation.com.

Index

Note: Page entries followed by "n" refer to footnotes.